VOLUME SEVEN

BY SANAMI MATOH

HAMBURG // LONDON // LOS ANGELES // TOKYO

FAKE Vol. 7
Created by Sanami Matoh

Translation - Nan Rymer
English Adaptation - Stuart Hazleton
Copy Editor - Aaron Sparrow
Retouch and Lettering - Tina Fulkerson
Cover Design - Raymond Makowski

Editor - Rob Tokar
Digital Imaging Manager - Chris Buford
Pre-Press Manager - Antonio DePietro
Production Managers - Jennifer Miller and Mutsumi Miyazaki
Art Director - Matt Alford
Managing Editor - Jill Freshney
VP of Production - Ron Klamert
President and C.O.O. - John Parker
Publisher and C.E.O. - Stuart Levy

A  Manga

TOKYOPOP Inc.
5900 Wilshire Blvd. Suite 2000
Los Angeles, CA 90036

E-mail: info@TOKYOPOP.com
Come visit us online at www.TOKYOPOP.com

ISBN: 1-59182-332-3

First TOKYOPOP printing: May 2004
10 9 8 7 6 5 4 3 2
Printed in the USA

THE STORY SO FAR...

Meet Ryo and Dee, two New York City cops with an attraction for action—and each other! When soft-spoken Detective Randy "Ryo" Maclean was transferred to the NYPD's 27th precinct, he was partnered with Dee Laytner--a cocky, confident cop with attitude to spare. Right from the start, Dee had strong feelings for Ryo and was not reluctant to share them. Ryo's feelings toward Dee were a mystery to both men…though neither can deny their existence any longer.

The detectives' first case together involved a drug-related homicide. The victim was a narcotics smuggler, survived only by his young son Bikky. Though a smart-mouthed street punk and a petty criminal-in-the-making, Bikky helped Dee and Ryo foil the drug-smuggling ring that killed his father. Seeing that the tough-talking boy was actually a frightened, sad child with nowhere to go, kind-hearted Ryo took Bikky in…much to Dee's chagrin.

In their second case, the detectives came to the rescue of a young pickpocket named Carol. Carol was stealing wallets to try to get enough money to bail her sick father out of jail before he died, but she ended up picking the pocket of a murderer whose wallet contained a key piece of evidence. In order to protect Carol from the killer and his cohorts, Ryo let her stay with him temporarily.

Even while Dee and Ryo's partnership grew into a bond of friendship, Bikky and Carol became close friends as well, despite the three years between them. Back at the precinct, a detective by the name of Jemmy "J.J." Adams arrived with a powerful, unrequited crush on Dee left over from their days at the Police Academy. To make matters even more complicated, Ryo and Dee also acquired a new supervisor, Chief Berkeley Rose…who had an obvious crush on Ryo.

It wasn't long before the emotionally explosive situation at the 27th Precinct became a literally explosive one, as the station was targeted by a serial-bomber. Quick thinking by Ryo and Dee managed to prevent any human casualties, but their building was a total goner. While awaiting new quarters, the officers of the 27th have been working their shifts from the Bronx Station…and Dee has been working Ryo non-stop!

-FAKE-

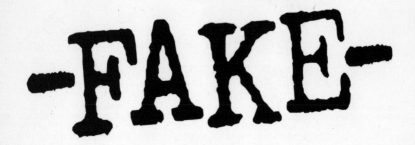

TABLE OF CONTENTS

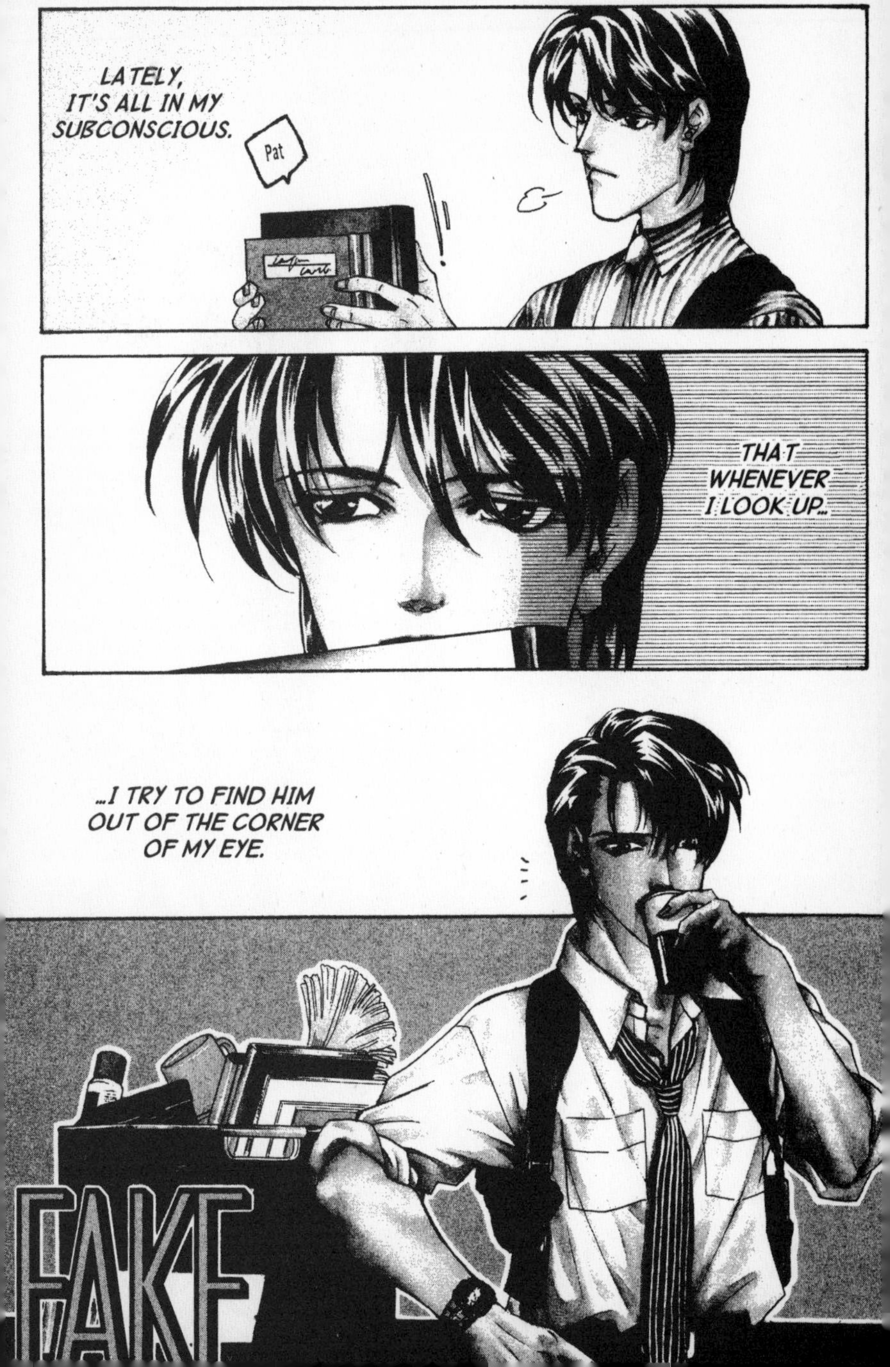
LATELY, IT'S ALL IN MY SUBCONSCIOUS.
Pat
THAT WHENEVER I LOOK UP...
...I TRY TO FIND HIM OUT OF THE CORNER OF MY EYE.
FAKE

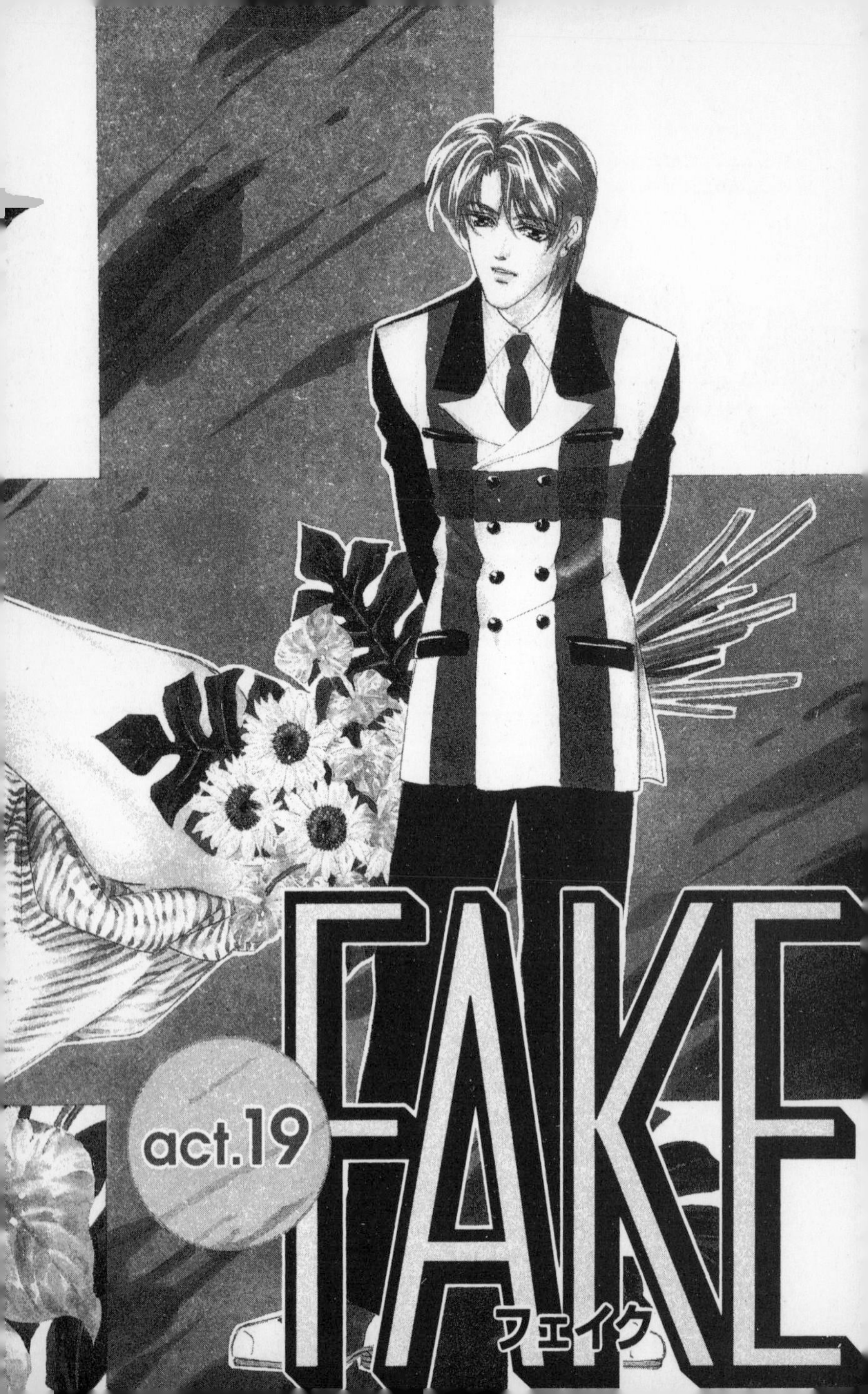
act.19
FAKE
フェイク

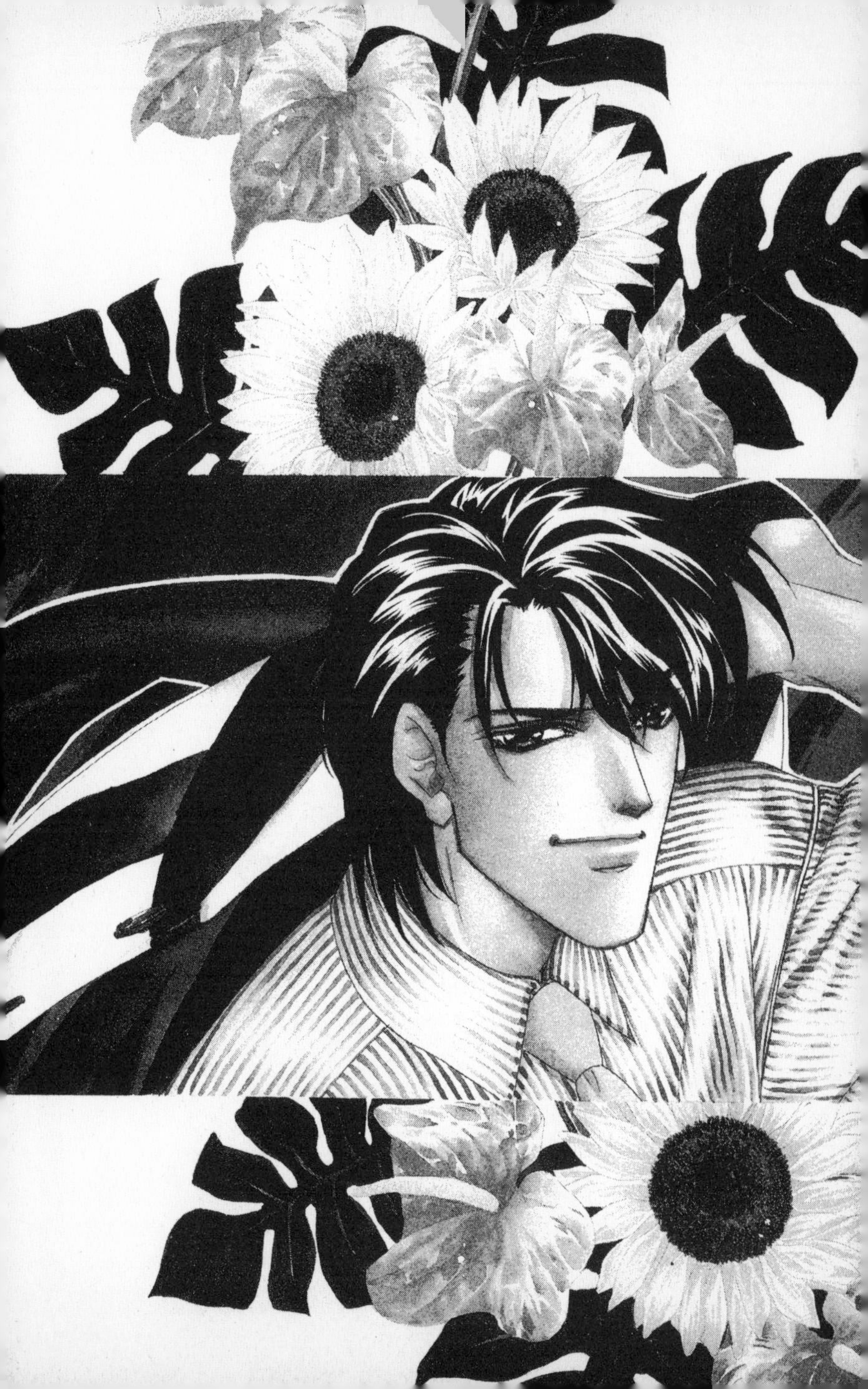

FAKE

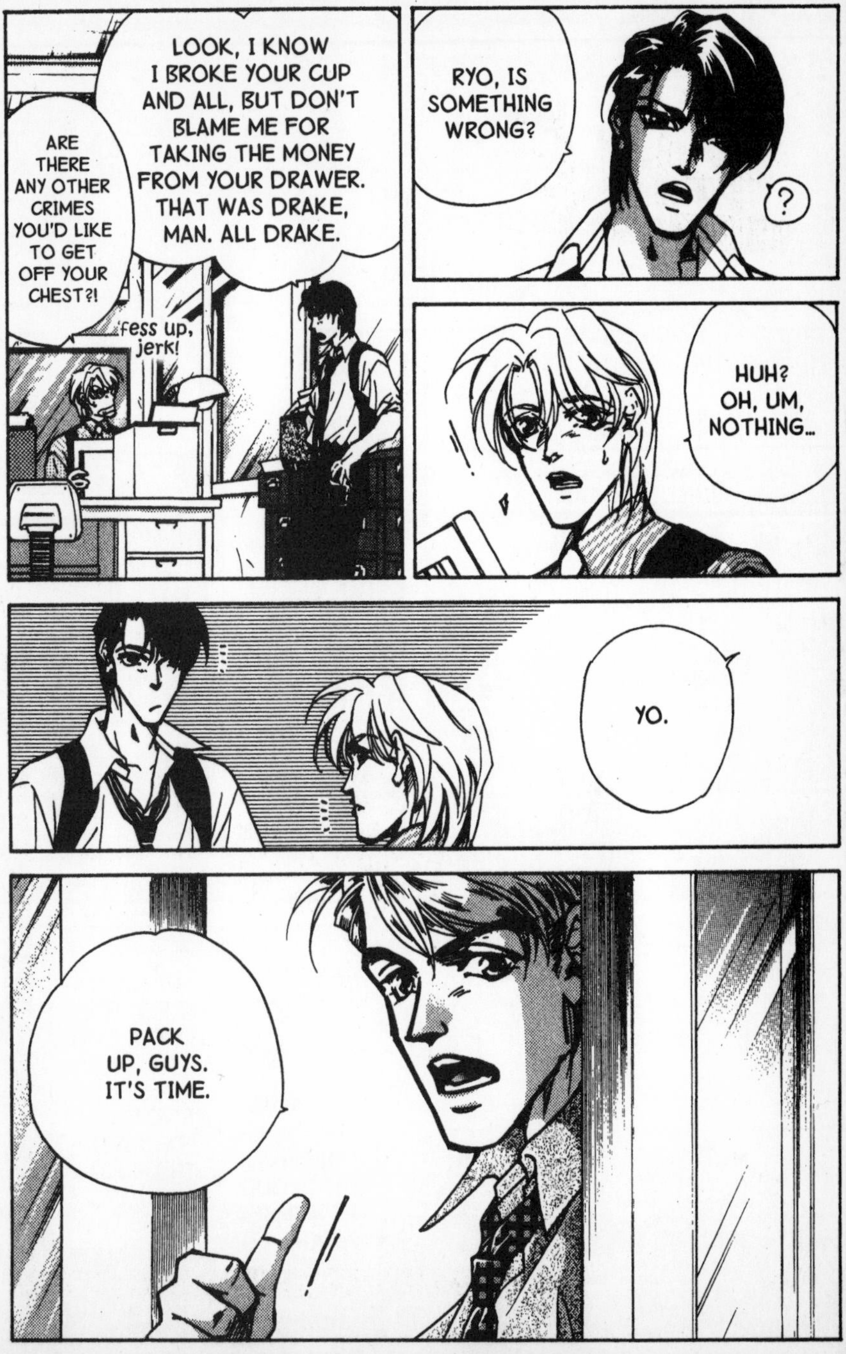
RYO, IS SOMETHING WRONG?
?
HUH? OH, UM, NOTHING...
LOOK, I KNOW I BROKE YOUR CUP AND ALL, BUT DON'T BLAME ME FOR TAKING THE MONEY FROM YOUR DRAWER. THAT WAS DRAKE, MAN. ALL DRAKE.
ARE THERE ANY OTHER CRIMES YOU'D LIKE TO GET OFF YOUR CHEST?!
'fess up, jerk!
YO.
PACK UP, GUYS. IT'S TIME.

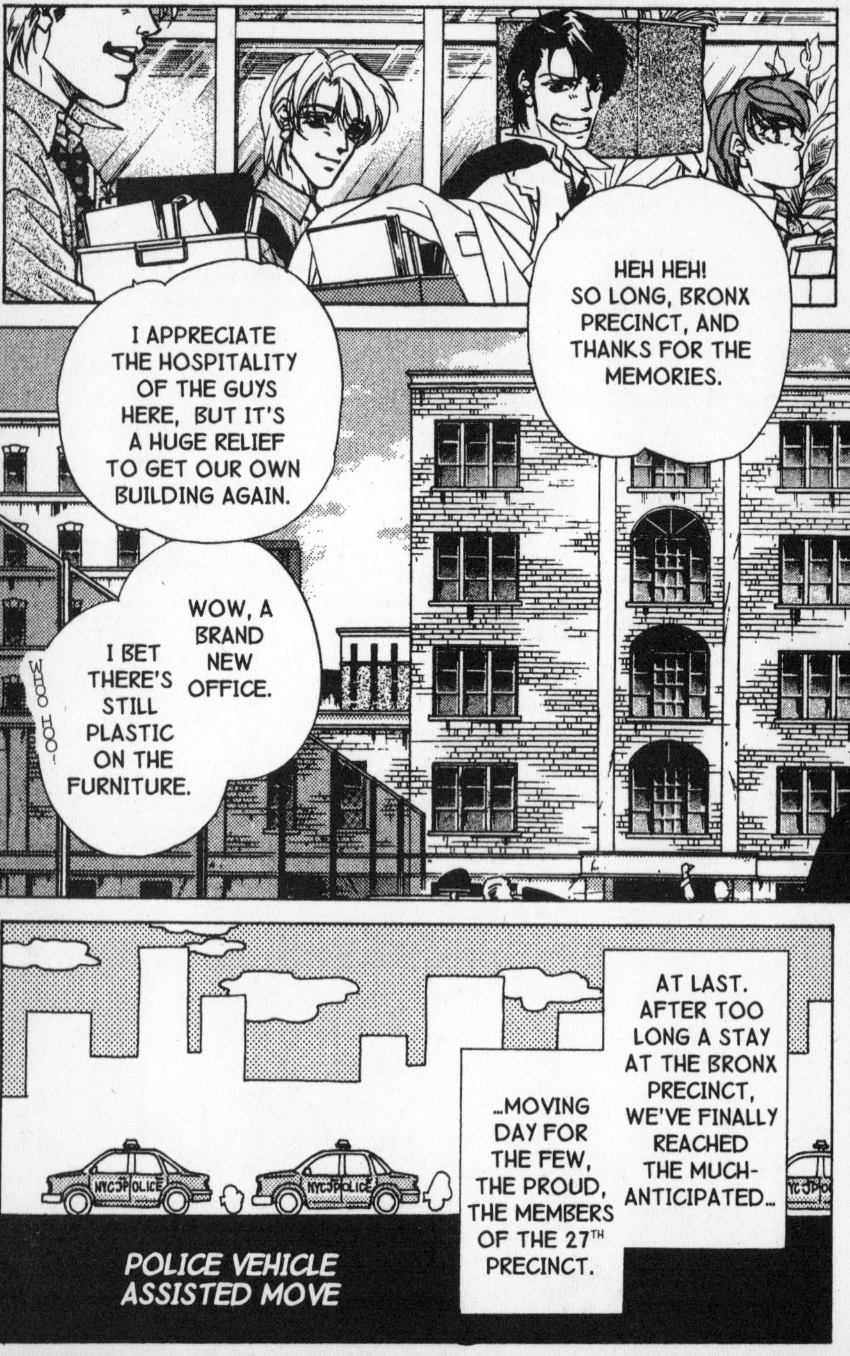
HEH HEH! SO LONG, BRONX PRECINCT, AND THANKS FOR THE MEMORIES.
I APPRECIATE THE HOSPITALITY OF THE GUYS HERE, BUT IT'S A HUGE RELIEF TO GET OUR OWN BUILDING AGAIN.
WOW, A BRAND NEW OFFICE.
I BET THERE'S STILL PLASTIC ON THE FURNITURE.
WHOO HOO!
AT LAST. AFTER TOO LONG A STAY AT THE BRONX PRECINCT, WE'VE FINALLY REACHED THE MUCH-ANTICIPATED...
...MOVING DAY FOR THE FEW, THE PROUD, THE MEMBERS OF THE 27TH PRECINCT.
POLICE VEHICLE ASSISTED MOVE

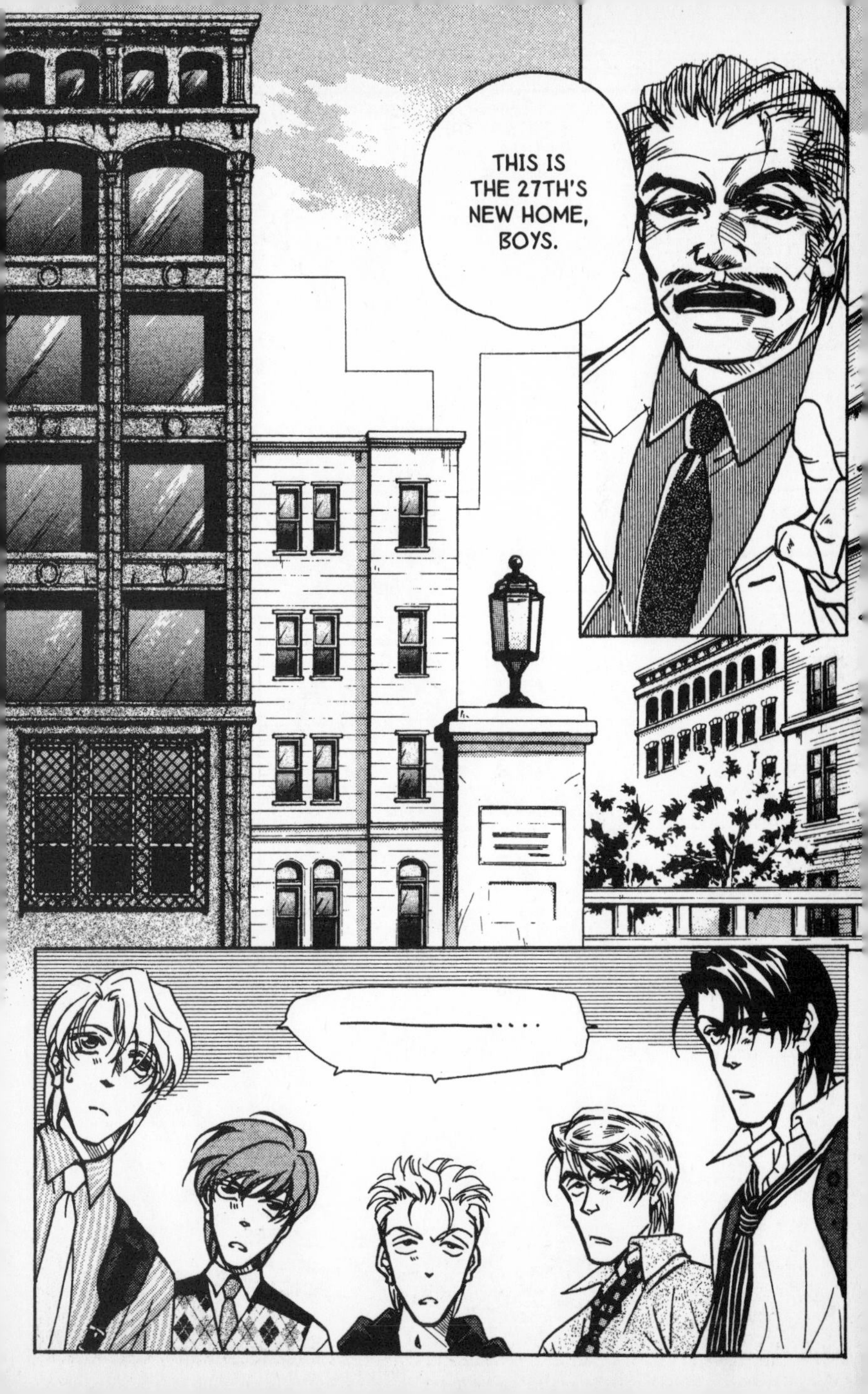
THIS IS THE 27TH'S NEW HOME, BOYS.
————————....

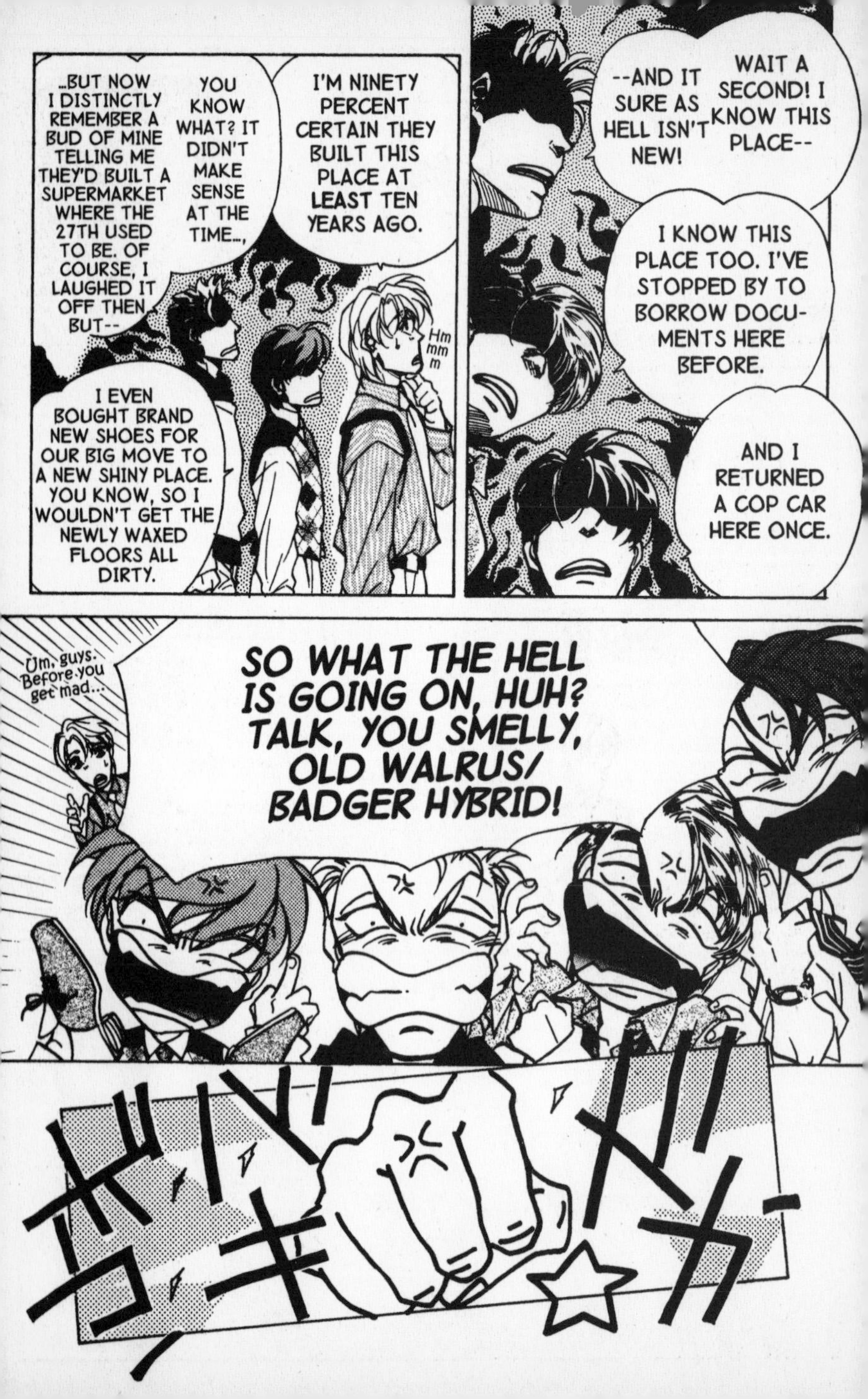

WAIT A SECOND! I KNOW THIS PLACE--
--AND IT SURE AS HELL ISN'T NEW!
I KNOW THIS PLACE TOO. I'VE STOPPED BY TO BORROW DOCU-MENTS HERE BEFORE.
AND I RETURNED A COP CAR HERE ONCE.
I'M NINETY PERCENT CERTAIN THEY BUILT THIS PLACE AT LEAST TEN YEARS AGO.
Hmmmm
YOU KNOW WHAT? IT DIDN'T MAKE SENSE AT THE TIME...,
...BUT NOW I DISTINCTLY REMEMBER A BUD OF MINE TELLING ME THEY'D BUILT A SUPERMARKET WHERE THE 27TH USED TO BE. OF COURSE, I LAUGHED IT OFF THEN BUT--
I EVEN BOUGHT BRAND NEW SHOES FOR OUR BIG MOVE TO A NEW SHINY PLACE. YOU KNOW, SO I WOULDN'T GET THE NEWLY WAXED FLOORS ALL DIRTY.
SO WHAT THE HELL IS GOING ON, HUH? TALK, YOU SMELLY, OLD WALRUS/ BADGER HYBRID!
Um, guys. Before you get mad...

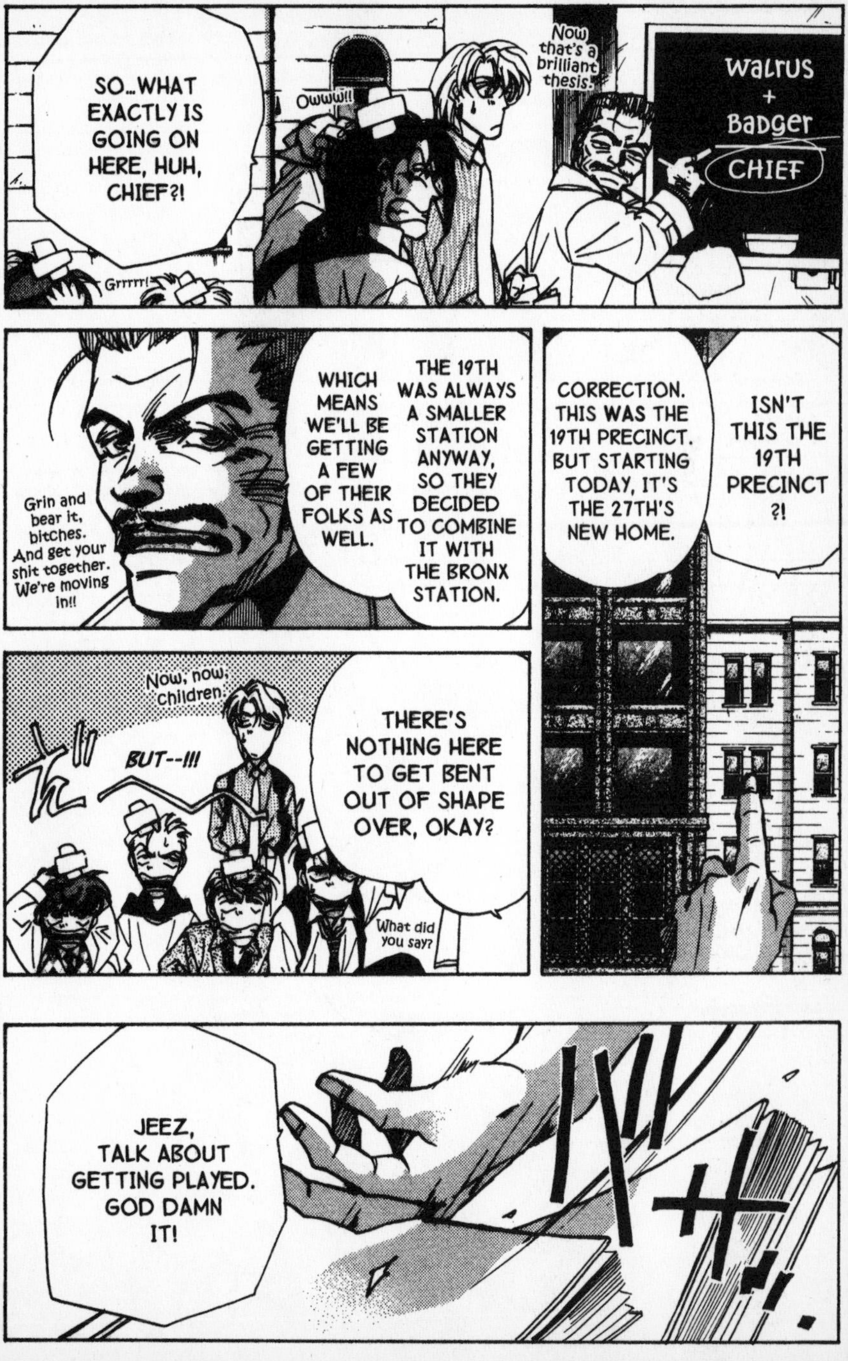
Now that's a brilliant thesis.
Walrus + Badger
CHIEF
Owww!!
SO...WHAT EXACTLY IS GOING ON HERE, HUH, CHIEF?!
Grrrrr!
ISN'T THIS THE 19TH PRECINCT?!
CORRECTION. THIS WAS THE 19TH PRECINCT. BUT STARTING TODAY, IT'S THE 27TH'S NEW HOME.
THE 19TH WAS ALWAYS A SMALLER STATION ANYWAY, SO THEY DECIDED TO COMBINE IT WITH THE BRONX STATION.
WHICH MEANS WE'LL BE GETTING A FEW OF THEIR FOLKS AS WELL.
Grin and bear it, bitches. And get your shit together. We're moving in!!
THERE'S NOTHING HERE TO GET BENT OUT OF SHAPE OVER, OKAY?
What did you say?
Now, now, children.
BUT--!!!
JEEZ, TALK ABOUT GETTING PLAYED. GOD DAMN IT!

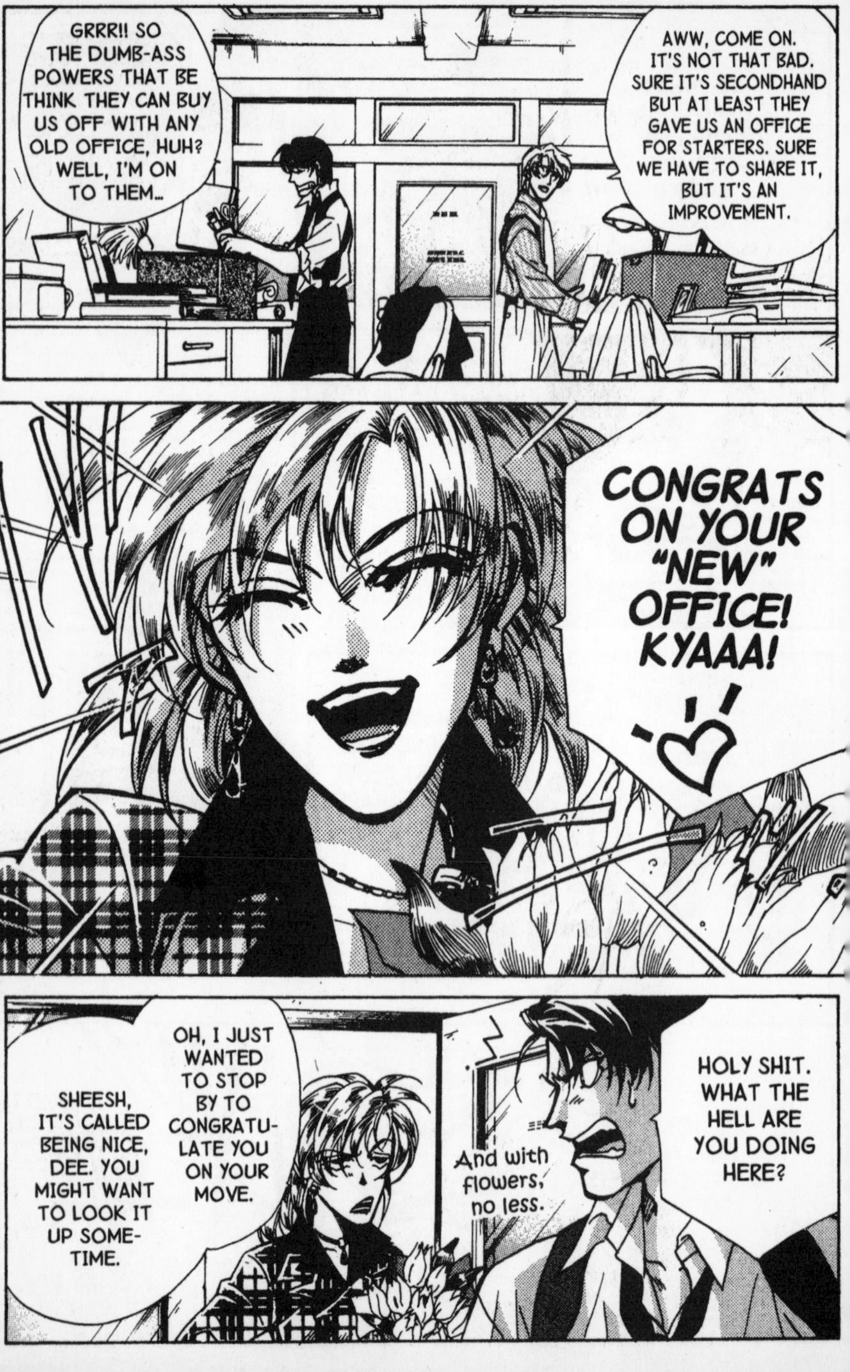
AWW, COME ON. IT'S NOT THAT BAD. SURE IT'S SECONDHAND BUT AT LEAST THEY GAVE US AN OFFICE FOR STARTERS. SURE WE HAVE TO SHARE IT, BUT IT'S AN IMPROVEMENT.
GRRR!! SO THE DUMB-ASS POWERS THAT BE THINK THEY CAN BUY US OFF WITH ANY OLD OFFICE, HUH? WELL, I'M ON TO THEM...
CONGRATS ON YOUR "NEW" OFFICE! KYAAA!
HOLY SHIT. WHAT THE HELL ARE YOU DOING HERE?
And with flowers, no less.
OH, I JUST WANTED TO STOP BY TO CONGRATU-LATE YOU ON YOUR MOVE.
SHEESH, IT'S CALLED BEING NICE, DEE. YOU MIGHT WANT TO LOOK IT UP SOME-TIME.

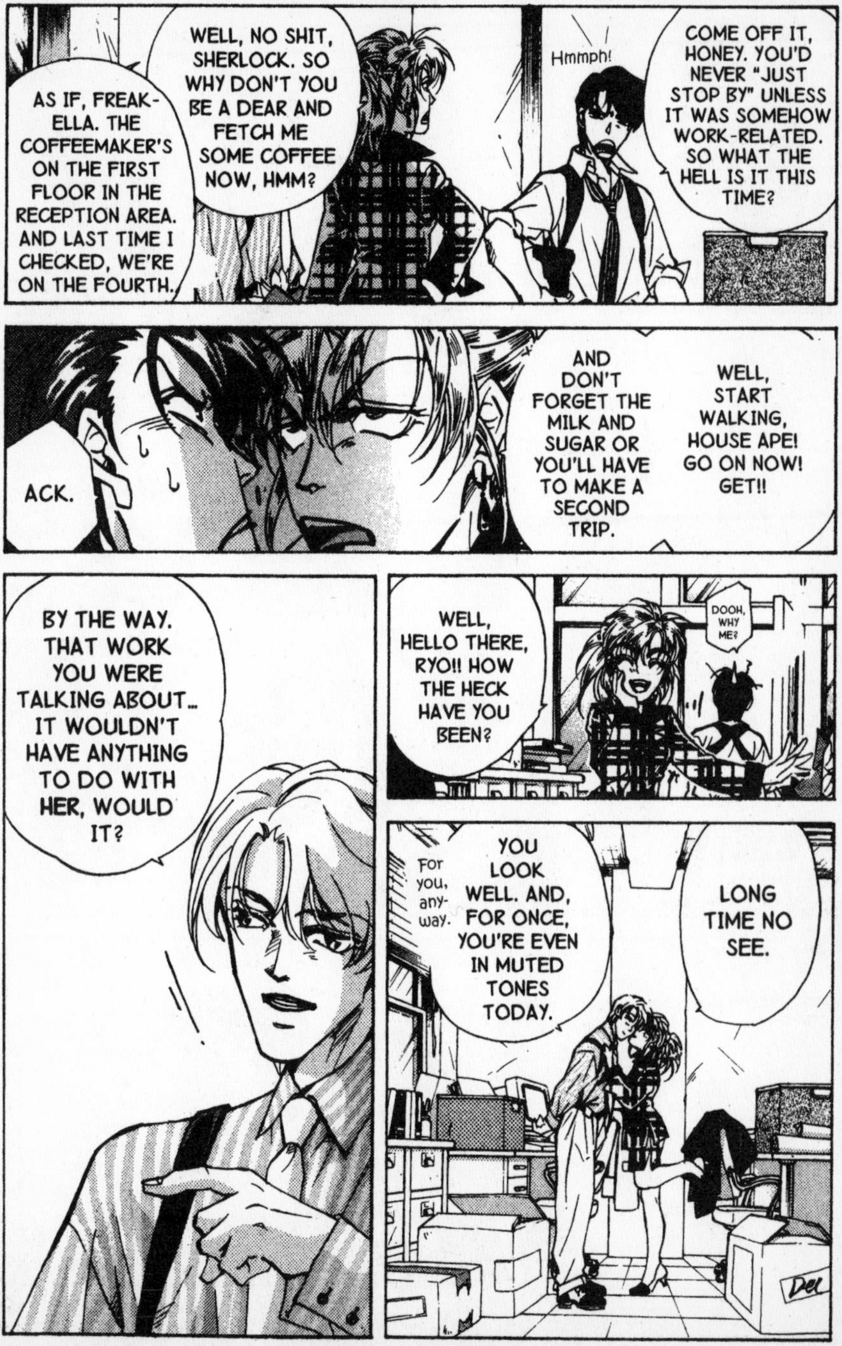
COME OFF IT, HONEY. YOU'D NEVER "JUST STOP BY" UNLESS IT WAS SOMEHOW WORK-RELATED. SO WHAT THE HELL IS IT THIS TIME?
Hmmph!
WELL, NO SHIT, SHERLOCK. SO WHY DON'T YOU BE A DEAR AND FETCH ME SOME COFFEE NOW, HMM?
AS IF, FREAK-ELLA. THE COFFEEMAKER'S ON THE FIRST FLOOR IN THE RECEPTION AREA. AND LAST TIME I CHECKED, WE'RE ON THE FOURTH.
WELL, START WALKING, HOUSE APE! GO ON NOW! GET!!
AND DON'T FORGET THE MILK AND SUGAR OR YOU'LL HAVE TO MAKE A SECOND TRIP.
ACK.
DOOH, WHY ME?
WELL, HELLO THERE, RYO!! HOW THE HECK HAVE YOU BEEN?
LONG TIME NO SEE.
YOU LOOK WELL. AND, FOR ONCE, YOU'RE EVEN IN MUTED TONES TODAY.
For you, any-way.
BY THE WAY. THAT WORK YOU WERE TALKING ABOUT... IT WOULDN'T HAVE ANYTHING TO DO WITH HER, WOULD IT?

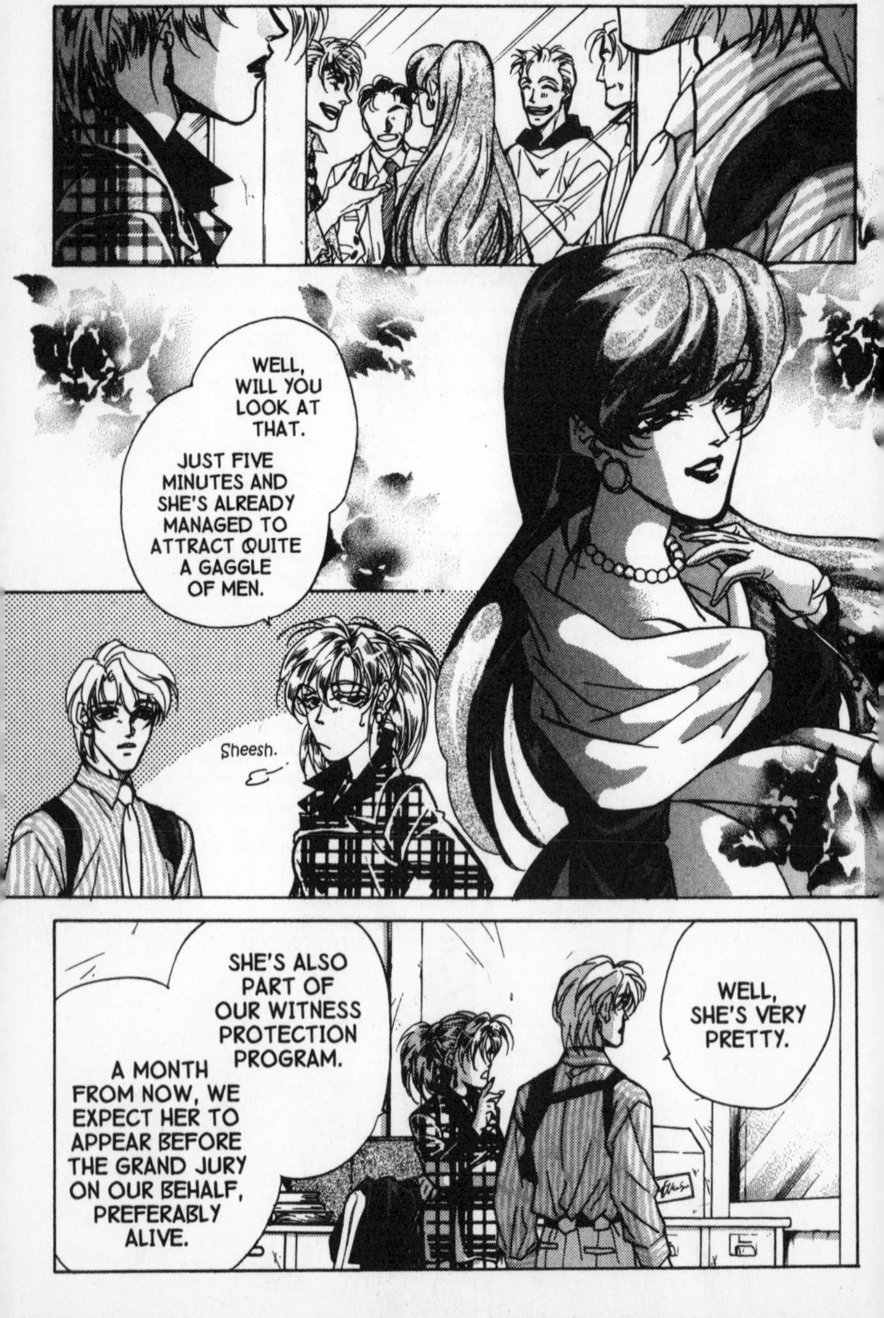
WELL, WILL YOU LOOK AT THAT.
JUST FIVE MINUTES AND SHE'S ALREADY MANAGED TO ATTRACT QUITE A GAGGLE OF MEN.
Sheesh.
WELL, SHE'S VERY PRETTY.
SHE'S ALSO PART OF OUR WITNESS PROTECTION PROGRAM.
A MONTH FROM NOW, WE EXPECT HER TO APPEAR BEFORE THE GRAND JURY ON OUR BEHALF, PREFERABLY ALIVE.

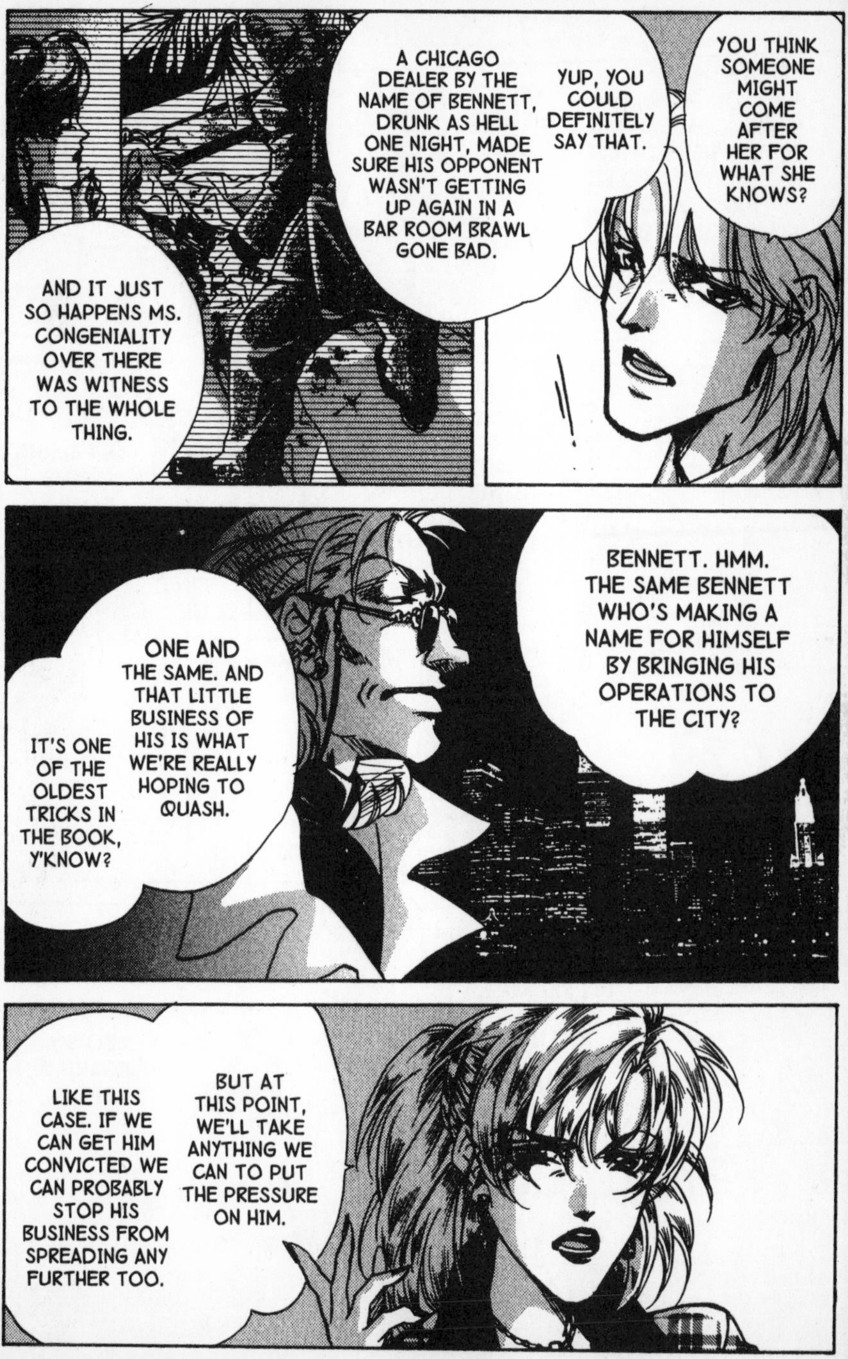
YOU THINK SOMEONE MIGHT COME AFTER HER FOR WHAT SHE KNOWS?
YUP, YOU COULD DEFINITELY SAY THAT.
A CHICAGO DEALER BY THE NAME OF BENNETT, DRUNK AS HELL ONE NIGHT, MADE SURE HIS OPPONENT WASN'T GETTING UP AGAIN IN A BAR ROOM BRAWL GONE BAD.
AND IT JUST SO HAPPENS MS. CONGENIALITY OVER THERE WAS WITNESS TO THE WHOLE THING.
BENNETT. HMM. THE SAME BENNETT WHO'S MAKING A NAME FOR HIMSELF BY BRINGING HIS OPERATIONS TO THE CITY?
ONE AND THE SAME. AND THAT LITTLE BUSINESS OF HIS IS WHAT WE'RE REALLY HOPING TO QUASH.
IT'S ONE OF THE OLDEST TRICKS IN THE BOOK, Y'KNOW?
BUT AT THIS POINT, WE'LL TAKE ANYTHING WE CAN TO PUT THE PRESSURE ON HIM.
LIKE THIS CASE. IF WE CAN GET HIM CONVICTED WE CAN PROBABLY STOP HIS BUSINESS FROM SPREADING ANY FURTHER TOO.

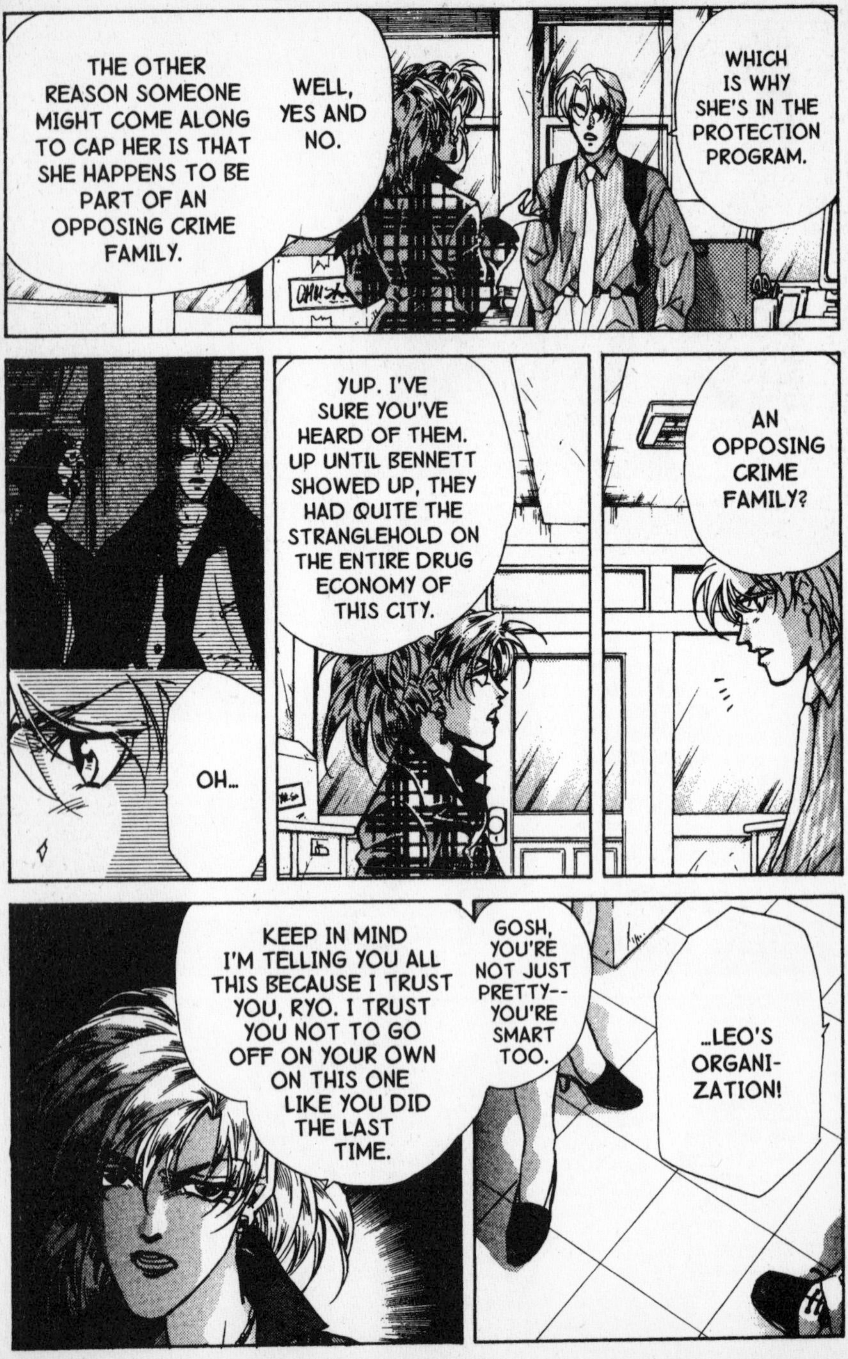
WHICH IS WHY SHE'S IN THE PROTECTION PROGRAM.
WELL, YES AND NO.
THE OTHER REASON SOMEONE MIGHT COME ALONG TO CAP HER IS THAT SHE HAPPENS TO BE PART OF AN OPPOSING CRIME FAMILY.
AN OPPOSING CRIME FAMILY?
YUP. I'VE SURE YOU'VE HEARD OF THEM. UP UNTIL BENNETT SHOWED UP, THEY HAD QUITE THE STRANGLEHOLD ON THE ENTIRE DRUG ECONOMY OF THIS CITY.
OH...
...LEO'S ORGANIZATION!
GOSH, YOU'RE NOT JUST PRETTY-- YOU'RE SMART TOO.
KEEP IN MIND I'M TELLING YOU ALL THIS BECAUSE I TRUST YOU, RYO. I TRUST YOU NOT TO GO OFF ON YOUR OWN ON THIS ONE LIKE YOU DID THE LAST TIME.

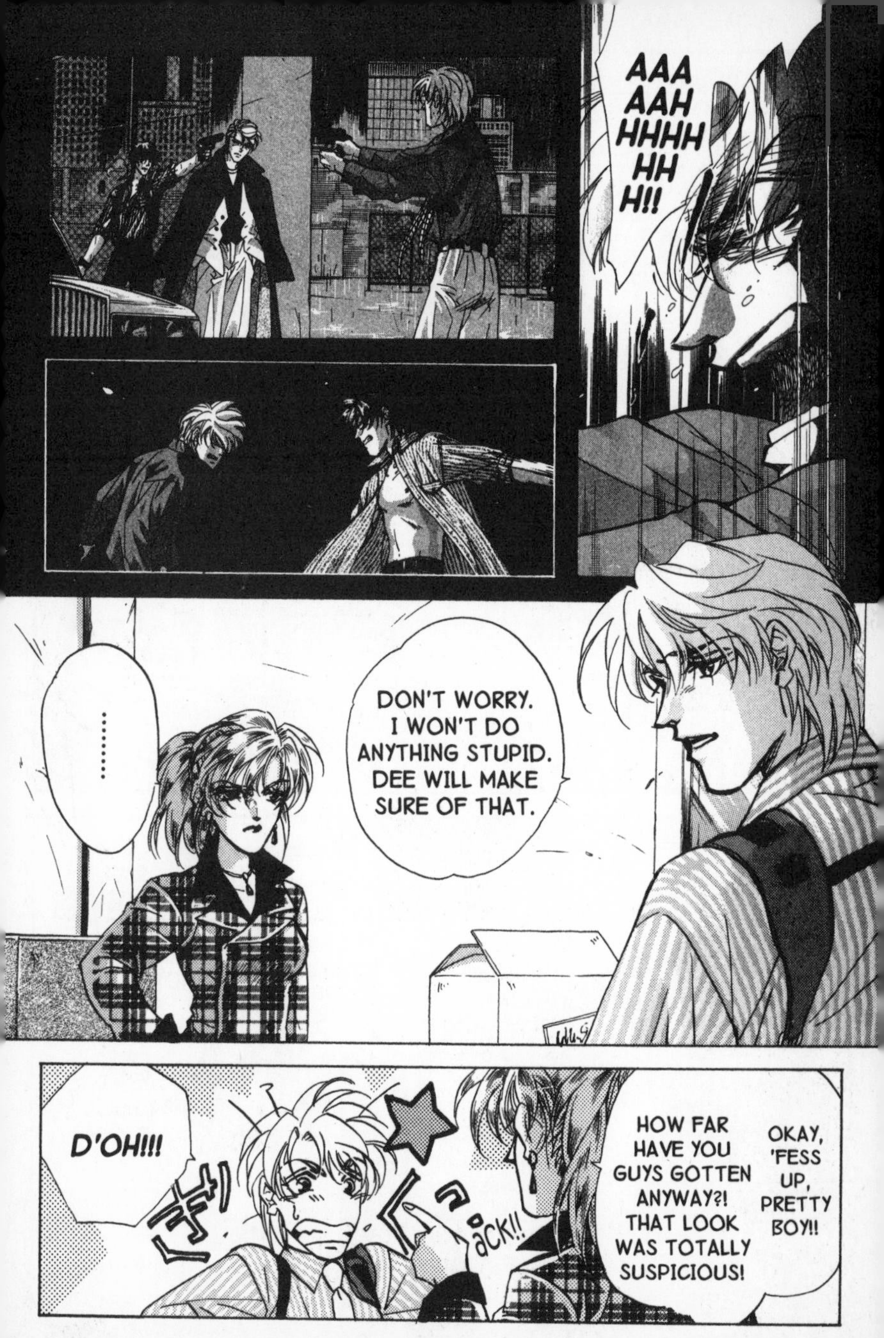
AAAAAHHHHHHHH!!
DON'T WORRY. I WON'T DO ANYTHING STUPID. DEE WILL MAKE SURE OF THAT.
......
OKAY, 'FESS UP, PRETTY BOY!!
HOW FAR HAVE YOU GUYS GOTTEN ANYWAY?! THAT LOOK WAS TOTALLY SUSPICIOUS!
ack!!
D'OH!!!

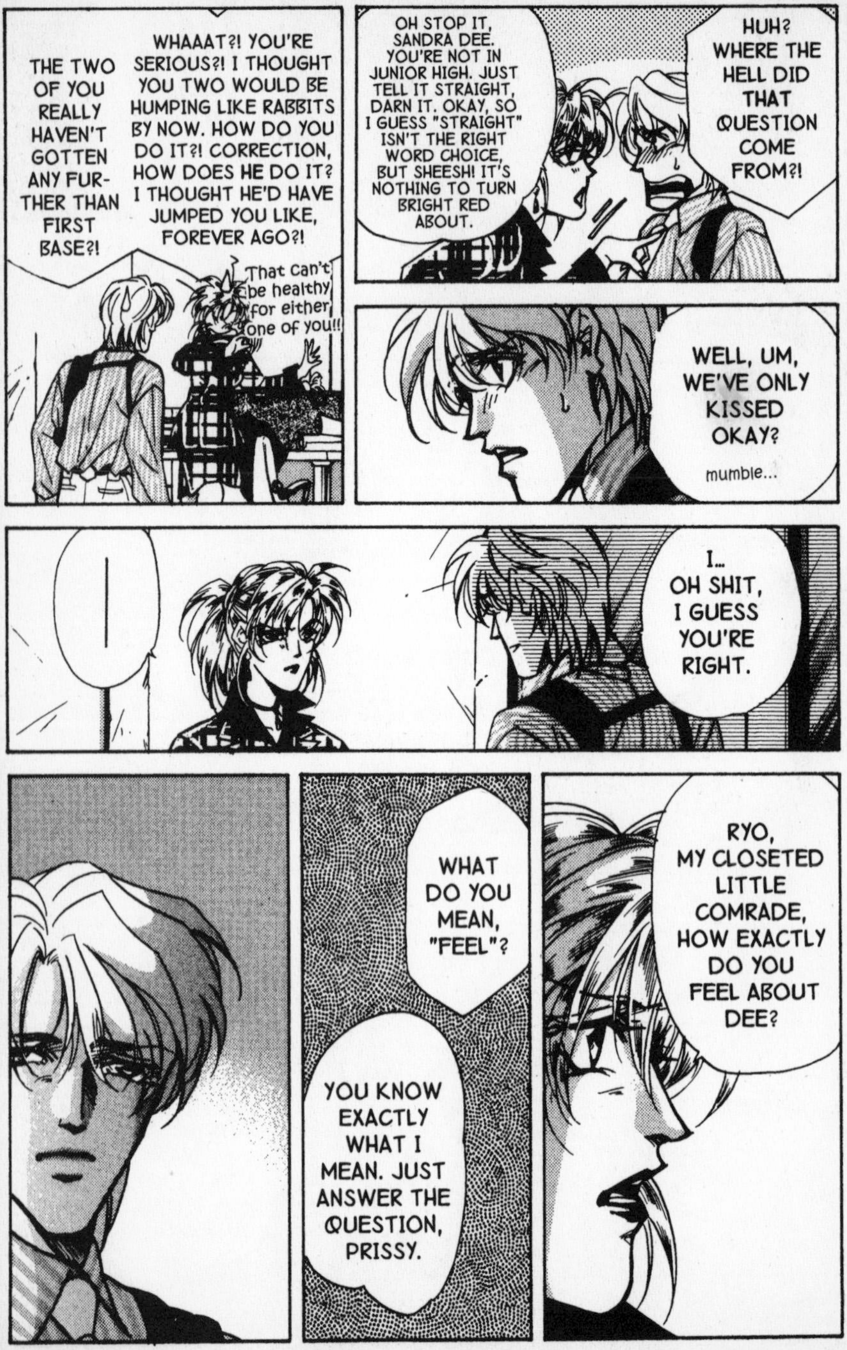
HUH? WHERE THE HELL DID THAT QUESTION COME FROM?!
OH STOP IT, SANDRA DEE. YOU'RE NOT IN JUNIOR HIGH. JUST TELL IT STRAIGHT, DARN IT. OKAY, SO I GUESS "STRAIGHT" ISN'T THE RIGHT WORD CHOICE, BUT SHEESH! IT'S NOTHING TO TURN BRIGHT RED ABOUT.
WELL, UM, WE'VE ONLY KISSED OKAY?
mumble...
WHAAAT?! YOU'RE SERIOUS?! I THOUGHT YOU TWO WOULD BE HUMPING LIKE RABBITS BY NOW. HOW DO YOU DO IT?! CORRECTION, HOW DOES HE DO IT? I THOUGHT HE'D HAVE JUMPED YOU LIKE, FOREVER AGO?!
THE TWO OF YOU REALLY HAVEN'T GOTTEN ANY FURTHER THAN FIRST BASE?!
That can't be healthy for either one of you!!
I... OH SHIT, I GUESS YOU'RE RIGHT.
|
RYO, MY CLOSETED LITTLE COMRADE, HOW EXACTLY DO YOU FEEL ABOUT DEE?
WHAT DO YOU MEAN, "FEEL"?
YOU KNOW EXACTLY WHAT I MEAN. JUST ANSWER THE QUESTION, PRISSY.

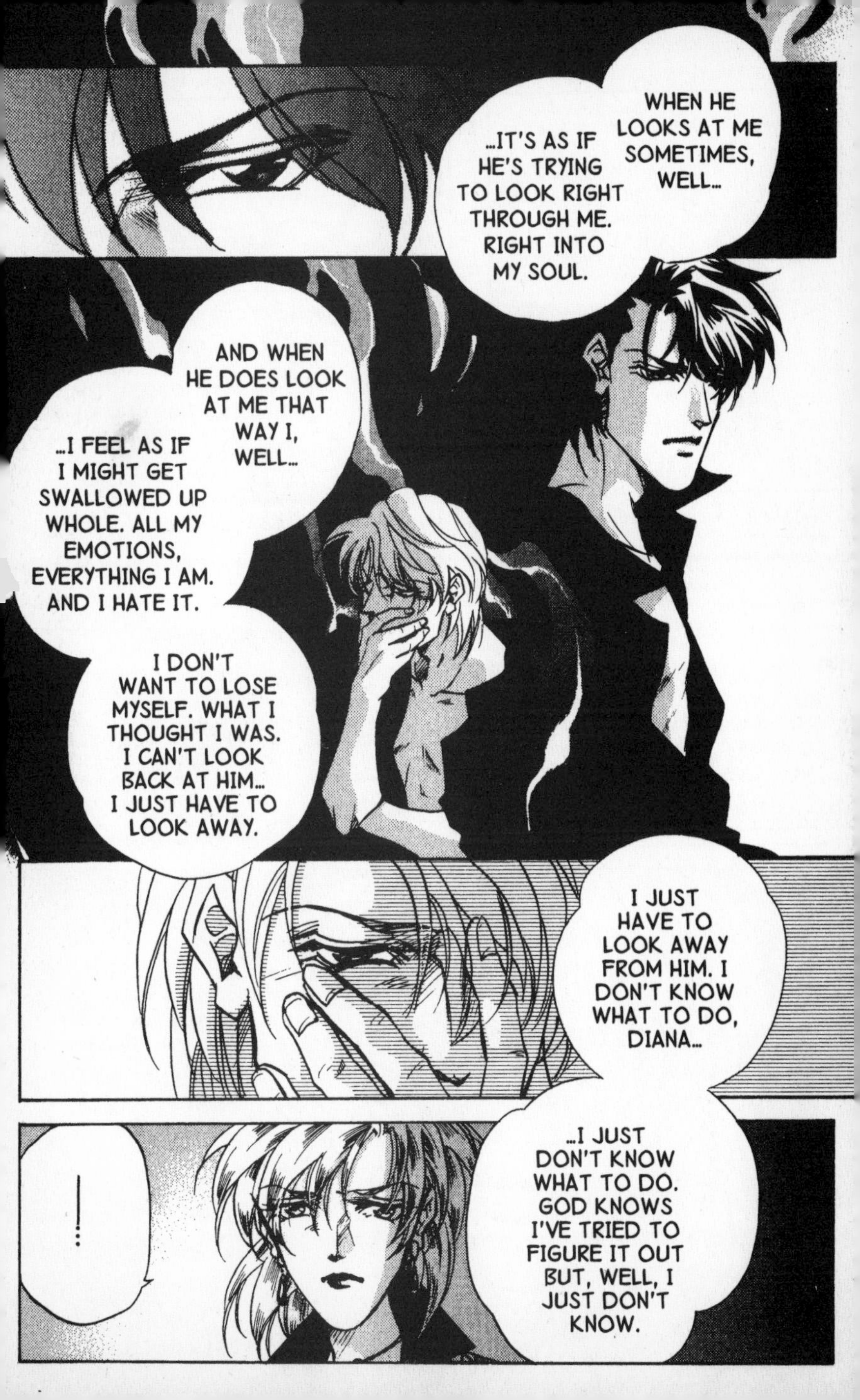

WHEN HE LOOKS AT ME SOMETIMES, WELL...
...IT'S AS IF HE'S TRYING TO LOOK RIGHT THROUGH ME. RIGHT INTO MY SOUL.
AND WHEN HE DOES LOOK AT ME THAT WAY I, WELL...
...I FEEL AS IF I MIGHT GET SWALLOWED UP WHOLE. ALL MY EMOTIONS, EVERYTHING I AM. AND I HATE IT.
I DON'T WANT TO LOSE MYSELF. WHAT I THOUGHT I WAS. I CAN'T LOOK BACK AT HIM... I JUST HAVE TO LOOK AWAY.
I JUST HAVE TO LOOK AWAY FROM HIM. I DON'T KNOW WHAT TO DO, DIANA...
...I JUST DON'T KNOW WHAT TO DO. GOD KNOWS I'VE TRIED TO FIGURE IT OUT BUT, WELL, I JUST DON'T KNOW.
......

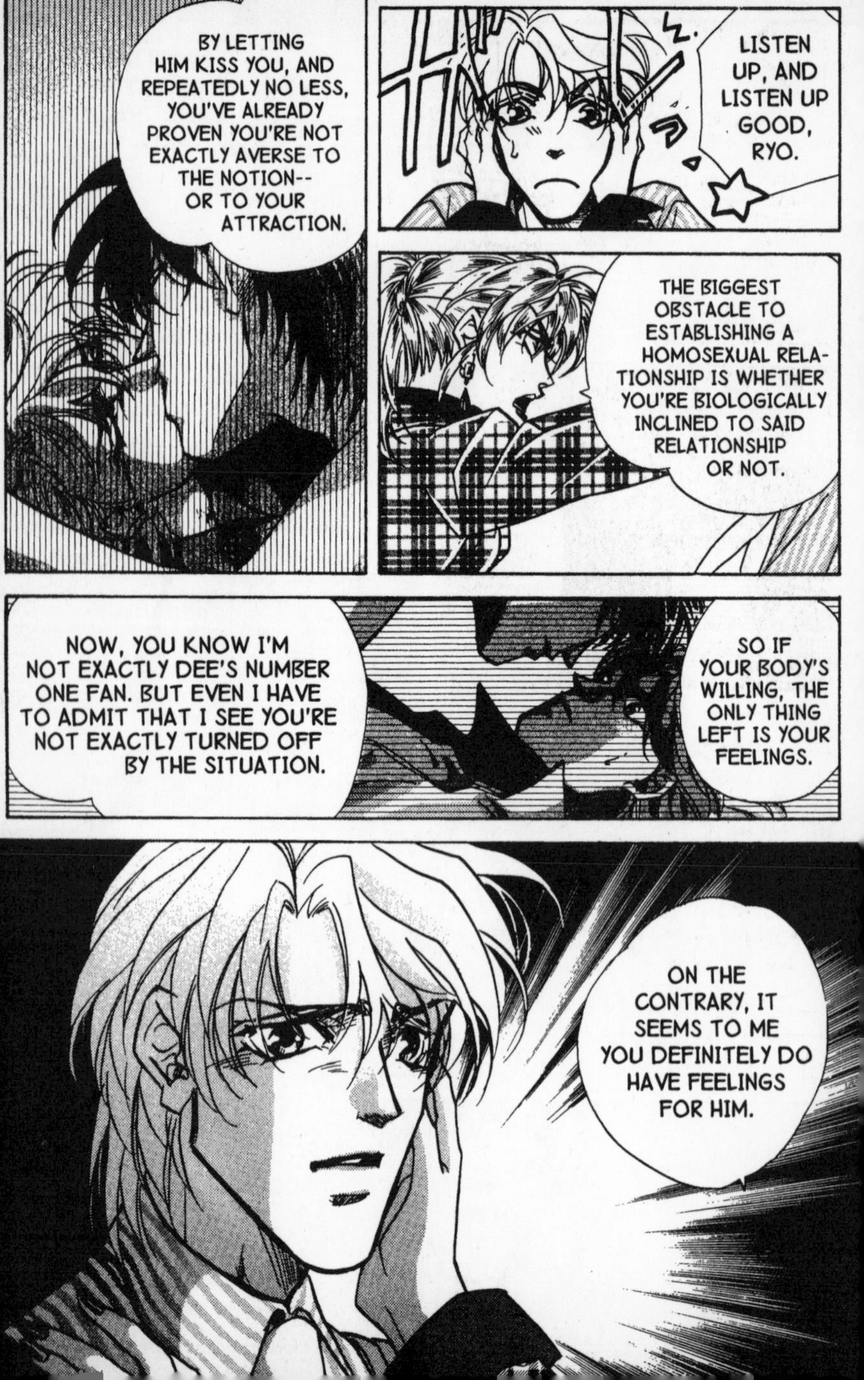
LISTEN UP, AND LISTEN UP GOOD, RYO.
THE BIGGEST OBSTACLE TO ESTABLISHING A HOMOSEXUAL RELA-TIONSHIP IS WHETHER YOU'RE BIOLOGICALLY INCLINED TO SAID RELATIONSHIP OR NOT.
BY LETTING HIM KISS YOU, AND REPEATEDLY NO LESS, YOU'VE ALREADY PROVEN YOU'RE NOT EXACTLY AVERSE TO THE NOTION-- OR TO YOUR ATTRACTION.
SO IF YOUR BODY'S WILLING, THE ONLY THING LEFT IS YOUR FEELINGS.
NOW, YOU KNOW I'M NOT EXACTLY DEE'S NUMBER ONE FAN. BUT EVEN I HAVE TO ADMIT THAT I SEE YOU'RE NOT EXACTLY TURNED OFF BY THE SITUATION.
ON THE CONTRARY, IT SEEMS TO ME YOU DEFINITELY DO HAVE FEELINGS FOR HIM.

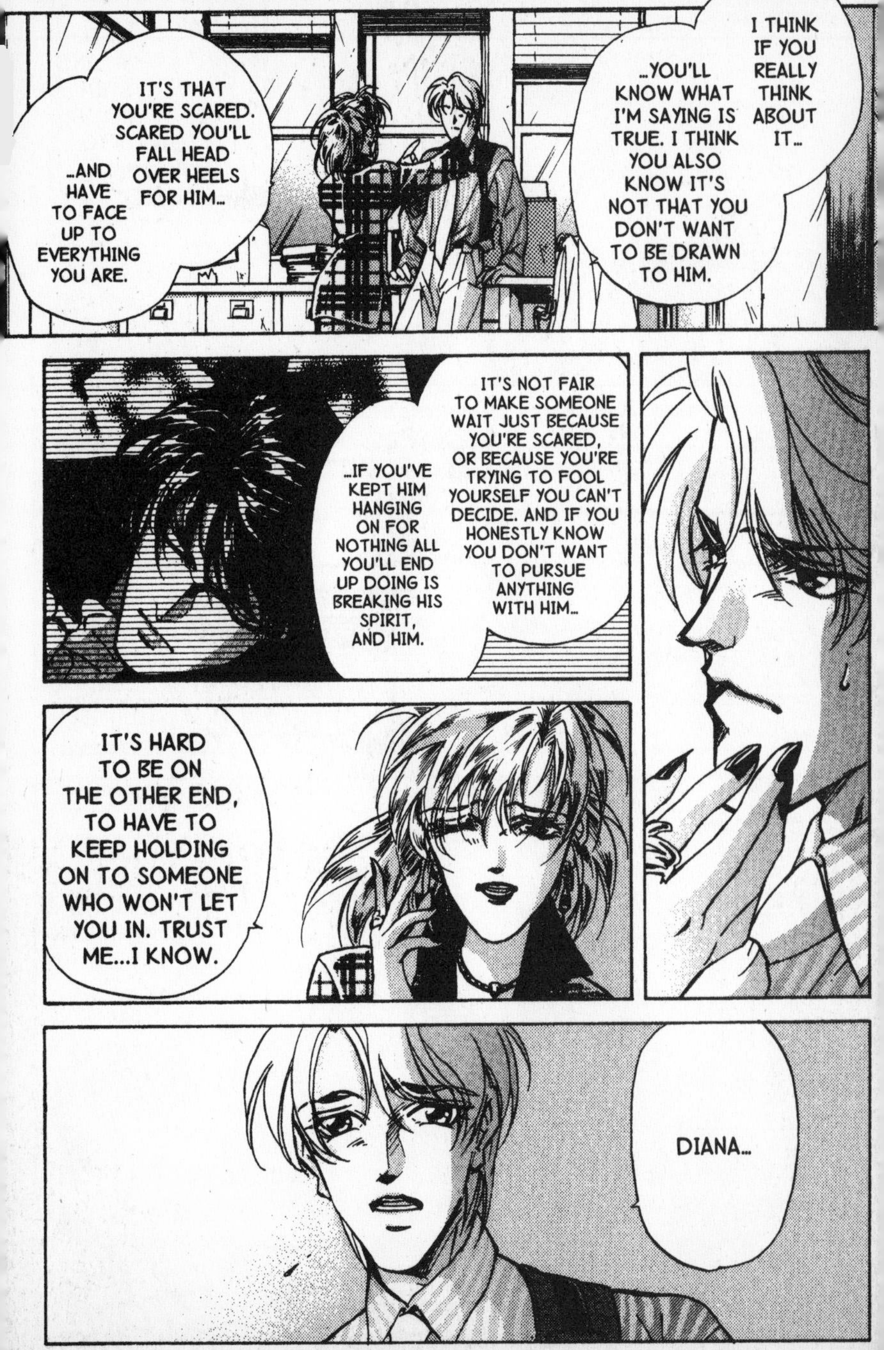
I THINK IF YOU REALLY THINK ABOUT IT...
...YOU'LL KNOW WHAT I'M SAYING IS TRUE. I THINK YOU ALSO KNOW IT'S NOT THAT YOU DON'T WANT TO BE DRAWN TO HIM.
IT'S THAT YOU'RE SCARED. SCARED YOU'LL FALL HEAD OVER HEELS FOR HIM...
...AND HAVE TO FACE UP TO EVERYTHING YOU ARE.
IT'S NOT FAIR TO MAKE SOMEONE WAIT JUST BECAUSE YOU'RE SCARED, OR BECAUSE YOU'RE TRYING TO FOOL YOURSELF YOU CAN'T DECIDE. AND IF YOU HONESTLY KNOW YOU DON'T WANT TO PURSUE ANYTHING WITH HIM...
...IF YOU'VE KEPT HIM HANGING ON FOR NOTHING ALL YOU'LL END UP DOING IS BREAKING HIS SPIRIT, AND HIM.
IT'S HARD TO BE ON THE OTHER END, TO HAVE TO KEEP HOLDING ON TO SOMEONE WHO WON'T LET YOU IN. TRUST ME...I KNOW.
DIANA...

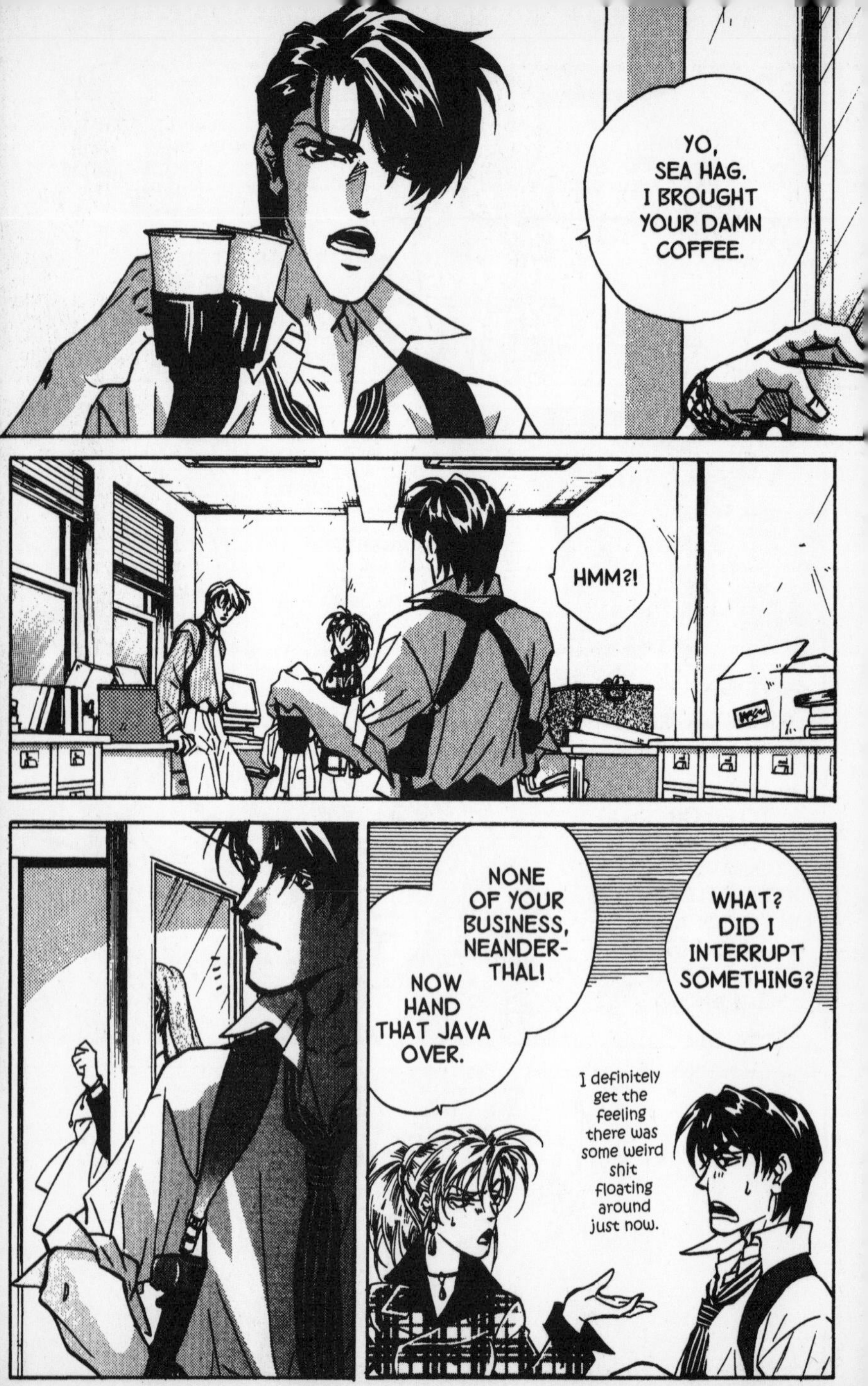
YO, SEA HAG. I BROUGHT YOUR DAMN COFFEE.
HMM?!
WHAT? DID I INTERRUPT SOMETHING?
NONE OF YOUR BUSINESS, NEANDER-THAL!
NOW HAND THAT JAVA OVER.
I definitely get the feeling there was some weird shit floating around just now.

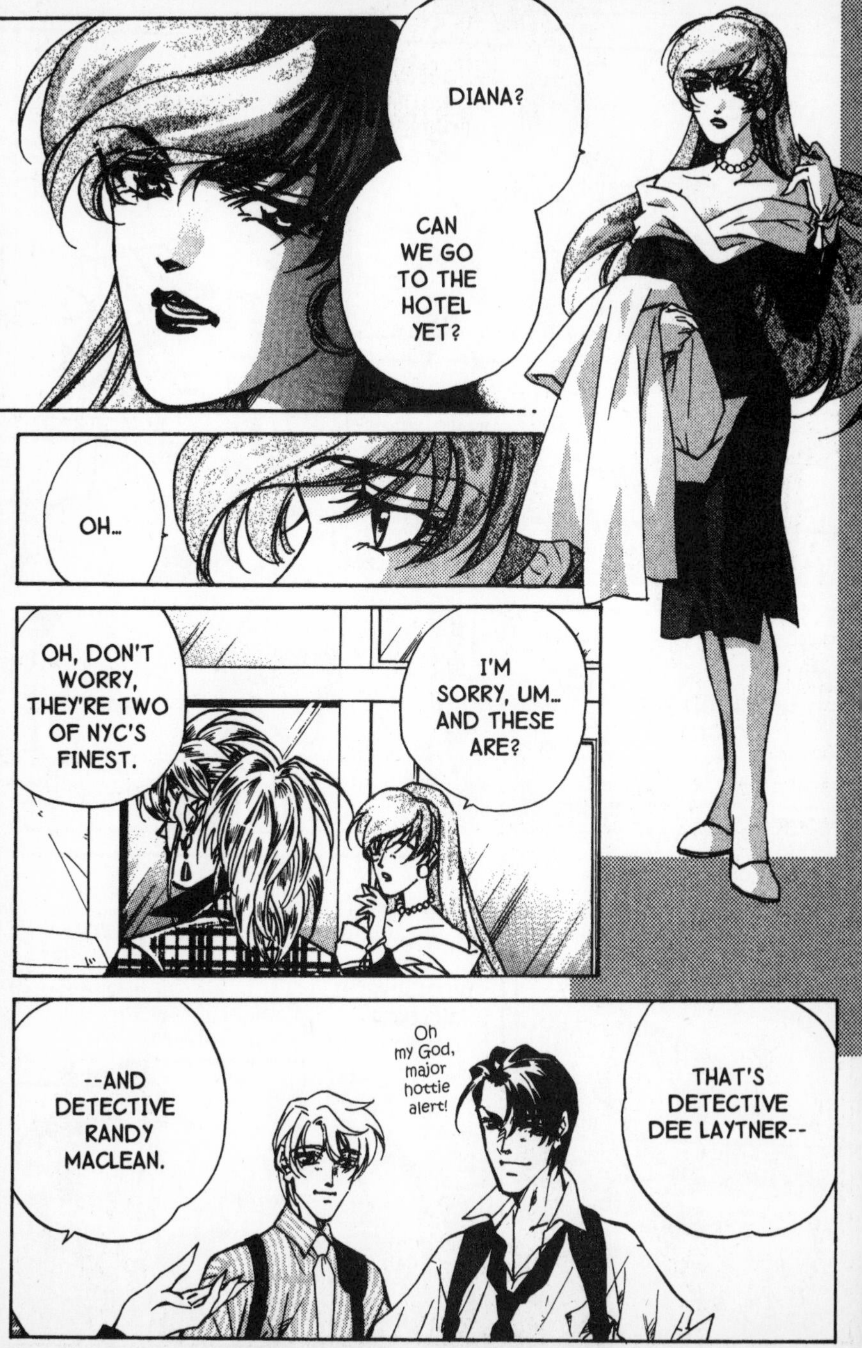
DIANA?
CAN WE GO TO THE HOTEL YET?
OH...
I'M SORRY, UM... AND THESE ARE?
OH, DON'T WORRY, THEY'RE TWO OF NYC'S FINEST.
THAT'S DETECTIVE DEE LAYTNER--
Oh my God, major hottie alert!
--AND DETECTIVE RANDY MACLEAN.

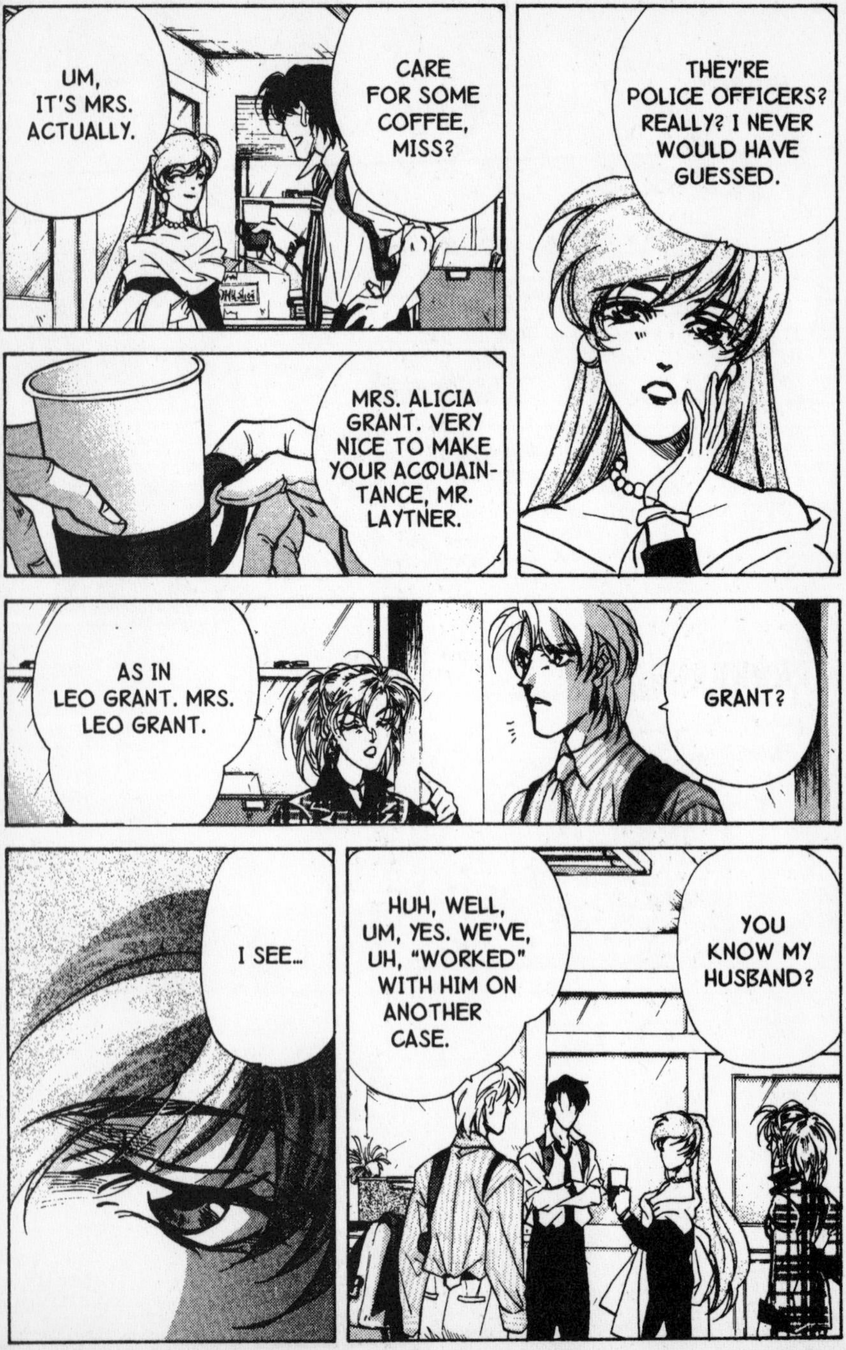
THEY'RE POLICE OFFICERS? REALLY? I NEVER WOULD HAVE GUESSED.
CARE FOR SOME COFFEE, MISS?
UM, IT'S MRS. ACTUALLY.
MRS. ALICIA GRANT. VERY NICE TO MAKE YOUR ACQUAIN-TANCE, MR. LAYTNER.
GRANT?
AS IN LEO GRANT. MRS. LEO GRANT.
YOU KNOW MY HUSBAND?
HUH, WELL, UM, YES. WE'VE, UH, "WORKED" WITH HIM ON ANOTHER CASE.
I SEE...

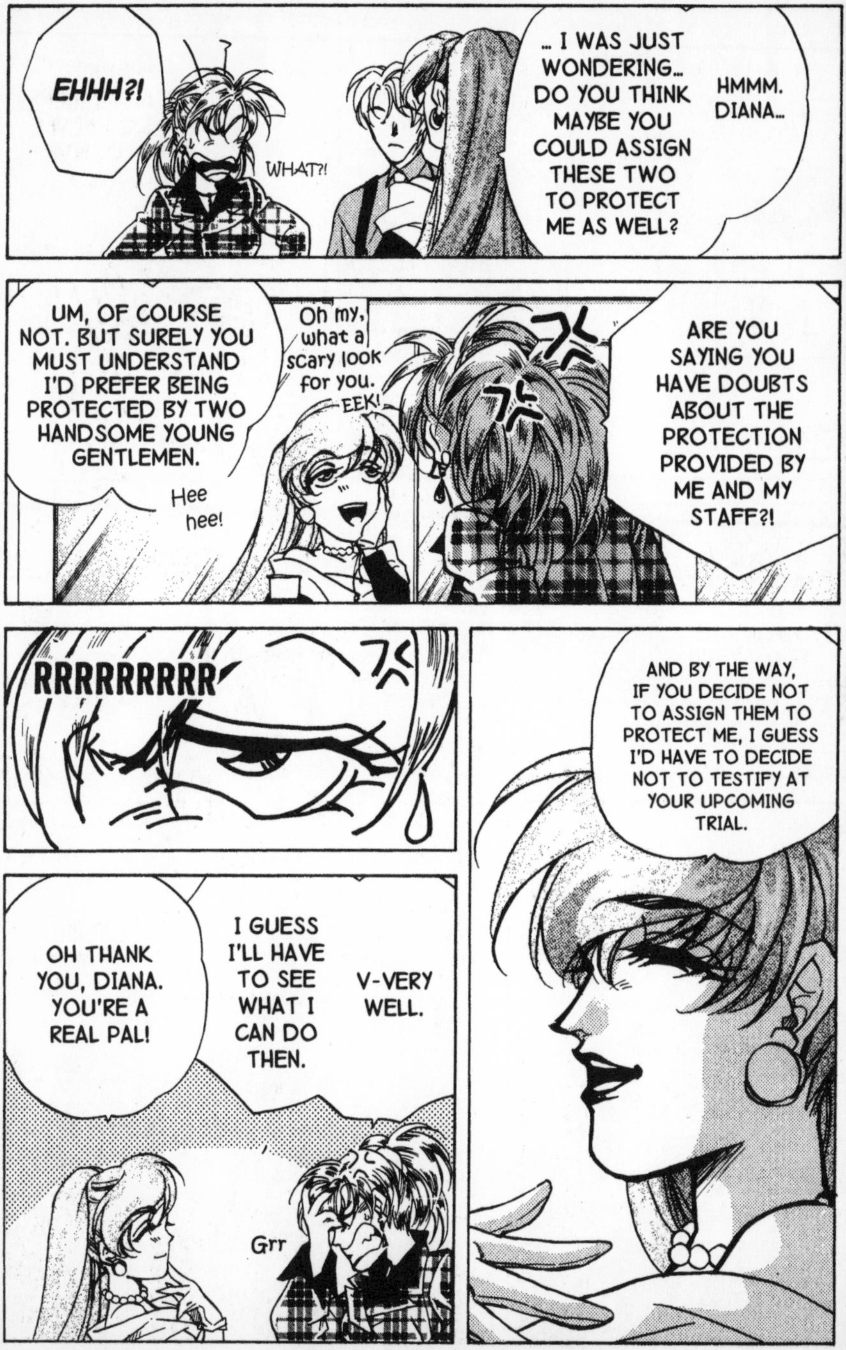
HMMM. DIANA...
... I WAS JUST WONDERING... DO YOU THINK MAYBE YOU COULD ASSIGN THESE TWO TO PROTECT ME AS WELL?
EHHH?!
WHAT?!
ARE YOU SAYING YOU HAVE DOUBTS ABOUT THE PROTECTION PROVIDED BY ME AND MY STAFF?!
Oh my, what a scary look for you.
EEK!
UM, OF COURSE NOT. BUT SURELY YOU MUST UNDERSTAND I'D PREFER BEING PROTECTED BY TWO HANDSOME YOUNG GENTLEMEN.
Hee hee!
AND BY THE WAY, IF YOU DECIDE NOT TO ASSIGN THEM TO PROTECT ME, I GUESS I'D HAVE TO DECIDE NOT TO TESTIFY AT YOUR UPCOMING TRIAL.
RRRRRRRRR
V-VERY WELL.
I GUESS I'LL HAVE TO SEE WHAT I CAN DO THEN.
OH THANK YOU, DIANA. YOU'RE A REAL PAL!
Grr

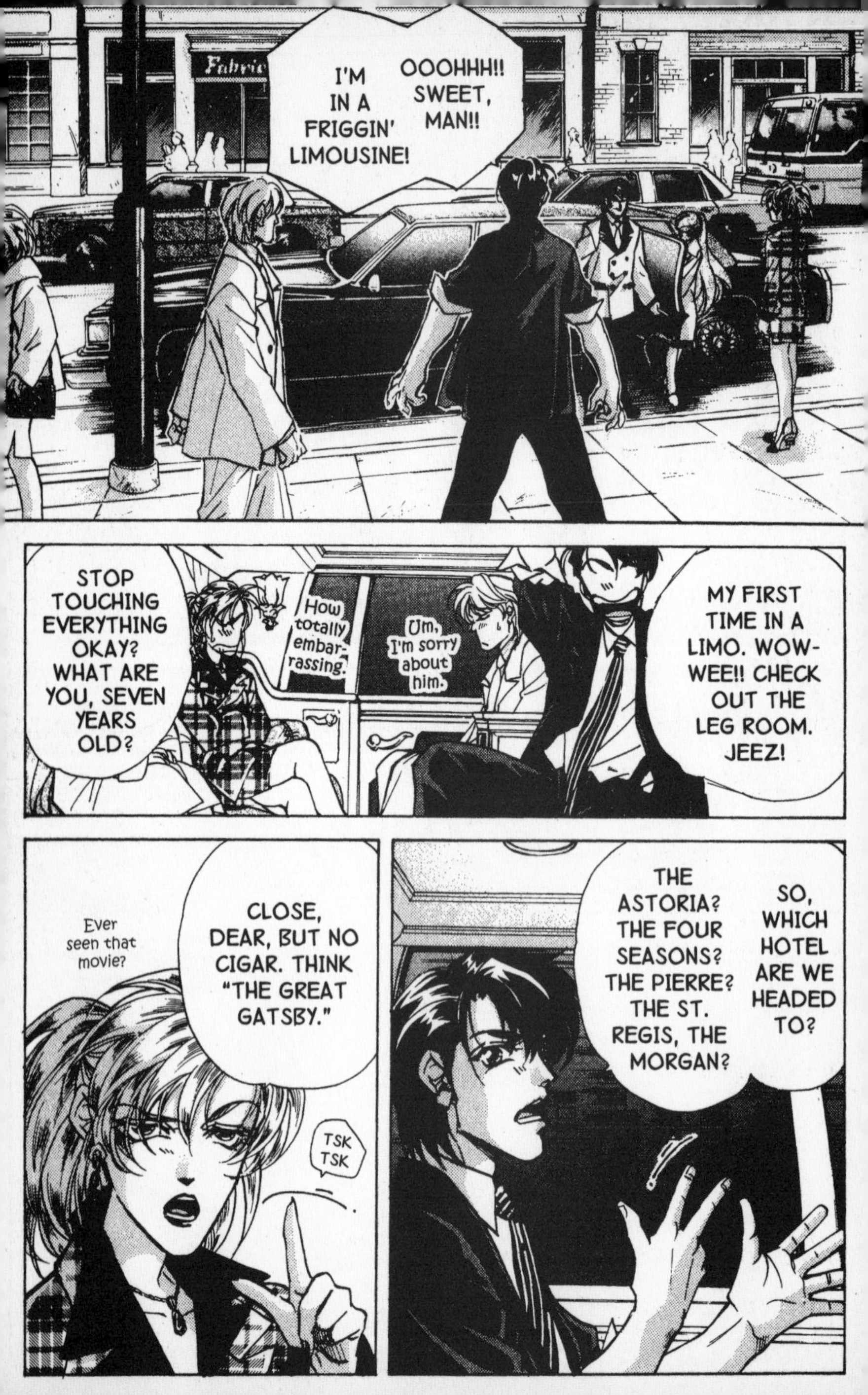
OOOHHH!! SWEET, MAN!!
I'M IN A FRIGGIN' LIMOUSINE!
MY FIRST TIME IN A LIMO. WOW-WEE!! CHECK OUT THE LEG ROOM. JEEZ!
Um, I'm sorry about him.
How totally embarrassing.
STOP TOUCHING EVERYTHING OKAY? WHAT ARE YOU, SEVEN YEARS OLD?
SO, WHICH HOTEL ARE WE HEADED TO?
THE ASTORIA? THE FOUR SEASONS? THE PIERRE? THE ST. REGIS, THE MORGAN?
CLOSE, DEAR, BUT NO CIGAR. THINK "THE GREAT GATSBY."
Ever seen that movie?
TSK TSK

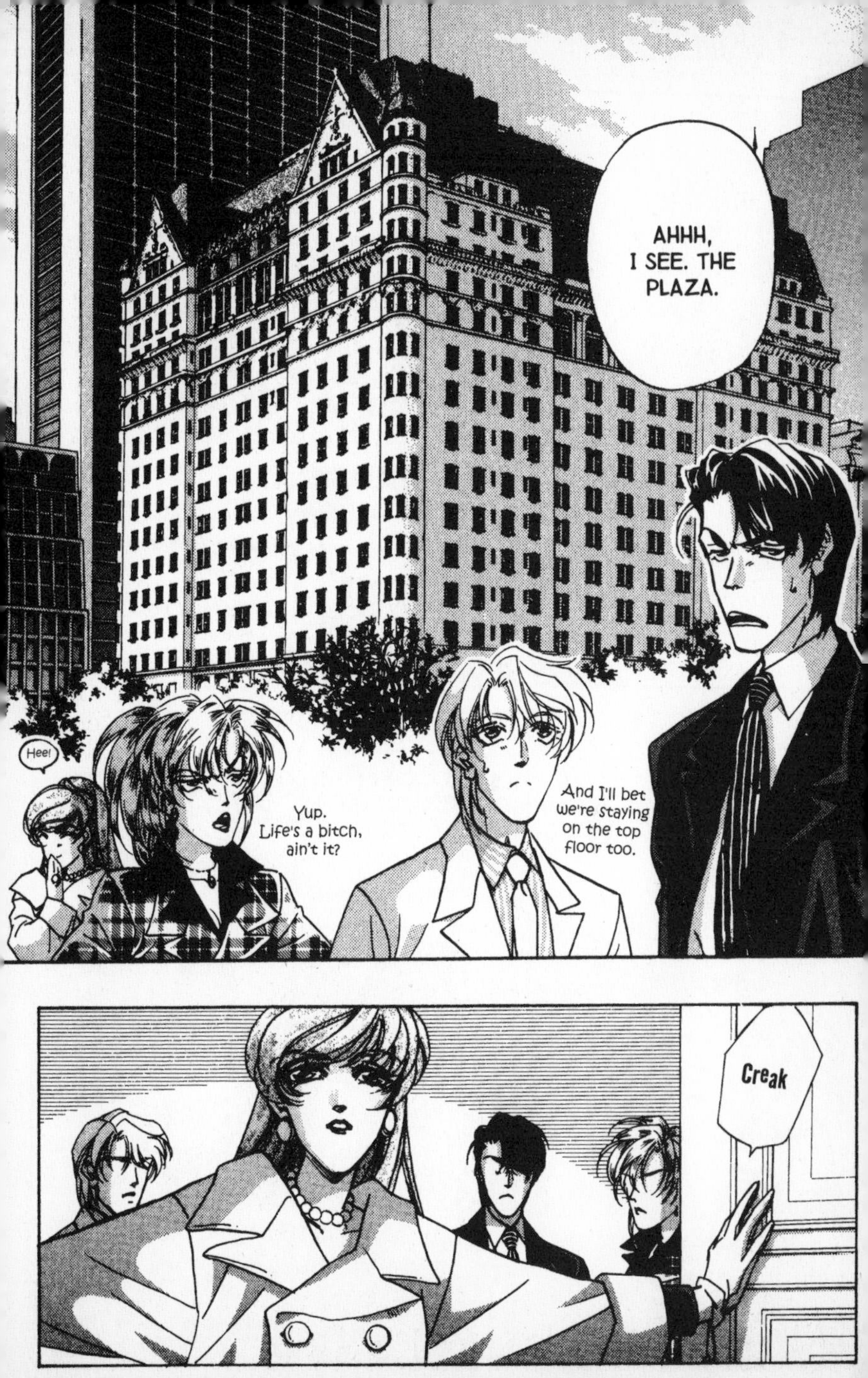
AHHH, I SEE. THE PLAZA.
And I'll bet we're staying on the top floor too.
Yup. Life's a bitch, ain't it?
Hee!
Creak

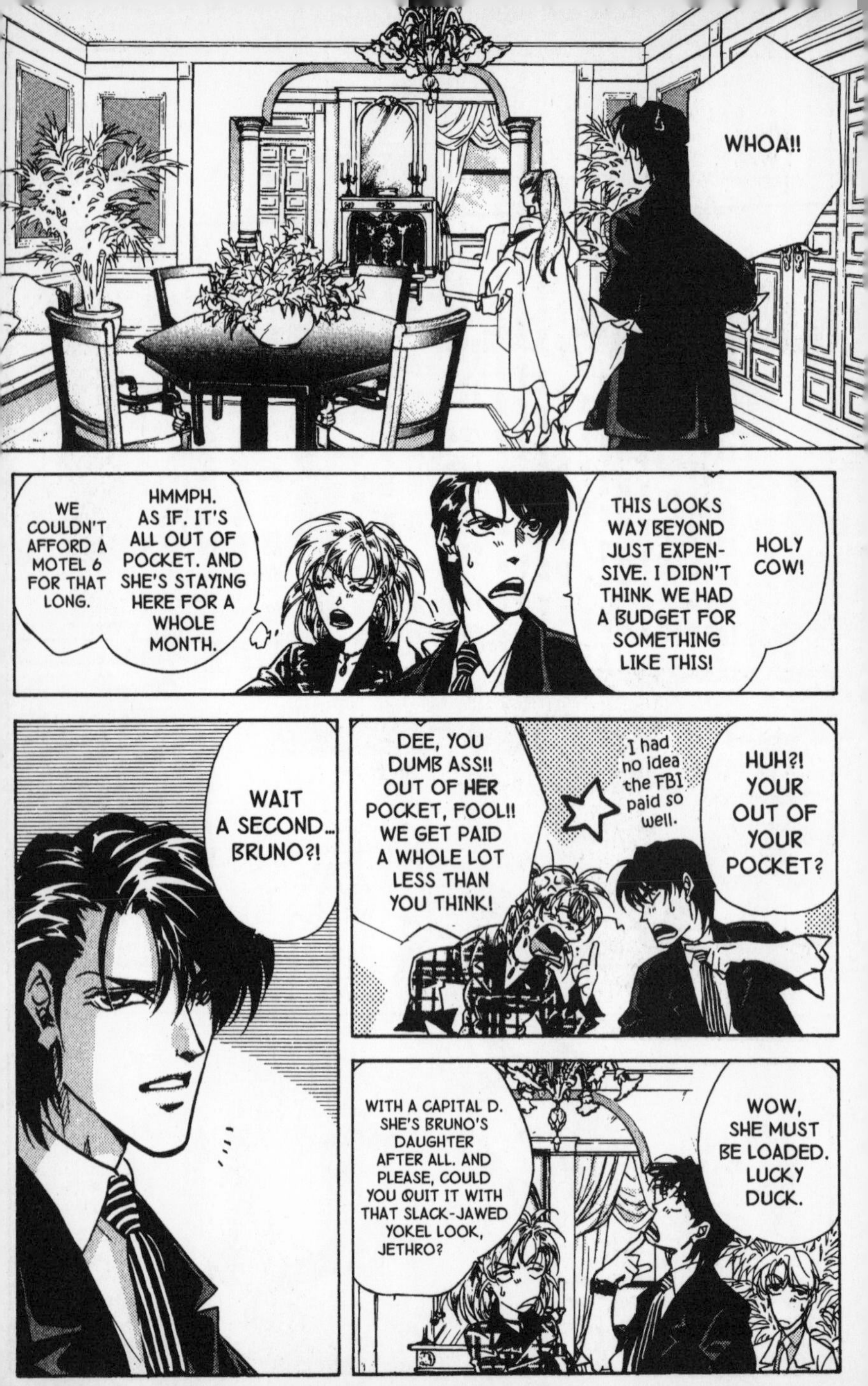
WHOA!!
HOLY COW!
THIS LOOKS WAY BEYOND JUST EXPEN-SIVE. I DIDN'T THINK WE HAD A BUDGET FOR SOMETHING LIKE THIS!
HMMPH. AS IF. IT'S ALL OUT OF POCKET. AND SHE'S STAYING HERE FOR A WHOLE MONTH.
WE COULDN'T AFFORD A MOTEL 6 FOR THAT LONG.
HUH?! YOUR OUT OF YOUR POCKET?
I had no idea the FBI paid so well.
DEE, YOU DUMB ASS!! OUT OF HER POCKET, FOOL!! WE GET PAID A WHOLE LOT LESS THAN YOU THINK!
WOW, SHE MUST BE LOADED. LUCKY DUCK.
WITH A CAPITAL D. SHE'S BRUNO'S DAUGHTER AFTER ALL. AND PLEASE, COULD YOU QUIT IT WITH THAT SLACK-JAWED YOKEL LOOK, JETHRO?
WAIT A SECOND... BRUNO?!

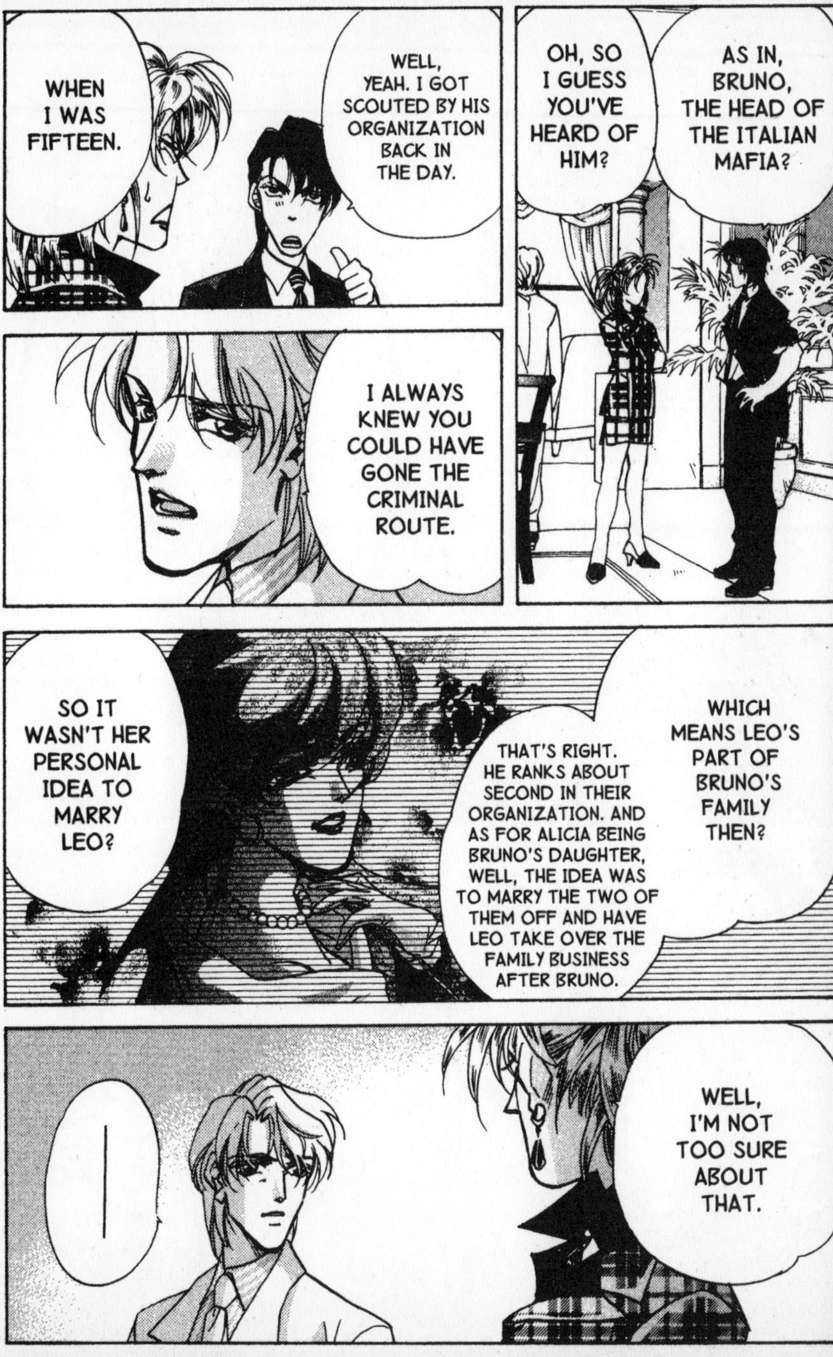
AS IN, BRUNO, THE HEAD OF THE ITALIAN MAFIA?
OH, SO I GUESS YOU'VE HEARD OF HIM?
WELL, YEAH. I GOT SCOUTED BY HIS ORGANIZATION BACK IN THE DAY.
WHEN I WAS FIFTEEN.
I ALWAYS KNEW YOU COULD HAVE GONE THE CRIMINAL ROUTE.
WHICH MEANS LEO'S PART OF BRUNO'S FAMILY THEN?
THAT'S RIGHT. HE RANKS ABOUT SECOND IN THEIR ORGANIZATION. AND AS FOR ALICIA BEING BRUNO'S DAUGHTER, WELL, THE IDEA WAS TO MARRY THE TWO OF THEM OFF AND HAVE LEO TAKE OVER THE FAMILY BUSINESS AFTER BRUNO.
SO IT WASN'T HER PERSONAL IDEA TO MARRY LEO?
WELL, I'M NOT TOO SURE ABOUT THAT.

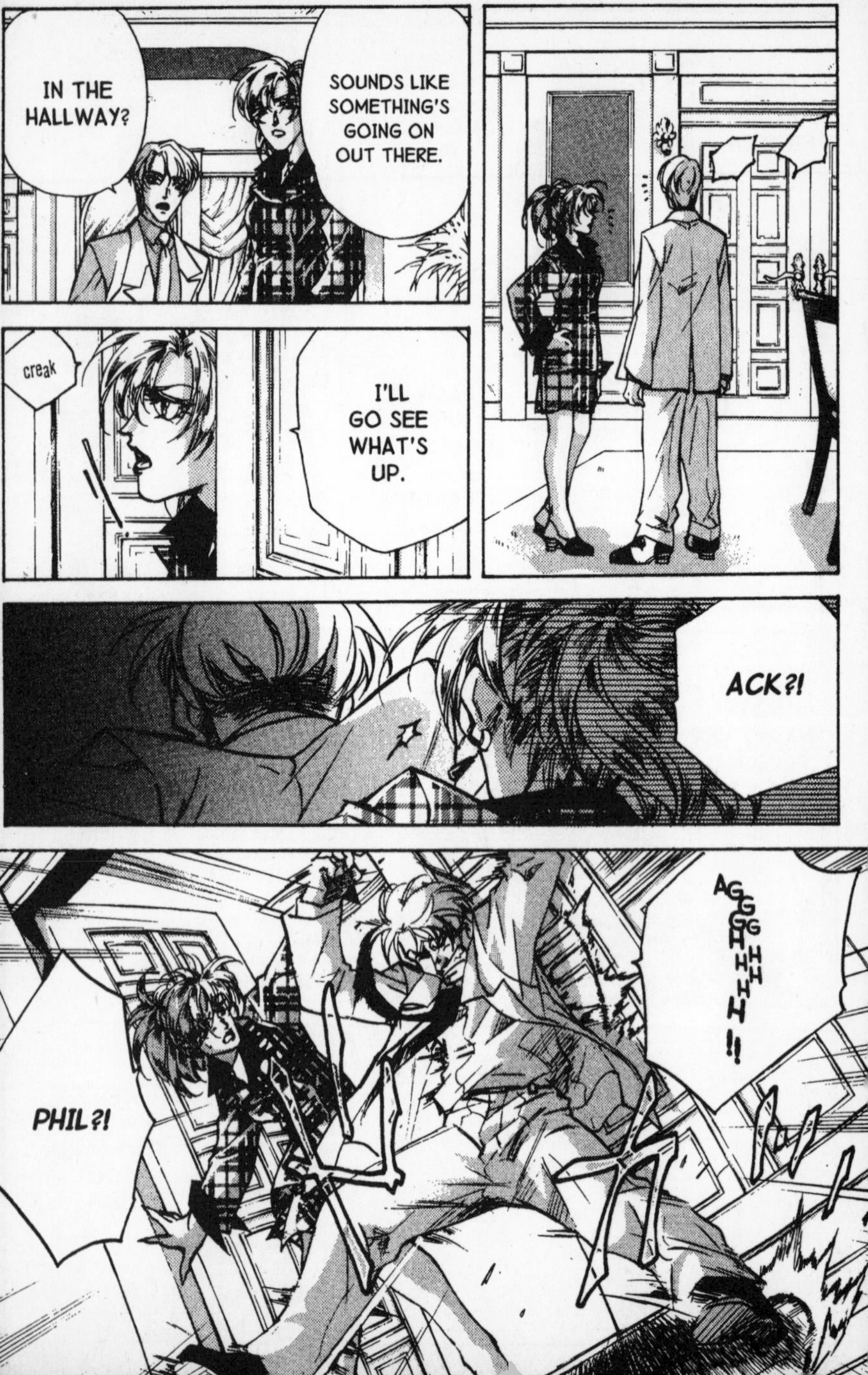

SOUNDS LIKE SOMETHING'S GOING ON OUT THERE.
IN THE HALLWAY?
I'LL GO SEE WHAT'S UP.
creak
ACK?!
AGGGHHHHH!!
PHIL?!

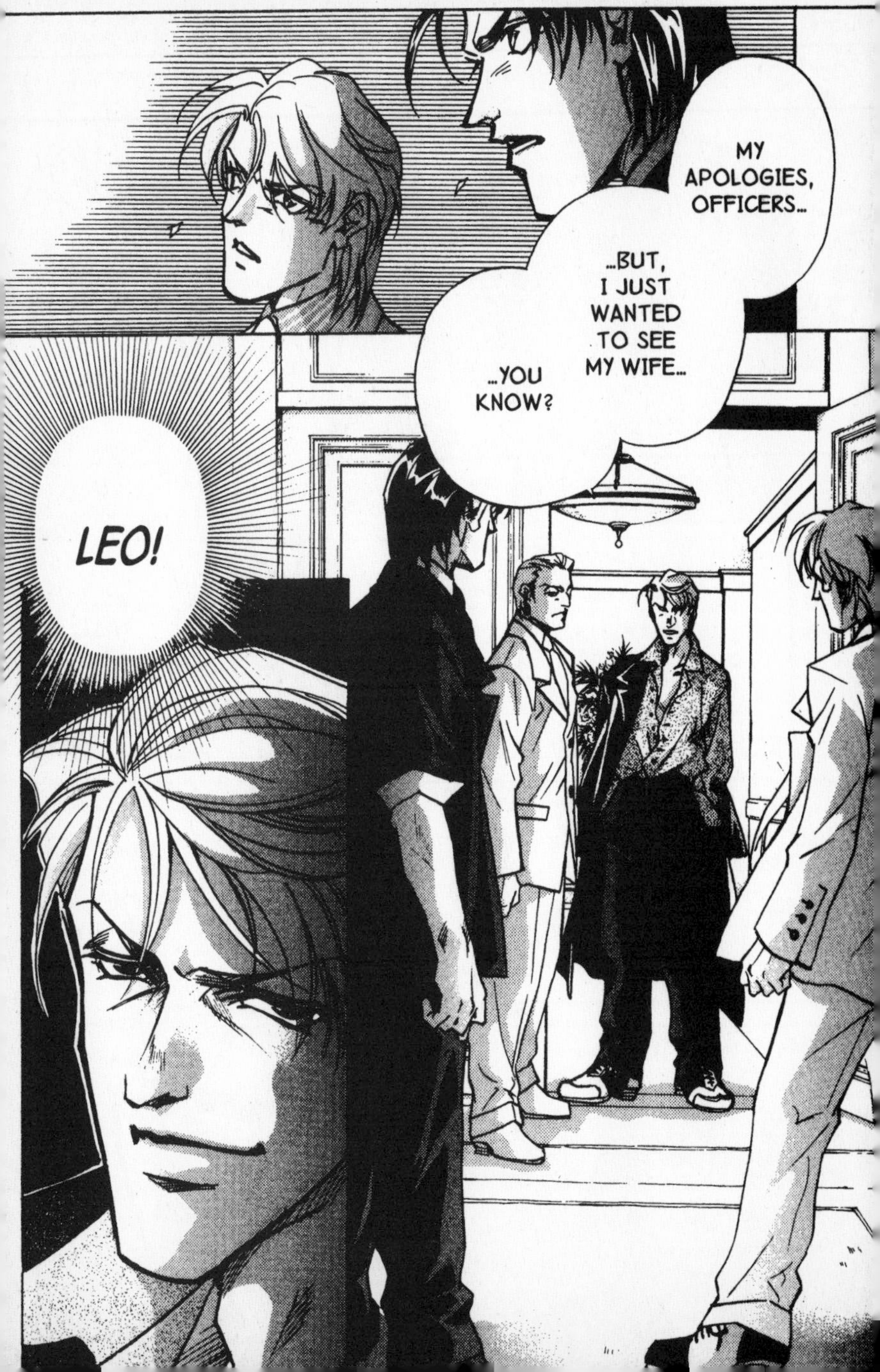
MY APOLOGIES, OFFICERS...
...BUT, I JUST WANTED TO SEE MY WIFE...
...YOU KNOW?
LEO!

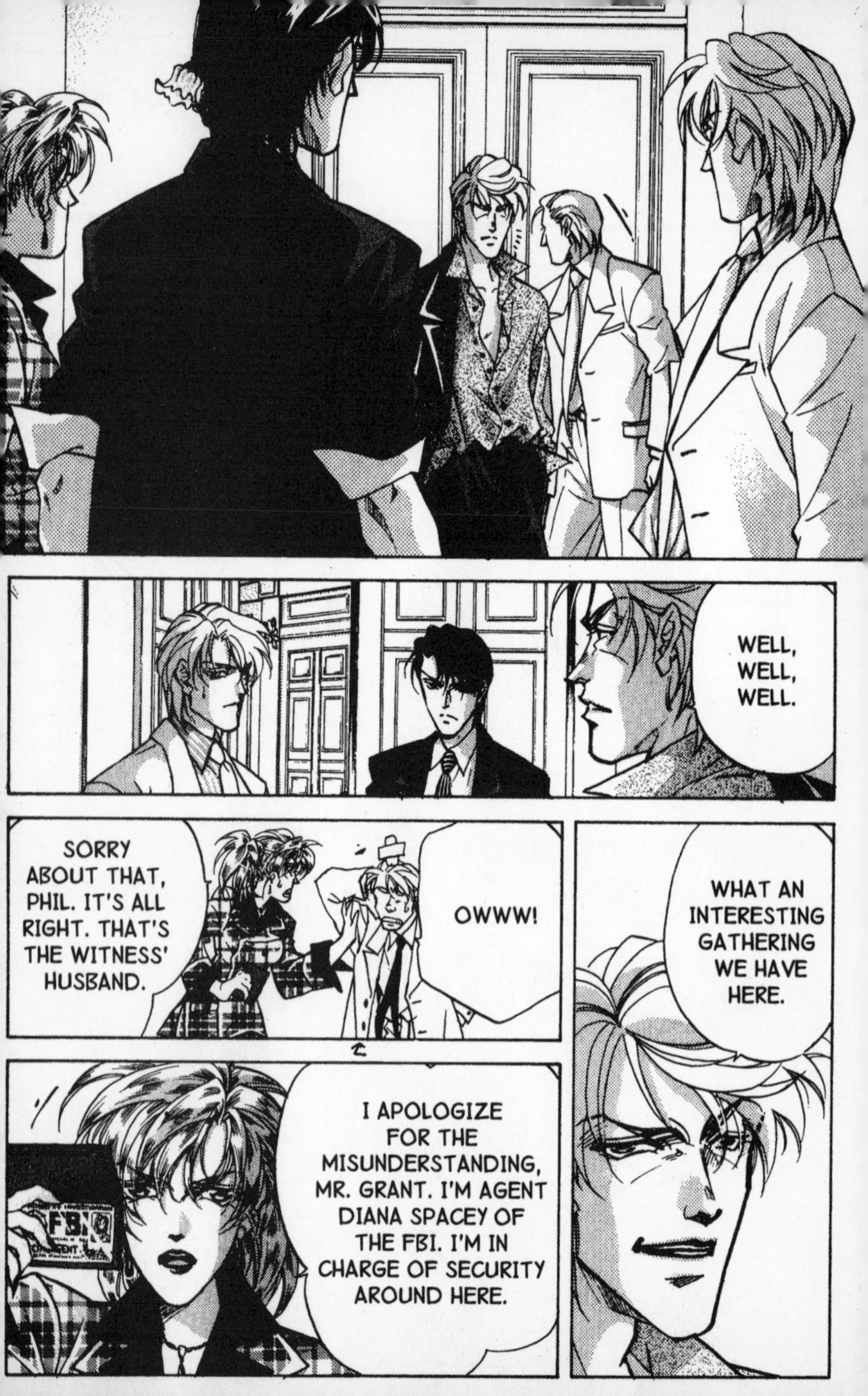
WELL, WELL, WELL.
WHAT AN INTERESTING GATHERING WE HAVE HERE.
OWWW!
SORRY ABOUT THAT, PHIL. IT'S ALL RIGHT. THAT'S THE WITNESS' HUSBAND.
I APOLOGIZE FOR THE MISUNDERSTANDING, MR. GRANT. I'M AGENT DIANA SPACEY OF THE FBI. I'M IN CHARGE OF SECURITY AROUND HERE.

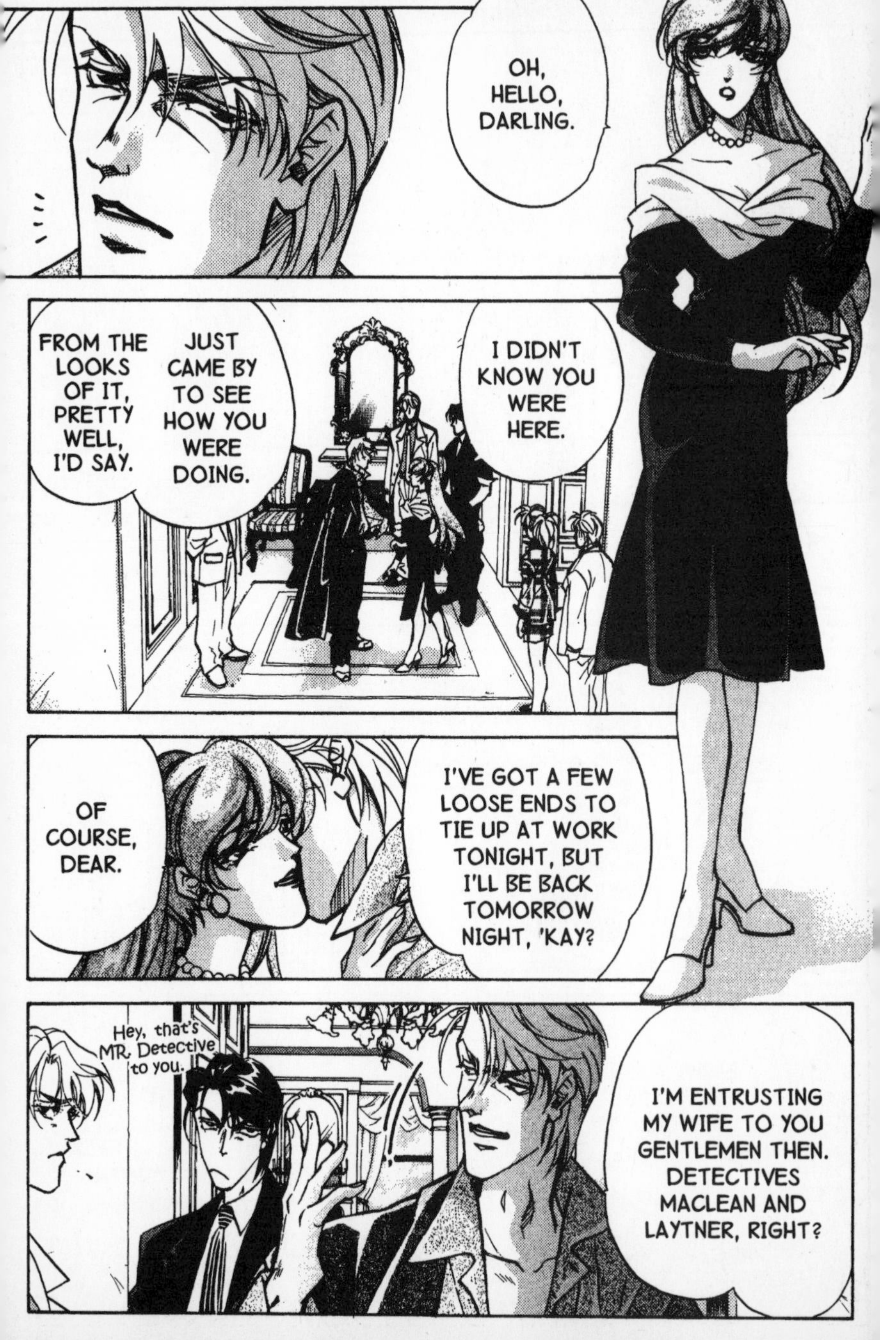
OH, HELLO, DARLING.
I DIDN'T KNOW YOU WERE HERE.
JUST CAME BY TO SEE HOW YOU WERE DOING.
FROM THE LOOKS OF IT, PRETTY WELL, I'D SAY.
I'VE GOT A FEW LOOSE ENDS TO TIE UP AT WORK TONIGHT, BUT I'LL BE BACK TOMORROW NIGHT, 'KAY?
OF COURSE, DEAR.
I'M ENTRUSTING MY WIFE TO YOU GENTLEMEN THEN. DETECTIVES MACLEAN AND LAYTNER, RIGHT?
Hey, that's MR. Detective to you.

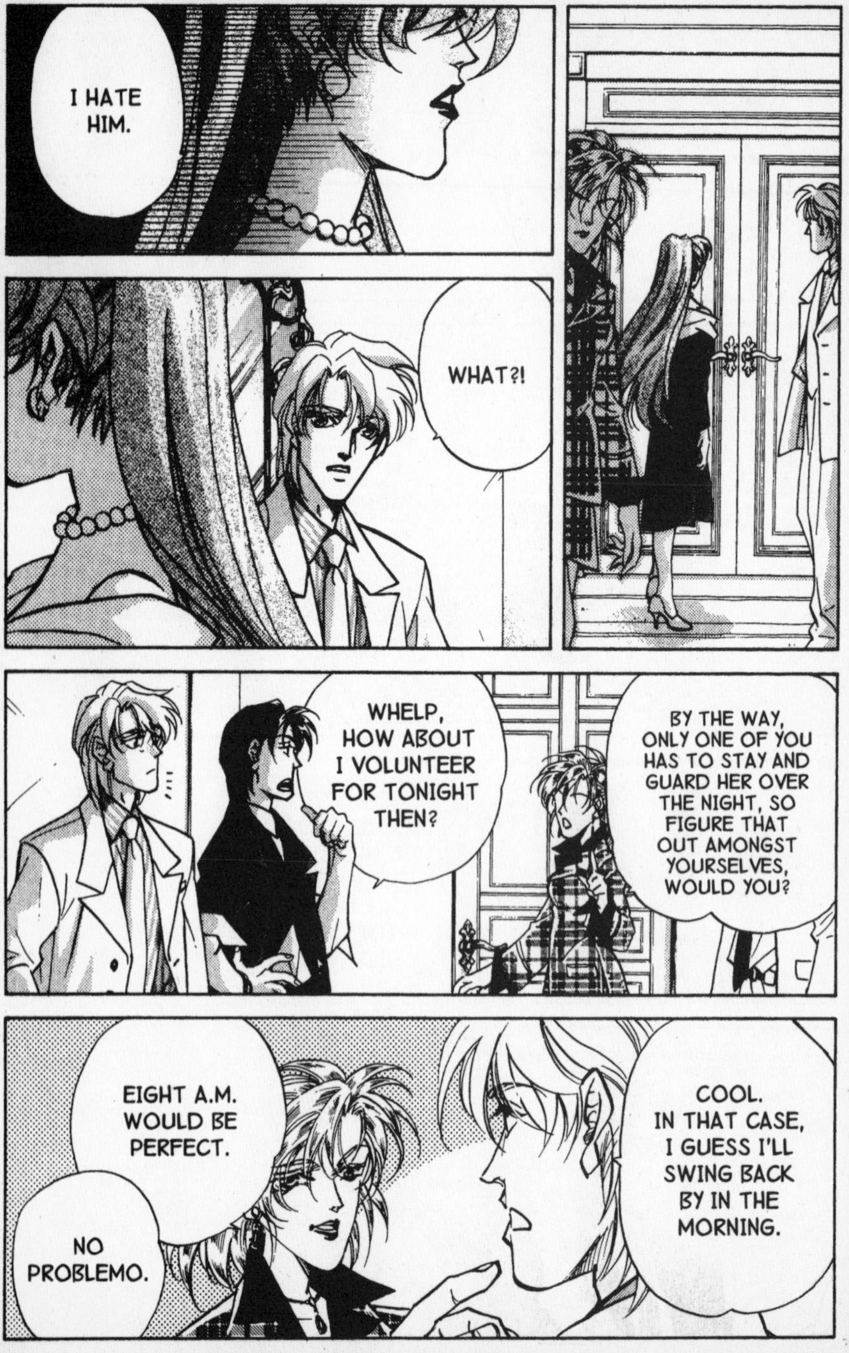
I HATE HIM.
WHAT?!
BY THE WAY, ONLY ONE OF YOU HAS TO STAY AND GUARD HER OVER THE NIGHT, SO FIGURE THAT OUT AMONGST YOURSELVES, WOULD YOU?
WHELP, HOW ABOUT I VOLUNTEER FOR TONIGHT THEN?
COOL. IN THAT CASE, I GUESS I'LL SWING BACK BY IN THE MORNING.
EIGHT A.M. WOULD BE PERFECT.
NO PROBLEMO.

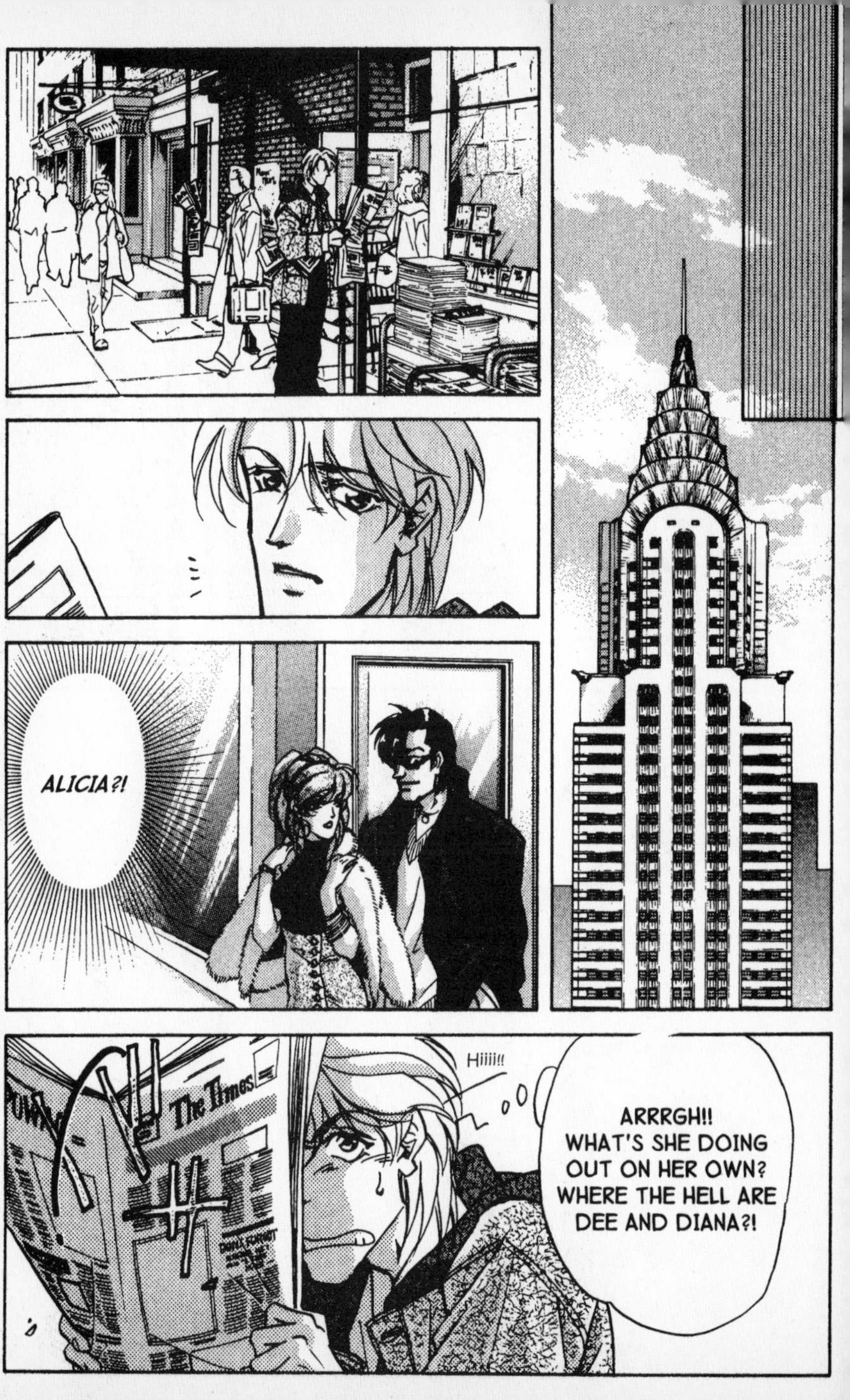
ALICIA?!
ARRRGH!! WHAT'S SHE DOING OUT ON HER OWN? WHERE THE HELL ARE DEE AND DIANA?!
Hiiii!!
The Times

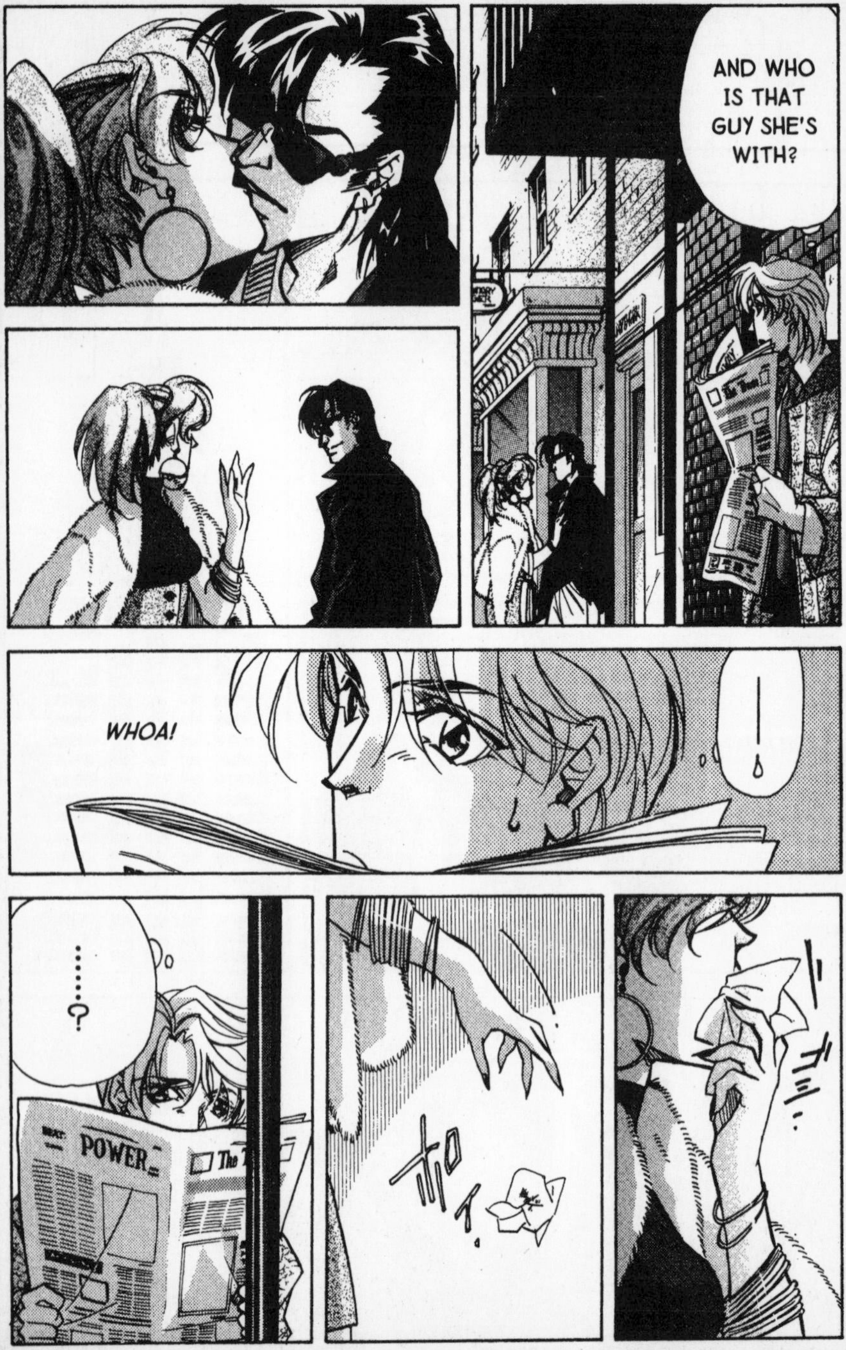
AND WHO IS THAT GUY SHE'S WITH?
!
WHOA!
ポイ
.....?

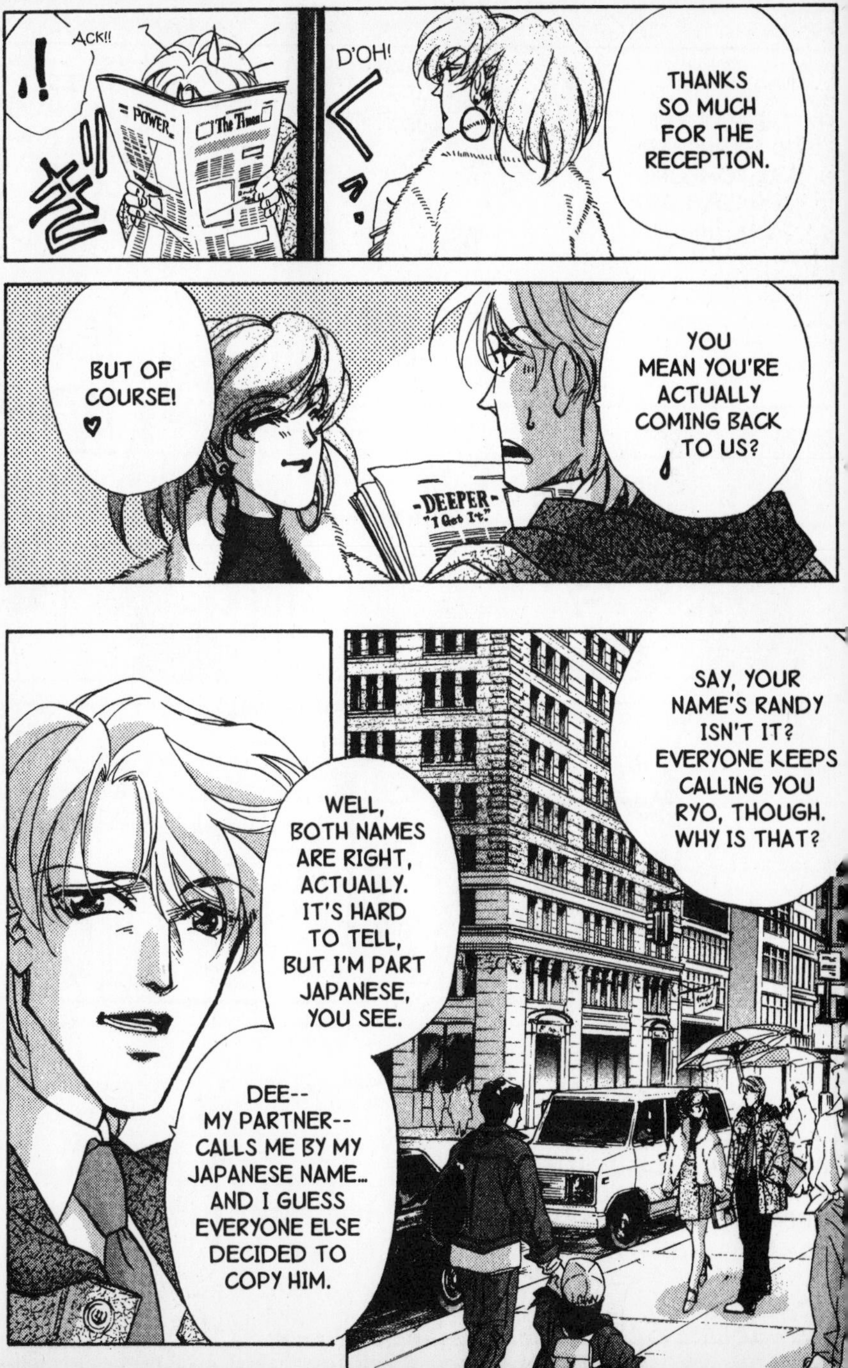
THANKS SO MUCH FOR THE RECEPTION.
D'OH!
ACK!!
POWER
The Times
YOU MEAN YOU'RE ACTUALLY COMING BACK TO US?
BUT OF COURSE! ♥
-DEEPER-
"I Got It."
SAY, YOUR NAME'S RANDY ISN'T IT? EVERYONE KEEPS CALLING YOU RYO, THOUGH. WHY IS THAT?
WELL, BOTH NAMES ARE RIGHT, ACTUALLY. IT'S HARD TO TELL, BUT I'M PART JAPANESE, YOU SEE.
DEE-- MY PARTNER-- CALLS ME BY MY JAPANESE NAME... AND I GUESS EVERYONE ELSE DECIDED TO COPY HIM.

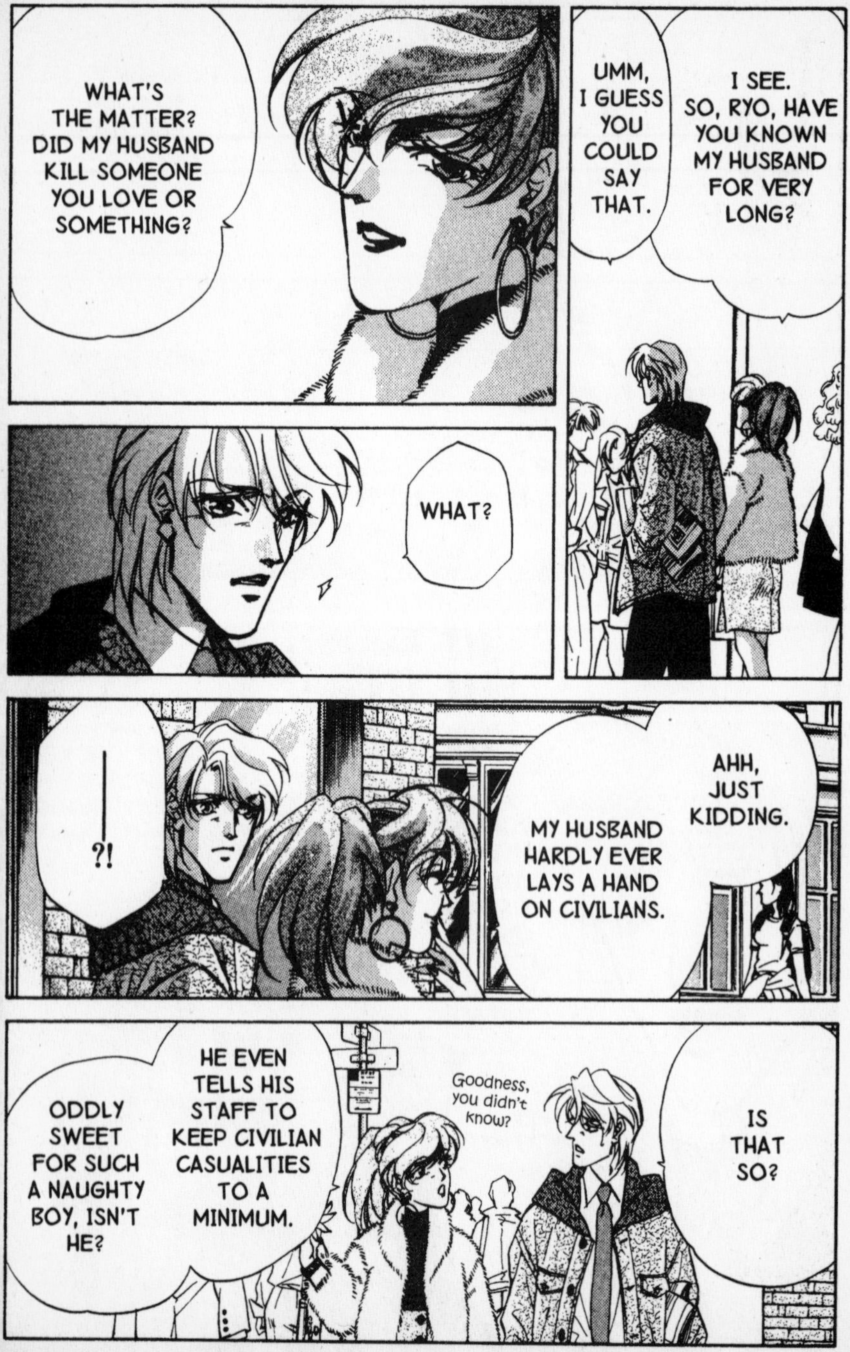
I SEE. SO, RYO, HAVE YOU KNOWN MY HUSBAND FOR VERY LONG?
UMM, I GUESS YOU COULD SAY THAT.
WHAT'S THE MATTER? DID MY HUSBAND KILL SOMEONE YOU LOVE OR SOMETHING?
WHAT?
AHH, JUST KIDDING.
MY HUSBAND HARDLY EVER LAYS A HAND ON CIVILIANS.
—?!
IS THAT SO?
Goodness, you didn't know?
HE EVEN TELLS HIS STAFF TO KEEP CIVILIAN CASUALITIES TO A MINIMUM.
ODDLY SWEET FOR SUCH A NAUGHTY BOY, ISN'T HE?

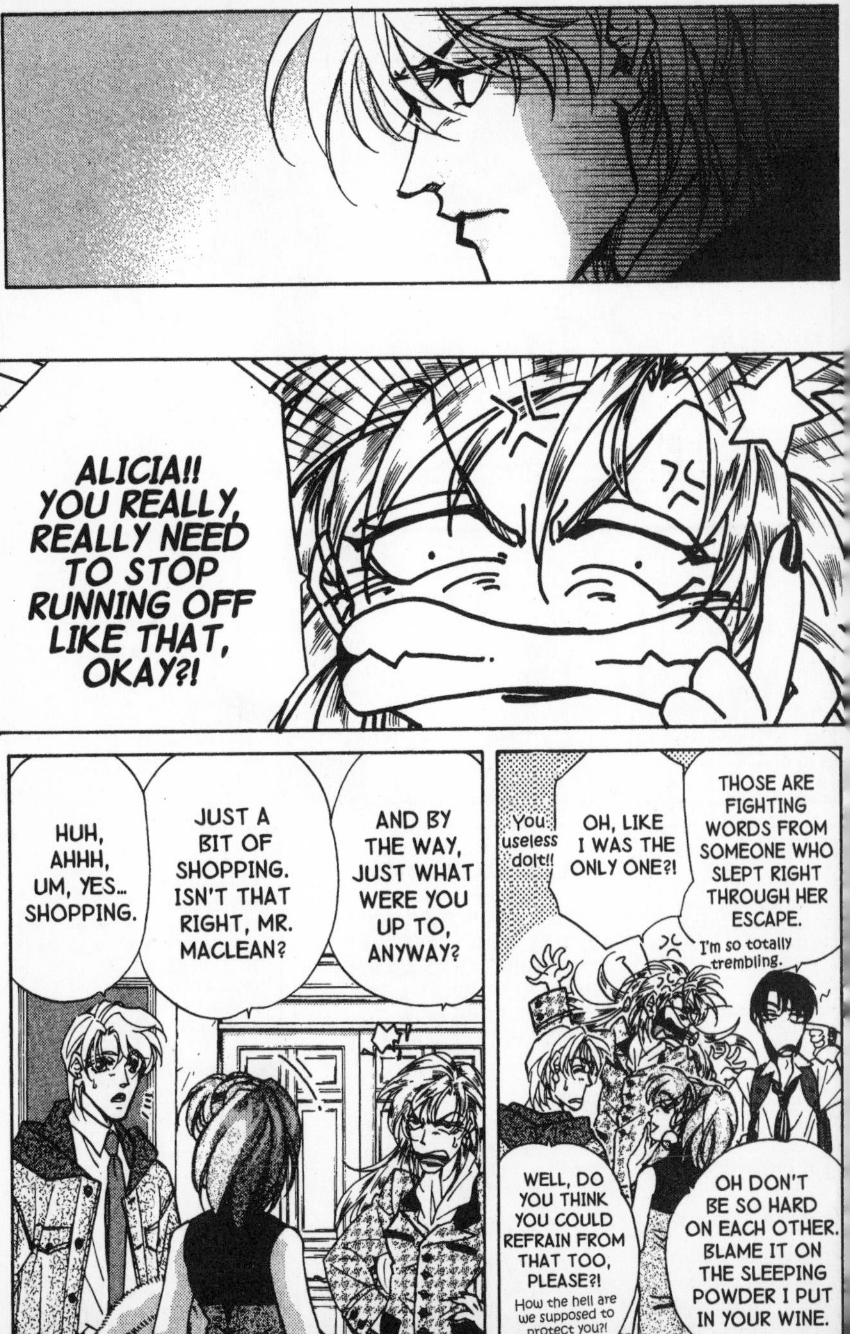
ALICIA!! YOU REALLY, REALLY NEED TO STOP RUNNING OFF LIKE THAT, OKAY?!
THOSE ARE FIGHTING WORDS FROM SOMEONE WHO SLEPT RIGHT THROUGH HER ESCAPE.
I'm so totally trembling.
OH, LIKE I WAS THE ONLY ONE?!
You useless dolt!!
OH DON'T BE SO HARD ON EACH OTHER. BLAME IT ON THE SLEEPING POWDER I PUT IN YOUR WINE.
WELL, DO YOU THINK YOU COULD REFRAIN FROM THAT TOO, PLEASE?!
How the hell are we supposed to protect you?!
AND BY THE WAY, JUST WHAT WERE YOU UP TO, ANYWAY?
JUST A BIT OF SHOPPING. ISN'T THAT RIGHT, MR. MACLEAN?
HUH, AHHH, UM, YES... SHOPPING.

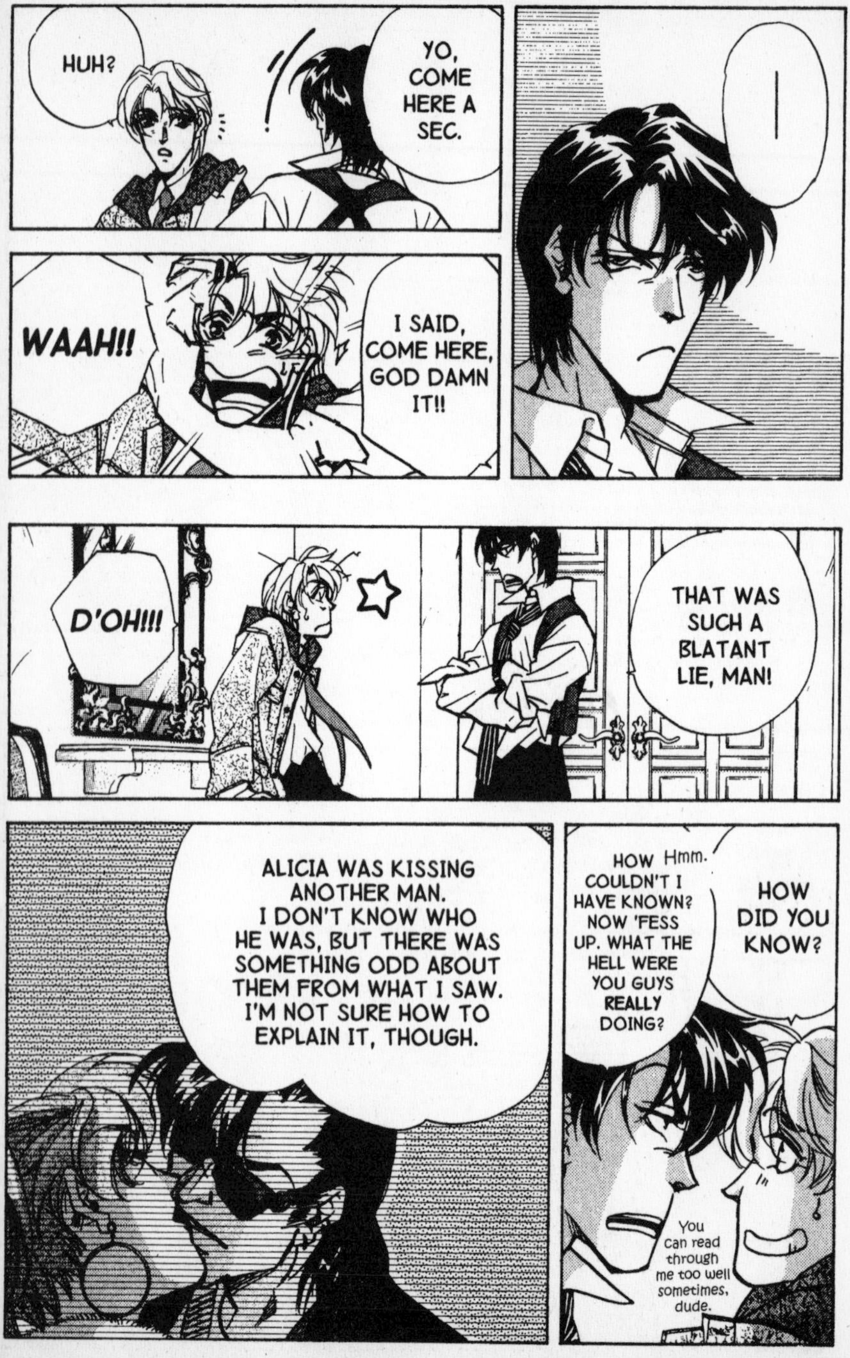
YO, COME HERE A SEC.
HUH?
I SAID, COME HERE, GOD DAMN IT!!
WAAH!!
THAT WAS SUCH A BLATANT LIE, MAN!
D'OH!!!
HOW DID YOU KNOW?
Hmm.
HOW COULDN'T I HAVE KNOWN? NOW 'FESS UP. WHAT THE HELL WERE YOU GUYS **REALLY** DOING?
You can read through me too well sometimes, dude.
ALICIA WAS KISSING ANOTHER MAN. I DON'T KNOW WHO HE WAS, BUT THERE WAS SOMETHING ODD ABOUT THEM FROM WHAT I SAW. I'M NOT SURE HOW TO EXPLAIN IT, THOUGH.

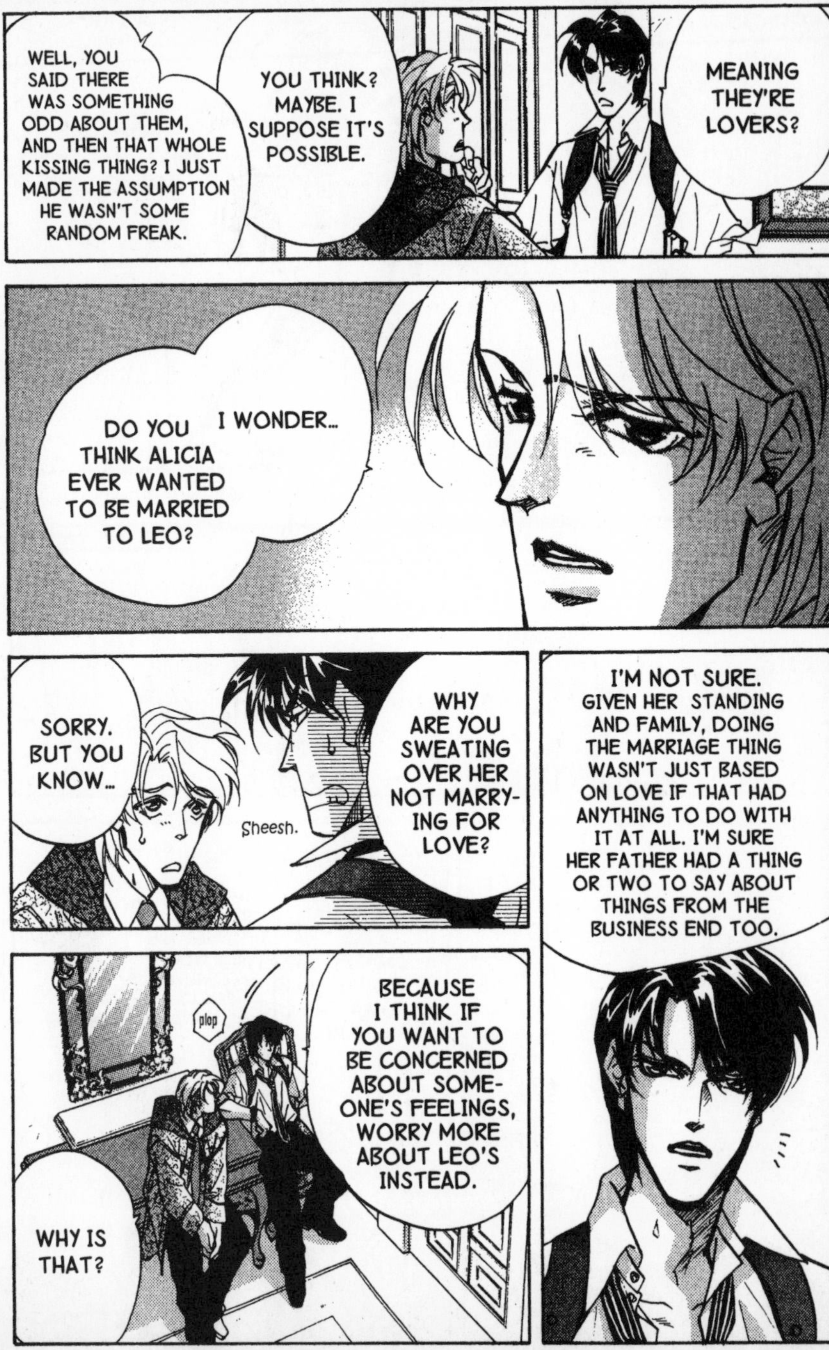
MEANING THEY'RE LOVERS?
YOU THINK? MAYBE. I SUPPOSE IT'S POSSIBLE.
WELL, YOU SAID THERE WAS SOMETHING ODD ABOUT THEM, AND THEN THAT WHOLE KISSING THING? I JUST MADE THE ASSUMPTION HE WASN'T SOME RANDOM FREAK.
I WONDER...
DO YOU THINK ALICIA EVER WANTED TO BE MARRIED TO LEO?
I'M NOT SURE. GIVEN HER STANDING AND FAMILY, DOING THE MARRIAGE THING WASN'T JUST BASED ON LOVE IF THAT HAD ANYTHING TO DO WITH IT AT ALL. I'M SURE HER FATHER HAD A THING OR TWO TO SAY ABOUT THINGS FROM THE BUSINESS END TOO.
WHY ARE YOU SWEATING OVER HER NOT MARRYING FOR LOVE?
Sheesh.
SORRY. BUT YOU KNOW...
BECAUSE I THINK IF YOU WANT TO BE CONCERNED ABOUT SOMEONE'S FEELINGS, WORRY MORE ABOUT LEO'S INSTEAD.
plop
WHY IS THAT?

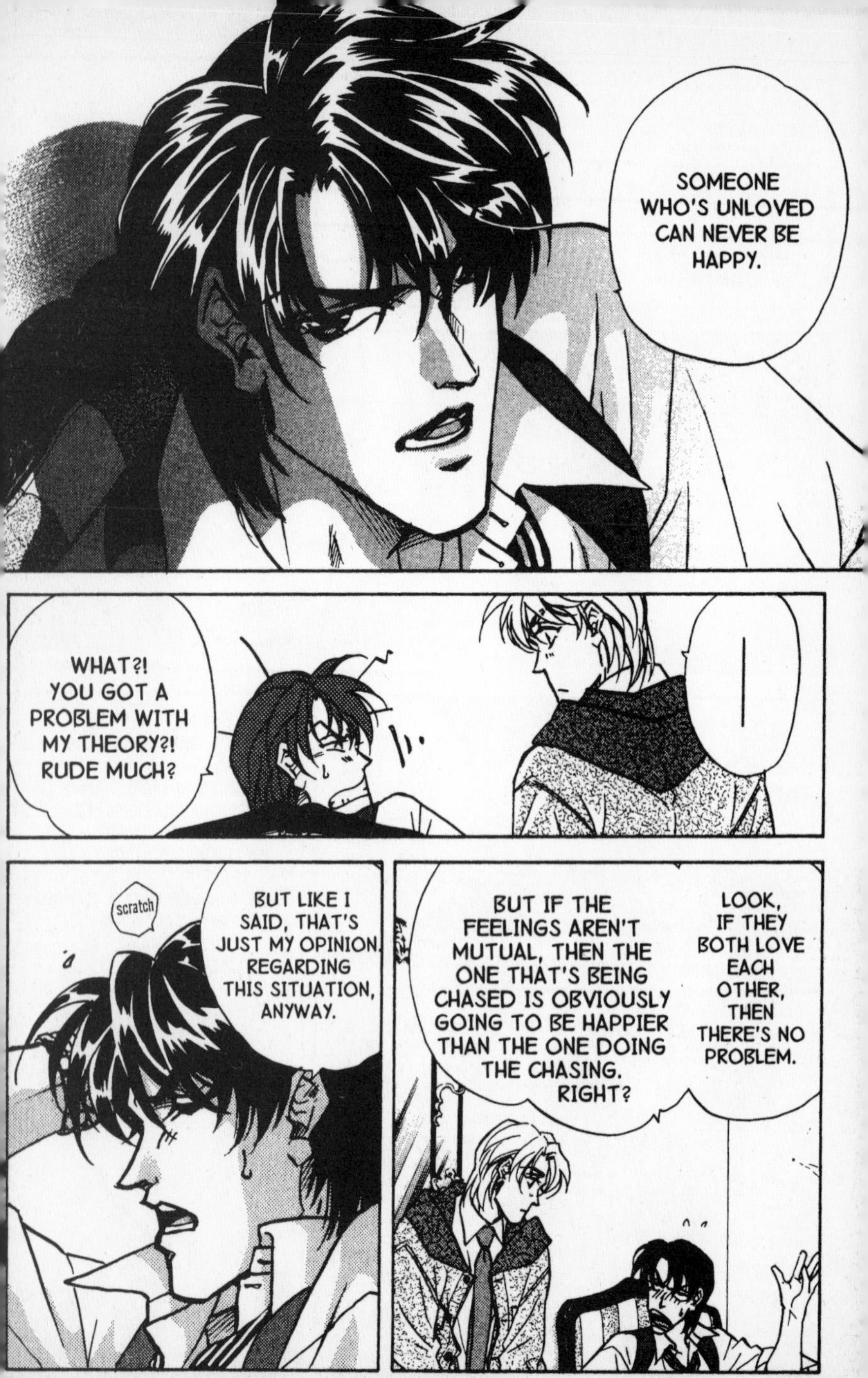
SOMEONE WHO'S UNLOVED CAN NEVER BE HAPPY.
WHAT?! YOU GOT A PROBLEM WITH MY THEORY?! RUDE MUCH?
LOOK, IF THEY BOTH LOVE EACH OTHER, THEN THERE'S NO PROBLEM.
BUT IF THE FEELINGS AREN'T MUTUAL, THEN THE ONE THAT'S BEING CHASED IS OBVIOUSLY GOING TO BE HAPPIER THAN THE ONE DOING THE CHASING. RIGHT?
scratch
BUT LIKE I SAID, THAT'S JUST MY OPINION. REGARDING THIS SITUATION, ANYWAY.

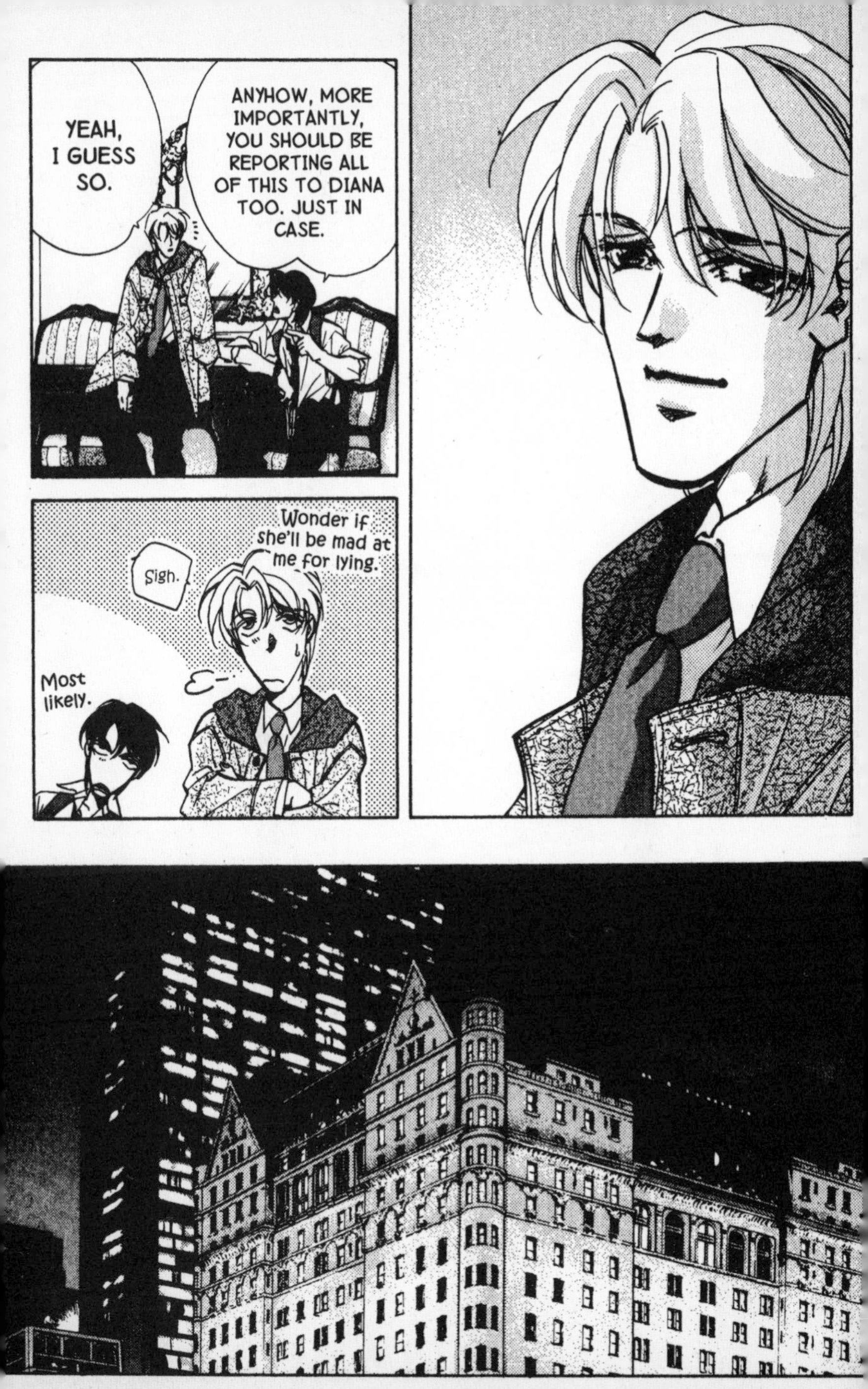
ANYHOW, MORE IMPORTANTLY, YOU SHOULD BE REPORTING ALL OF THIS TO DIANA TOO. JUST IN CASE.
YEAH, I GUESS SO.
Wonder if she'll be mad at me for lying.
Sigh.
Most likely.

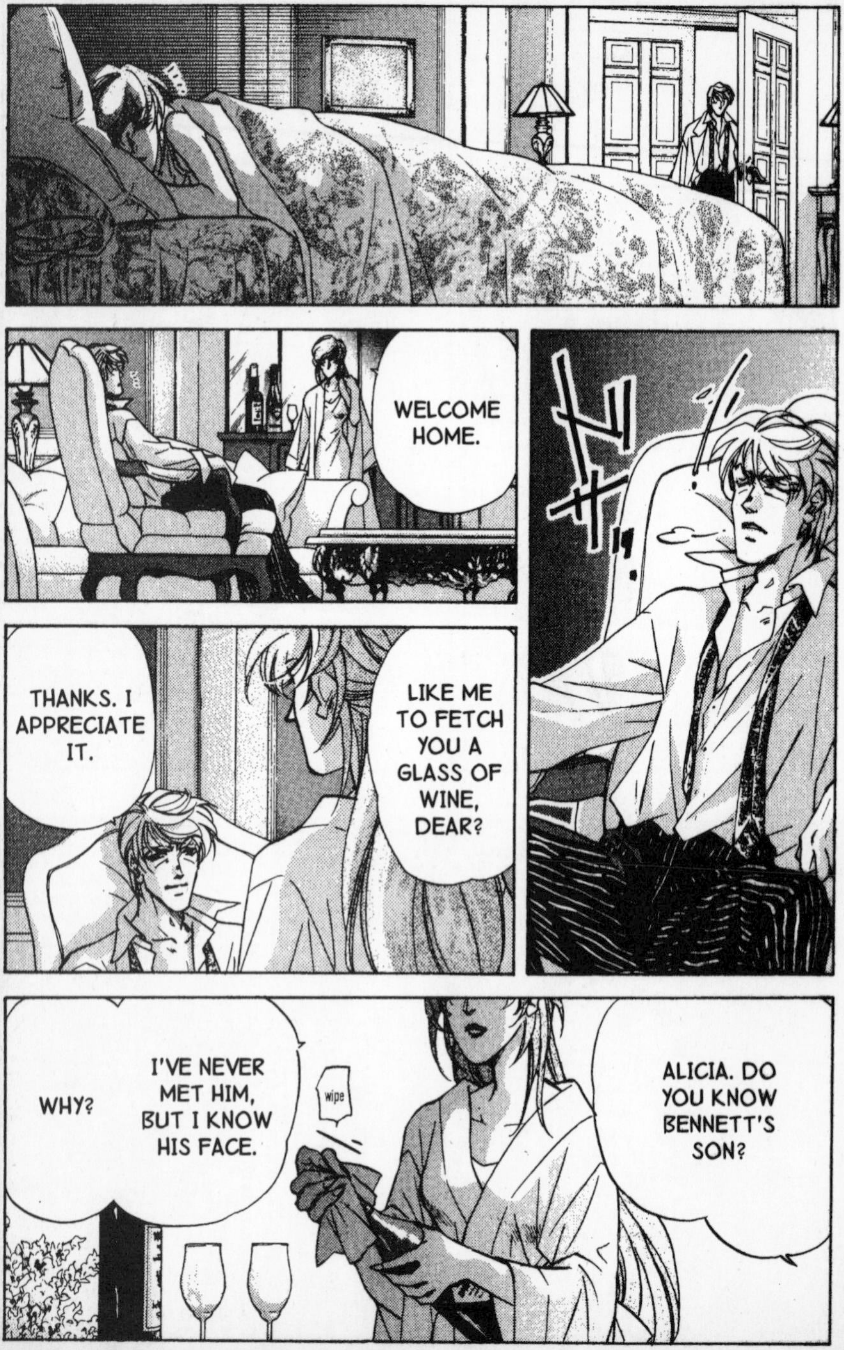
WELCOME HOME.
LIKE ME TO FETCH YOU A GLASS OF WINE, DEAR?
THANKS. I APPRECIATE IT.
ALICIA. DO YOU KNOW BENNETT'S SON?
wipe
I'VE NEVER MET HIM, BUT I KNOW HIS FACE.
WHY?

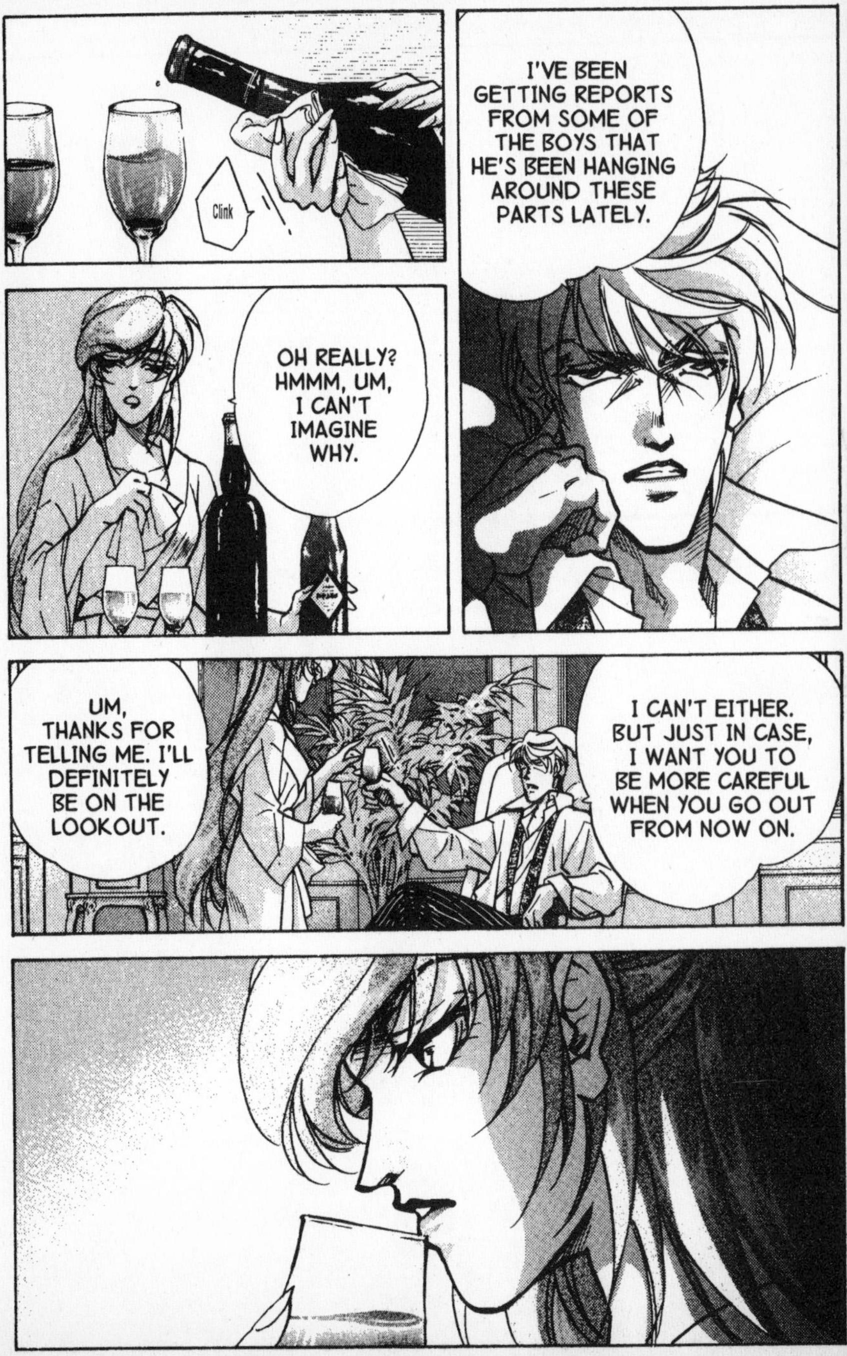
I'VE BEEN GETTING REPORTS FROM SOME OF THE BOYS THAT HE'S BEEN HANGING AROUND THESE PARTS LATELY.
Clink
OH REALLY? HMMM, UM, I CAN'T IMAGINE WHY.
I CAN'T EITHER. BUT JUST IN CASE, I WANT YOU TO BE MORE CAREFUL WHEN YOU GO OUT FROM NOW ON.
UM, THANKS FOR TELLING ME. I'LL DEFINITELY BE ON THE LOOKOUT.

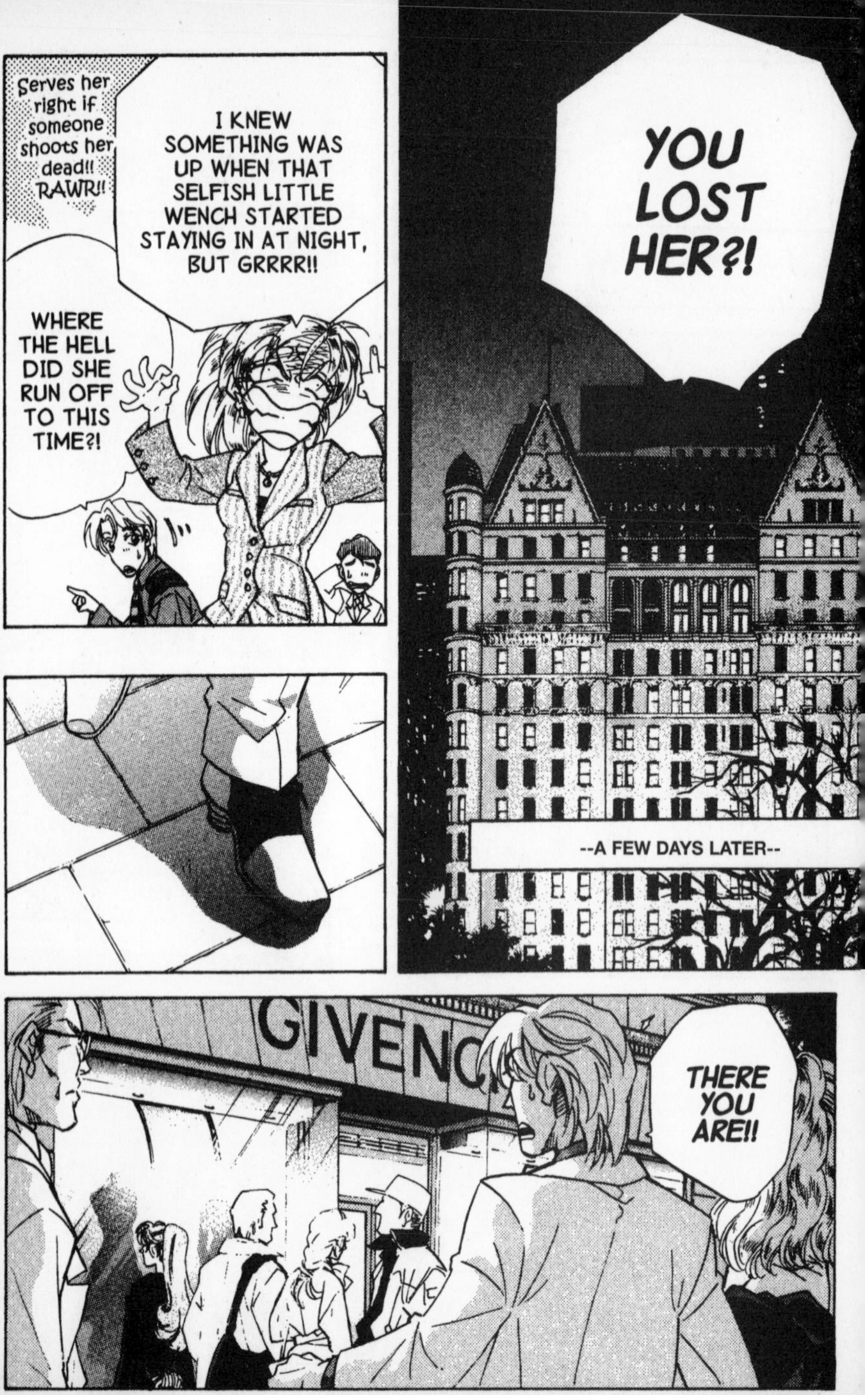
YOU LOST HER?!
--A FEW DAYS LATER--
I KNEW SOMETHING WAS UP WHEN THAT SELFISH LITTLE WENCH STARTED STAYING IN AT NIGHT, BUT GRRRR!!
Serves her right if someone shoots her dead!! RAWR!!
WHERE THE HELL DID SHE RUN OFF TO THIS TIME?!
THERE YOU ARE!!

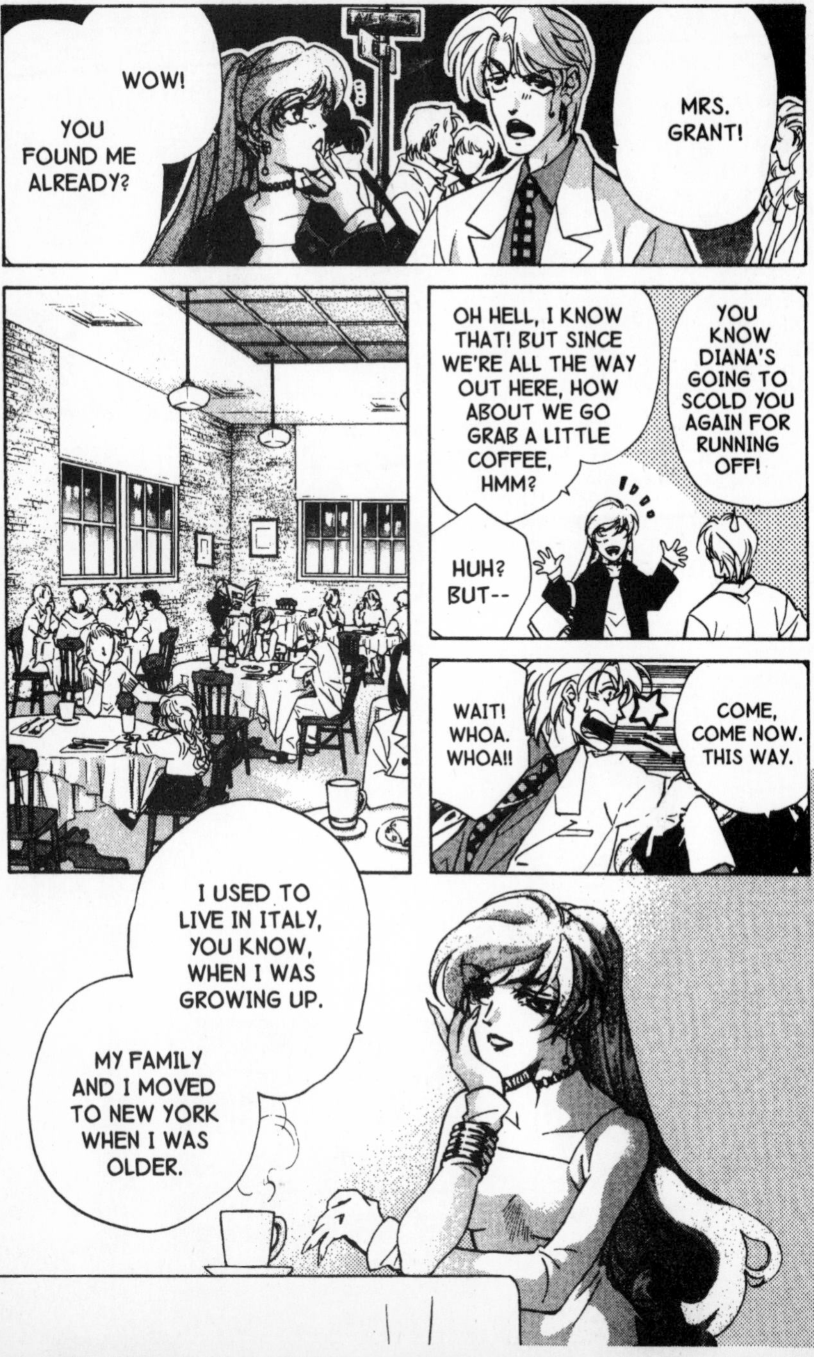
MRS. GRANT!
WOW! YOU FOUND ME ALREADY?
YOU KNOW DIANA'S GOING TO SCOLD YOU AGAIN FOR RUNNING OFF!
OH HELL, I KNOW THAT! BUT SINCE WE'RE ALL THE WAY OUT HERE, HOW ABOUT WE GO GRAB A LITTLE COFFEE, HMM?
HUH? BUT--
COME, COME NOW. THIS WAY.
WAIT! WHOA. WHOA!!
I USED TO LIVE IN ITALY, YOU KNOW, WHEN I WAS GROWING UP.
MY FAMILY AND I MOVED TO NEW YORK WHEN I WAS OLDER.

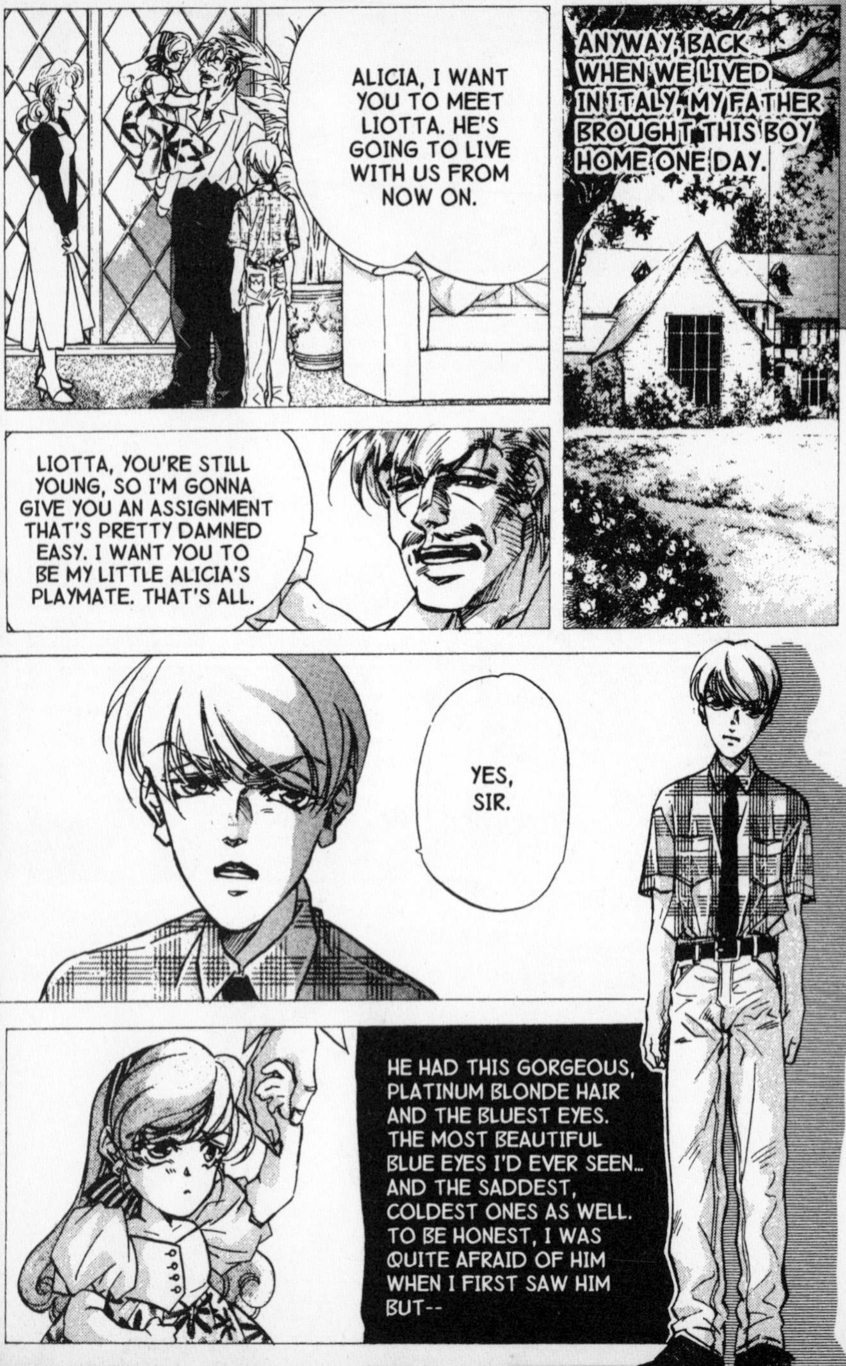
ANYWAY, BACK WHEN WE LIVED IN ITALY, MY FATHER BROUGHT THIS BOY HOME ONE DAY.
ALICIA, I WANT YOU TO MEET LIOTTA. HE'S GOING TO LIVE WITH US FROM NOW ON.
LIOTTA, YOU'RE STILL YOUNG, SO I'M GONNA GIVE YOU AN ASSIGNMENT THAT'S PRETTY DAMNED EASY. I WANT YOU TO BE MY LITTLE ALICIA'S PLAYMATE. THAT'S ALL.
YES, SIR.
HE HAD THIS GORGEOUS, PLATINUM BLONDE HAIR AND THE BLUEST EYES. THE MOST BEAUTIFUL BLUE EYES I'D EVER SEEN... AND THE SADDEST, COLDEST ONES AS WELL. TO BE HONEST, I WAS QUITE AFRAID OF HIM WHEN I FIRST SAW HIM BUT--

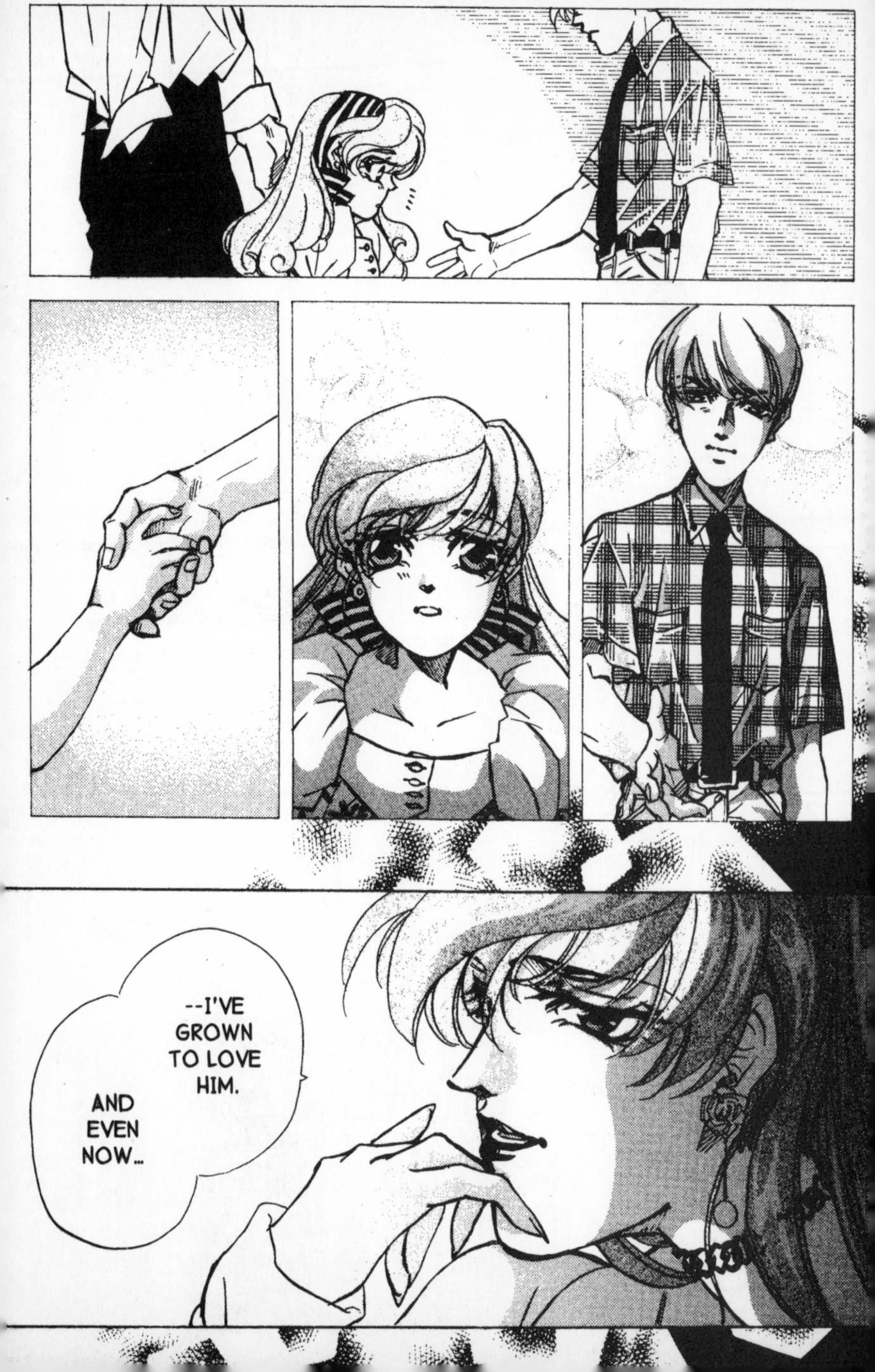
--I'VE GROWN TO LOVE HIM.
AND EVEN NOW...

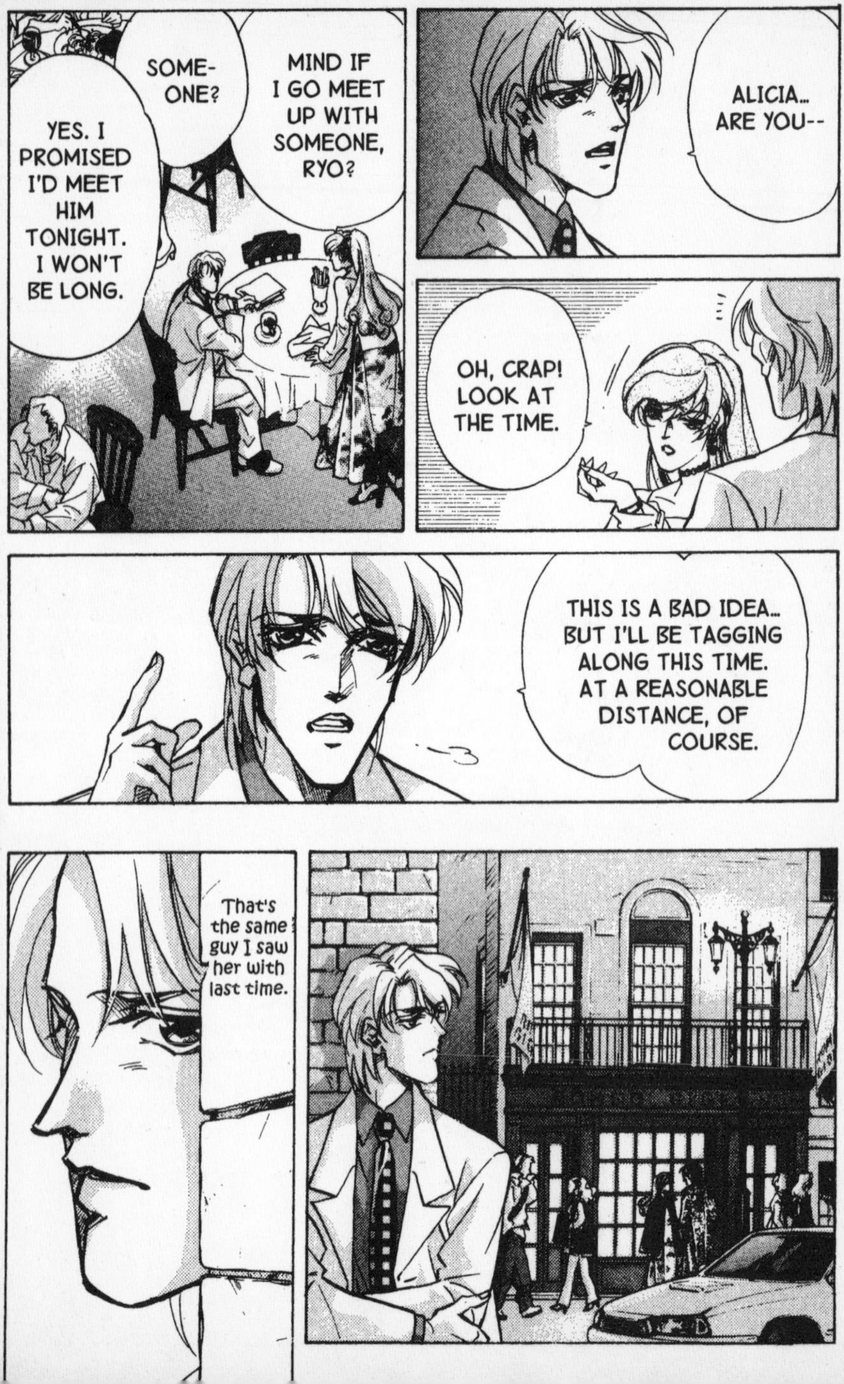
ALICIA... ARE YOU--
OH, CRAP! LOOK AT THE TIME.
MIND IF I GO MEET UP WITH SOMEONE, RYO?
SOME-ONE?
YES. I PROMISED I'D MEET HIM TONIGHT. I WON'T BE LONG.
THIS IS A BAD IDEA... BUT I'LL BE TAGGING ALONG THIS TIME. AT A REASONABLE DISTANCE, OF COURSE.
That's the same guy I saw her with last time.

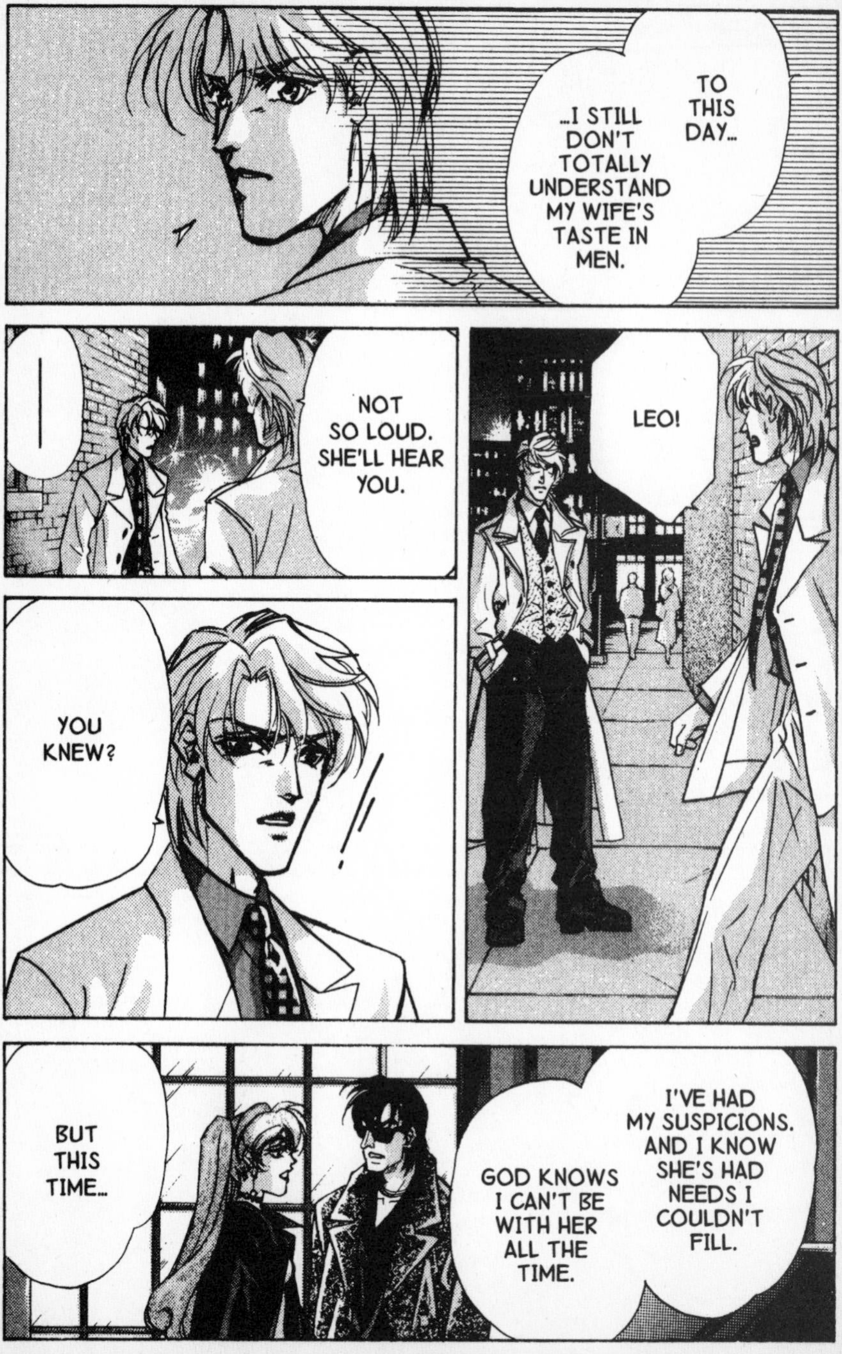
TO THIS DAY...
...I STILL DON'T TOTALLY UNDERSTAND MY WIFE'S TASTE IN MEN.
LEO!
NOT SO LOUD. SHE'LL HEAR YOU.
—
YOU KNEW?
I'VE HAD MY SUSPICIONS. AND I KNOW SHE'S HAD NEEDS I COULDN'T FILL.
GOD KNOWS I CAN'T BE WITH HER ALL THE TIME.
BUT THIS TIME...

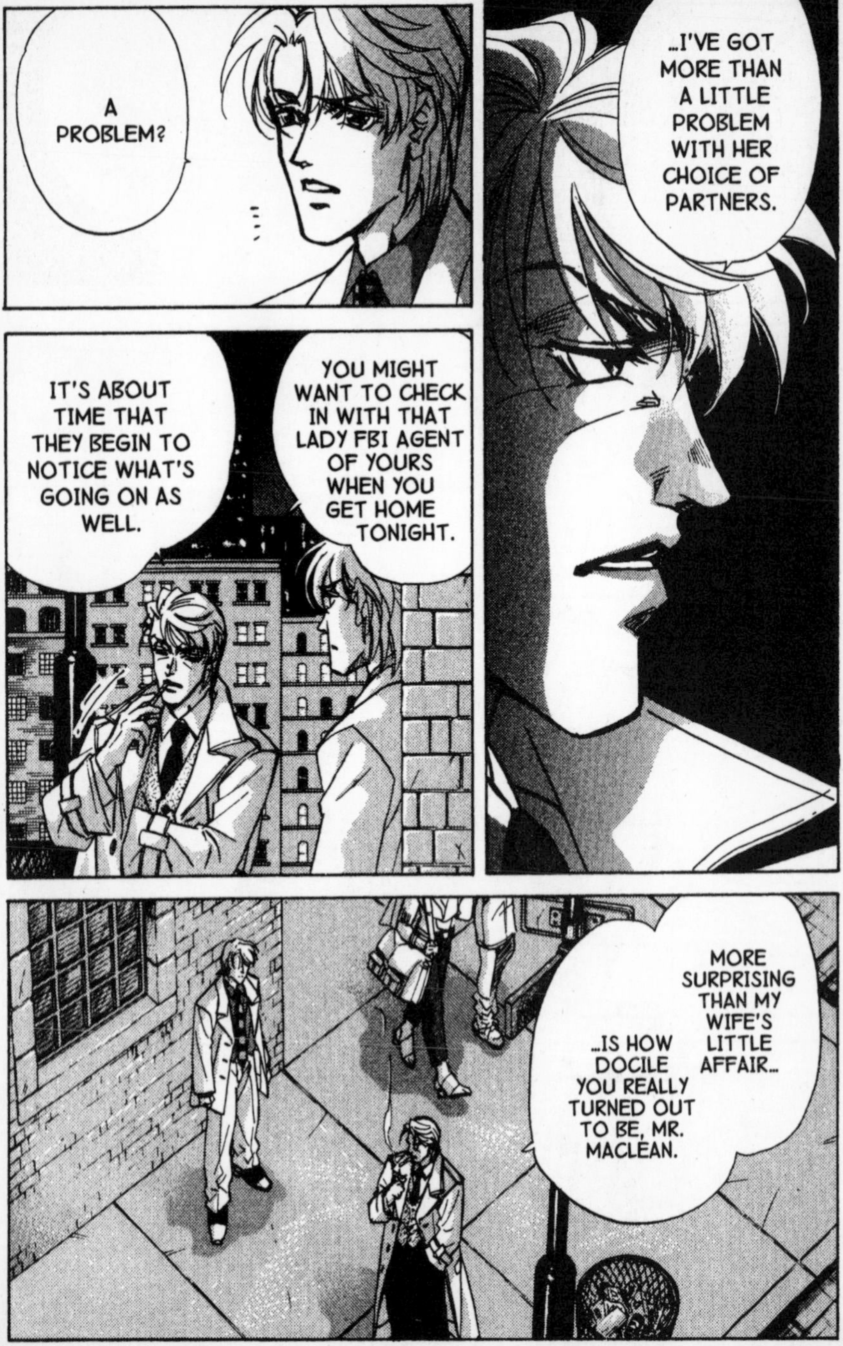
...I'VE GOT MORE THAN A LITTLE PROBLEM WITH HER CHOICE OF PARTNERS.
A PROBLEM?
YOU MIGHT WANT TO CHECK IN WITH THAT LADY FBI AGENT OF YOURS WHEN YOU GET HOME TONIGHT.
IT'S ABOUT TIME THAT THEY BEGIN TO NOTICE WHAT'S GOING ON AS WELL.
MORE SURPRISING THAN MY WIFE'S LITTLE AFFAIR...
...IS HOW DOCILE YOU REALLY TURNED OUT TO BE, MR. MACLEAN.

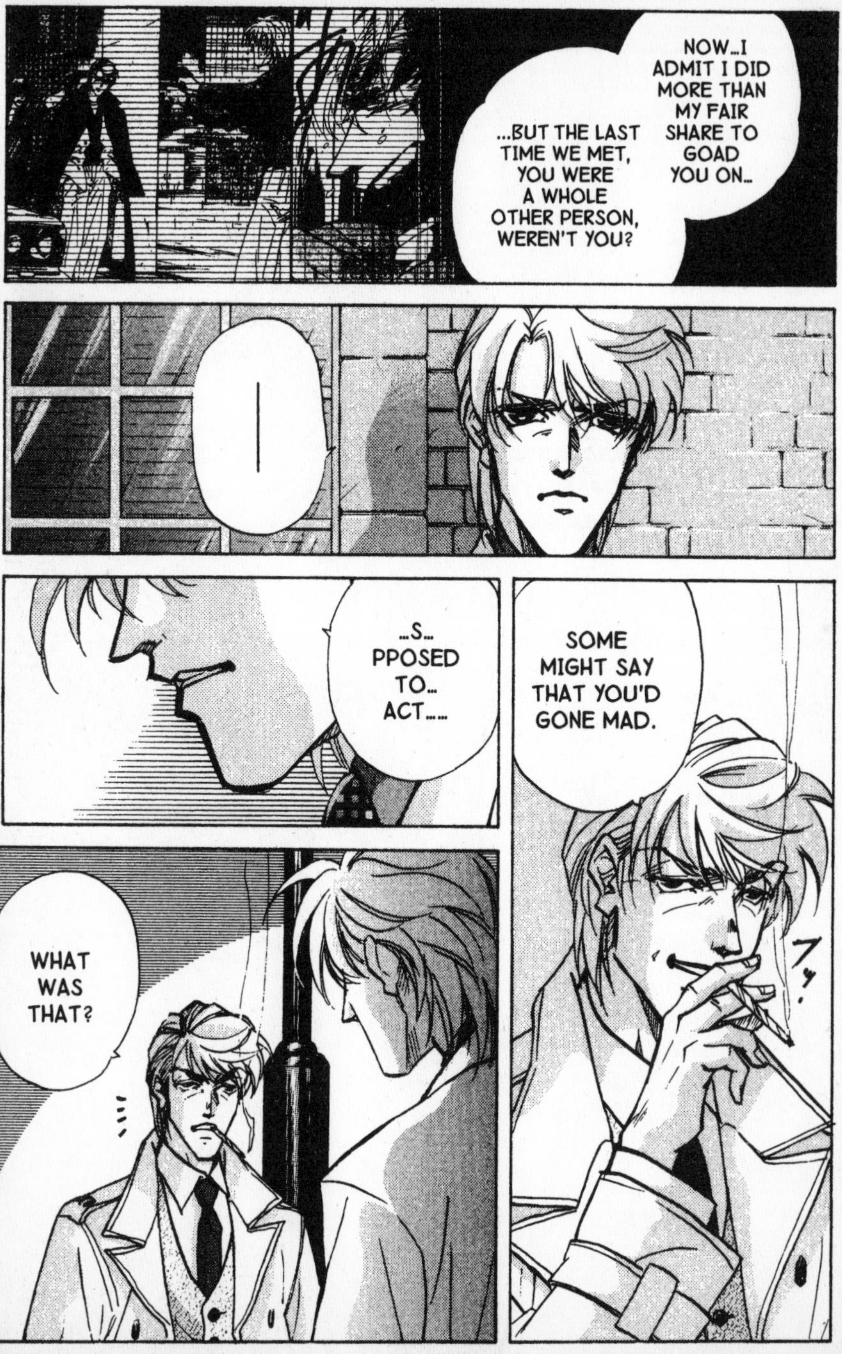
NOW...I ADMIT I DID MORE THAN MY FAIR SHARE TO GOAD YOU ON...
...BUT THE LAST TIME WE MET, YOU WERE A WHOLE OTHER PERSON, WEREN'T YOU?
—
SOME MIGHT SAY THAT YOU'D GONE MAD.
...S... PPOSED TO... ACT.....
WHAT WAS THAT?

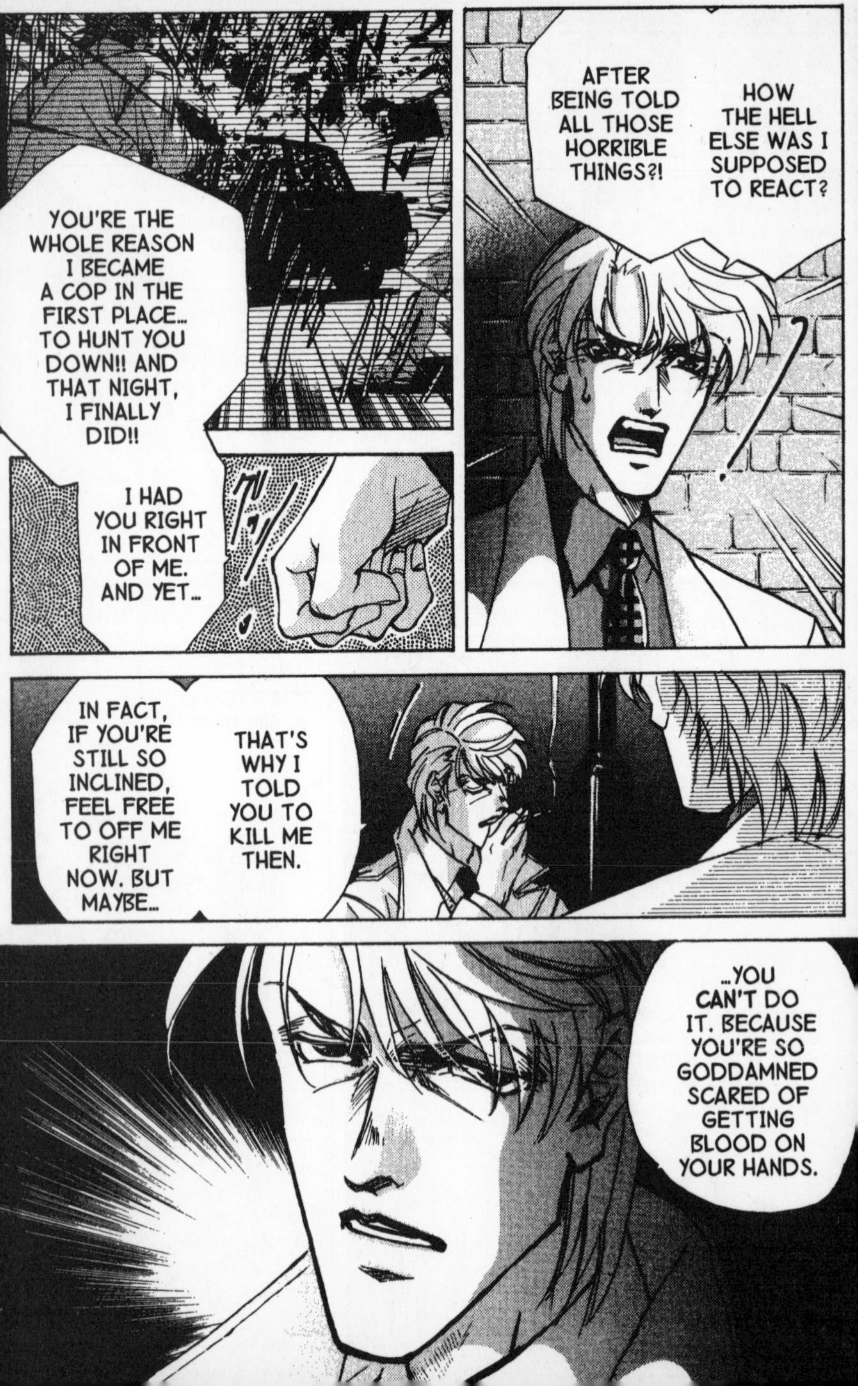
HOW THE HELL ELSE WAS I SUPPOSED TO REACT?
AFTER BEING TOLD ALL THOSE HORRIBLE THINGS?!
YOU'RE THE WHOLE REASON I BECAME A COP IN THE FIRST PLACE... TO HUNT YOU DOWN!! AND THAT NIGHT, I FINALLY DID!!
I HAD YOU RIGHT IN FRONT OF ME. AND YET...
THAT'S WHY I TOLD YOU TO KILL ME THEN.
IN FACT, IF YOU'RE STILL SO INCLINED, FEEL FREE TO OFF ME RIGHT NOW. BUT MAYBE...
...YOU CAN'T DO IT. BECAUSE YOU'RE SO GODDAMNED SCARED OF GETTING BLOOD ON YOUR HANDS.

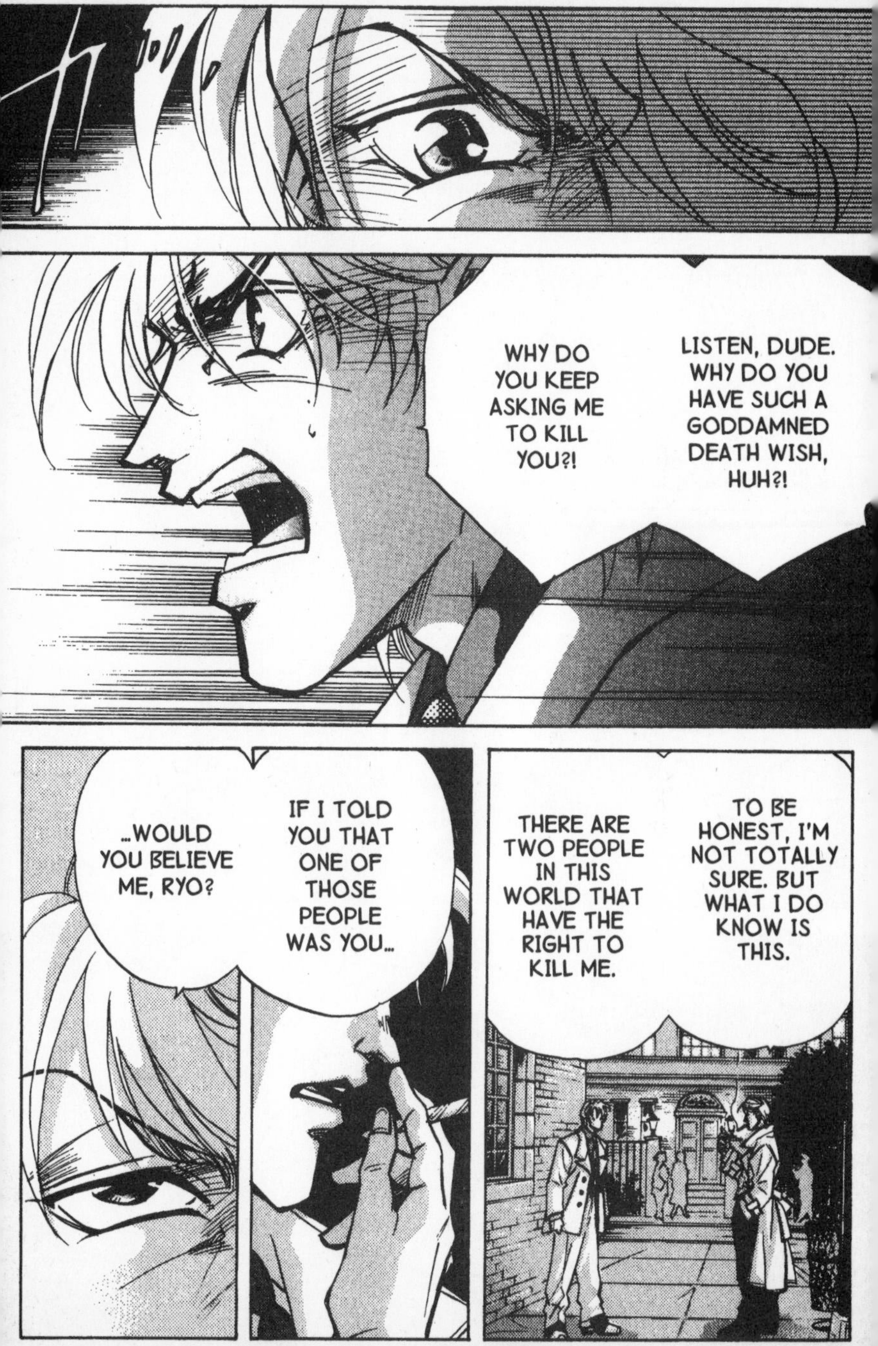
LISTEN, DUDE. WHY DO YOU HAVE SUCH A GODDAMNED DEATH WISH, HUH?!
WHY DO YOU KEEP ASKING ME TO KILL YOU?!
TO BE HONEST, I'M NOT TOTALLY SURE. BUT WHAT I DO KNOW IS THIS.
THERE ARE TWO PEOPLE IN THIS WORLD THAT HAVE THE RIGHT TO KILL ME.
IF I TOLD YOU THAT ONE OF THOSE PEOPLE WAS YOU...
...WOULD YOU BELIEVE ME, RYO?

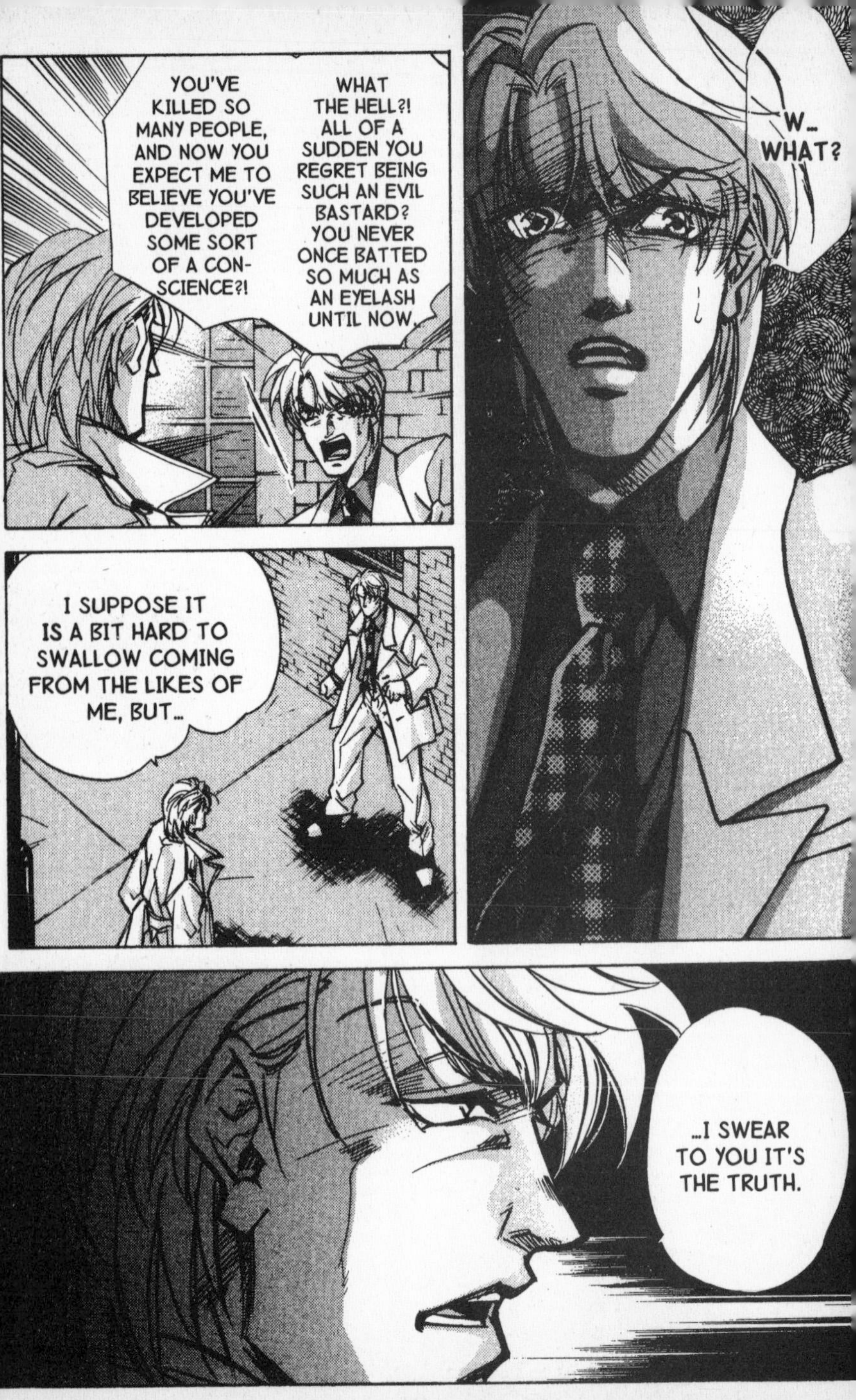
W... WHAT?
WHAT THE HELL?! ALL OF A SUDDEN YOU REGRET BEING SUCH AN EVIL BASTARD? YOU NEVER ONCE BATTED SO MUCH AS AN EYELASH UNTIL NOW.
YOU'VE KILLED SO MANY PEOPLE, AND NOW YOU EXPECT ME TO BELIEVE YOU'VE DEVELOPED SOME SORT OF A CON-SCIENCE?!
I SUPPOSE IT IS A BIT HARD TO SWALLOW COMING FROM THE LIKES OF ME, BUT...
...I SWEAR TO YOU IT'S THE TRUTH.

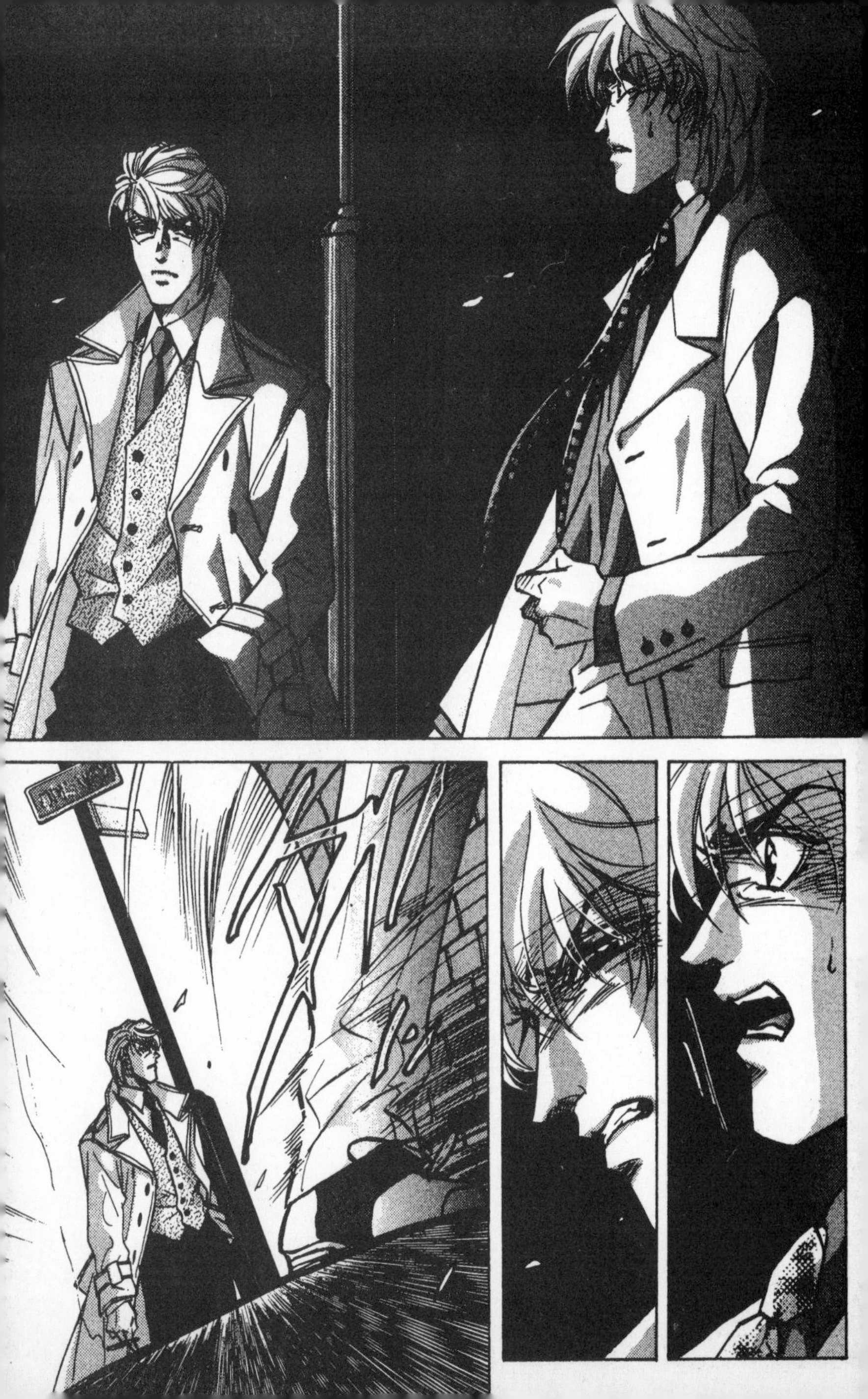

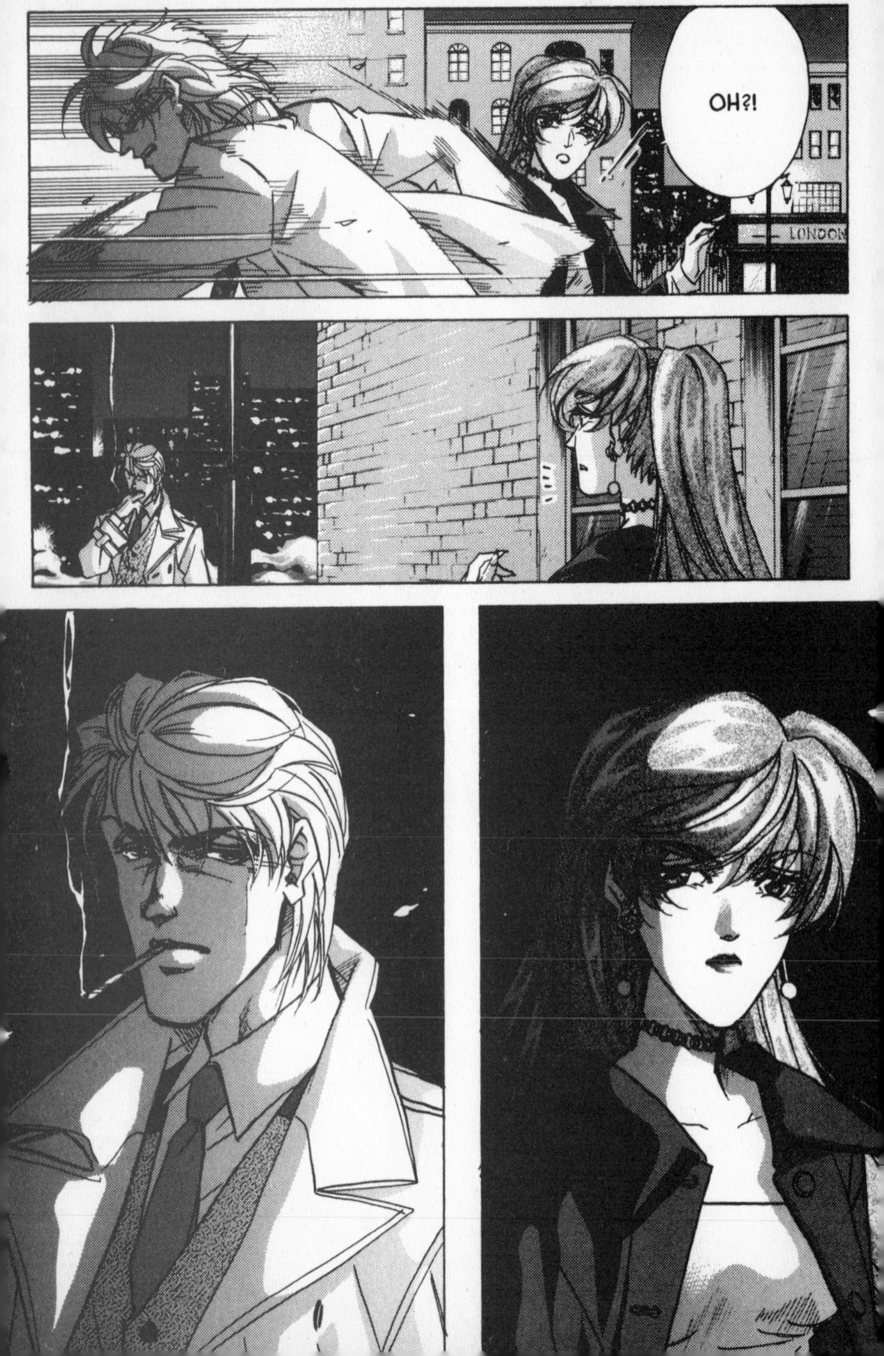
OH?!
LONDON

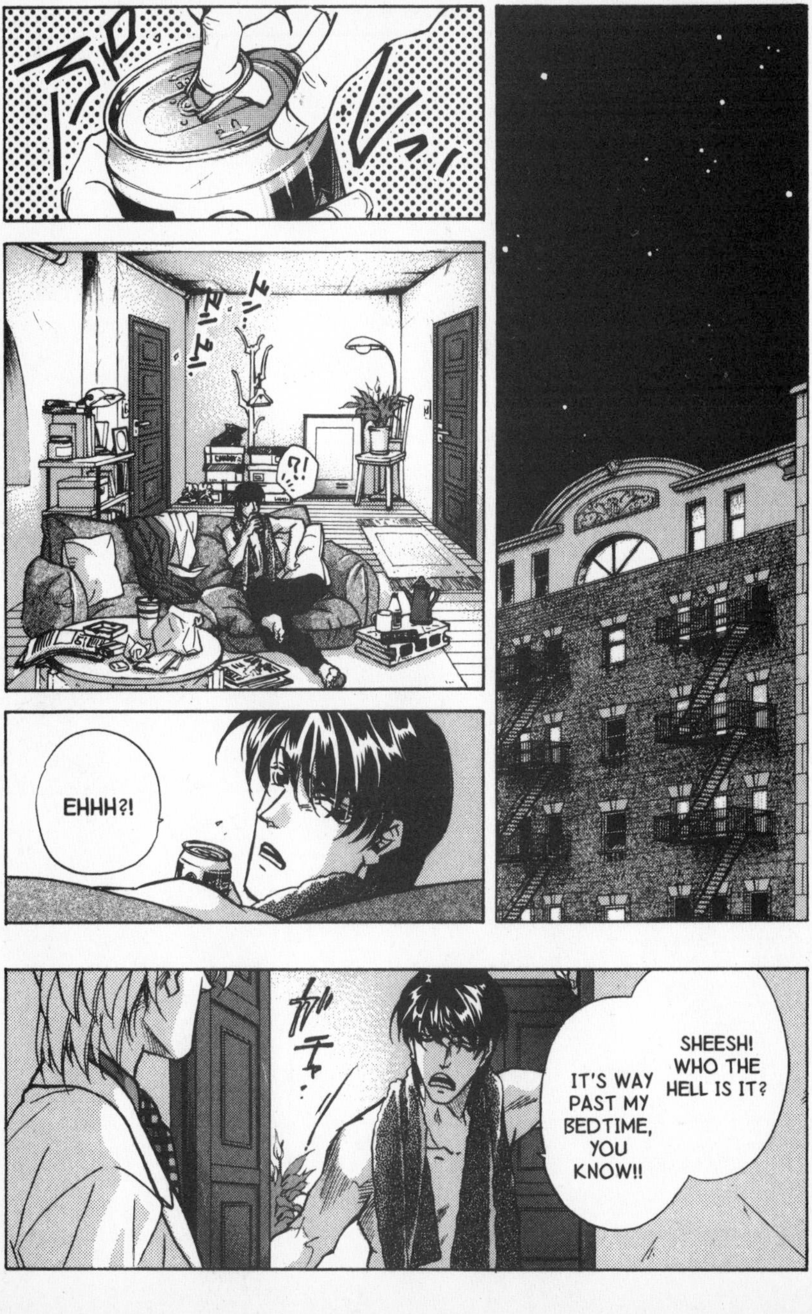
EHHH?!
SHEESH! WHO THE HELL IS IT?
IT'S WAY PAST MY BEDTIME, YOU KNOW!!

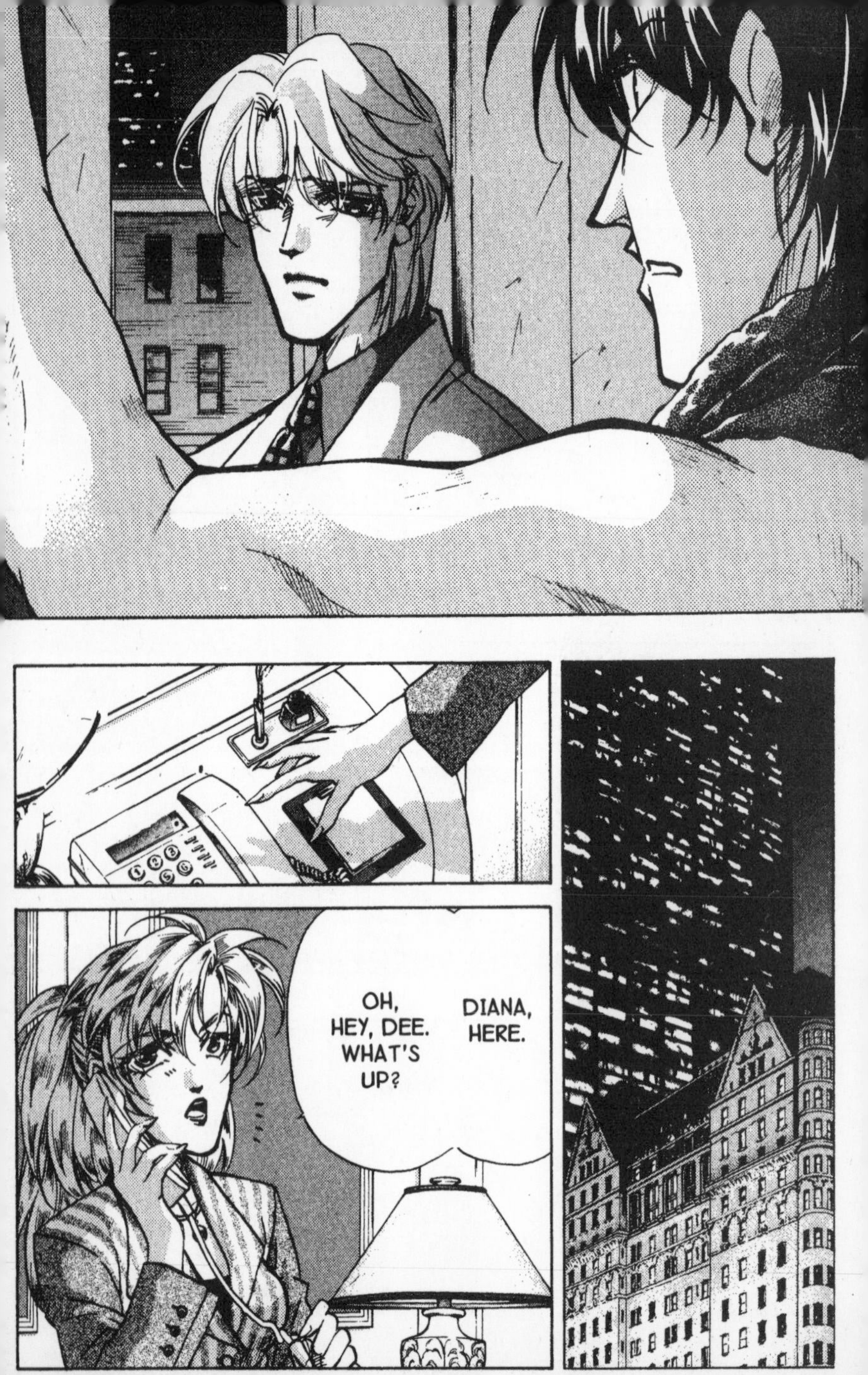
DIANA, HERE.
OH, HEY, DEE. WHAT'S UP?

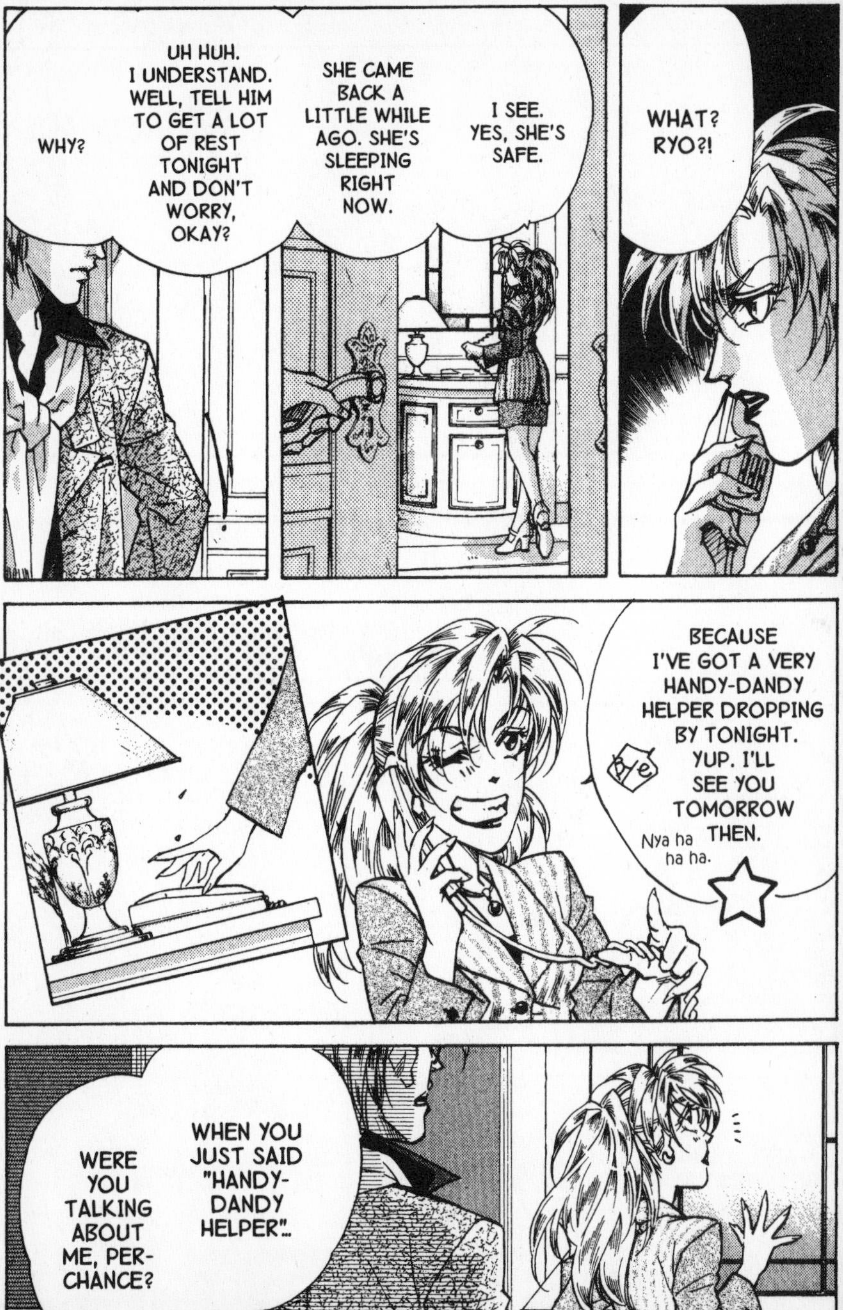
WHAT? RYO?!
I SEE. YES, SHE'S SAFE.
SHE CAME BACK A LITTLE WHILE AGO. SHE'S SLEEPING RIGHT NOW.
UH HUH. I UNDERSTAND. WELL, TELL HIM TO GET A LOT OF REST TONIGHT AND DON'T WORRY, OKAY?
WHY?
BECAUSE I'VE GOT A VERY HANDY-DANDY HELPER DROPPING BY TONIGHT. YUP. I'LL SEE YOU TOMORROW THEN.
Nya ha ha ha.
WHEN YOU JUST SAID "HANDY-DANDY HELPER"...
WERE YOU TALKING ABOUT ME, PER-CHANCE?

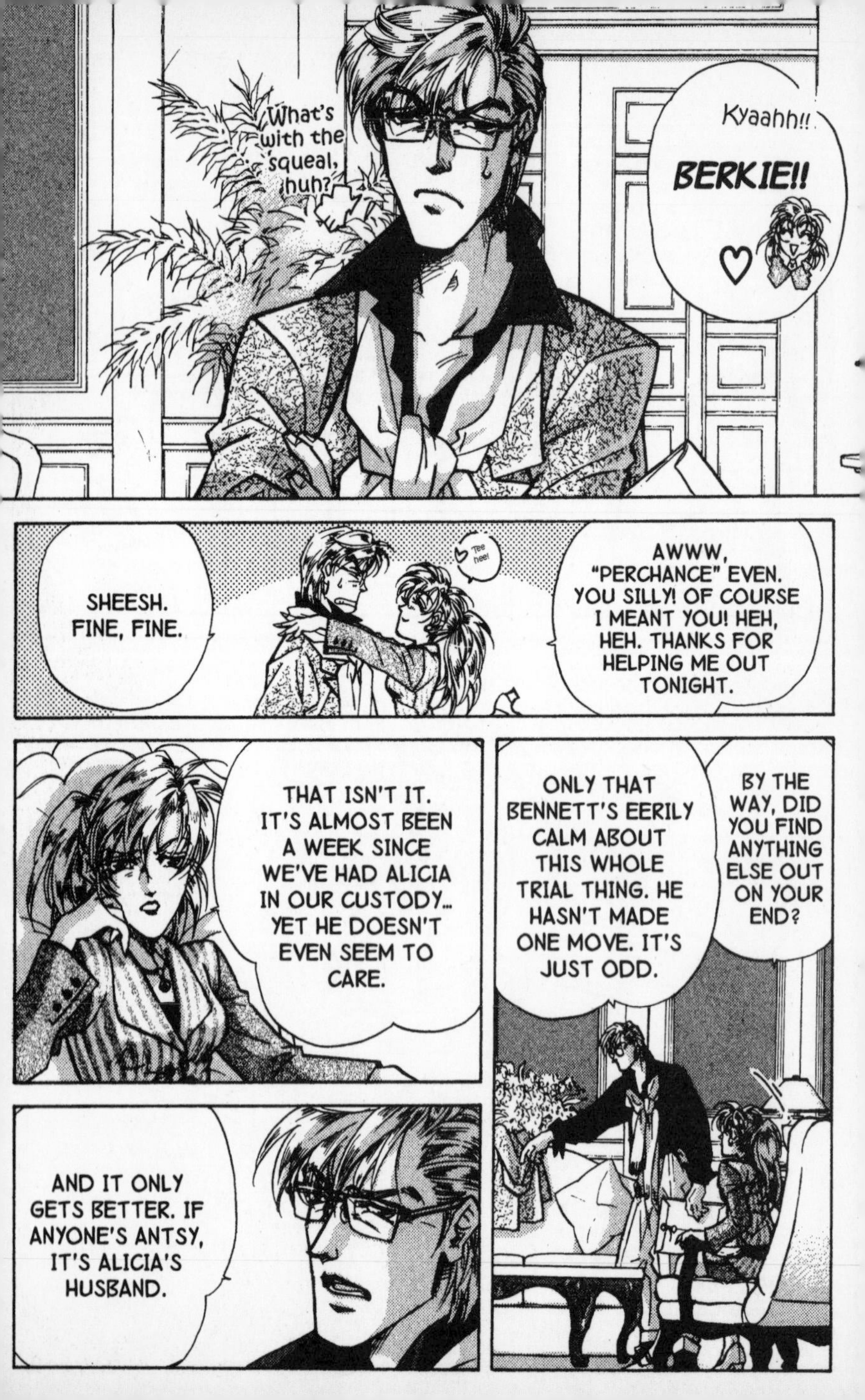
Kyaahh!!
BERKIE!!
What's with the squeal, huh?
AWWW, "PERCHANCE" EVEN. YOU SILLY! OF COURSE I MEANT YOU! HEH, HEH. THANKS FOR HELPING ME OUT TONIGHT.
Tee hee!
SHEESH. FINE, FINE.
BY THE WAY, DID YOU FIND ANYTHING ELSE OUT ON YOUR END?
ONLY THAT BENNETT'S EERILY CALM ABOUT THIS WHOLE TRIAL THING. HE HASN'T MADE ONE MOVE. IT'S JUST ODD.
THAT ISN'T IT. IT'S ALMOST BEEN A WEEK SINCE WE'VE HAD ALICIA IN OUR CUSTODY... YET HE DOESN'T EVEN SEEM TO CARE.
AND IT ONLY GETS BETTER. IF ANYONE'S ANTSY, IT'S ALICIA'S HUSBAND.

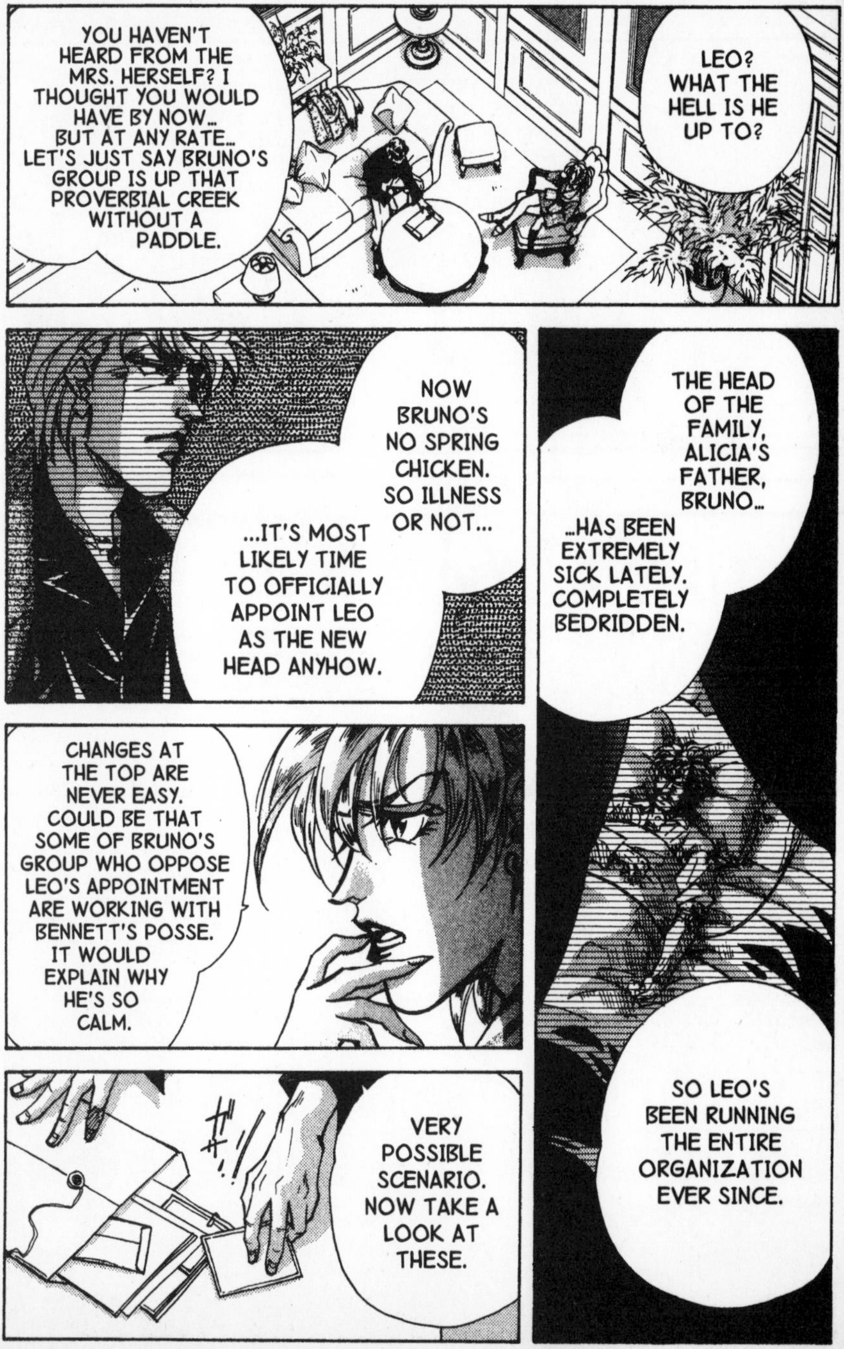
LEO? WHAT THE HELL IS HE UP TO?
YOU HAVEN'T HEARD FROM THE MRS. HERSELF? I THOUGHT YOU WOULD HAVE BY NOW... BUT AT ANY RATE... LET'S JUST SAY BRUNO'S GROUP IS UP THAT PROVERBIAL CREEK WITHOUT A PADDLE.
THE HEAD OF THE FAMILY, ALICIA'S FATHER, BRUNO...
...HAS BEEN EXTREMELY SICK LATELY. COMPLETELY BEDRIDDEN.
SO LEO'S BEEN RUNNING THE ENTIRE ORGANIZATION EVER SINCE.
NOW BRUNO'S NO SPRING CHICKEN. SO ILLNESS OR NOT...
...IT'S MOST LIKELY TIME TO OFFICIALLY APPOINT LEO AS THE NEW HEAD ANYHOW.
CHANGES AT THE TOP ARE NEVER EASY. COULD BE THAT SOME OF BRUNO'S GROUP WHO OPPOSE LEO'S APPOINTMENT ARE WORKING WITH BENNETT'S POSSE. IT WOULD EXPLAIN WHY HE'S SO CALM.
VERY POSSIBLE SCENARIO. NOW TAKE A LOOK AT THESE.

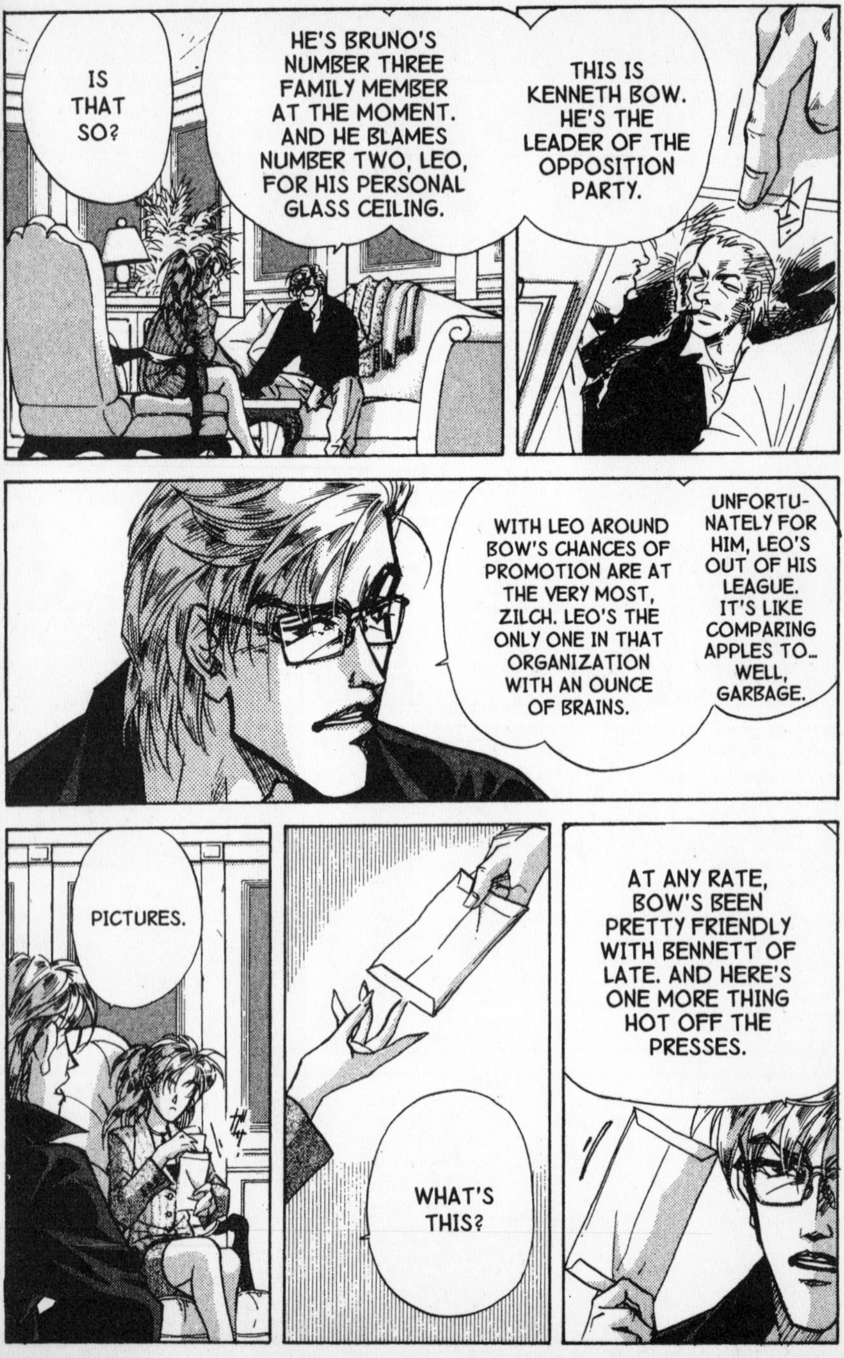
THIS IS KENNETH BOW. HE'S THE LEADER OF THE OPPOSITION PARTY.
HE'S BRUNO'S NUMBER THREE FAMILY MEMBER AT THE MOMENT. AND HE BLAMES NUMBER TWO, LEO, FOR HIS PERSONAL GLASS CEILING.
IS THAT SO?
UNFORTU-NATELY FOR HIM, LEO'S OUT OF HIS LEAGUE. IT'S LIKE COMPARING APPLES TO... WELL, GARBAGE.
WITH LEO AROUND BOW'S CHANCES OF PROMOTION ARE AT THE VERY MOST, ZILCH. LEO'S THE ONLY ONE IN THAT ORGANIZATION WITH AN OUNCE OF BRAINS.
AT ANY RATE, BOW'S BEEN PRETTY FRIENDLY WITH BENNETT OF LATE. AND HERE'S ONE MORE THING HOT OFF THE PRESSES.
WHAT'S THIS?
PICTURES.

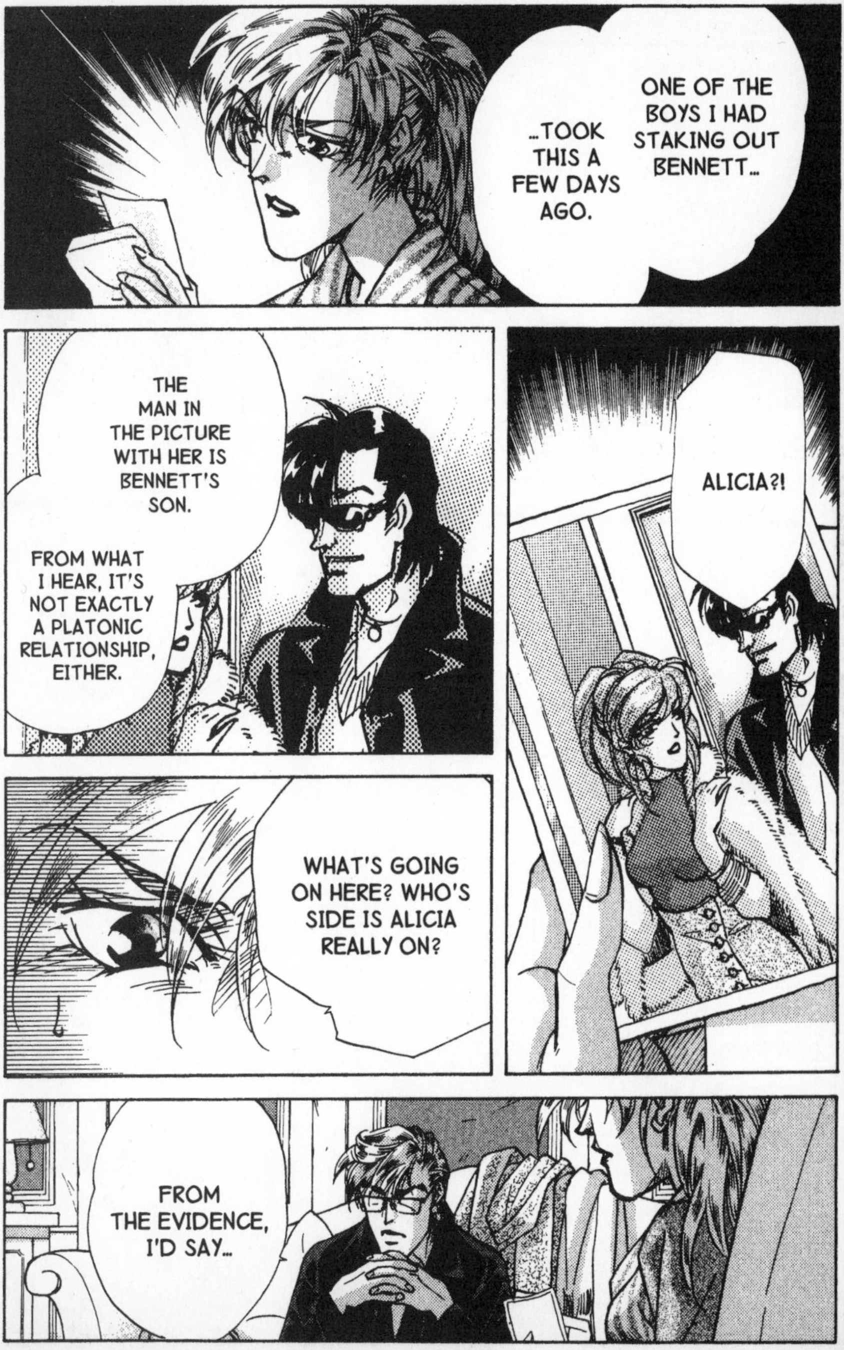
ONE OF THE BOYS I HAD STAKING OUT BENNETT...
...TOOK THIS A FEW DAYS AGO.
ALICIA?!
THE MAN IN THE PICTURE WITH HER IS BENNETT'S SON.
FROM WHAT I HEAR, IT'S NOT EXACTLY A PLATONIC RELATIONSHIP, EITHER.
WHAT'S GOING ON HERE? WHO'S SIDE IS ALICIA REALLY ON?
FROM THE EVIDENCE, I'D SAY...

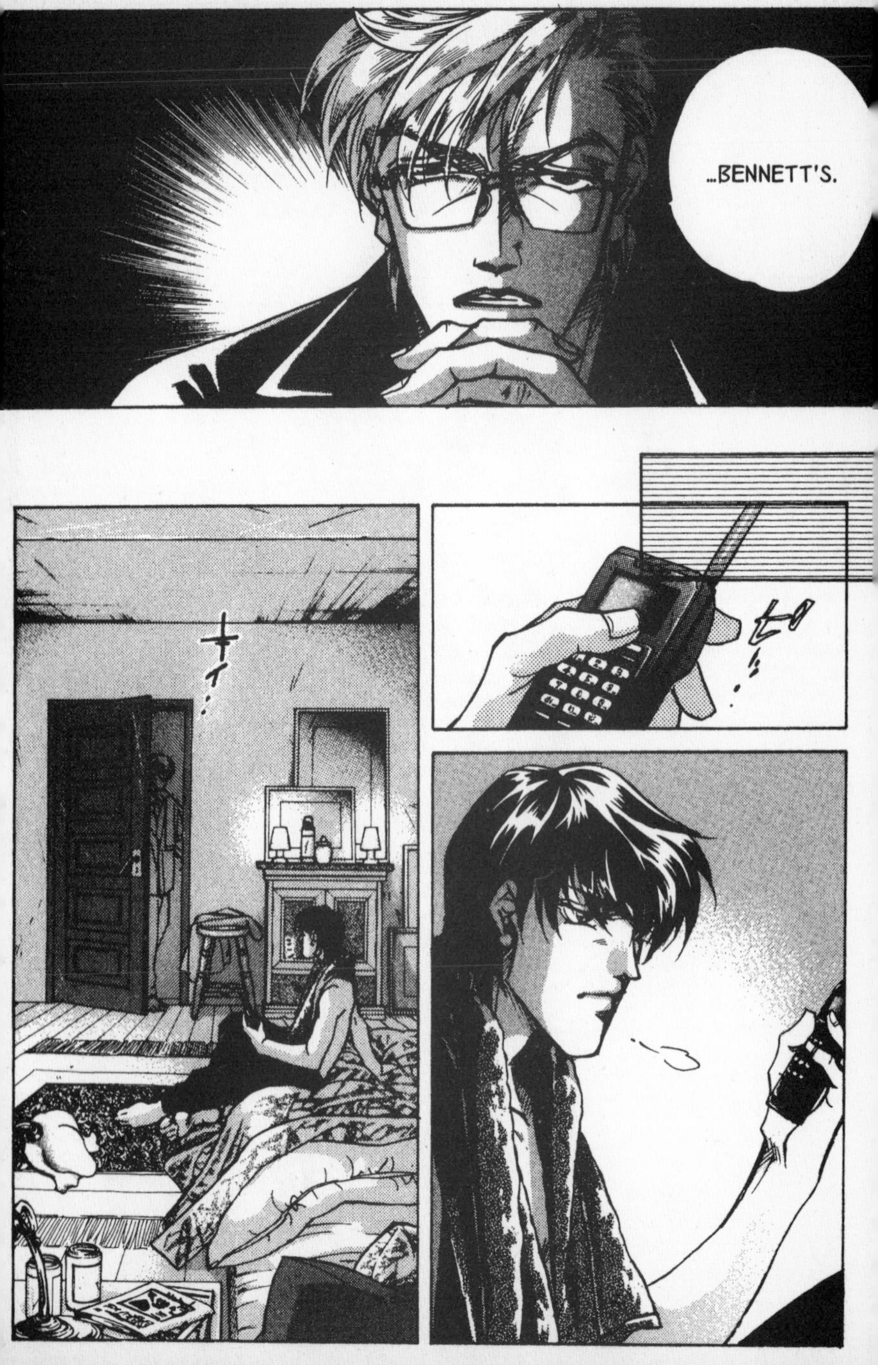
...BENNETT'S.

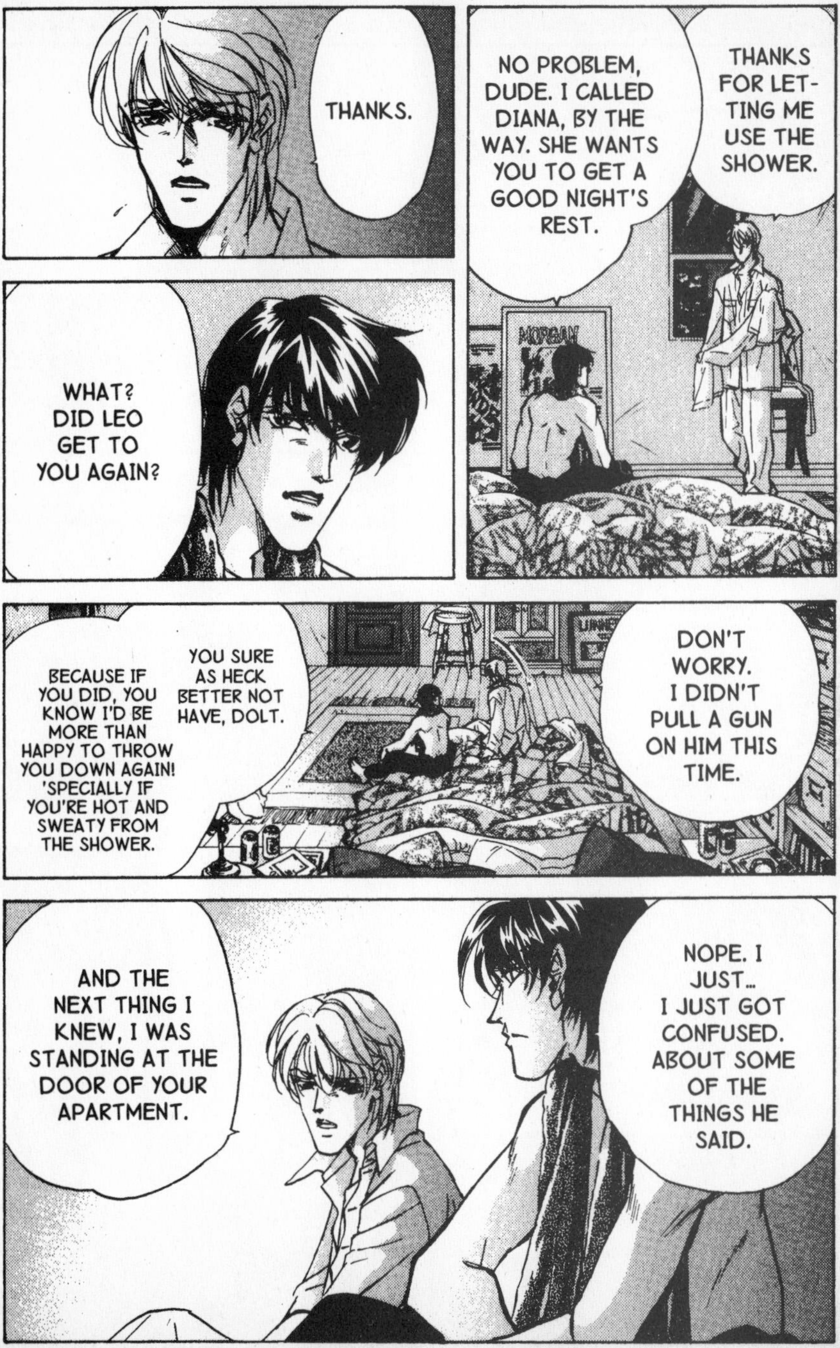
THANKS FOR LET-TING ME USE THE SHOWER.
NO PROBLEM, DUDE. I CALLED DIANA, BY THE WAY. SHE WANTS YOU TO GET A GOOD NIGHT'S REST.
THANKS.
WHAT? DID LEO GET TO YOU AGAIN?
DON'T WORRY. I DIDN'T PULL A GUN ON HIM THIS TIME.
YOU SURE AS HECK BETTER NOT HAVE, DOLT.
BECAUSE IF YOU DID, YOU KNOW I'D BE MORE THAN HAPPY TO THROW YOU DOWN AGAIN! 'SPECIALLY IF YOU'RE HOT AND SWEATY FROM THE SHOWER.
NOPE. I JUST... I JUST GOT CONFUSED. ABOUT SOME OF THE THINGS HE SAID.
AND THE NEXT THING I KNEW, I WAS STANDING AT THE DOOR OF YOUR APARTMENT.

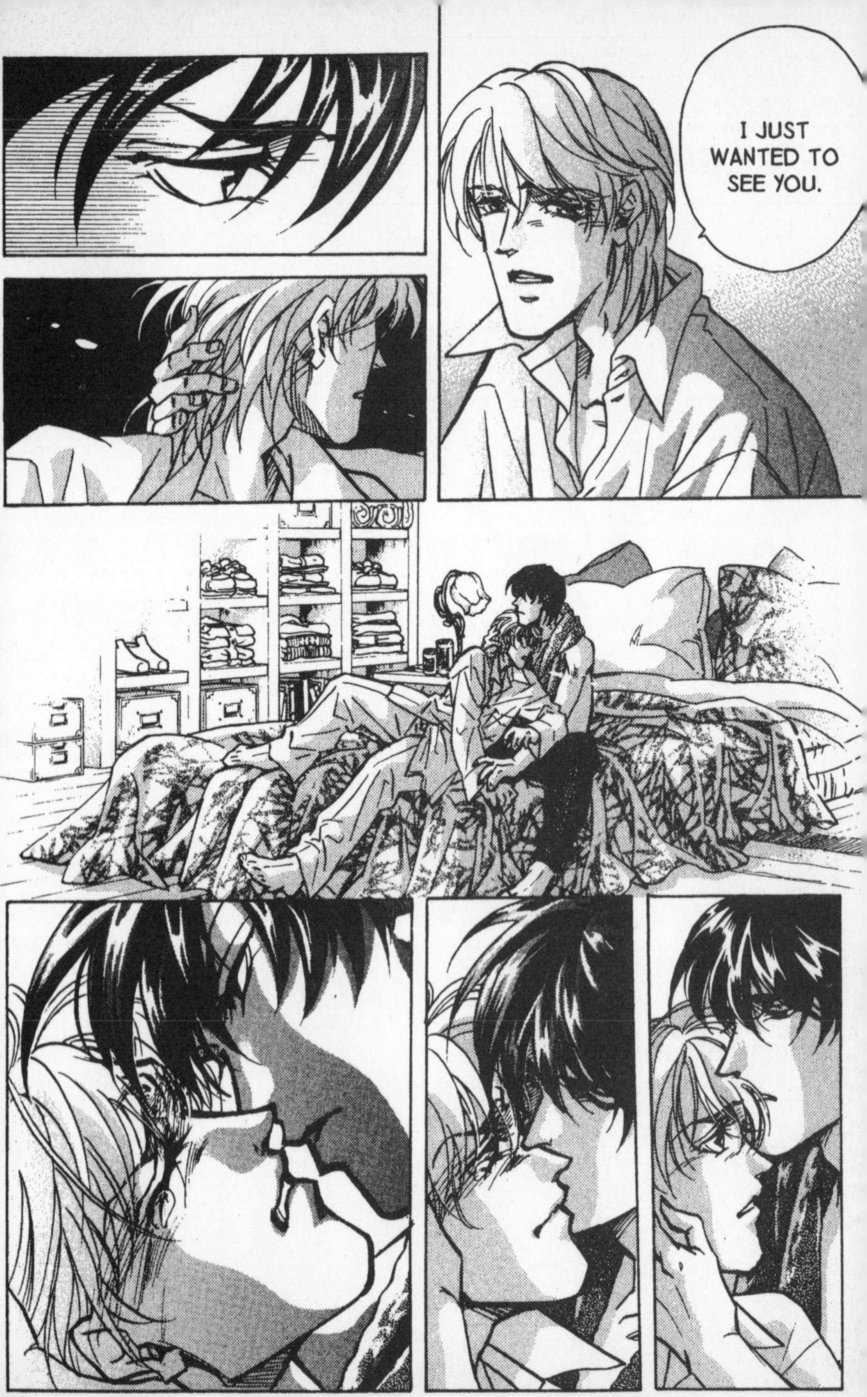
I JUST WANTED TO SEE YOU.

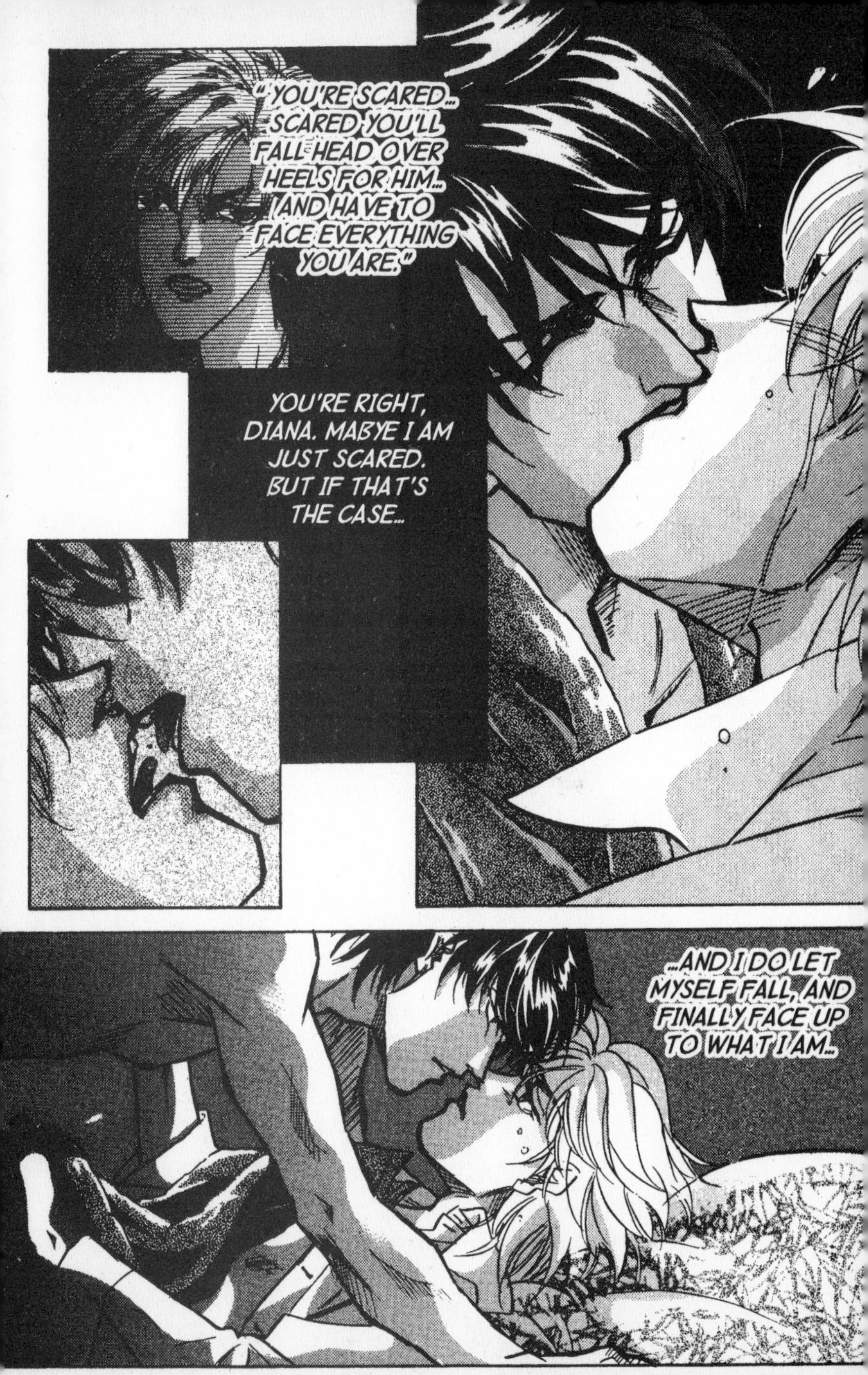
"YOU'RE SCARED... SCARED YOU'LL FALL HEAD OVER HEELS FOR HIM... AND HAVE TO FACE EVERYTHING YOU ARE."
YOU'RE RIGHT, DIANA. MABYE I AM JUST SCARED. BUT IF THAT'S THE CASE...
...AND I DO LET MYSELF FALL, AND FINALLY FACE UP TO WHAT I AM...

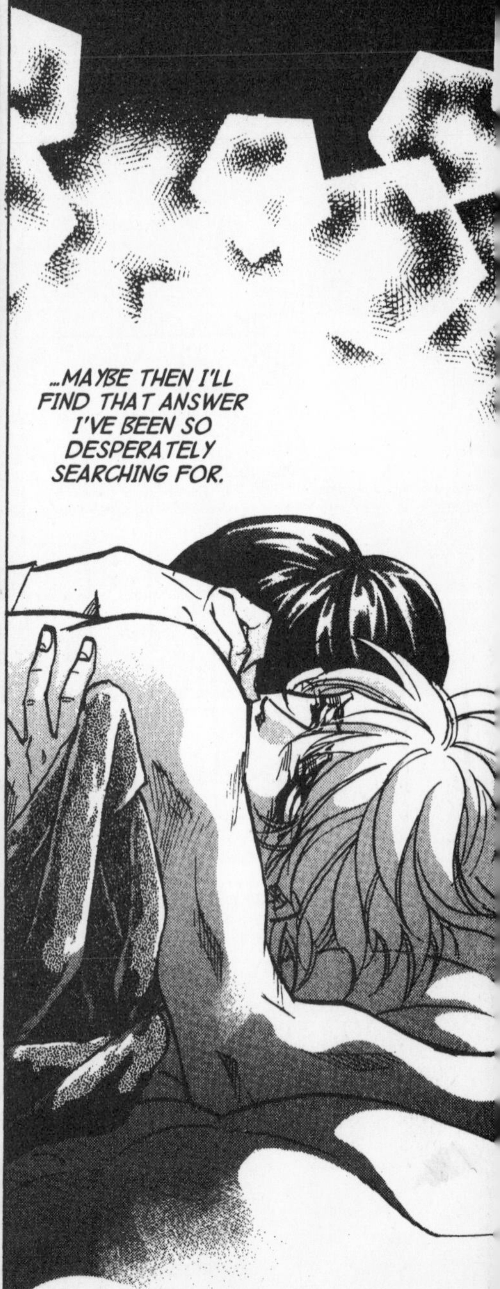
...MAYBE THEN I'LL FIND THAT ANSWER I'VE BEEN SO DESPERATELY SEARCHING FOR.

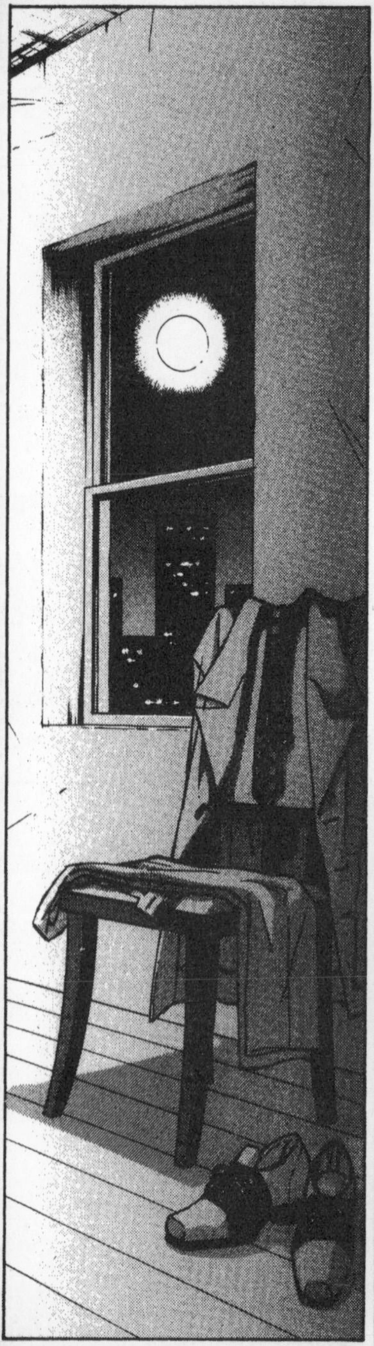

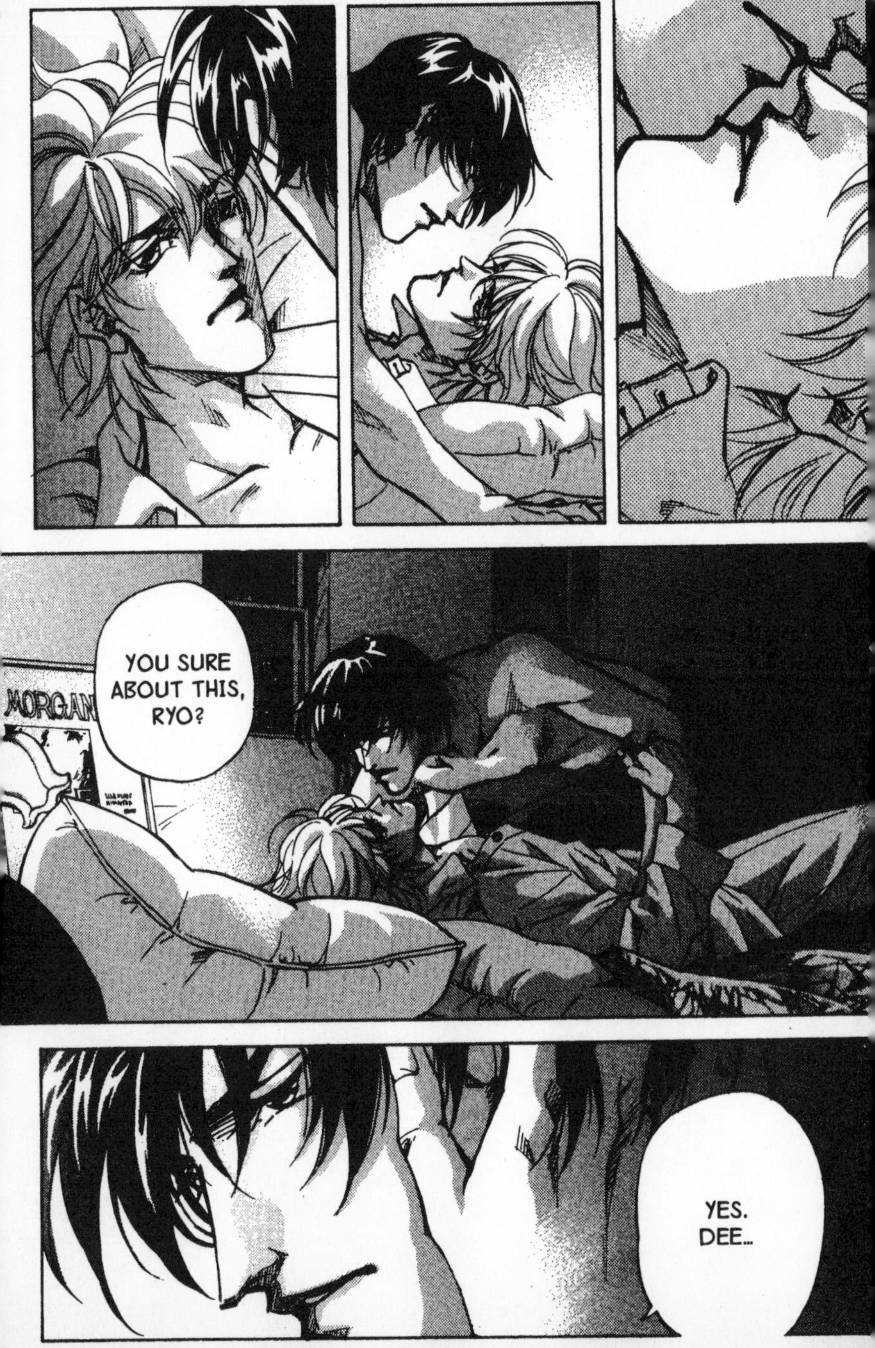
MORGAN
YOU SURE ABOUT THIS, RYO?
YES. DEE...

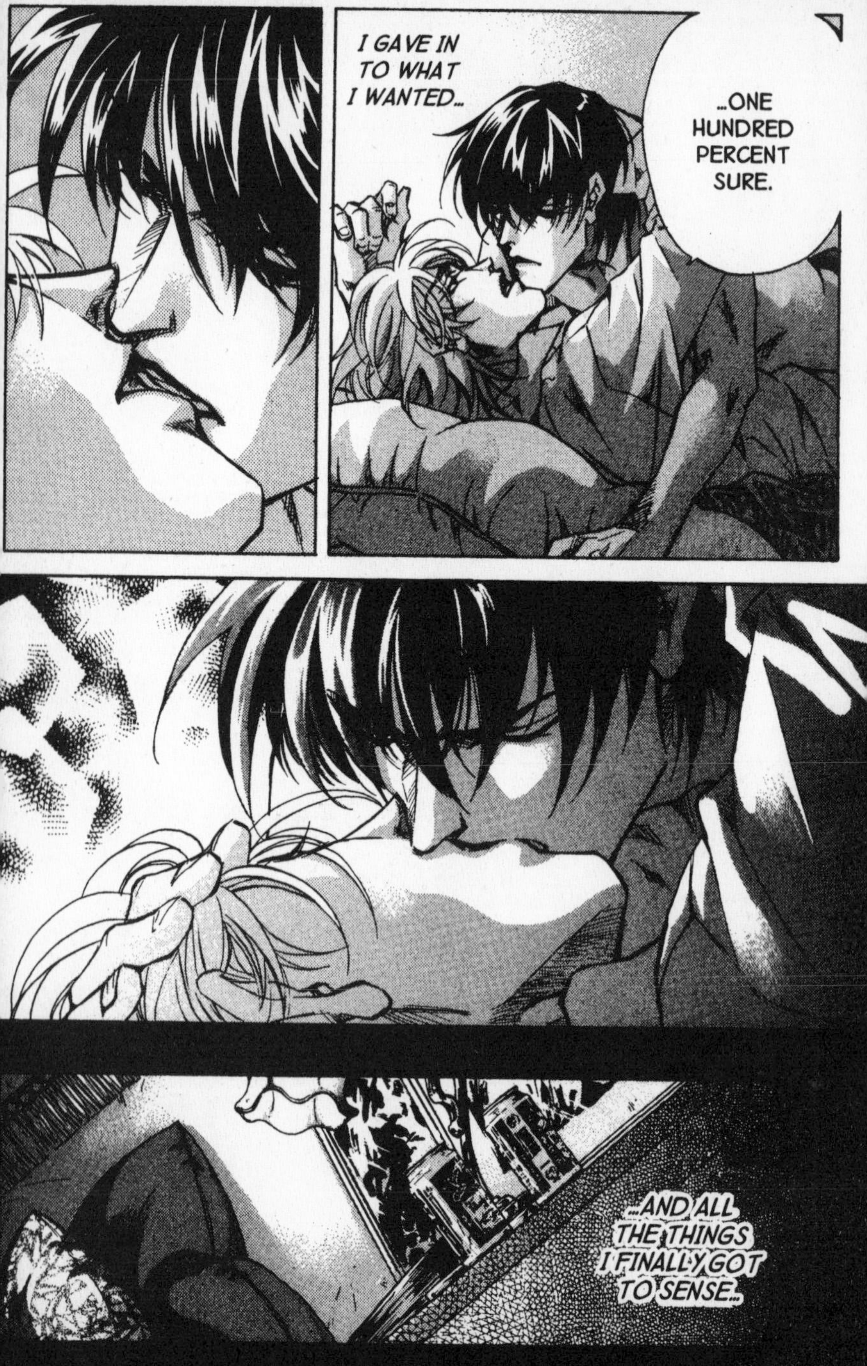
...ONE HUNDRED PERCENT SURE.
I GAVE IN TO WHAT I WANTED...
...AND ALL THE THINGS I FINALLY GOT TO SENSE...

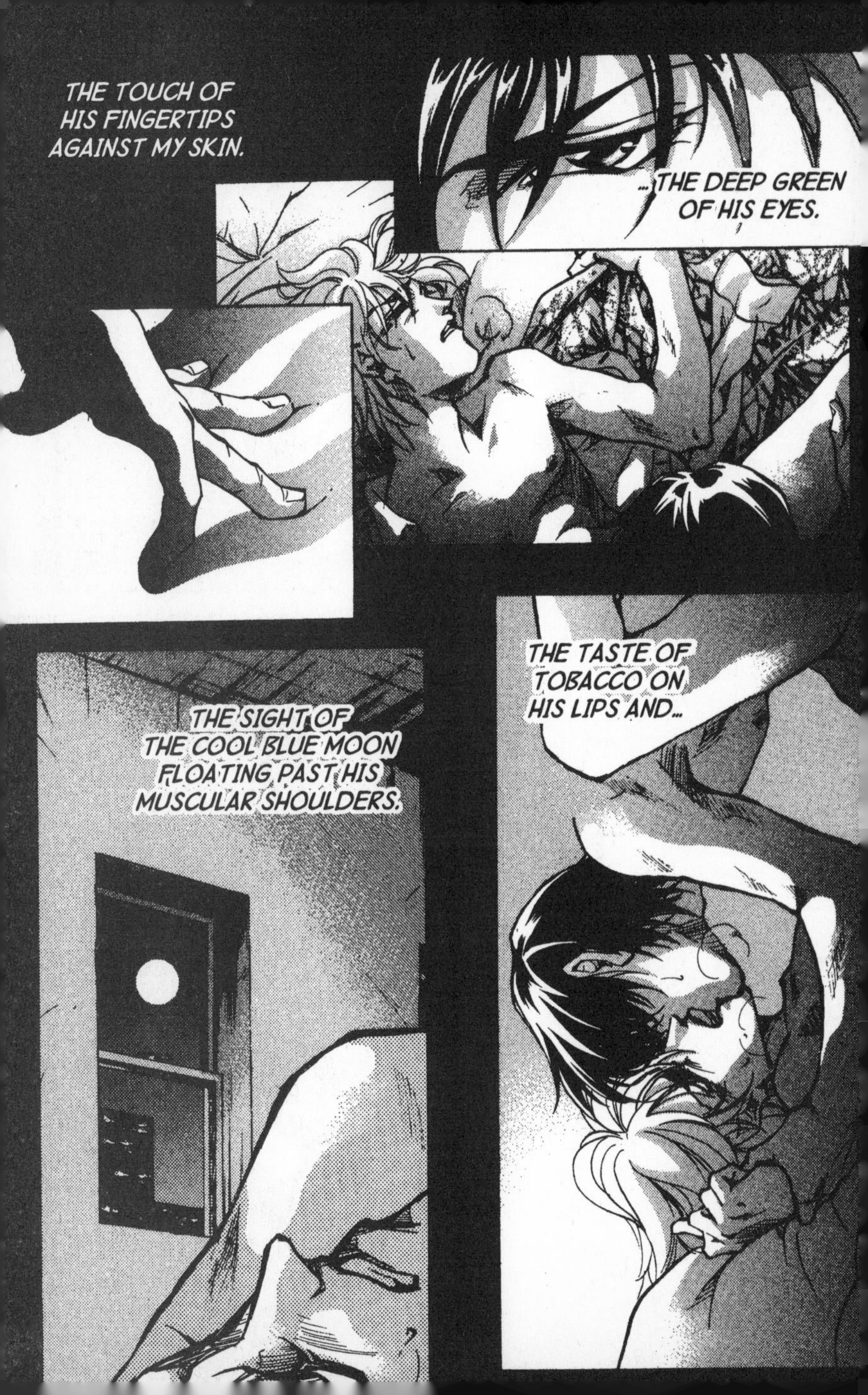
...THE DEEP GREEN OF HIS EYES.
THE TOUCH OF HIS FINGERTIPS AGAINST MY SKIN.
THE TASTE OF TOBACCO ON HIS LIPS AND...
THE SIGHT OF THE COOL BLUE MOON FLOATING PAST HIS MUSCULAR SHOULDERS.

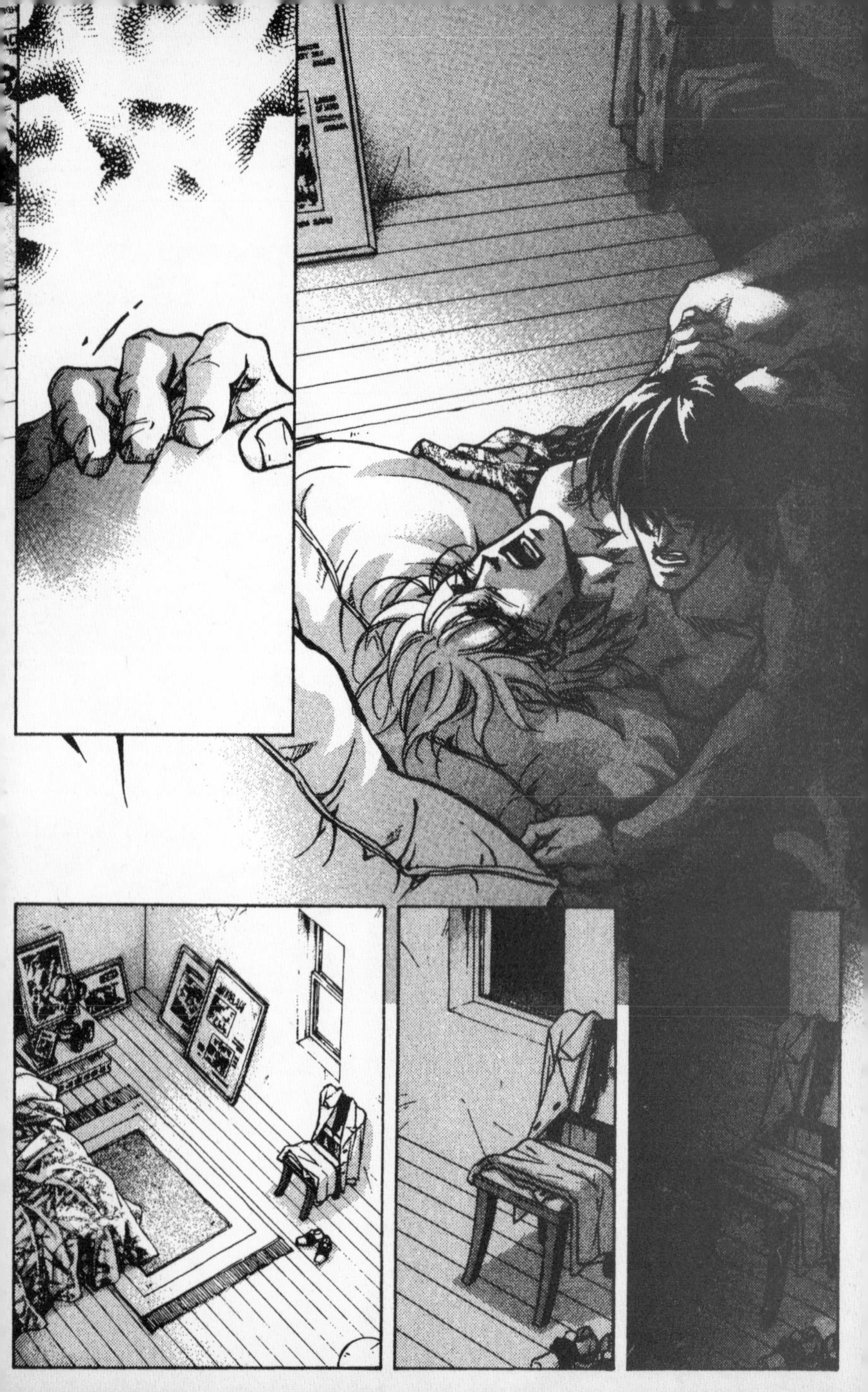

AND THEN, WHEN I WOKE UP...

...I REMEMBER HEARING HIS SOFT, PEACEFUL BREATHING AS HE SLEPT WRAPPED WITHIN MY ARMS.

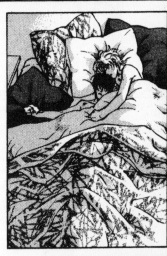

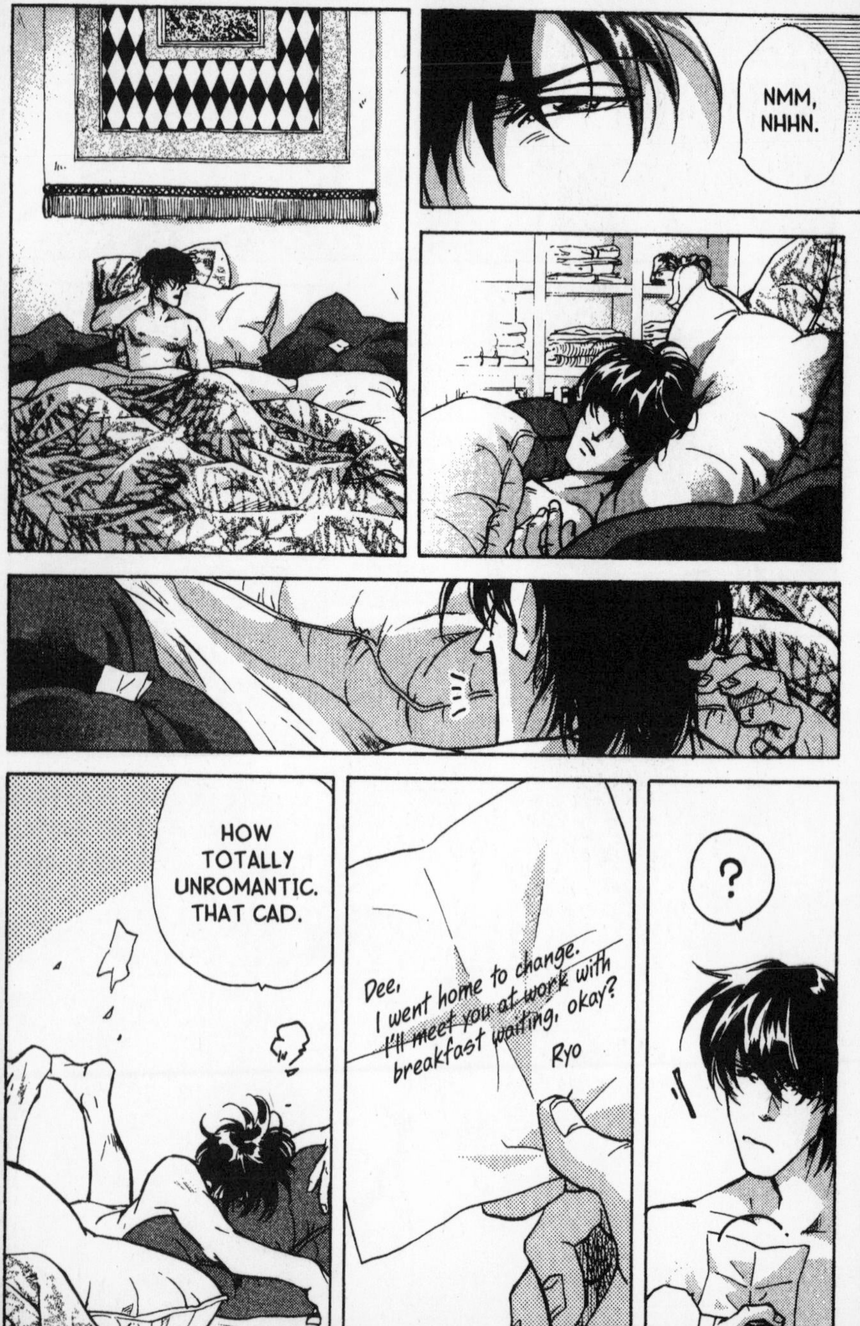
NMM, NHHN.
?
Dee,
I went home to change.
I'll meet you at work with breakfast waiting, okay?
Ryo
HOW TOTALLY UNROMANTIC. THAT CAD.

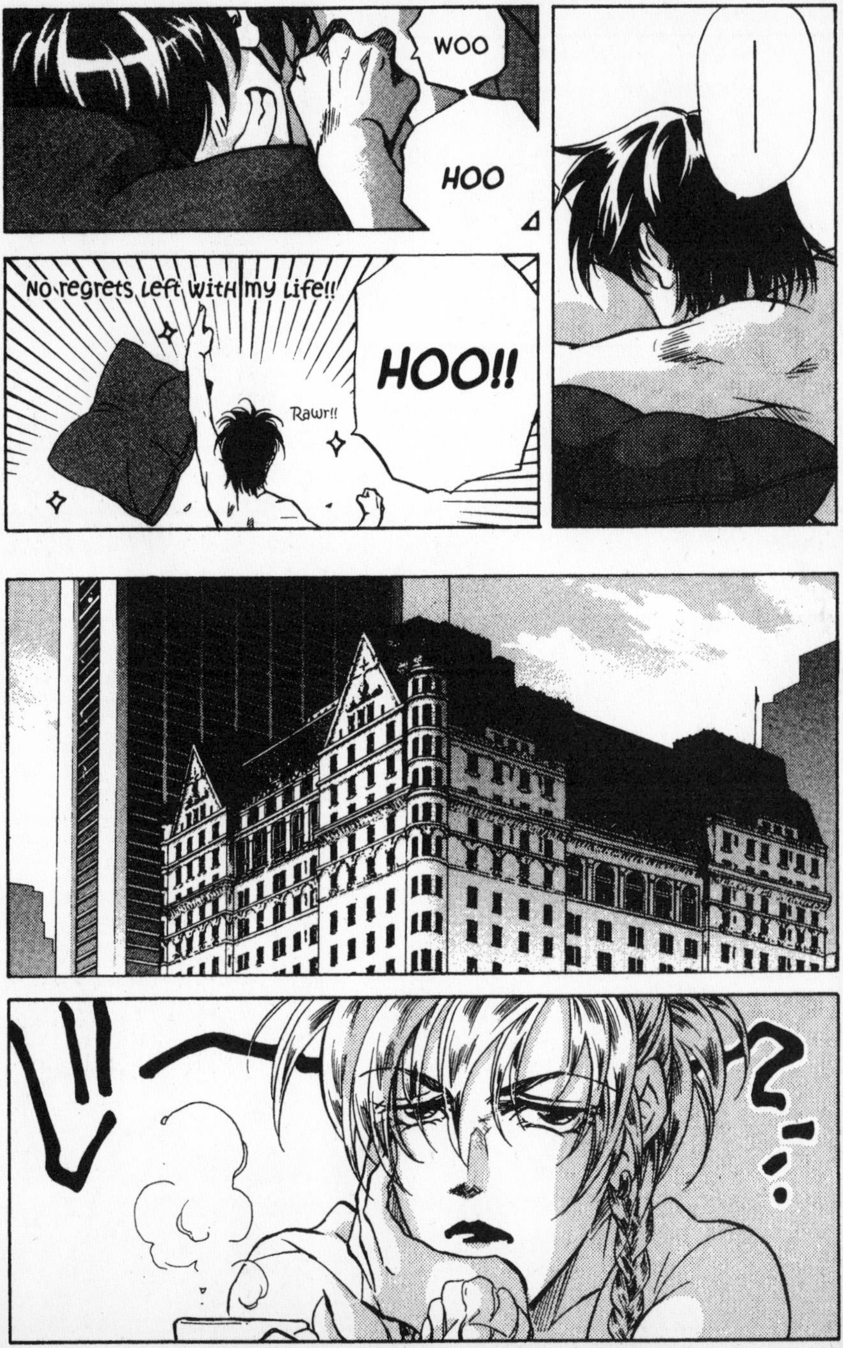
WOO
HOO
HOO!!
No regrets left with my life!!
Rawr!!

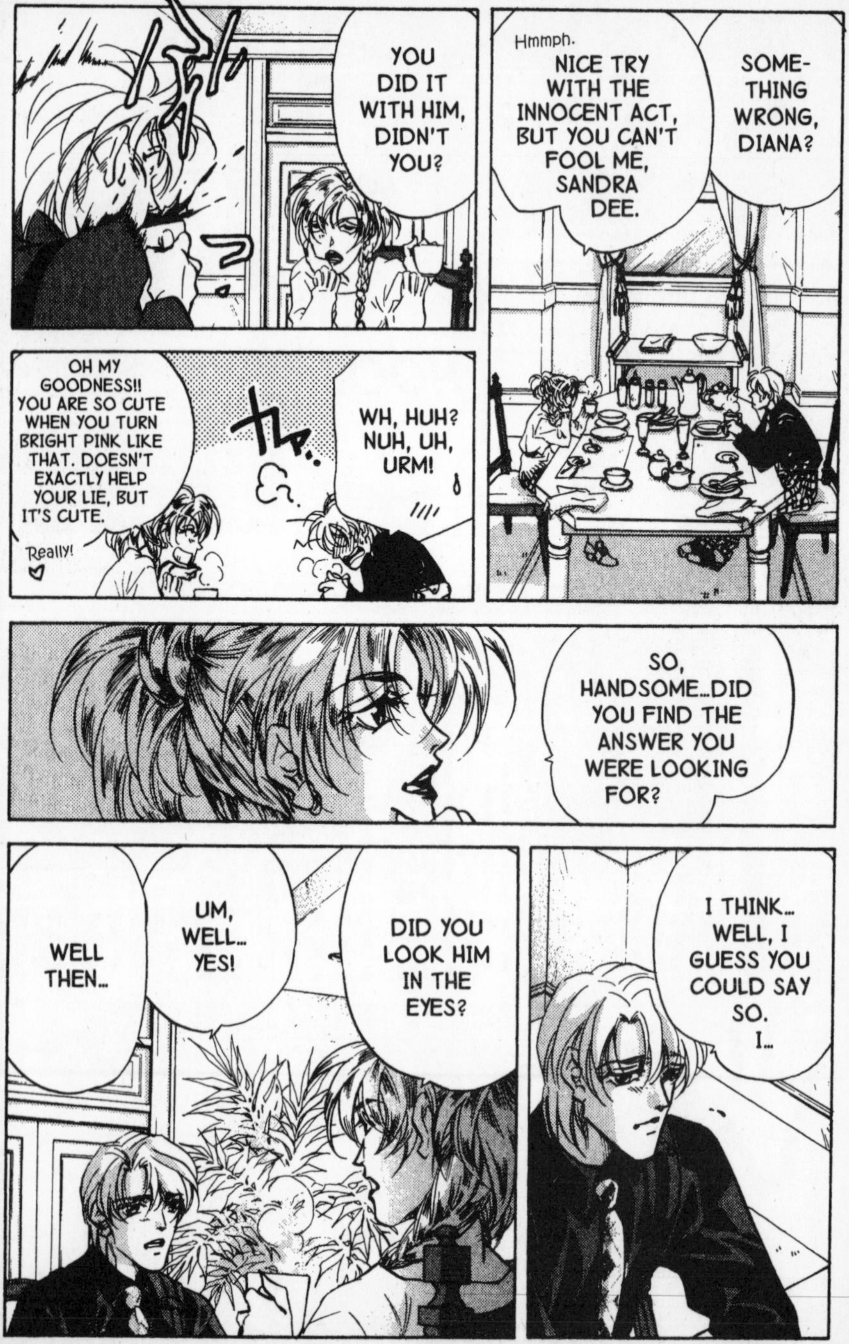
SOME-THING WRONG, DIANA?
Hmmph.
NICE TRY WITH THE INNOCENT ACT, BUT YOU CAN'T FOOL ME, SANDRA DEE.
YOU DID IT WITH HIM, DIDN'T YOU?
WH, HUH? NUH, UH, URM!
OH MY GOODNESS!! YOU ARE SO CUTE WHEN YOU TURN BRIGHT PINK LIKE THAT. DOESN'T EXACTLY HELP YOUR LIE, BUT IT'S CUTE.
Really!
SO, HANDSOME...DID YOU FIND THE ANSWER YOU WERE LOOKING FOR?
I THINK... WELL, I GUESS YOU COULD SAY SO.
I...
DID YOU LOOK HIM IN THE EYES?
UM, WELL... YES!
WELL THEN...

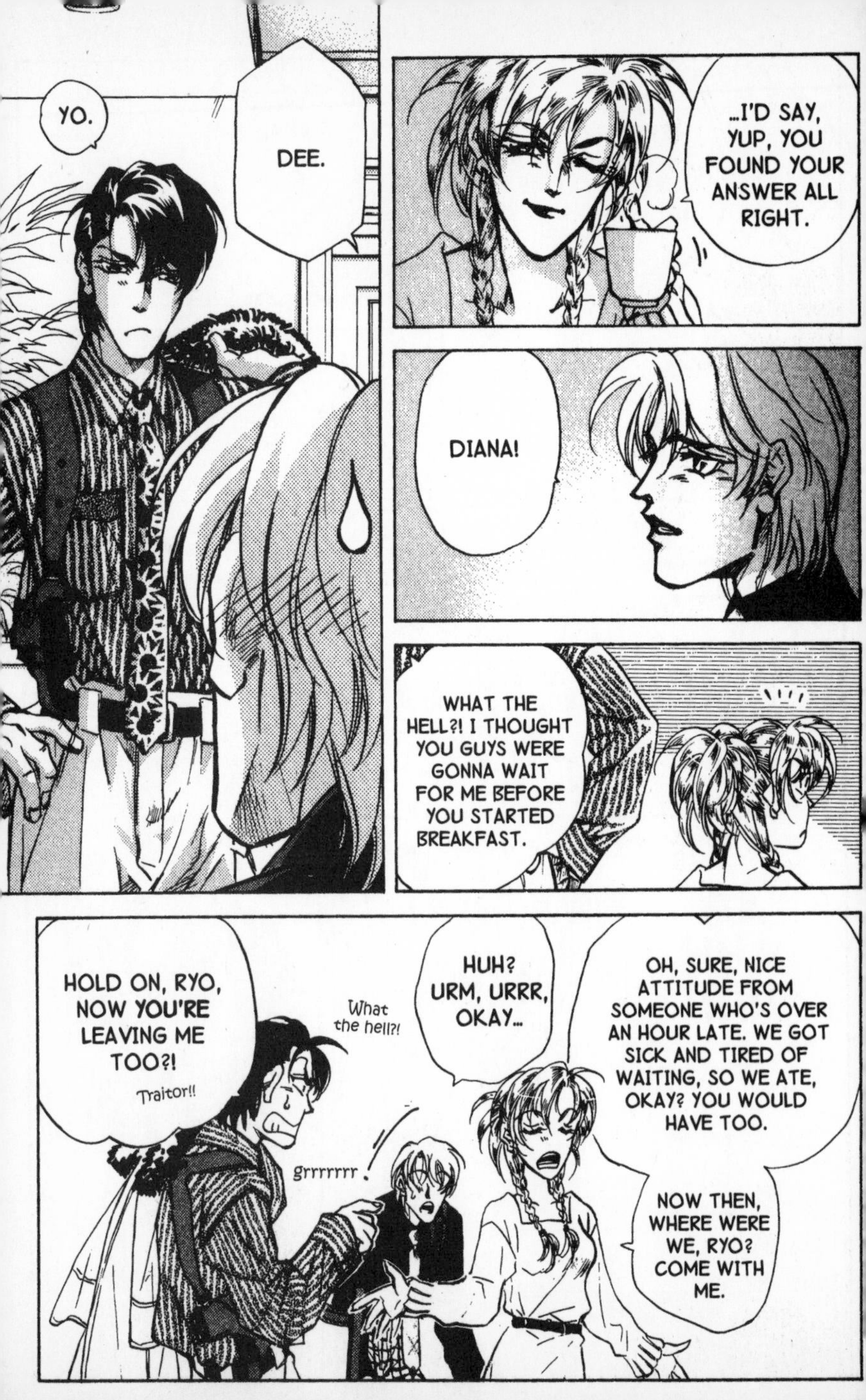
...I'D SAY, YUP, YOU FOUND YOUR ANSWER ALL RIGHT.
DIANA!
WHAT THE HELL?! I THOUGHT YOU GUYS WERE GONNA WAIT FOR ME BEFORE YOU STARTED BREAKFAST.
DEE.
YO.
OH, SURE, NICE ATTITUDE FROM SOMEONE WHO'S OVER AN HOUR LATE. WE GOT SICK AND TIRED OF WAITING, SO WE ATE, OKAY? YOU WOULD HAVE TOO.
NOW THEN, WHERE WERE WE, RYO? COME WITH ME.
HUH? URM, URRR, OKAY...
What the hell?!
HOLD ON, RYO, NOW YOU'RE LEAVING ME TOO?!
Traitor!!
grrrrrrr

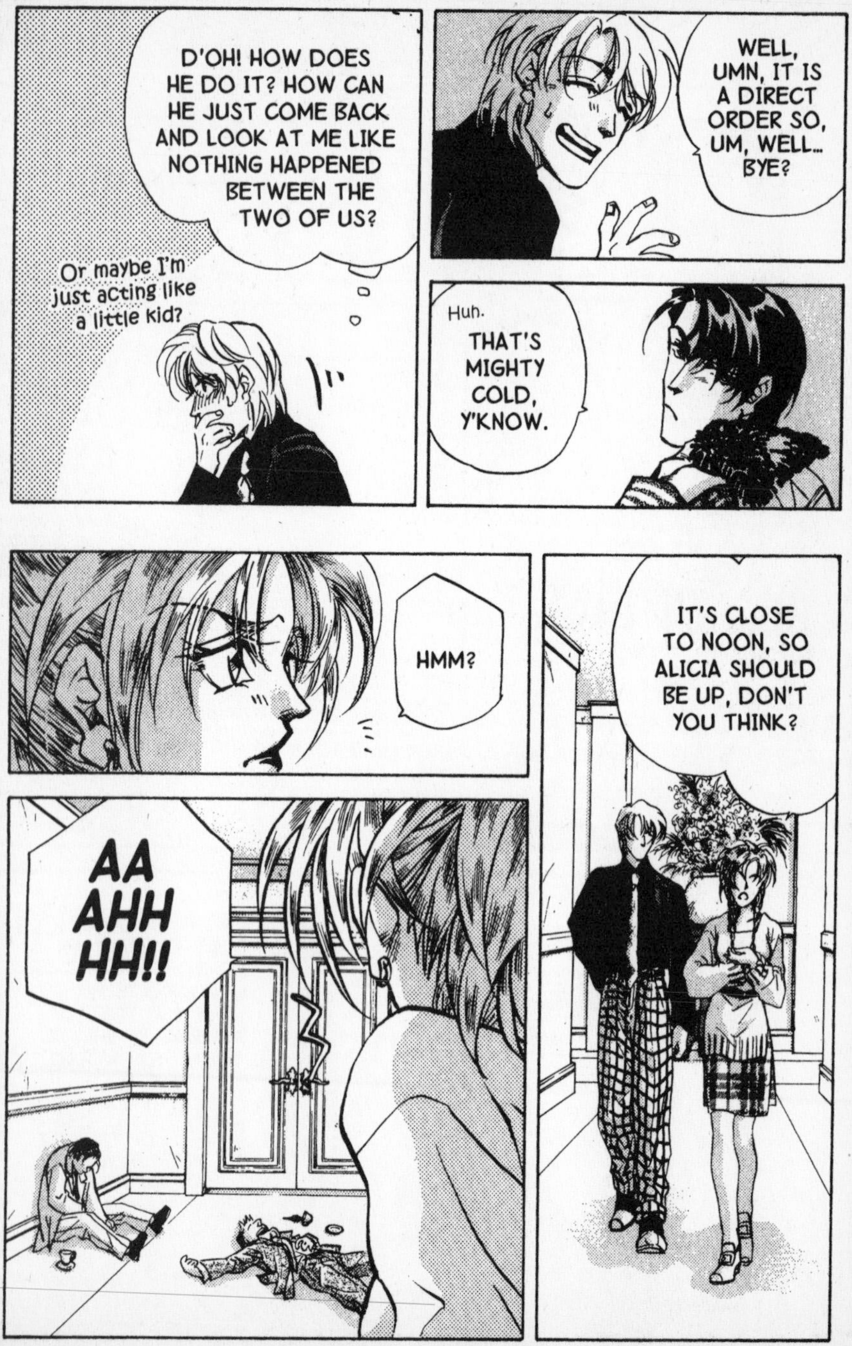
WELL, UMN, IT IS A DIRECT ORDER SO, UM, WELL... BYE?
Huh.
THAT'S MIGHTY COLD, Y'KNOW.
D'OH! HOW DOES HE DO IT? HOW CAN HE JUST COME BACK AND LOOK AT ME LIKE NOTHING HAPPENED BETWEEN THE TWO OF US?
Or maybe I'm just acting like a little kid?
IT'S CLOSE TO NOON, SO ALICIA SHOULD BE UP, DON'T YOU THINK?
HMM?
AA AHH HH!!

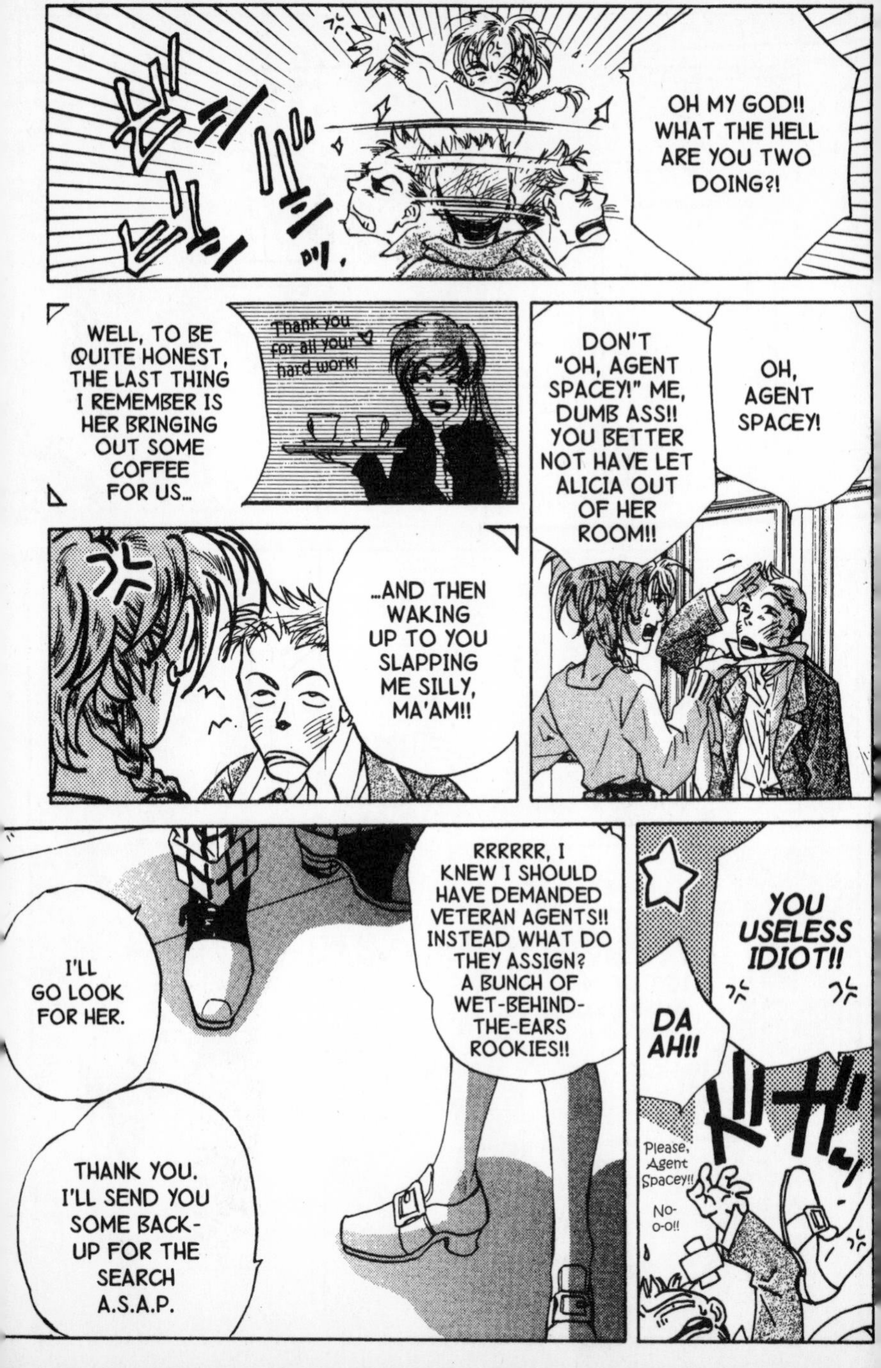
OH MY GOD!! WHAT THE HELL ARE YOU TWO DOING?!
OH, AGENT SPACEY!
DON'T "OH, AGENT SPACEY!" ME, DUMB ASS!! YOU BETTER NOT HAVE LET ALICIA OUT OF HER ROOM!!
WELL, TO BE QUITE HONEST, THE LAST THING I REMEMBER IS HER BRINGING OUT SOME COFFEE FOR US...
Thank you for all your hard work!
...AND THEN WAKING UP TO YOU SLAPPING ME SILLY, MA'AM!!
YOU USELESS IDIOT!!
DA AH!!
Please, Agent Spacey!!
No-o-o!!
RRRRRR, I KNEW I SHOULD HAVE DEMANDED VETERAN AGENTS!! INSTEAD WHAT DO THEY ASSIGN? A BUNCH OF WET-BEHIND-THE-EARS ROOKIES!!
I'LL GO LOOK FOR HER.
THANK YOU. I'LL SEND YOU SOME BACK-UP FOR THE SEARCH A.S.A.P.

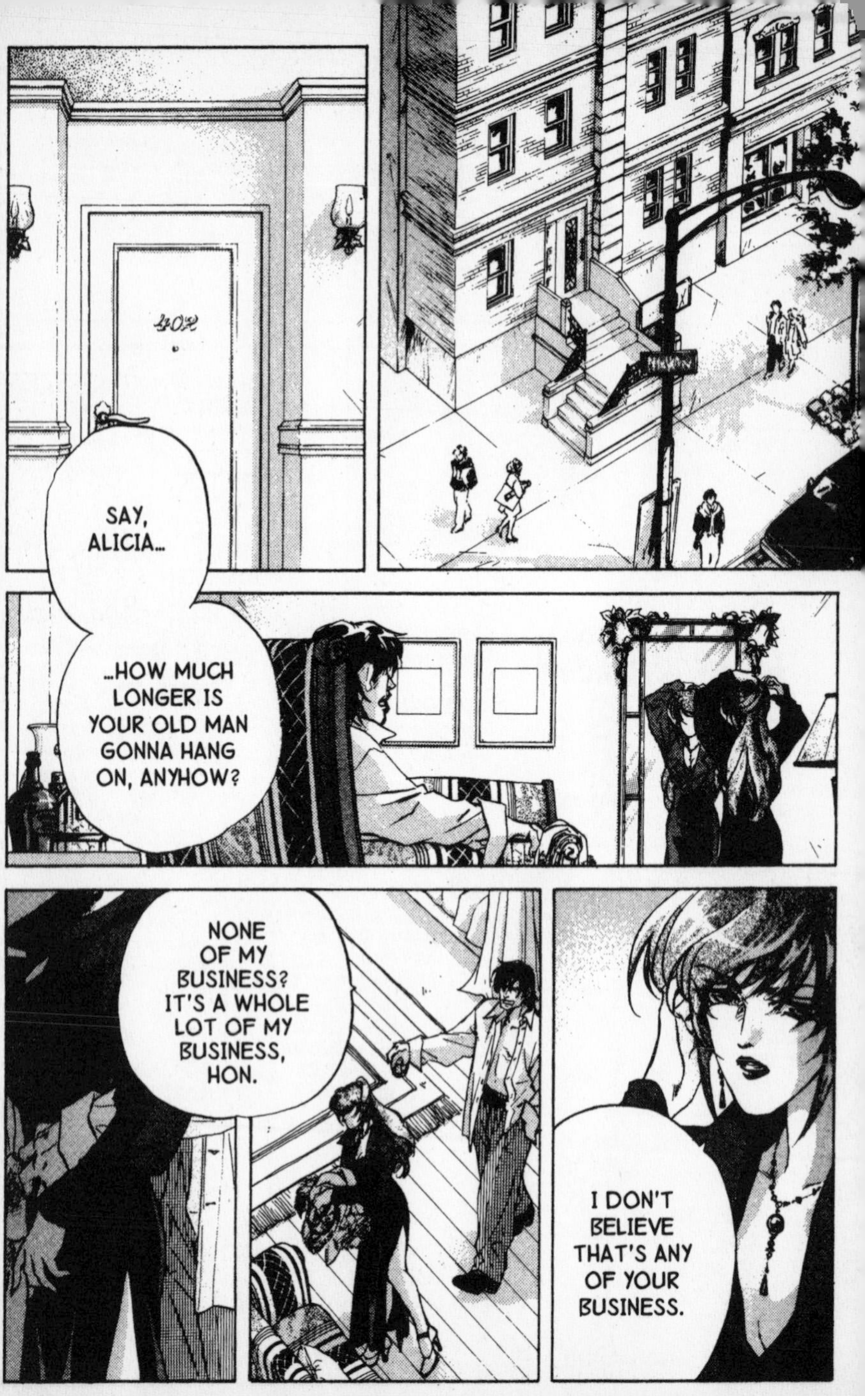
SAY, ALICIA...
...HOW MUCH LONGER IS YOUR OLD MAN GONNA HANG ON, ANYHOW?
I DON'T BELIEVE THAT'S ANY OF YOUR BUSINESS.
NONE OF MY BUSINESS? IT'S A WHOLE LOT OF MY BUSINESS, HON.

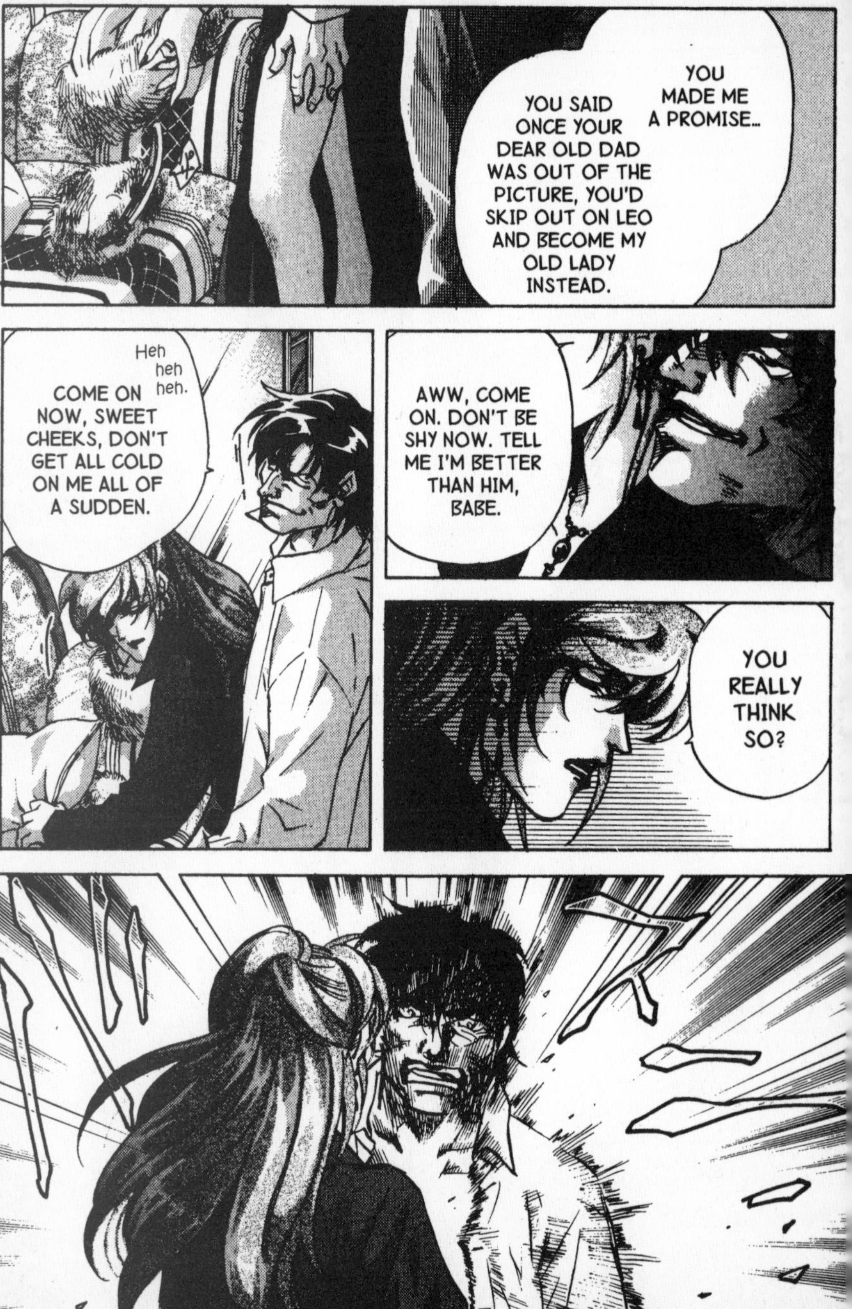
YOU MADE ME A PROMISE...
YOU SAID ONCE YOUR DEAR OLD DAD WAS OUT OF THE PICTURE, YOU'D SKIP OUT ON LEO AND BECOME MY OLD LADY INSTEAD.
AWW, COME ON. DON'T BE SHY NOW. TELL ME I'M BETTER THAN HIM, BABE.
YOU REALLY THINK SO?
Heh heh heh.
COME ON NOW, SWEET CHEEKS, DON'T GET ALL COLD ON ME ALL OF A SUDDEN.

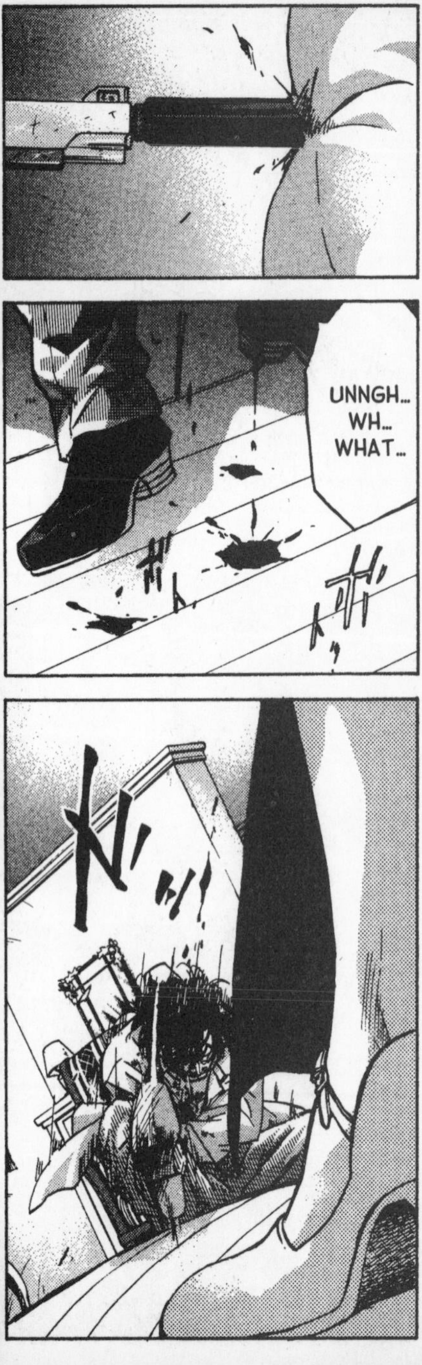
UNNGH... WH... WHAT...
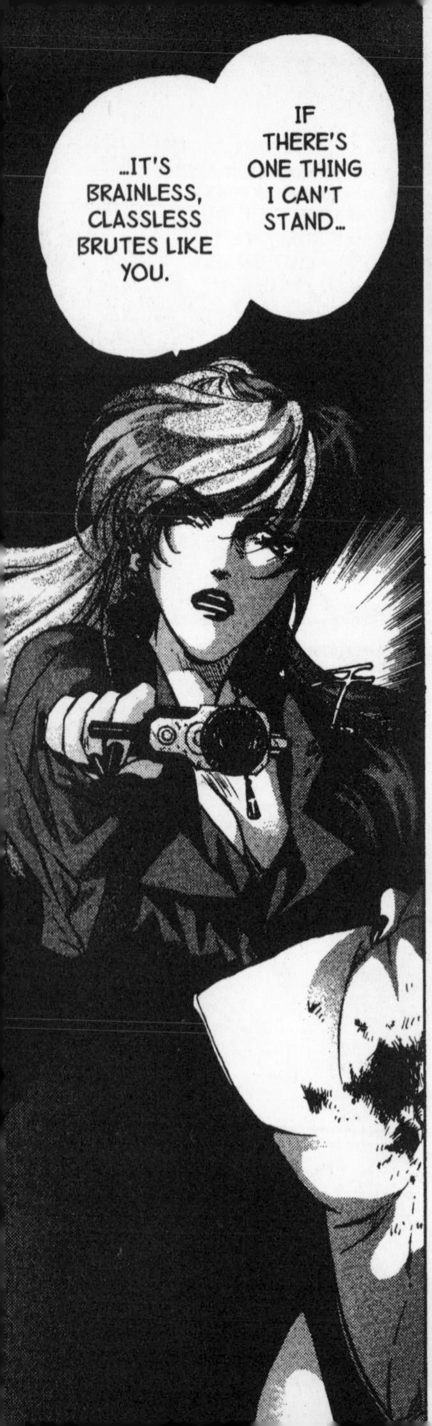
IF THERE'S ONE THING I CAN'T STAND...
...IT'S BRAINLESS, CLASSLESS BRUTES LIKE YOU.

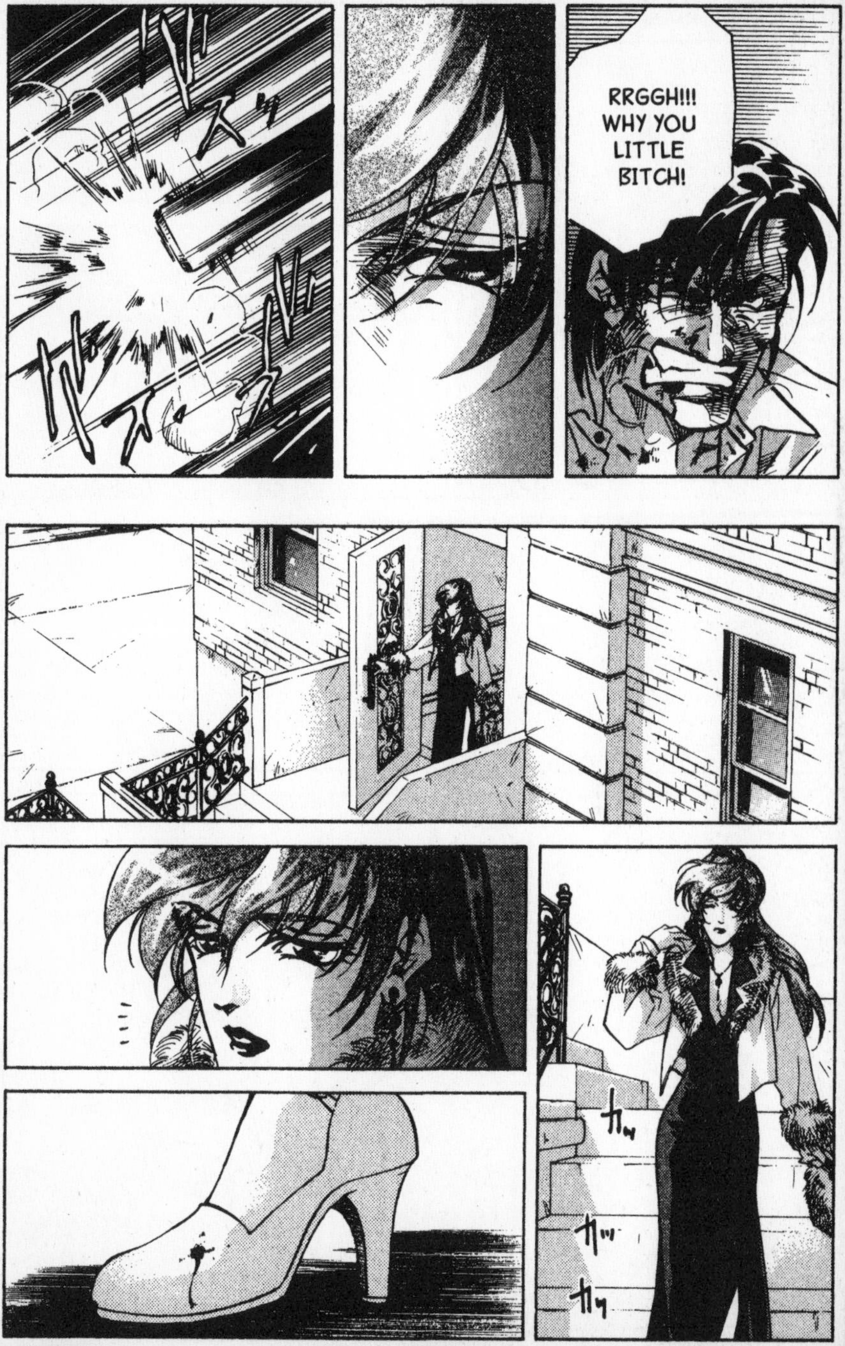
RRGGH!!! WHY YOU LITTLE BITCH!

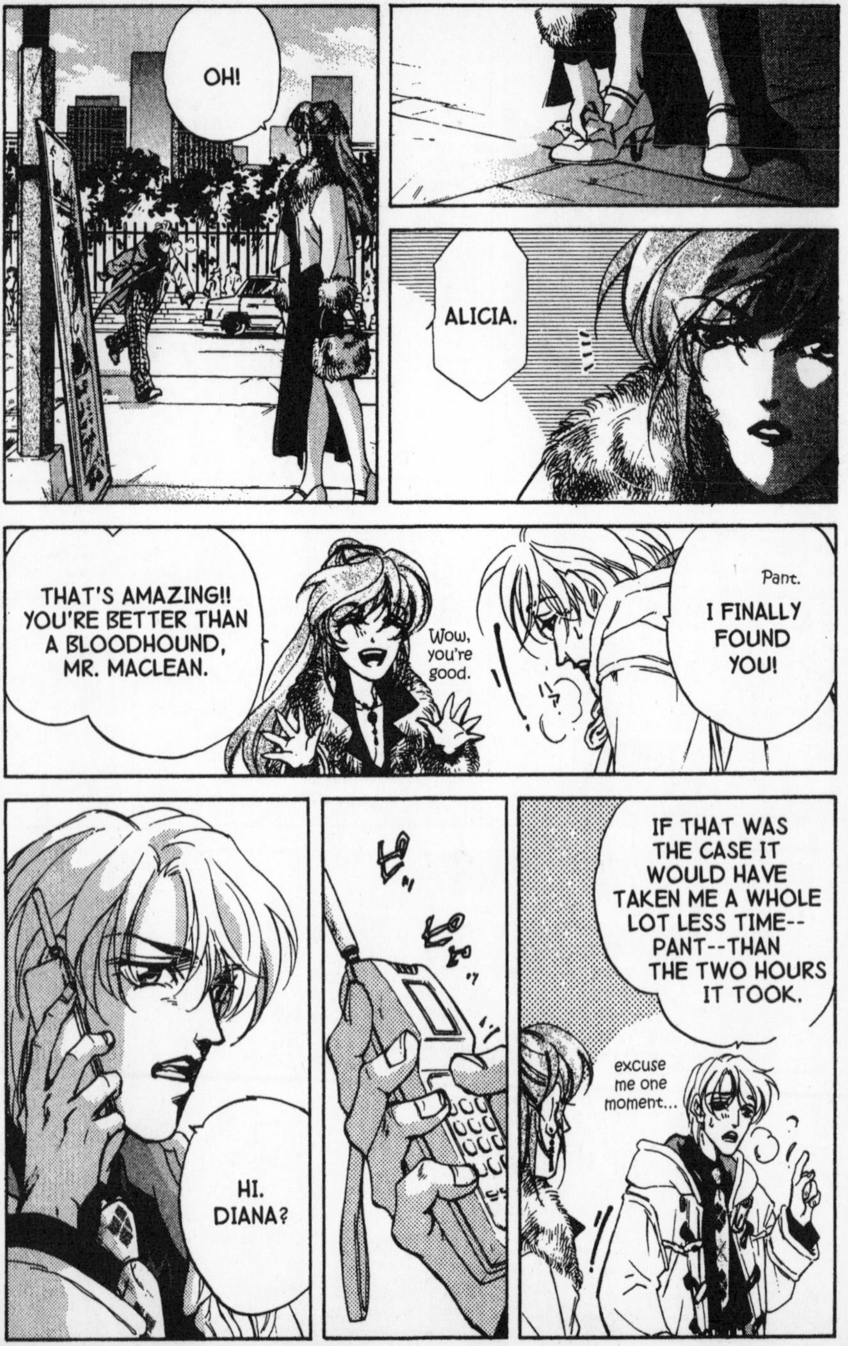
ALICIA.
OH!
Pant.
I FINALLY FOUND YOU!
Wow, you're good.
THAT'S AMAZING!! YOU'RE BETTER THAN A BLOODHOUND, MR. MACLEAN.
IF THAT WAS THE CASE IT WOULD HAVE TAKEN ME A WHOLE LOT LESS TIME-- PANT--THAN THE TWO HOURS IT TOOK.
excuse me one moment...
HI. DIANA?

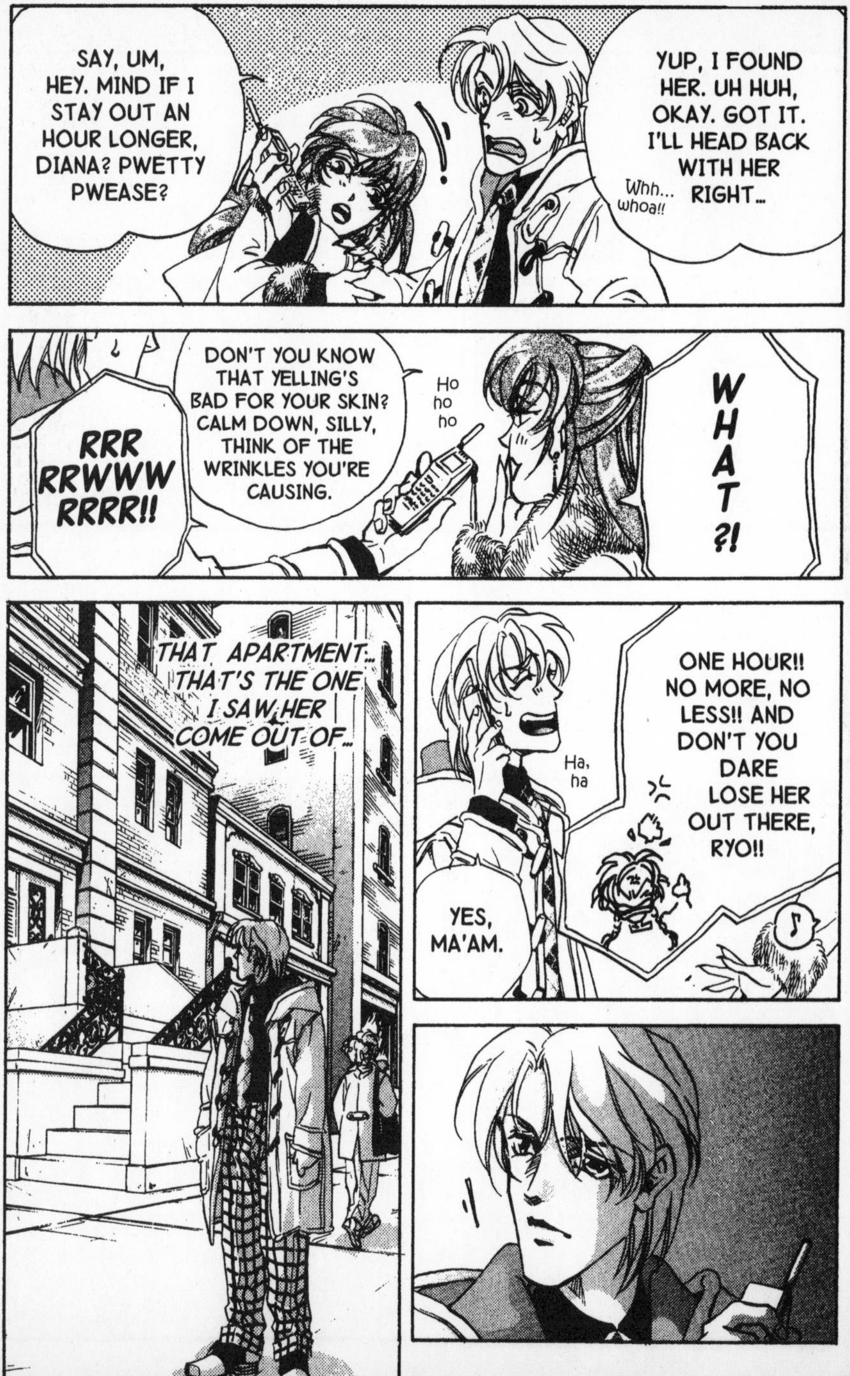
YUP, I FOUND HER. UH HUH, OKAY. GOT IT. I'LL HEAD BACK WITH HER RIGHT...
Whh... whoa!!
SAY, UM, HEY. MIND IF I STAY OUT AN HOUR LONGER, DIANA? PWETTY PWEASE?
WHAT?!
Ho ho ho
DON'T YOU KNOW THAT YELLING'S BAD FOR YOUR SKIN? CALM DOWN, SILLY, THINK OF THE WRINKLES YOU'RE CAUSING.
RRR RRWWW RRRR!!
ONE HOUR!! NO MORE, NO LESS!! AND DON'T YOU DARE LOSE HER OUT THERE, RYO!!
Ha, ha
YES, MA'AM.
THAT APARTMENT... THAT'S THE ONE I SAW HER COME OUT OF...

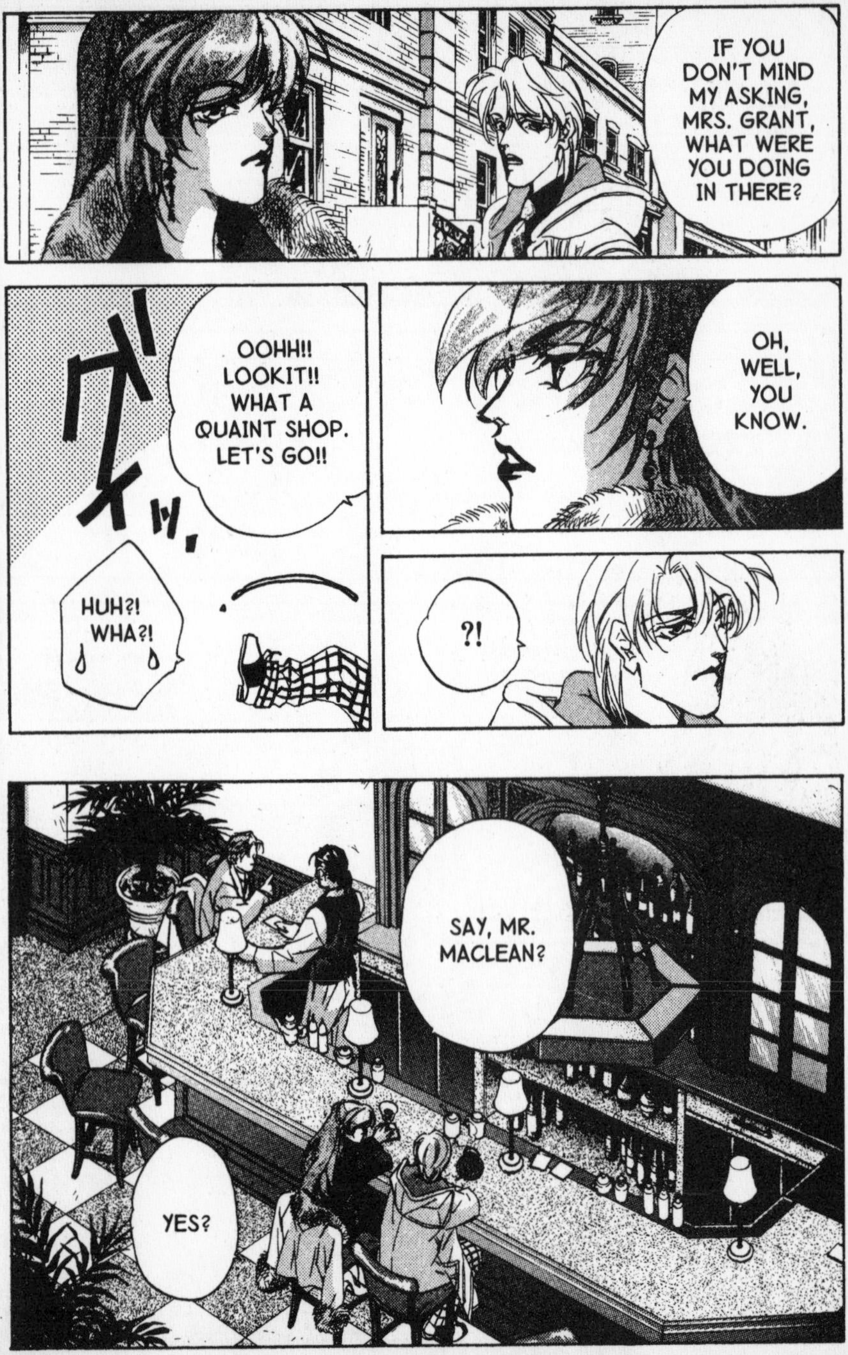
IF YOU DON'T MIND MY ASKING, MRS. GRANT, WHAT WERE YOU DOING IN THERE?
OH, WELL, YOU KNOW.
?!
OOHH!! LOOKIT!! WHAT A QUAINT SHOP. LET'S GO!!
グイッ
HUH?! WHA?!
SAY, MR. MACLEAN?
YES?

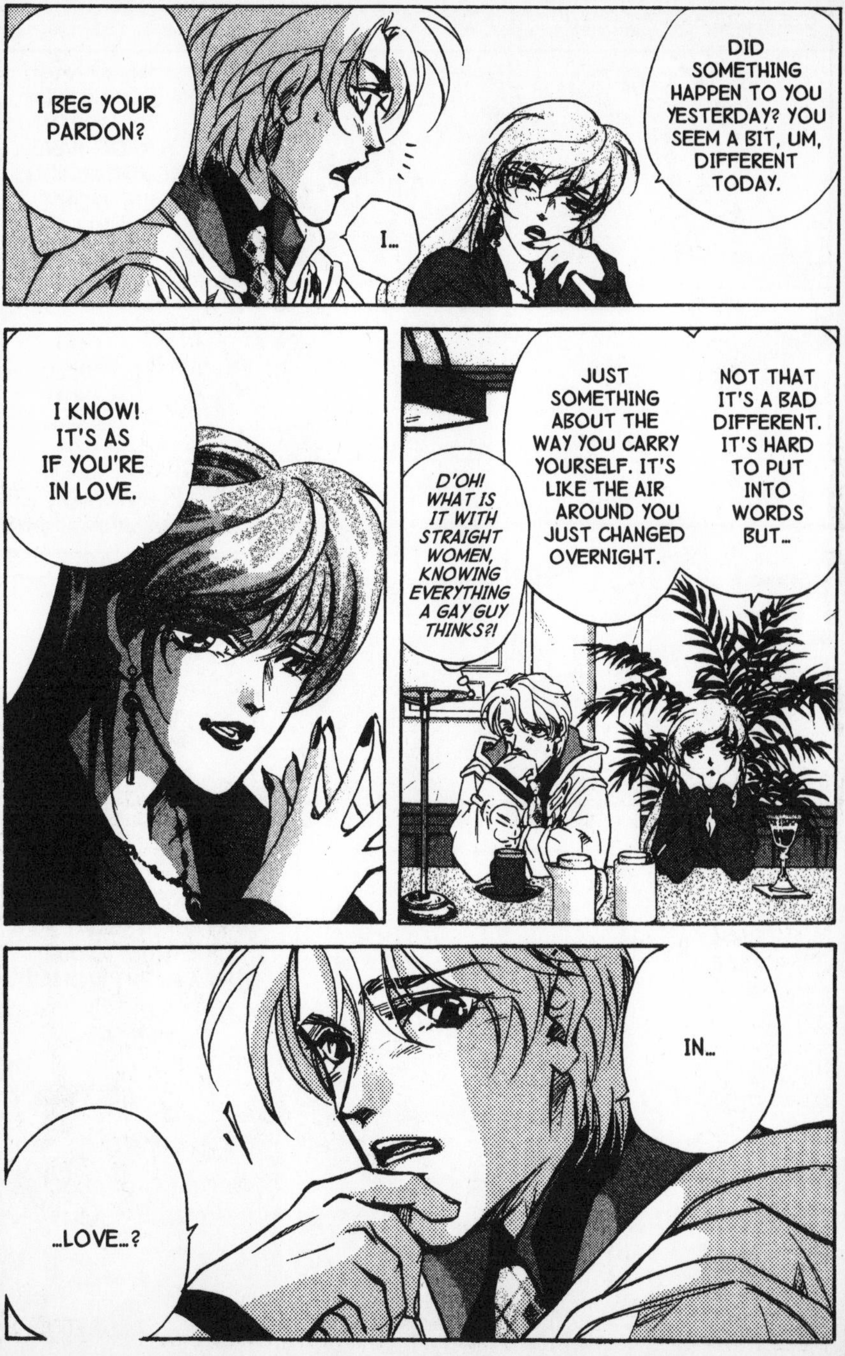
DID SOMETHING HAPPEN TO YOU YESTERDAY? YOU SEEM A BIT, UM, DIFFERENT TODAY.
I BEG YOUR PARDON?
I...
NOT THAT IT'S A BAD DIFFERENT. IT'S HARD TO PUT INTO WORDS BUT...
JUST SOMETHING ABOUT THE WAY YOU CARRY YOURSELF. IT'S LIKE THE AIR AROUND YOU JUST CHANGED OVERNIGHT.
D'OH! WHAT IS IT WITH STRAIGHT WOMEN, KNOWING EVERYTHING A GAY GUY THINKS?!
I KNOW! IT'S AS IF YOU'RE IN LOVE.
IN...
...LOVE...?

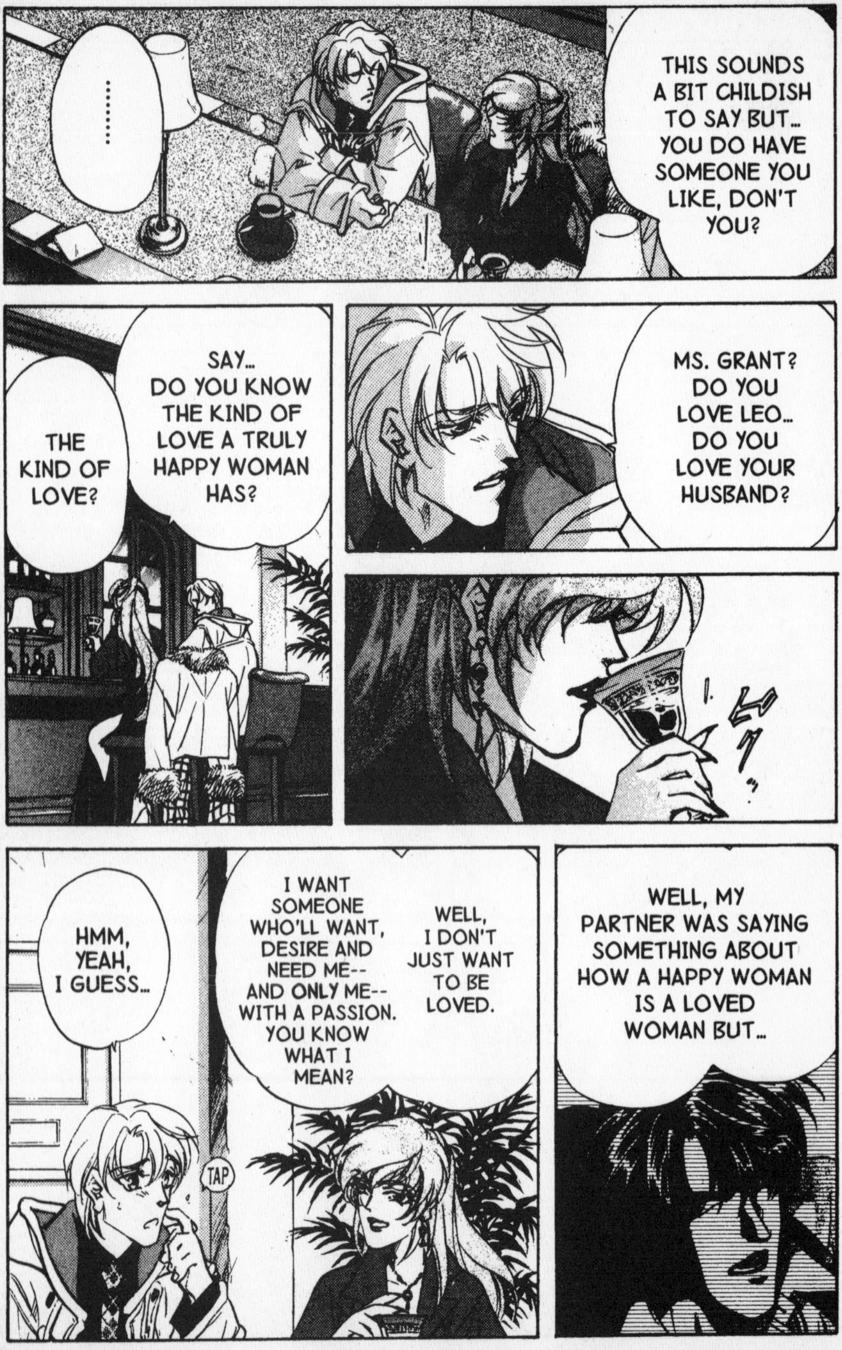
THIS SOUNDS A BIT CHILDISH TO SAY BUT... YOU DO HAVE SOMEONE YOU LIKE, DON'T YOU?
......
MS. GRANT? DO YOU LOVE LEO... DO YOU LOVE YOUR HUSBAND?
SAY... DO YOU KNOW THE KIND OF LOVE A TRULY HAPPY WOMAN HAS?
THE KIND OF LOVE?
WELL, MY PARTNER WAS SAYING SOMETHING ABOUT HOW A HAPPY WOMAN IS A LOVED WOMAN BUT...
WELL, I DON'T JUST WANT TO BE LOVED.
I WANT SOMEONE WHO'LL WANT, DESIRE AND NEED ME-- AND ONLY ME-- WITH A PASSION. YOU KNOW WHAT I MEAN?
HMM, YEAH, I GUESS...
TAP

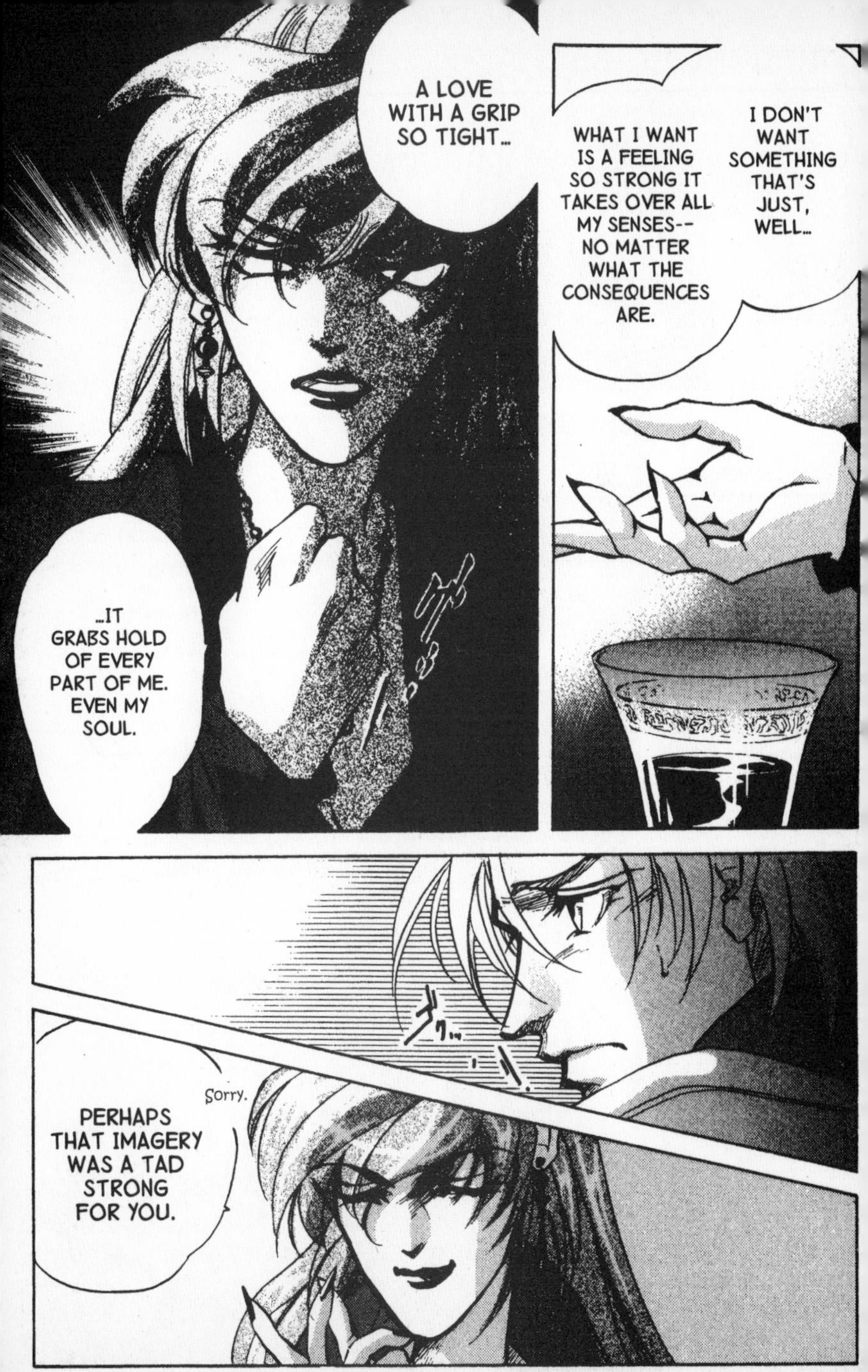
I DON'T WANT SOMETHING THAT'S JUST, WELL...
WHAT I WANT IS A FEELING SO STRONG IT TAKES OVER ALL MY SENSES-- NO MATTER WHAT THE CONSEQUENCES ARE.
A LOVE WITH A GRIP SO TIGHT...
...IT GRABS HOLD OF EVERY PART OF ME. EVEN MY SOUL.
Sorry.
PERHAPS THAT IMAGERY WAS A TAD STRONG FOR YOU.

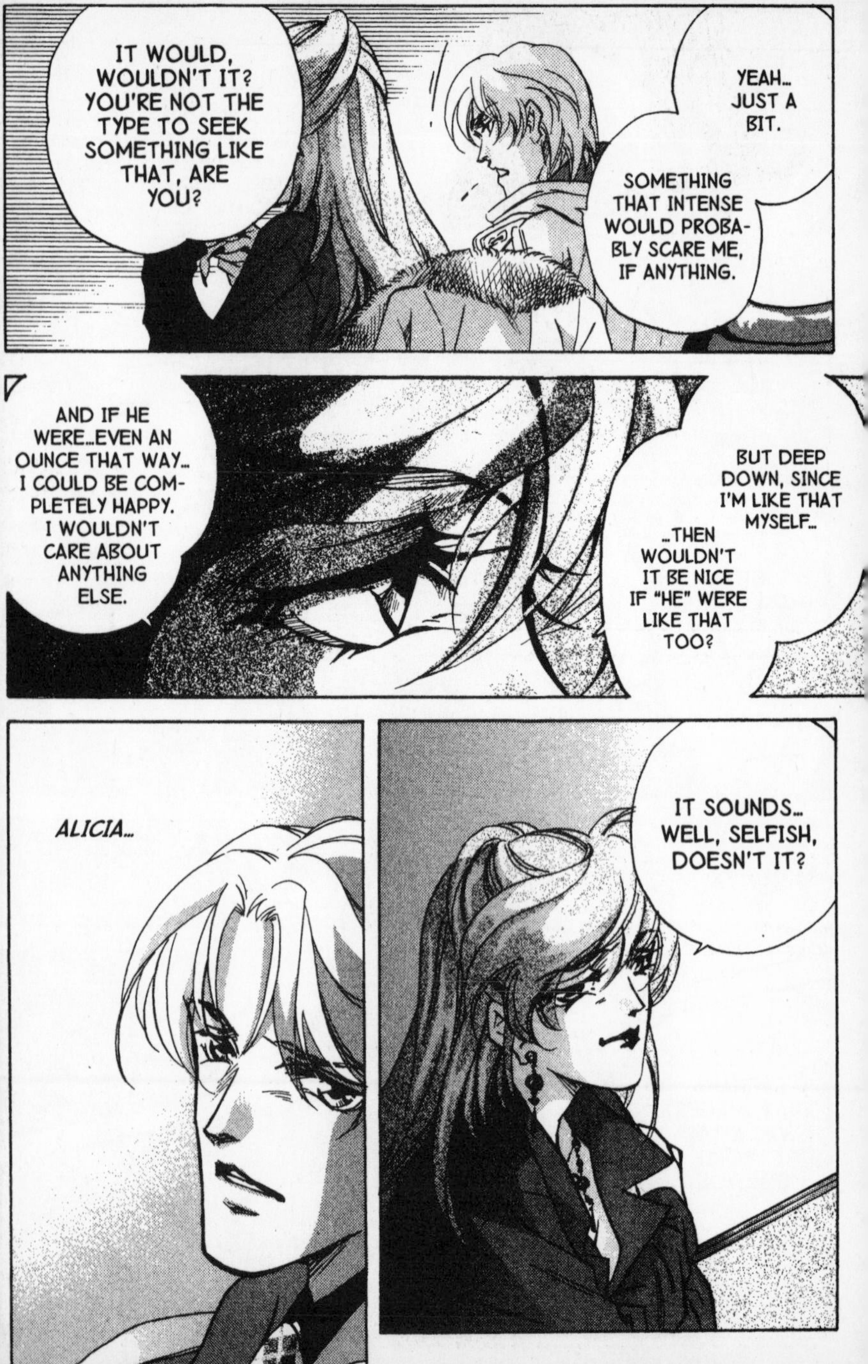
YEAH... JUST A BIT.
SOMETHING THAT INTENSE WOULD PROBABLY SCARE ME, IF ANYTHING.
IT WOULD, WOULDN'T IT? YOU'RE NOT THE TYPE TO SEEK SOMETHING LIKE THAT, ARE YOU?
BUT DEEP DOWN, SINCE I'M LIKE THAT MYSELF...
...THEN WOULDN'T IT BE NICE IF "HE" WERE LIKE THAT TOO?
AND IF HE WERE...EVEN AN OUNCE THAT WAY... I COULD BE COMPLETELY HAPPY. I WOULDN'T CARE ABOUT ANYTHING ELSE.
IT SOUNDS... WELL, SELFISH, DOESN'T IT?
ALICIA...

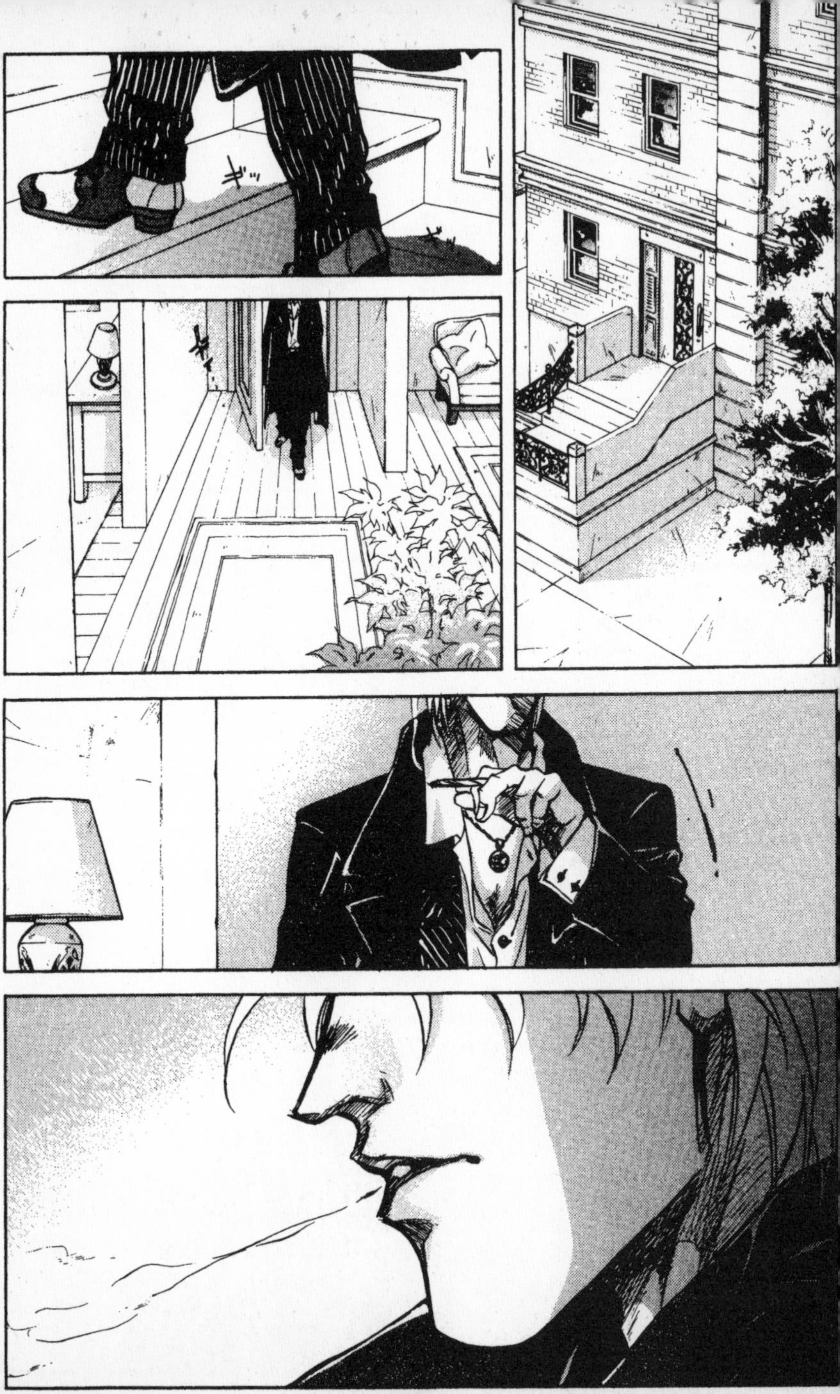

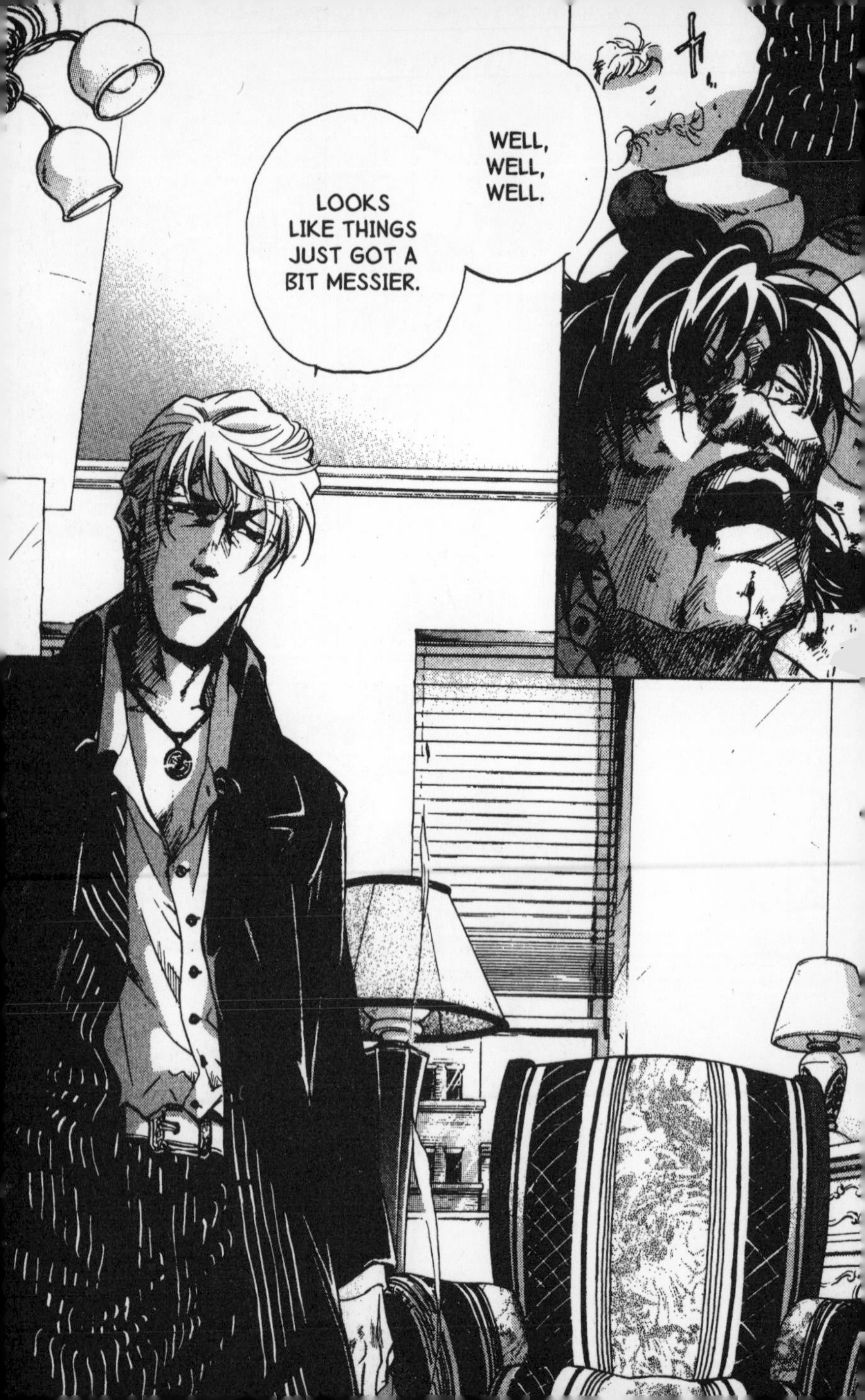
WELL, WELL, WELL.
LOOKS LIKE THINGS JUST GOT A BIT MESSIER.

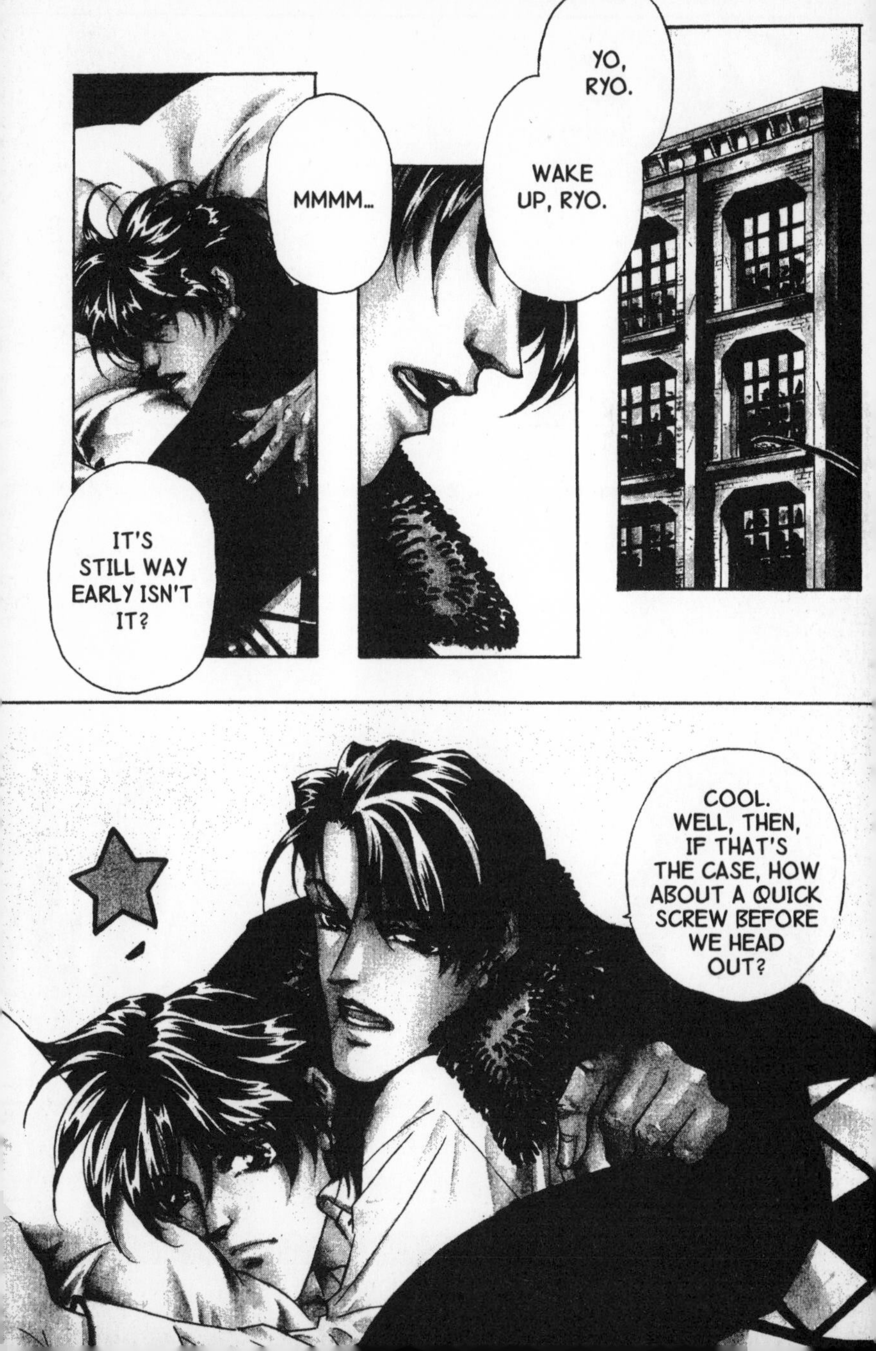
YO, RYO.
WAKE UP, RYO.
MMMM...
IT'S STILL WAY EARLY ISN'T IT?
COOL. WELL, THEN, IF THAT'S THE CASE, HOW ABOUT A QUICK SCREW BEFORE WE HEAD OUT?

FAKE

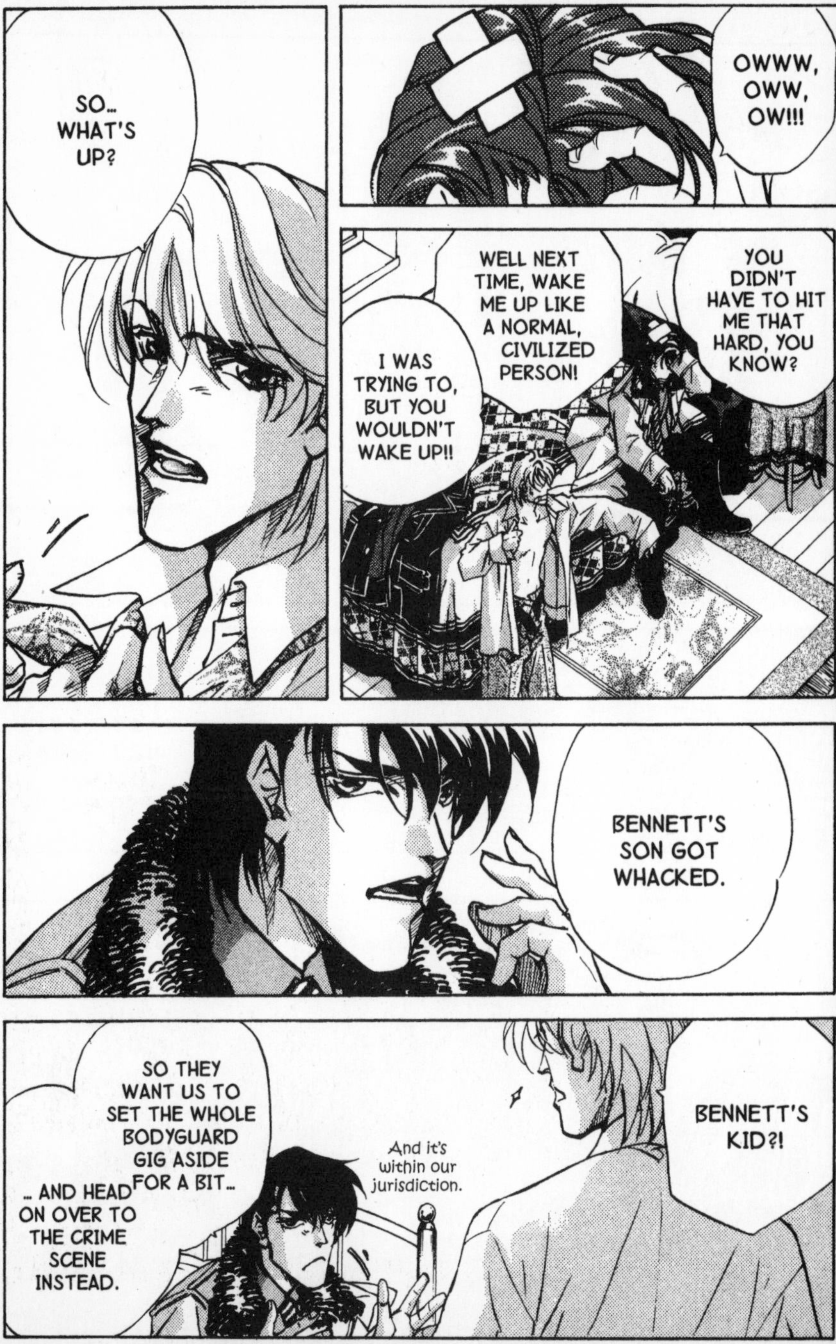

OWWW, OWW, OW!!!
YOU DIDN'T HAVE TO HIT ME THAT HARD, YOU KNOW?
WELL NEXT TIME, WAKE ME UP LIKE A NORMAL, CIVILIZED PERSON!
I WAS TRYING TO, BUT YOU WOULDN'T WAKE UP!!
SO... WHAT'S UP?
BENNETT'S SON GOT WHACKED.
BENNETT'S KID?!
SO THEY WANT US TO SET THE WHOLE BODYGUARD GIG ASIDE FOR A BIT...
... AND HEAD ON OVER TO THE CRIME SCENE INSTEAD.
And it's within our jurisdiction.

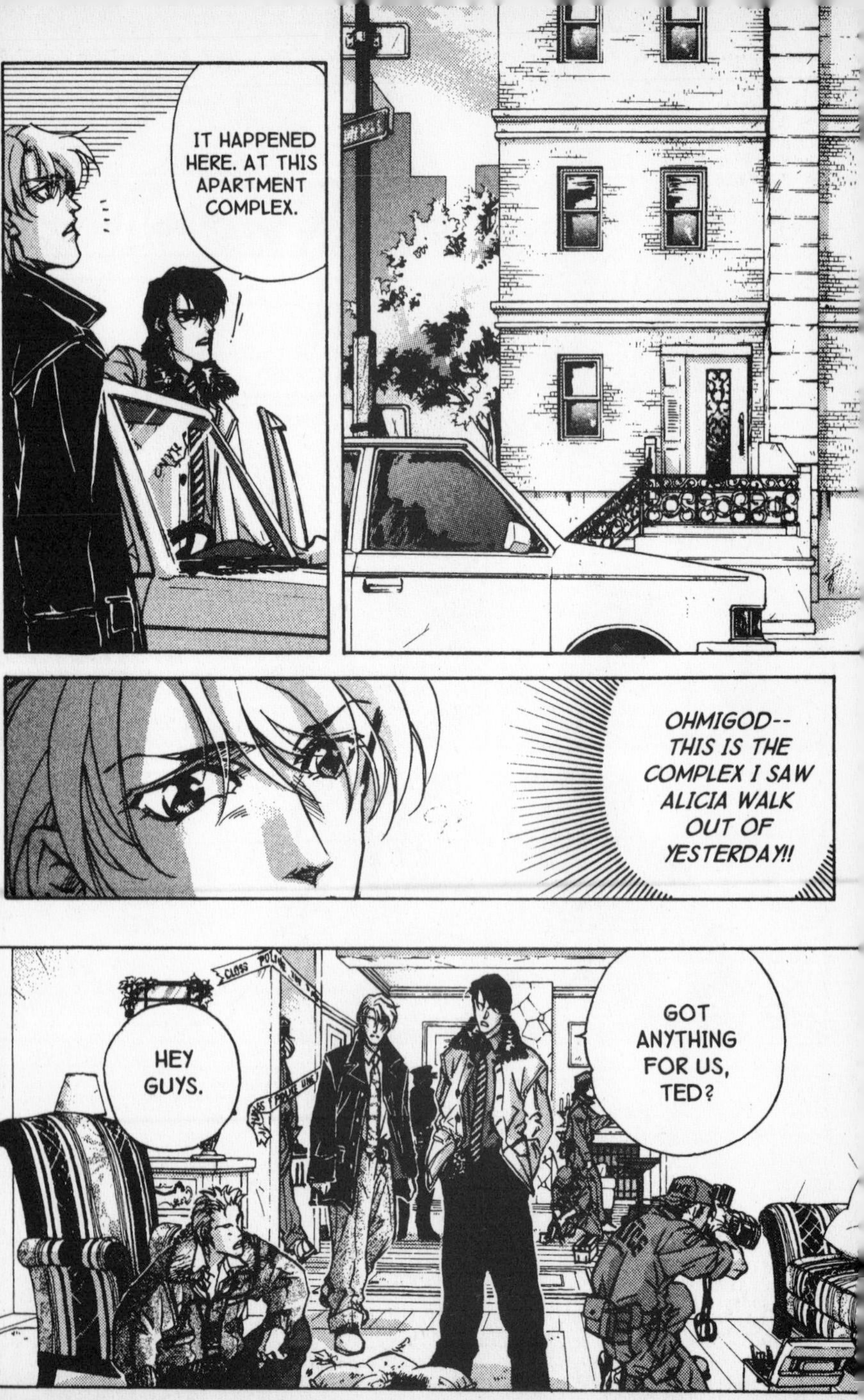
IT HAPPENED HERE. AT THIS APARTMENT COMPLEX.
OHMIGOD-- THIS IS THE COMPLEX I SAW ALICIA WALK OUT OF YESTERDAY!!
GOT ANYTHING FOR US, TED?
HEY GUYS.

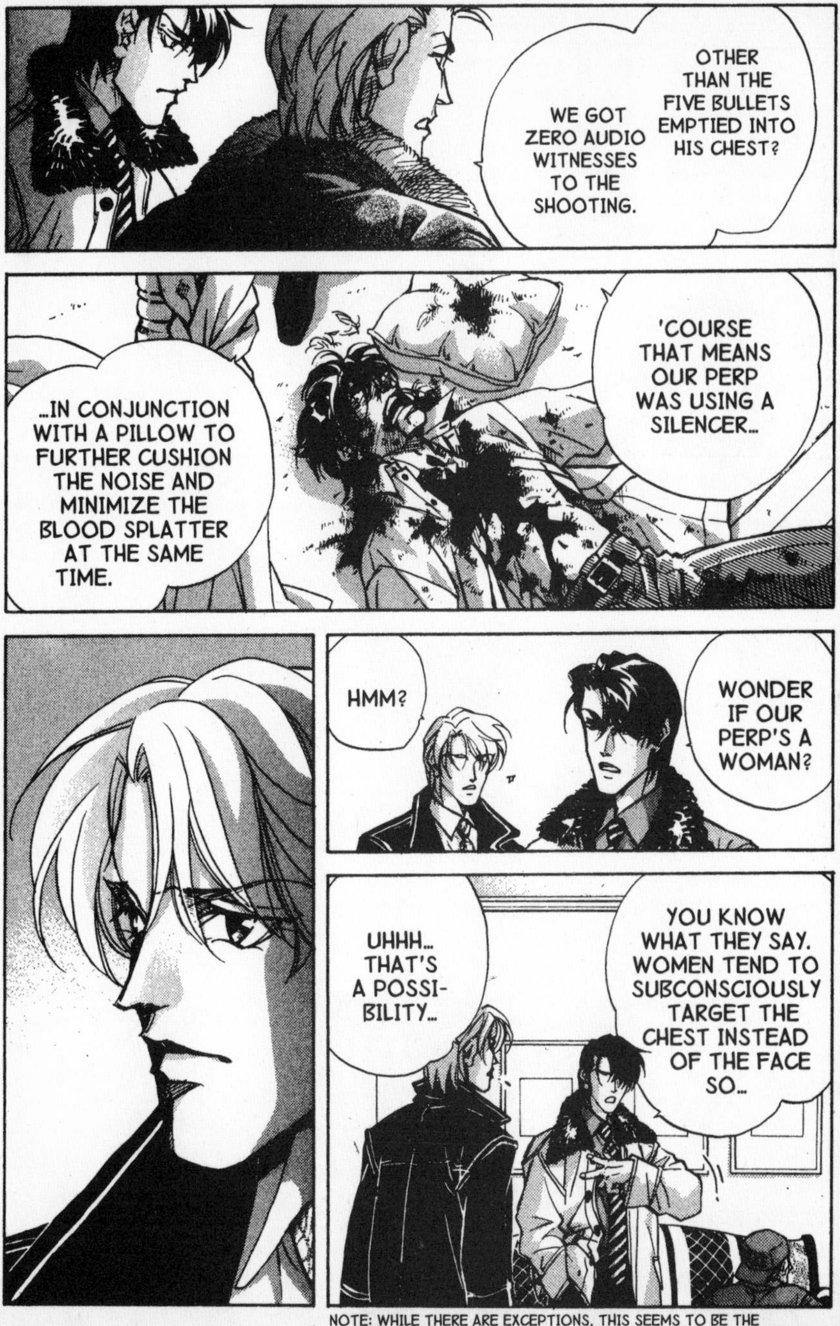
OTHER THAN THE FIVE BULLETS EMPTIED INTO HIS CHEST?
WE GOT ZERO AUDIO WITNESSES TO THE SHOOTING.
'COURSE THAT MEANS OUR PERP WAS USING A SILENCER...
...IN CONJUNCTION WITH A PILLOW TO FURTHER CUSHION THE NOISE AND MINIMIZE THE BLOOD SPLATTER AT THE SAME TIME.
WONDER IF OUR PERP'S A WOMAN?
HMM?
YOU KNOW WHAT THEY SAY. WOMEN TEND TO SUBCONSCIOUSLY TARGET THE CHEST INSTEAD OF THE FACE SO...
UHHH... THAT'S A POSSI-BILITY...

NOTE: WHILE THERE ARE EXCEPTIONS, THIS SEEMS TO BE THE GENERALLY ACCEPTED THEORY IN REGARD TO MURDER INVESTIGATIONS.

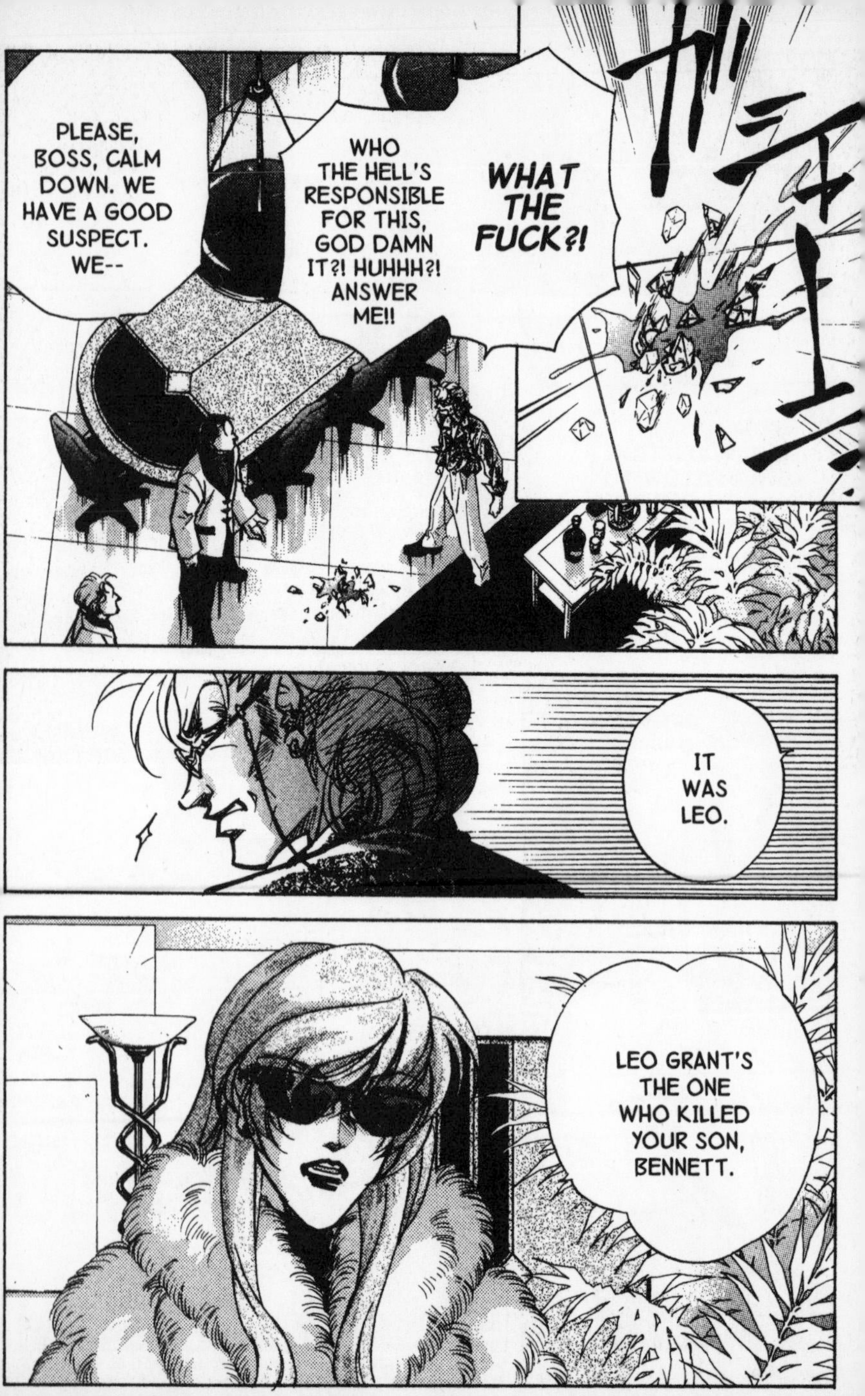
WHAT THE FUCK?!
WHO THE HELL'S RESPONSIBLE FOR THIS, GOD DAMN IT?! HUHHH?! ANSWER ME!!
PLEASE, BOSS, CALM DOWN. WE HAVE A GOOD SUSPECT. WE--
IT WAS LEO.
LEO GRANT'S THE ONE WHO KILLED YOUR SON, BENNETT.

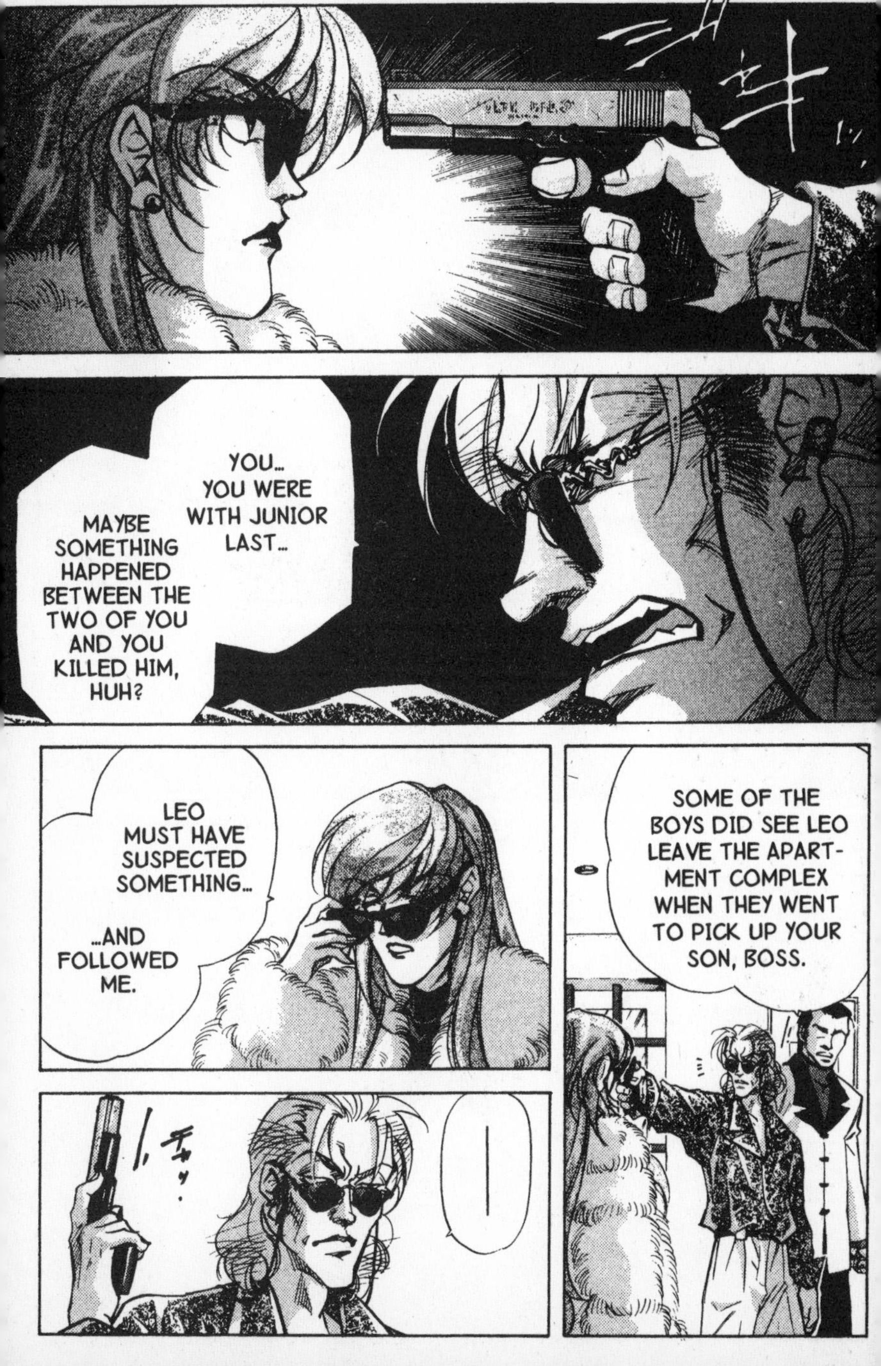
YOU... YOU WERE WITH JUNIOR LAST...
MAYBE SOMETHING HAPPENED BETWEEN THE TWO OF YOU AND YOU KILLED HIM, HUH?
SOME OF THE BOYS DID SEE LEO LEAVE THE APARTMENT COMPLEX WHEN THEY WENT TO PICK UP YOUR SON, BOSS.
LEO MUST HAVE SUSPECTED SOMETHING...
...AND FOLLOWED ME.

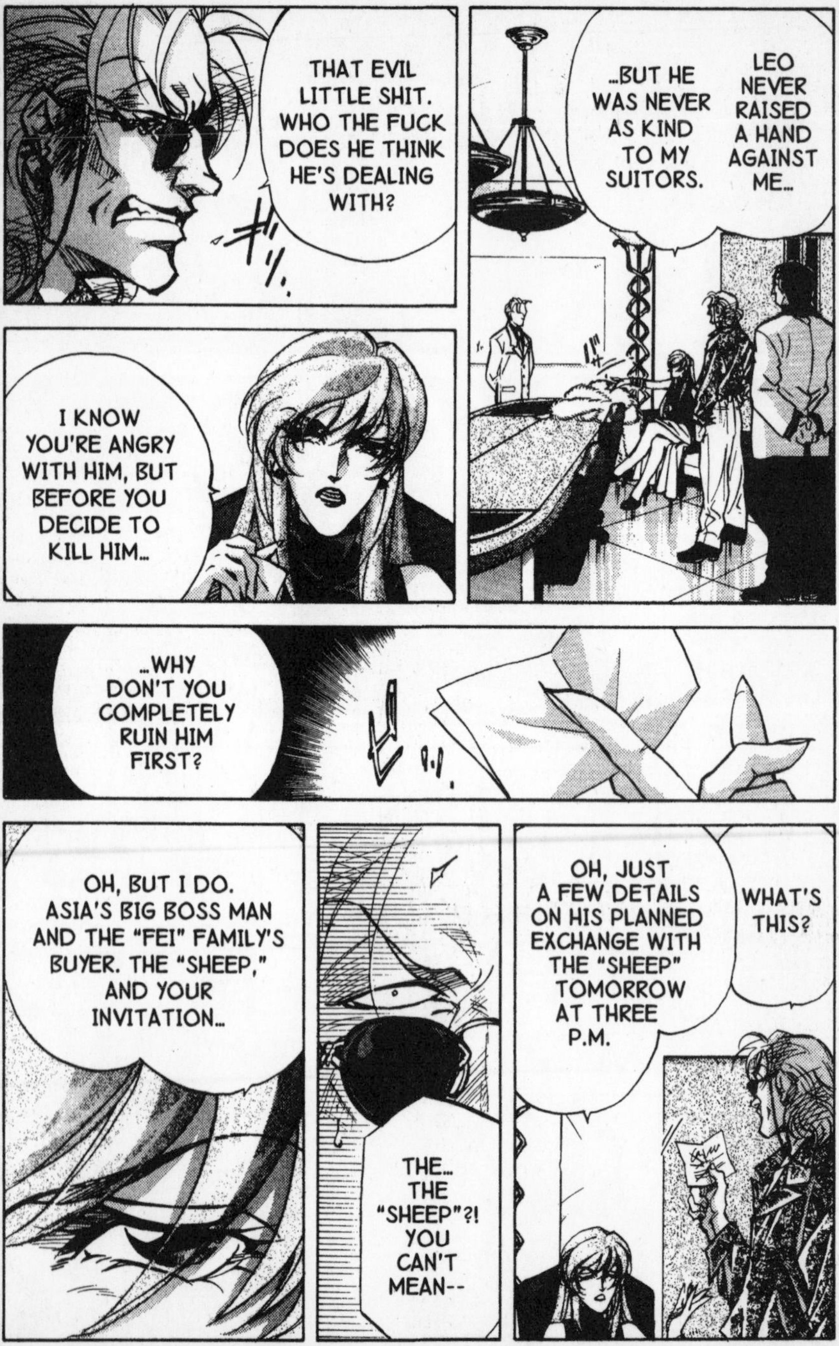
LEO NEVER RAISED A HAND AGAINST ME...
...BUT HE WAS NEVER AS KIND TO MY SUITORS.
THAT EVIL LITTLE SHIT. WHO THE FUCK DOES HE THINK HE'S DEALING WITH?
I KNOW YOU'RE ANGRY WITH HIM, BUT BEFORE YOU DECIDE TO KILL HIM...
...WHY DON'T YOU COMPLETELY RUIN HIM FIRST?
WHAT'S THIS?
OH, JUST A FEW DETAILS ON HIS PLANNED EXCHANGE WITH THE "SHEEP" TOMORROW AT THREE P.M.
THE... THE "SHEEP"?! YOU CAN'T MEAN--
OH, BUT I DO. ASIA'S BIG BOSS MAN AND THE "FEI" FAMILY'S BUYER. THE "SHEEP," AND YOUR INVITATION...

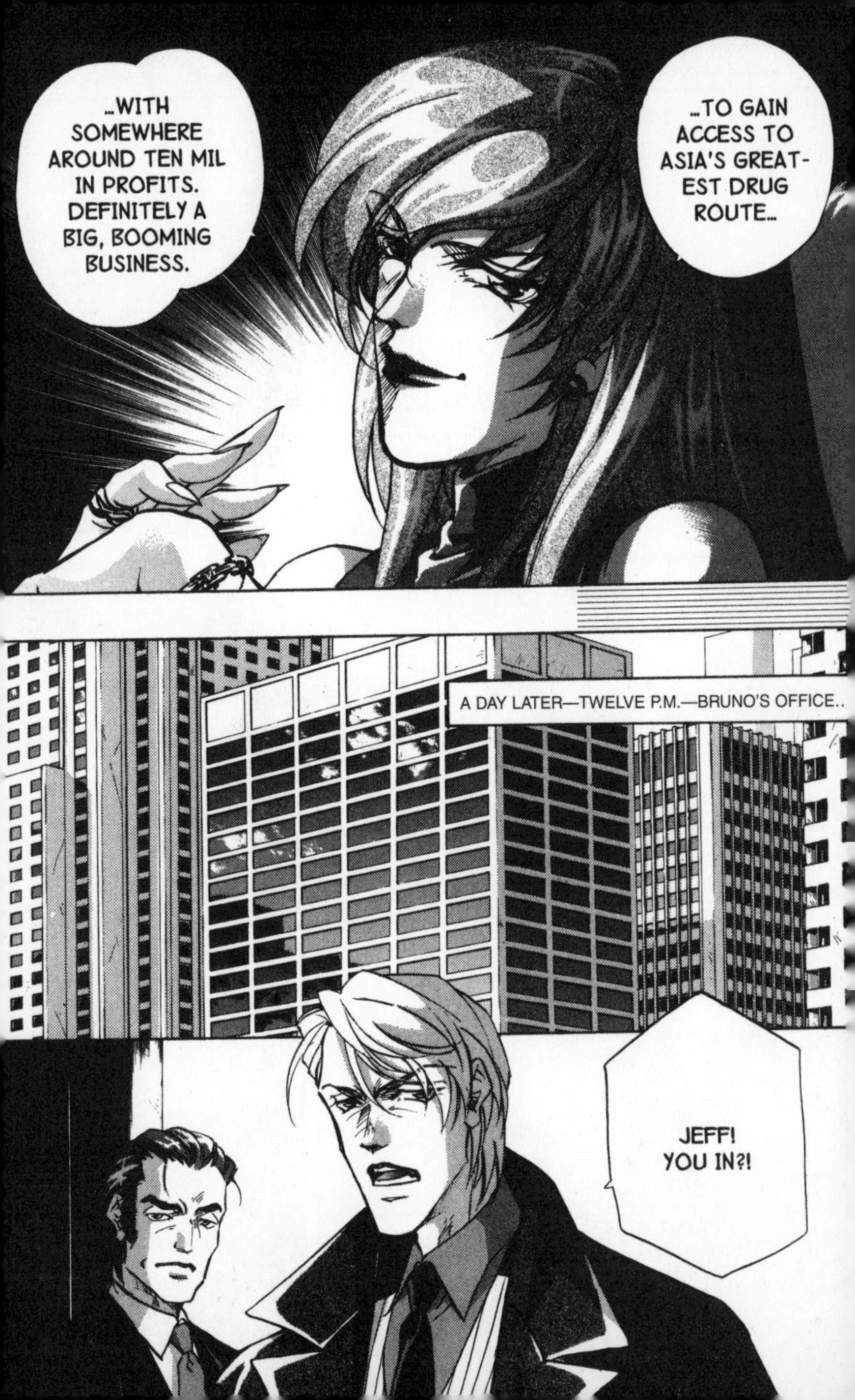
...TO GAIN ACCESS TO ASIA'S GREAT-EST DRUG ROUTE...
...WITH SOMEWHERE AROUND TEN MIL IN PROFITS. DEFINITELY A BIG, BOOMING BUSINESS.
A DAY LATER—TWELVE P.M.—BRUNO'S OFFICE..
JEFF! YOU IN?!

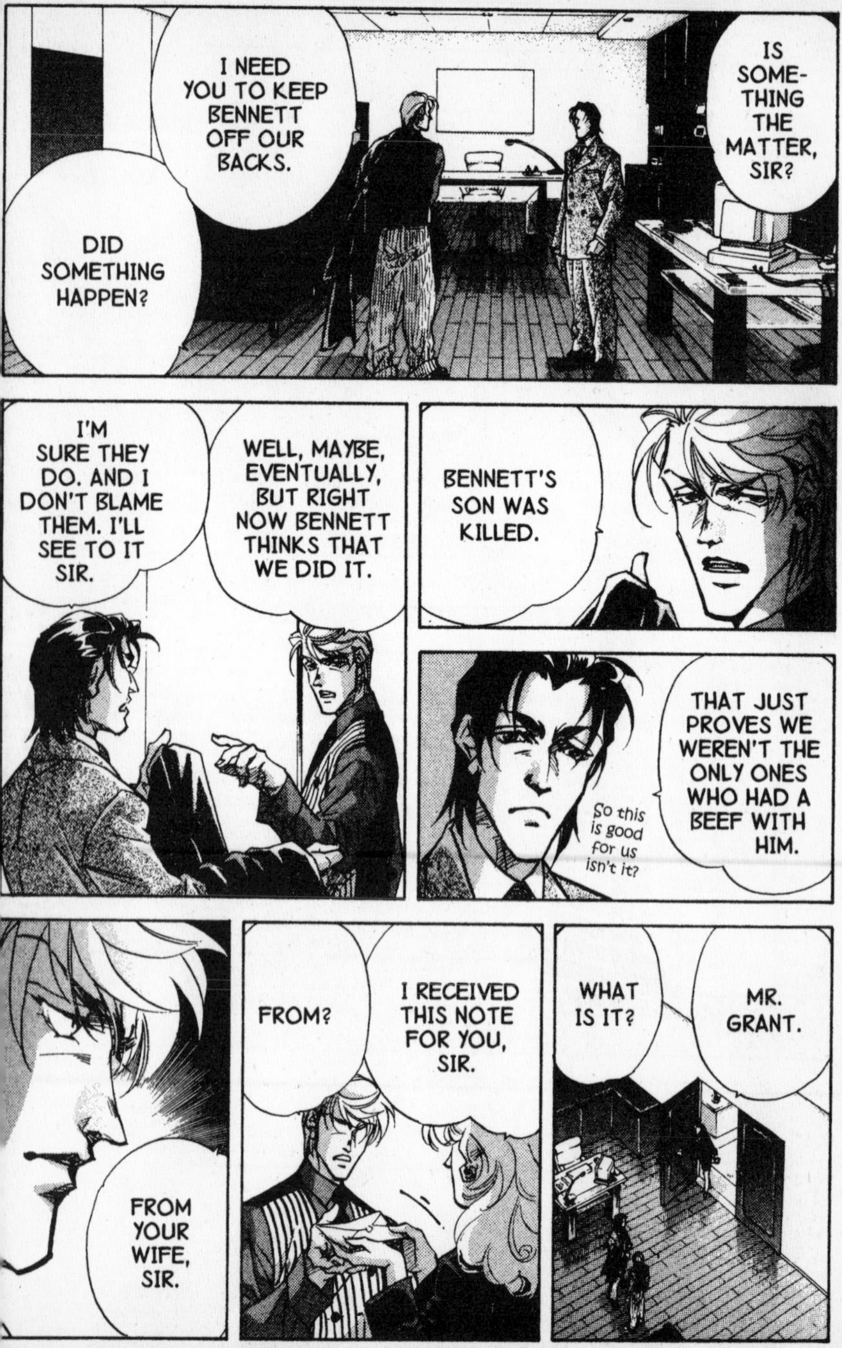
IS SOMETHING THE MATTER, SIR?
I NEED YOU TO KEEP BENNETT OFF OUR BACKS.
DID SOMETHING HAPPEN?
BENNETT'S SON WAS KILLED.
THAT JUST PROVES WE WEREN'T THE ONLY ONES WHO HAD A BEEF WITH HIM.
So this is good for us isn't it?
WELL, MAYBE, EVENTUALLY, BUT RIGHT NOW BENNETT THINKS THAT WE DID IT.
I'M SURE THEY DO. AND I DON'T BLAME THEM. I'LL SEE TO IT SIR.
MR. GRANT.
WHAT IS IT?
I RECEIVED THIS NOTE FOR YOU, SIR.
FROM?
FROM YOUR WIFE, SIR.

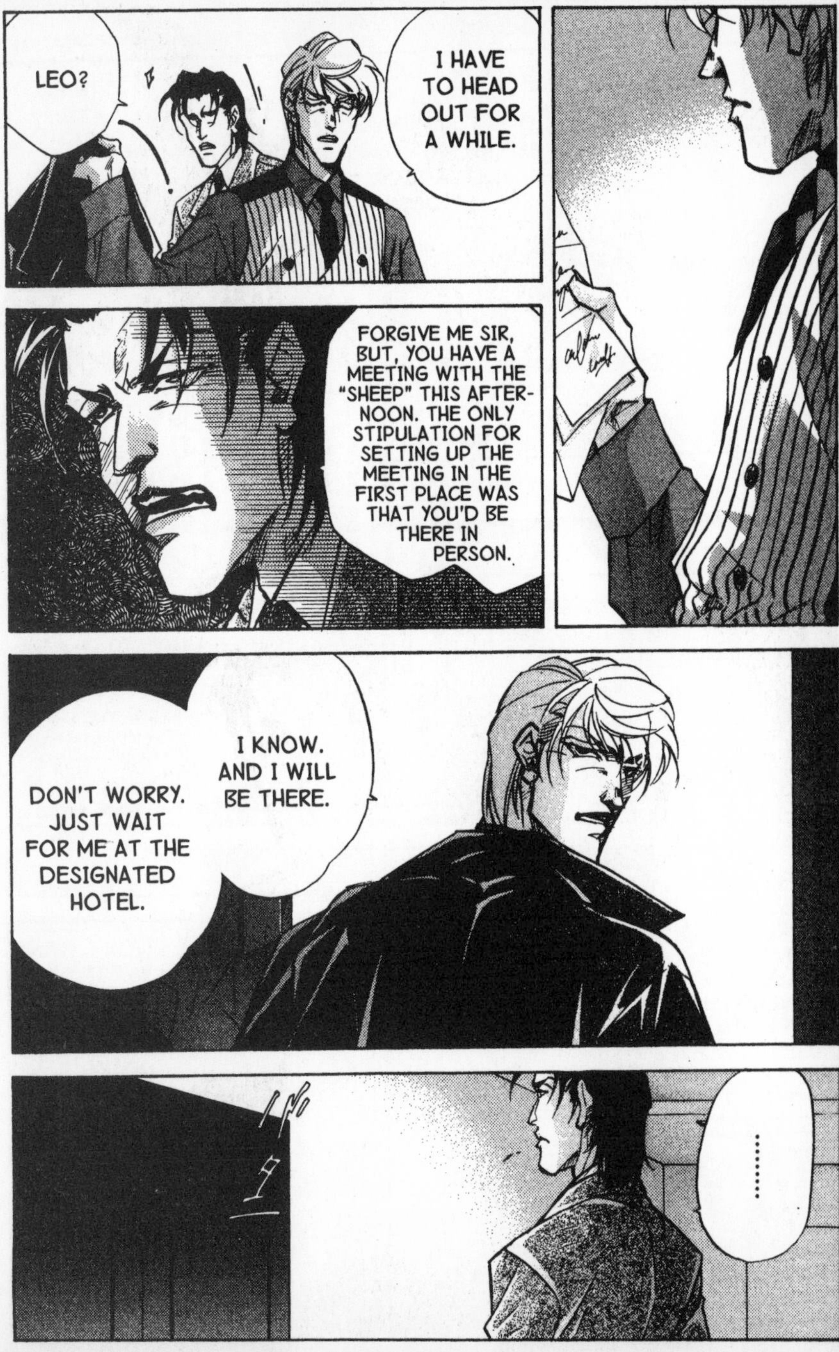
I HAVE TO HEAD OUT FOR A WHILE.
LEO?
FORGIVE ME SIR, BUT, YOU HAVE A MEETING WITH THE "SHEEP" THIS AFTERNOON. THE ONLY STIPULATION FOR SETTING UP THE MEETING IN THE FIRST PLACE WAS THAT YOU'D BE THERE IN PERSON.
I KNOW. AND I WILL BE THERE.
DON'T WORRY. JUST WAIT FOR ME AT THE DESIGNATED HOTEL.
....

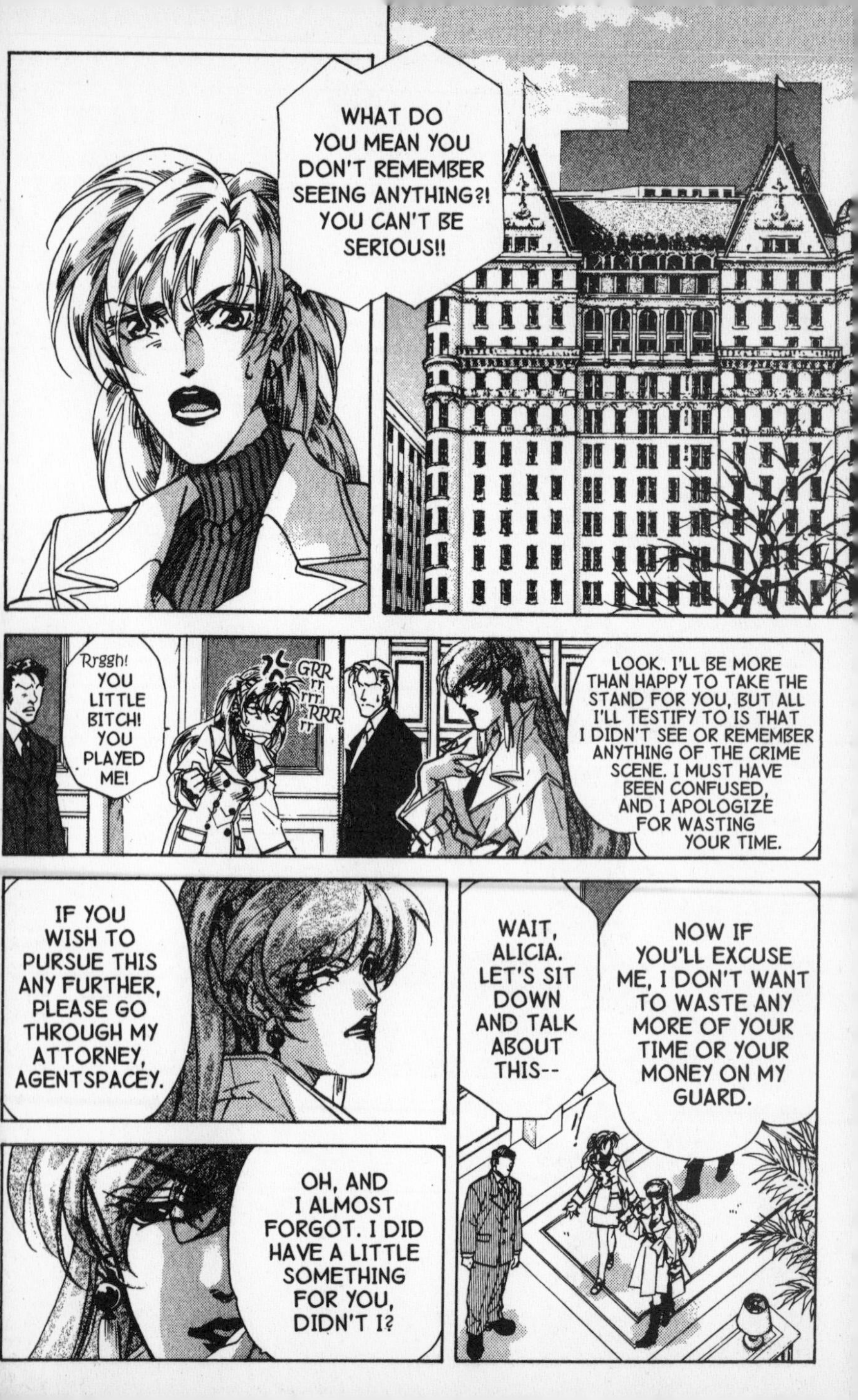
WHAT DO YOU MEAN YOU DON'T REMEMBER SEEING ANYTHING?! YOU CAN'T BE SERIOUS!!
LOOK. I'LL BE MORE THAN HAPPY TO TAKE THE STAND FOR YOU, BUT ALL I'LL TESTIFY TO IS THAT I DIDN'T SEE OR REMEMBER ANYTHING OF THE CRIME SCENE. I MUST HAVE BEEN CONFUSED, AND I APOLOGIZE FOR WASTING YOUR TIME.
GRR rr rrr RRR rr
Rrggh! YOU LITTLE BITCH! YOU PLAYED ME!
NOW IF YOU'LL EXCUSE ME, I DON'T WANT TO WASTE ANY MORE OF YOUR TIME OR YOUR MONEY ON MY GUARD.
WAIT, ALICIA. LET'S SIT DOWN AND TALK ABOUT THIS--
IF YOU WISH TO PURSUE THIS ANY FURTHER, PLEASE GO THROUGH MY ATTORNEY, AGENTSPACEY.
OH, AND I ALMOST FORGOT. I DID HAVE A LITTLE SOMETHING FOR YOU, DIDN'T I?

?!

IT'S AN INVITATION REALLY, TO TEA. THREE P.M. TODAY, AT THE ST. REGIS HOTEL. I HOPE YOU'LL BRING ALL YOUR FRIENDS FROM THE D.E.A.*

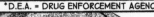

*D.E.A. = DRUG ENFORCEMENT AGENCY.

I'M SURE YOU'LL FIND THE COMPANY DELIGHTFUL.

WHAT ON EARTH DO YOU THINK SHE MEANS BY INVITING US TO TEA?

GOOD DAY.

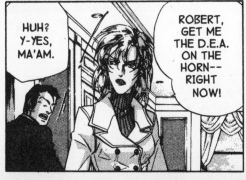

HUH? Y-YES, MA'AM.

ROBERT, GET ME THE D.E.A. ON THE HORN-- RIGHT NOW!

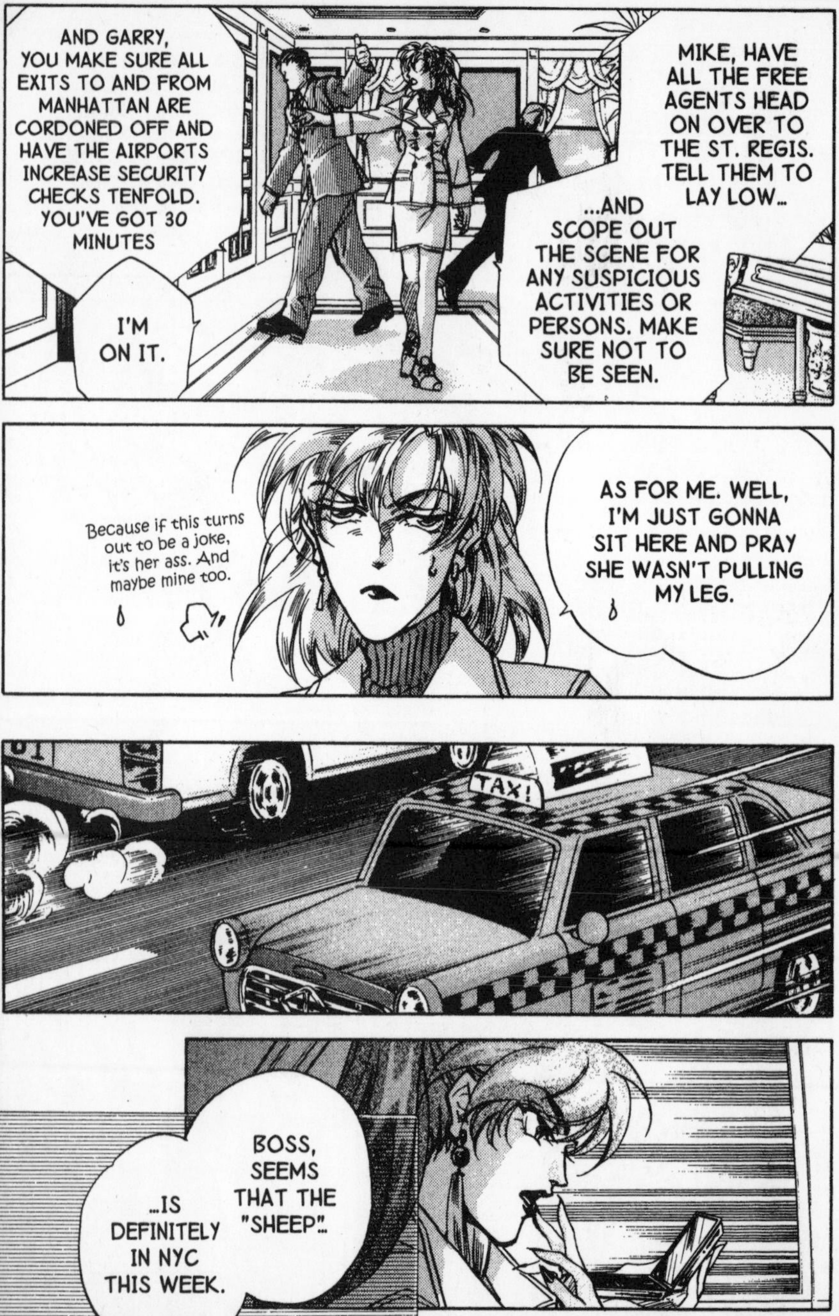
MIKE, HAVE ALL THE FREE AGENTS HEAD ON OVER TO THE ST. REGIS. TELL THEM TO LAY LOW...
...AND SCOPE OUT THE SCENE FOR ANY SUSPICIOUS ACTIVITIES OR PERSONS. MAKE SURE NOT TO BE SEEN.
AND GARRY, YOU MAKE SURE ALL EXITS TO AND FROM MANHATTAN ARE CORDONED OFF AND HAVE THE AIRPORTS INCREASE SECURITY CHECKS TENFOLD. YOU'VE GOT 30 MINUTES
I'M ON IT.
AS FOR ME. WELL, I'M JUST GONNA SIT HERE AND PRAY SHE WASN'T PULLING MY LEG.
Because if this turns out to be a joke, it's her ass. And maybe mine too.
TAXI
BOSS, SEEMS THAT THE "SHEEP"...
...IS DEFINITELY IN NYC THIS WEEK.

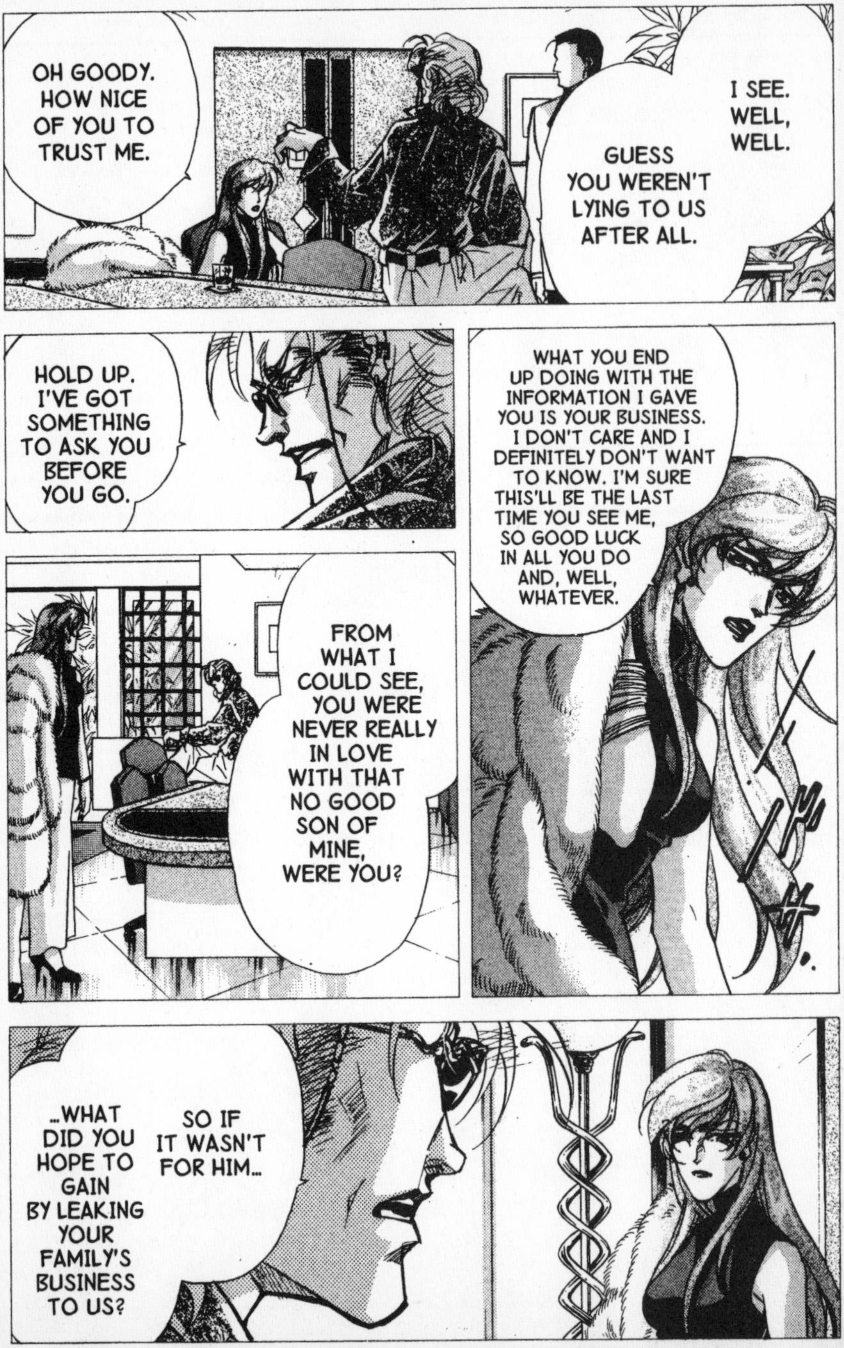
I SEE. WELL, WELL.
GUESS YOU WEREN'T LYING TO US AFTER ALL.
OH GOODY. HOW NICE OF YOU TO TRUST ME.
WHAT YOU END UP DOING WITH THE INFORMATION I GAVE YOU IS YOUR BUSINESS. I DON'T CARE AND I DEFINITELY DON'T WANT TO KNOW. I'M SURE THIS'LL BE THE LAST TIME YOU SEE ME, SO GOOD LUCK IN ALL YOU DO AND, WELL, WHATEVER.
HOLD UP. I'VE GOT SOMETHING TO ASK YOU BEFORE YOU GO.
FROM WHAT I COULD SEE, YOU WERE NEVER REALLY IN LOVE WITH THAT NO GOOD SON OF MINE, WERE YOU?
SO IF IT WASN'T FOR HIM...
...WHAT DID YOU HOPE TO GAIN BY LEAKING YOUR FAMILY'S BUSINESS TO US?

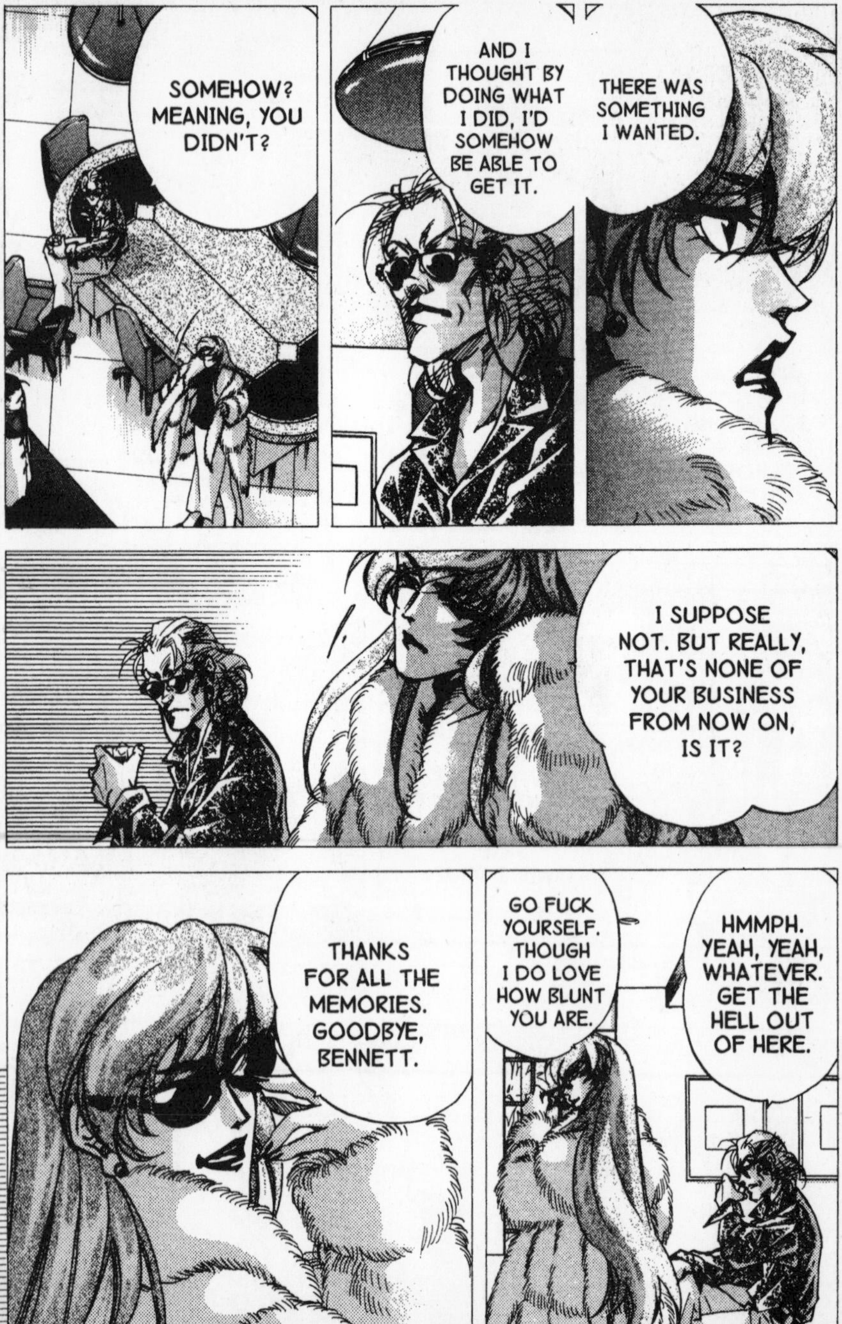
THERE WAS SOMETHING I WANTED.
AND I THOUGHT BY DOING WHAT I DID, I'D SOMEHOW BE ABLE TO GET IT.
SOMEHOW? MEANING, YOU DIDN'T?
I SUPPOSE NOT. BUT REALLY, THAT'S NONE OF YOUR BUSINESS FROM NOW ON, IS IT?
GO FUCK YOURSELF. THOUGH I DO LOVE HOW BLUNT YOU ARE.
HMMPH. YEAH, YEAH, WHATEVER. GET THE HELL OUT OF HERE.
THANKS FOR ALL THE MEMORIES. GOODBYE, BENNETT.

KLAK

WE'VE GOT A MURDER TO INVESTIGATE. WHAT DO YOU MEAN IT CAME FROM ABOVE? CHIEF?

HUH? WHAT? YOU WANT US TO CORDON OFF WHERE?! WHAT THE HELL IS GOING ON? WHY DO WE HAVE TO DO THAT?

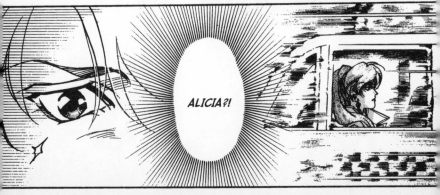

ALICIA?!

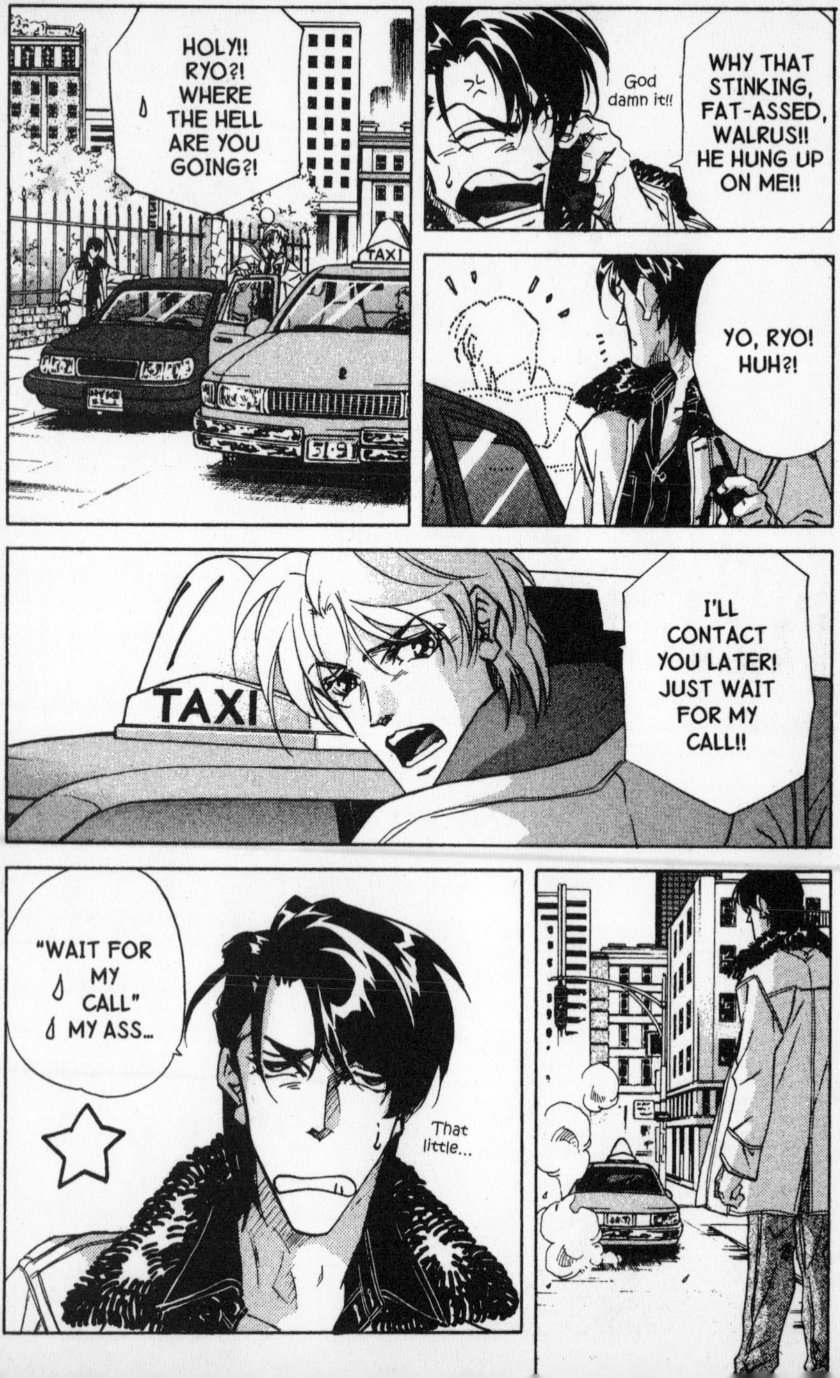
God damn it!!
WHY THAT STINKING, FAT-ASSED, WALRUS!! HE HUNG UP ON ME!!
YO, RYO! HUH?!
HOLY!! RYO?! WHERE THE HELL ARE YOU GOING?!
TAXI
I'LL CONTACT YOU LATER! JUST WAIT FOR MY CALL!!
TAXI
"WAIT FOR MY CALL" MY ASS...
That little...

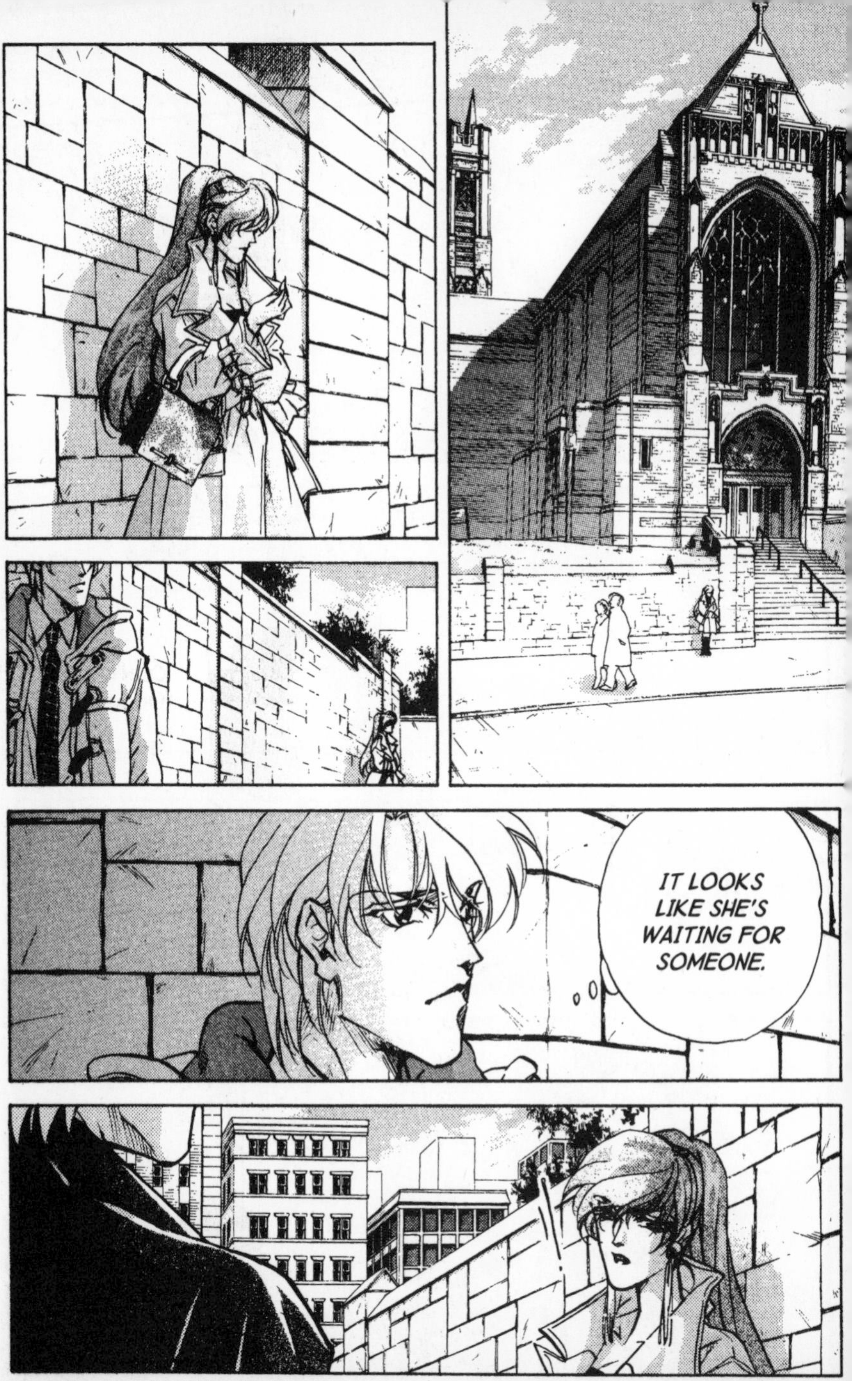
IT LOOKS LIKE SHE'S WAITING FOR SOMEONE.

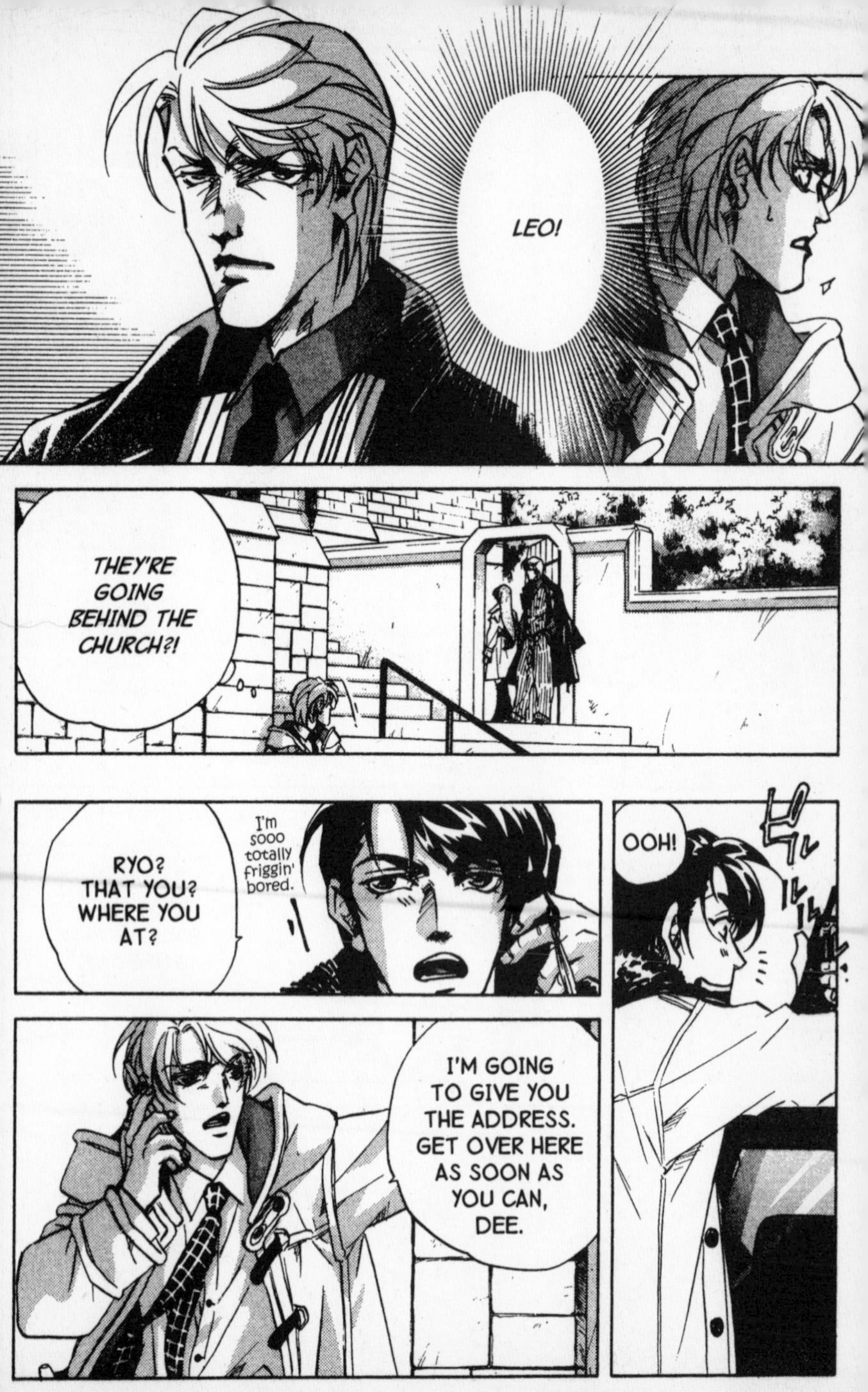

LEO!
THEY'RE GOING BEHIND THE CHURCH?!
OOH!
I'm sooo totally friggin' bored.
RYO? THAT YOU? WHERE YOU AT?
I'M GOING TO GIVE YOU THE ADDRESS. GET OVER HERE AS SOON AS YOU CAN, DEE.

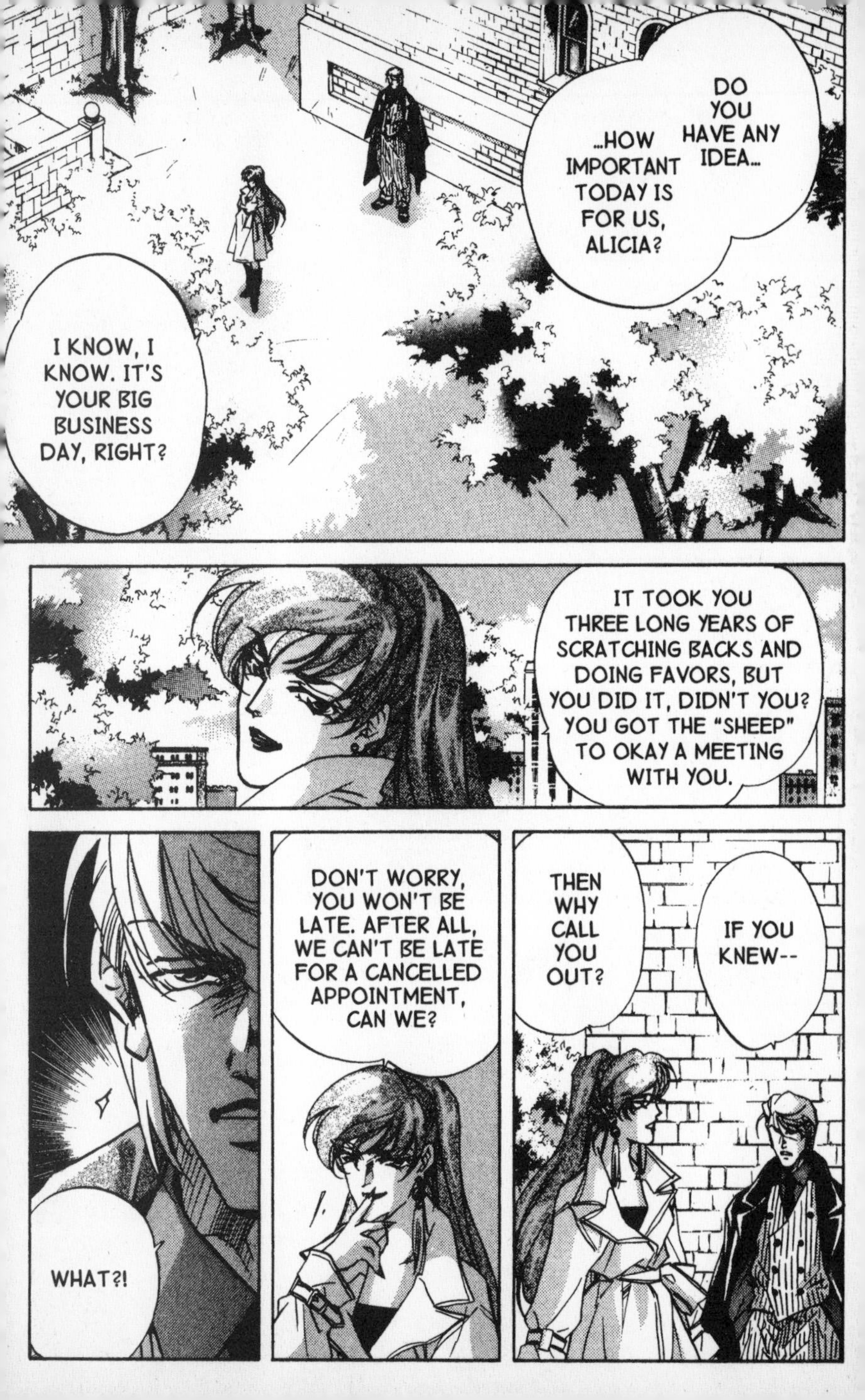
DO YOU HAVE ANY IDEA...
...HOW IMPORTANT TODAY IS FOR US, ALICIA?
I KNOW, I KNOW. IT'S YOUR BIG BUSINESS DAY, RIGHT?
IT TOOK YOU THREE LONG YEARS OF SCRATCHING BACKS AND DOING FAVORS, BUT YOU DID IT, DIDN'T YOU? YOU GOT THE "SHEEP" TO OKAY A MEETING WITH YOU.
IF YOU KNEW--
THEN WHY CALL YOU OUT?
DON'T WORRY, YOU WON'T BE LATE. AFTER ALL, WE CAN'T BE LATE FOR A CANCELLED APPOINTMENT, CAN WE?
WHAT?!

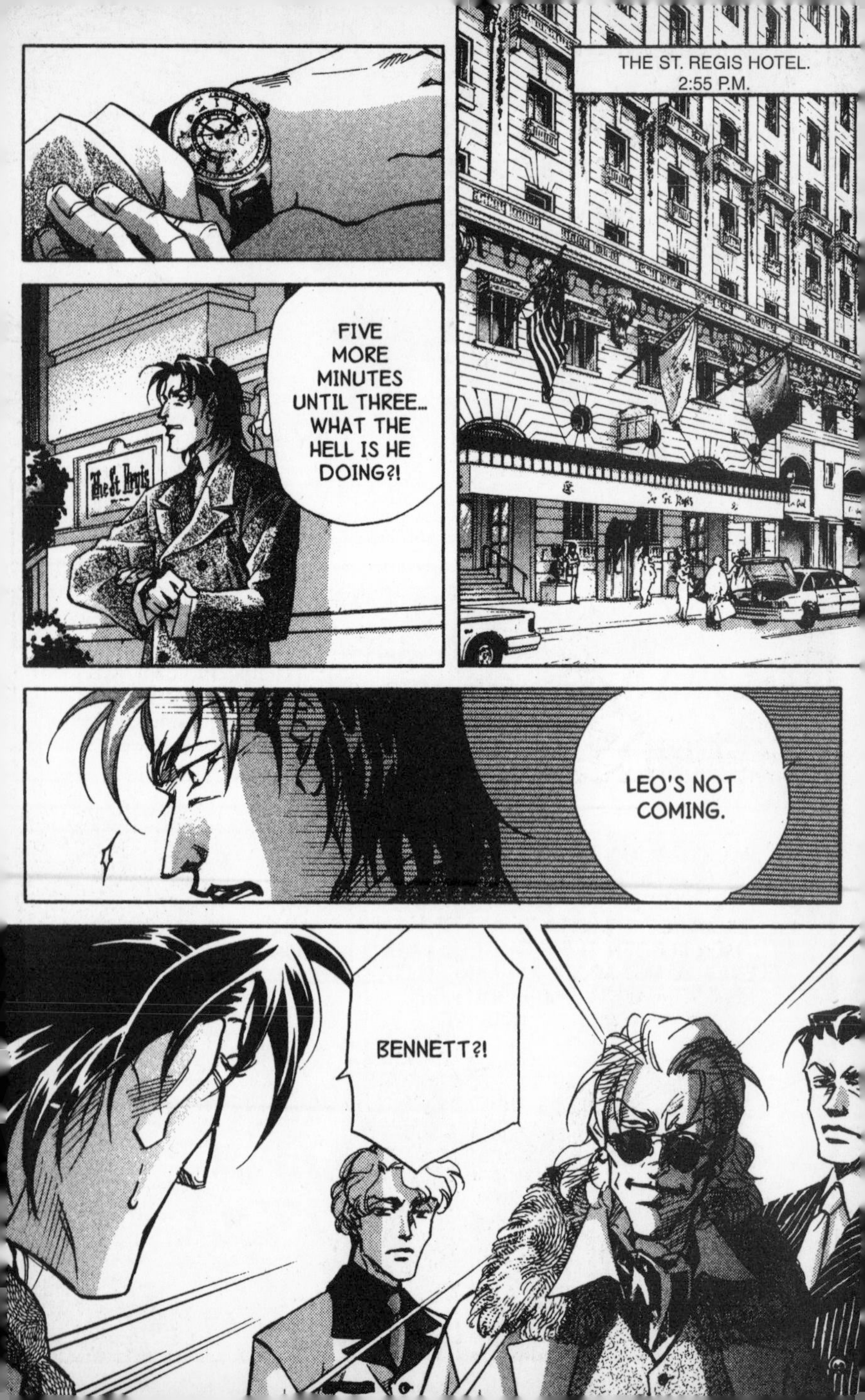
THE ST. REGIS HOTEL. 2:55 P.M.
FIVE MORE MINUTES UNTIL THREE... WHAT THE HELL IS HE DOING?!
LEO'S NOT COMING.
BENNETT?!

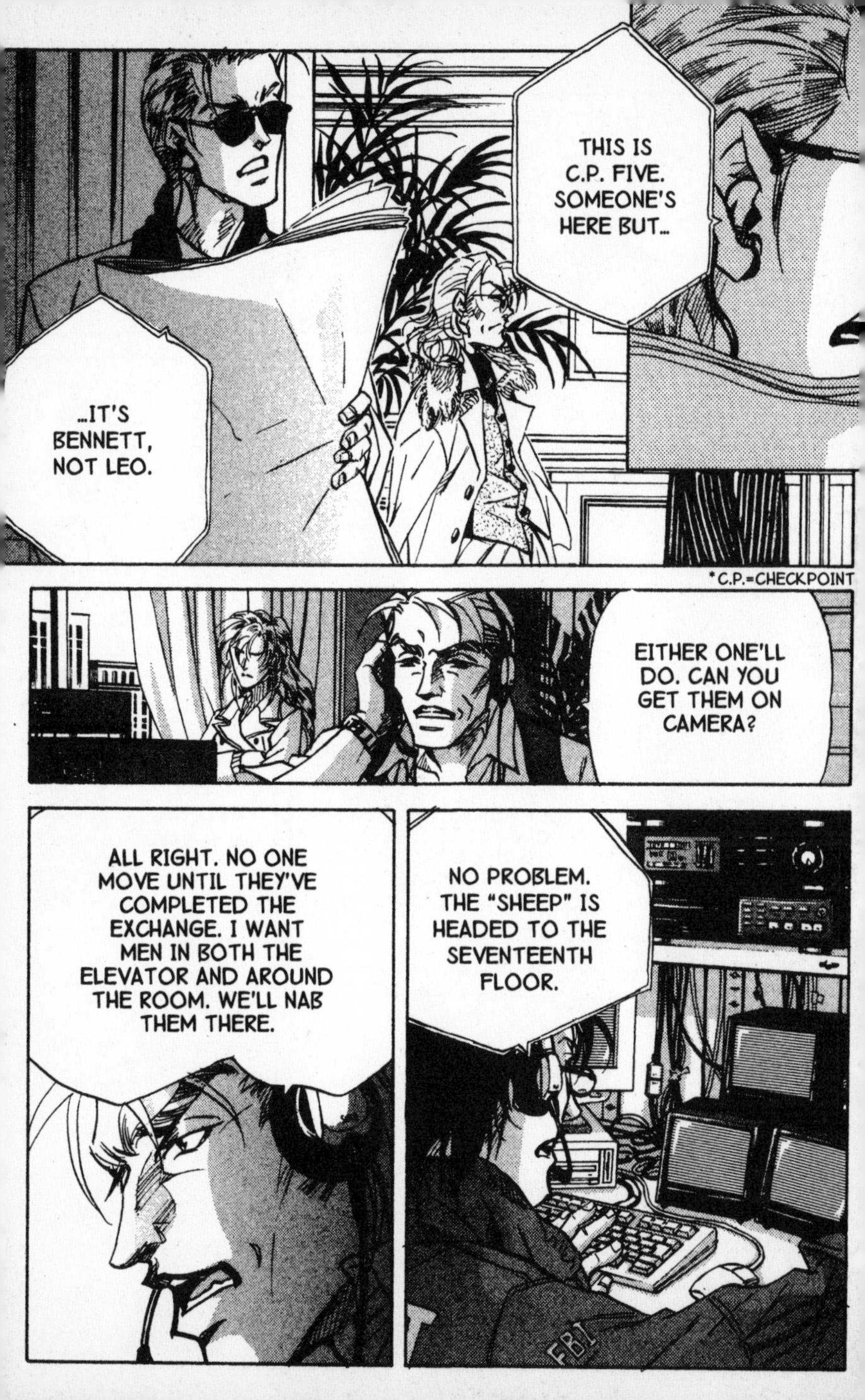
THIS IS C.P. FIVE. SOMEONE'S HERE BUT...
*C.P.=CHECKPOINT
...IT'S BENNETT, NOT LEO.
EITHER ONE'LL DO. CAN YOU GET THEM ON CAMERA?
NO PROBLEM. THE "SHEEP" IS HEADED TO THE SEVENTEENTH FLOOR.
ALL RIGHT. NO ONE MOVE UNTIL THEY'VE COMPLETED THE EXCHANGE. I WANT MEN IN BOTH THE ELEVATOR AND AROUND THE ROOM. WE'LL NAB THEM THERE.

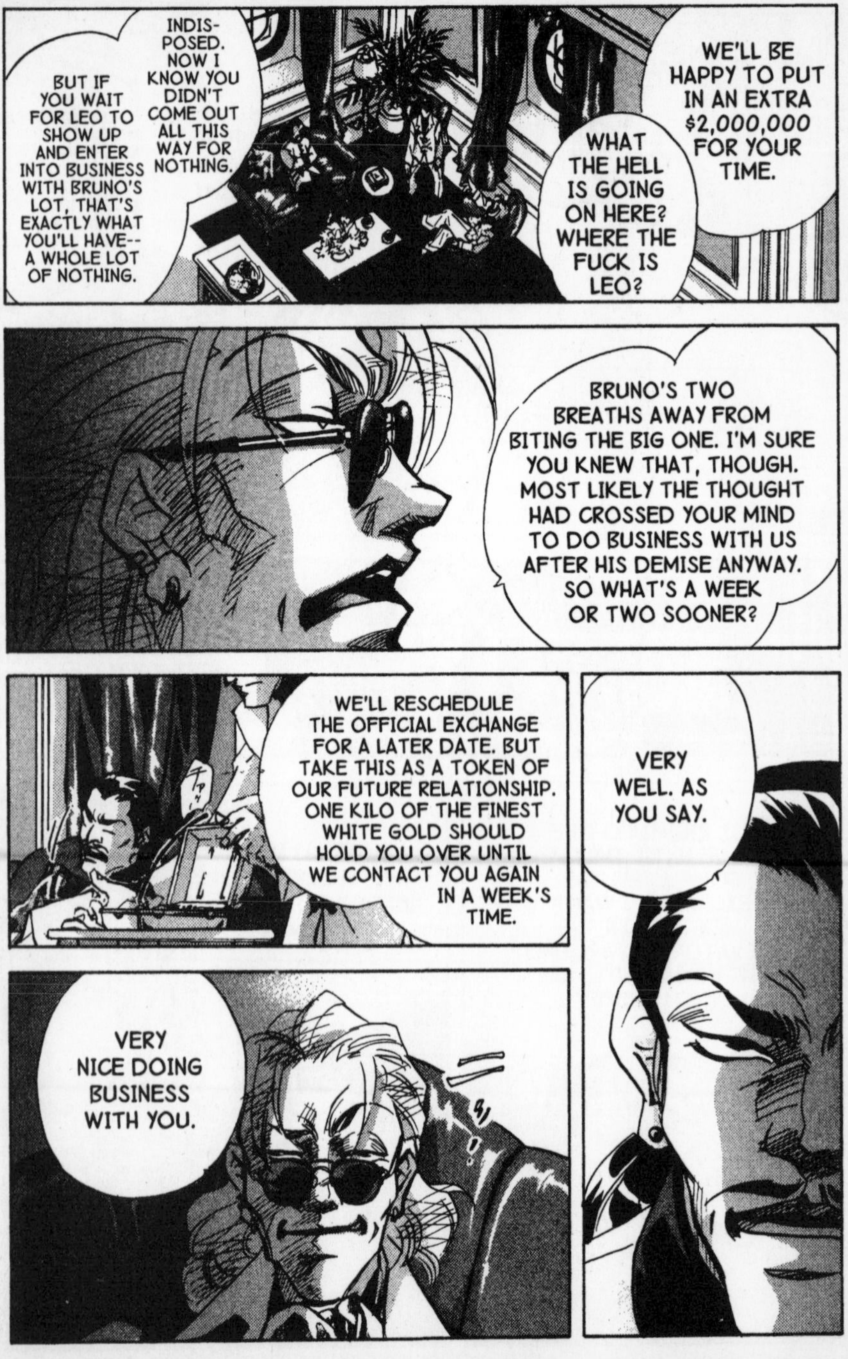
WE'LL BE HAPPY TO PUT IN AN EXTRA $2,000,000 FOR YOUR TIME.
WHAT THE HELL IS GOING ON HERE? WHERE THE FUCK IS LEO?
INDIS-POSED. NOW I KNOW YOU DIDN'T COME OUT ALL THIS WAY FOR NOTHING.
BUT IF YOU WAIT FOR LEO TO SHOW UP AND ENTER INTO BUSINESS WITH BRUNO'S LOT, THAT'S EXACTLY WHAT YOU'LL HAVE-- A WHOLE LOT OF NOTHING.
BRUNO'S TWO BREATHS AWAY FROM BITING THE BIG ONE. I'M SURE YOU KNEW THAT, THOUGH. MOST LIKELY THE THOUGHT HAD CROSSED YOUR MIND TO DO BUSINESS WITH US AFTER HIS DEMISE ANYWAY. SO WHAT'S A WEEK OR TWO SOONER?
VERY WELL. AS YOU SAY.
WE'LL RESCHEDULE THE OFFICIAL EXCHANGE FOR A LATER DATE. BUT TAKE THIS AS A TOKEN OF OUR FUTURE RELATIONSHIP. ONE KILO OF THE FINEST WHITE GOLD SHOULD HOLD YOU OVER UNTIL WE CONTACT YOU AGAIN IN A WEEK'S TIME.
VERY NICE DOING BUSINESS WITH YOU.

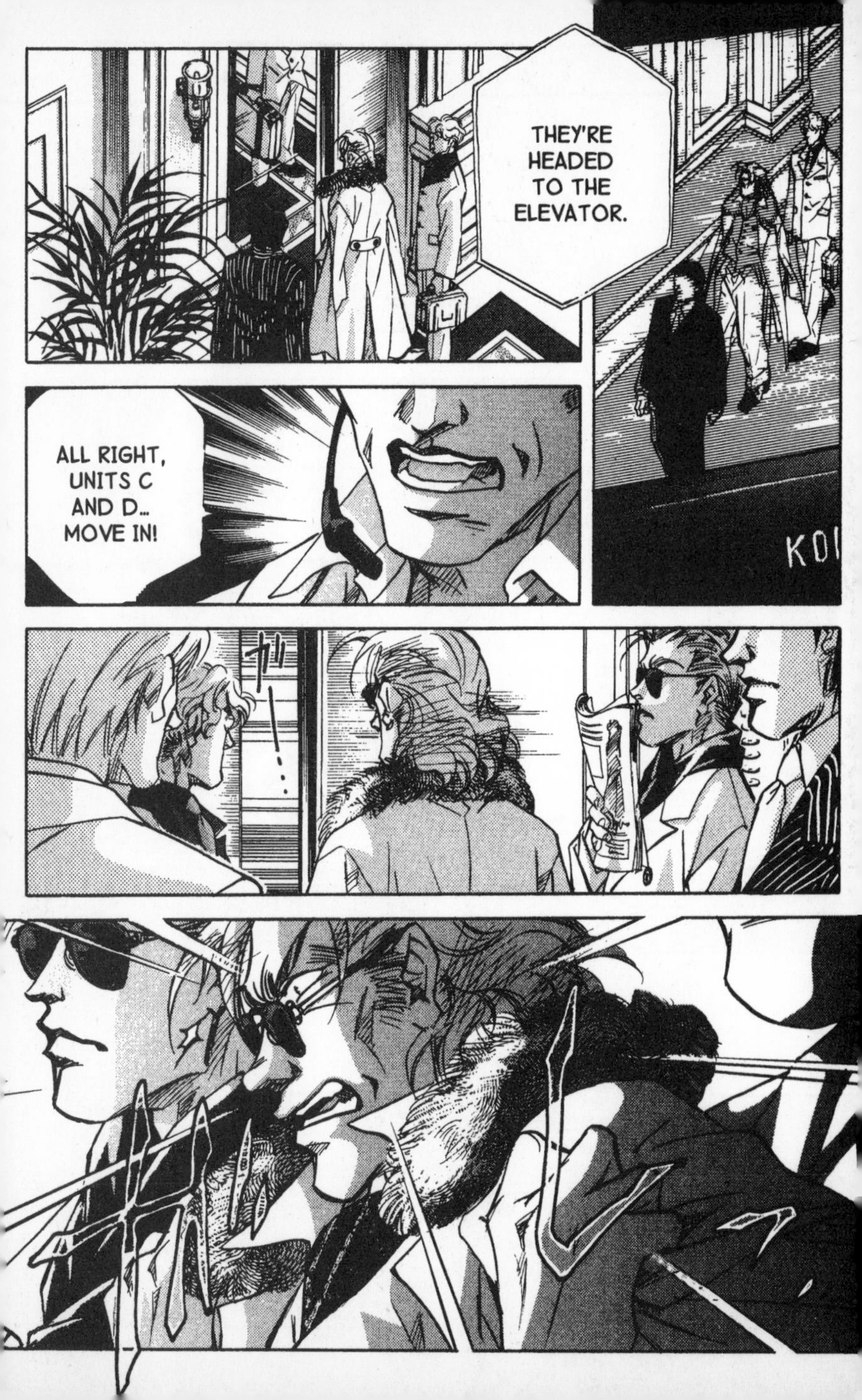
KO
THEY'RE HEADED TO THE ELEVATOR.
ALL RIGHT, UNITS C AND D... MOVE IN!

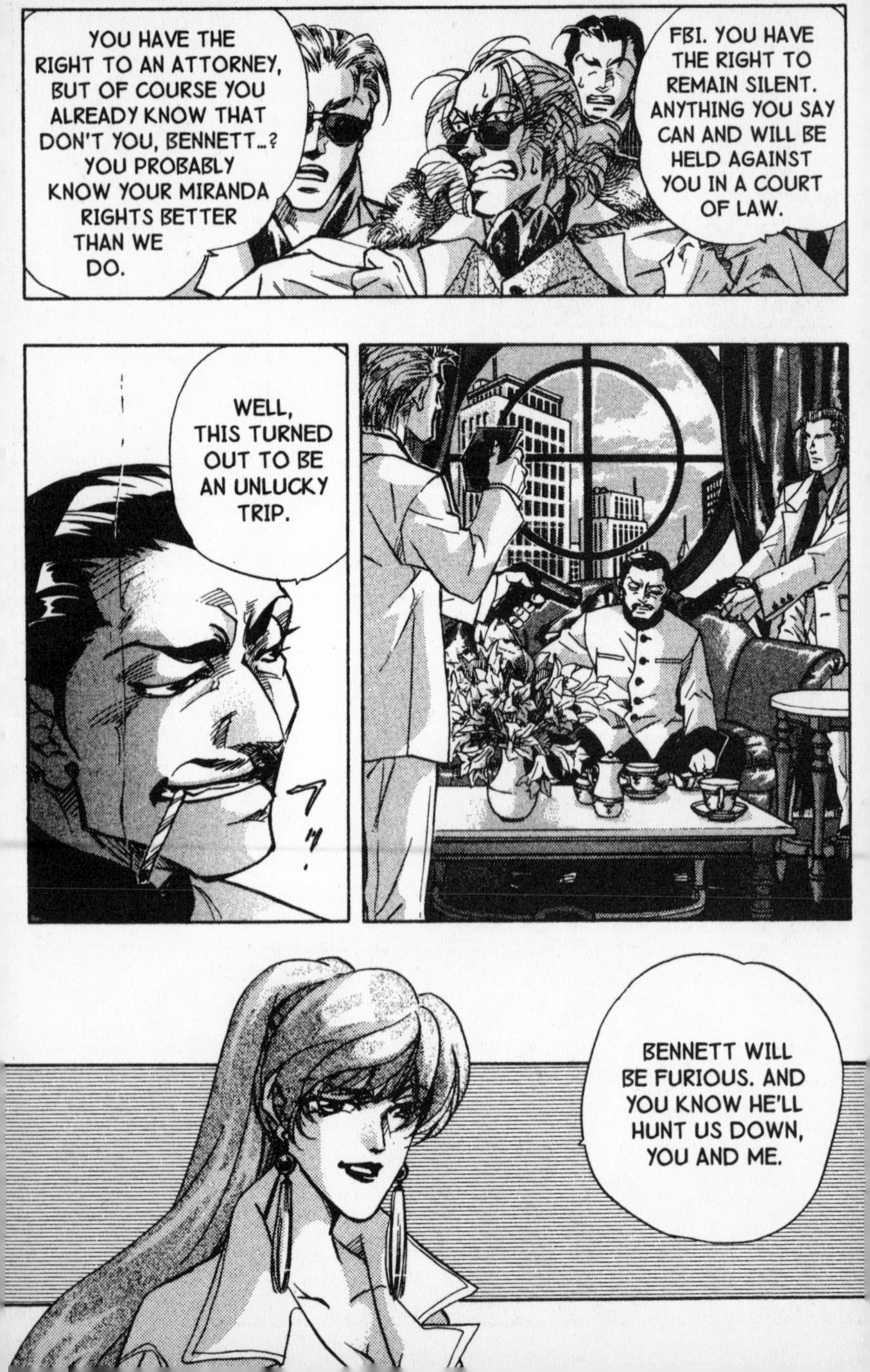
FBI. YOU HAVE THE RIGHT TO REMAIN SILENT. ANYTHING YOU SAY CAN AND WILL BE HELD AGAINST YOU IN A COURT OF LAW.
YOU HAVE THE RIGHT TO AN ATTORNEY, BUT OF COURSE YOU ALREADY KNOW THAT DON'T YOU, BENNETT...? YOU PROBABLY KNOW YOUR MIRANDA RIGHTS BETTER THAN WE DO.
WELL, THIS TURNED OUT TO BE AN UNLUCKY TRIP.
BENNETT WILL BE FURIOUS. AND YOU KNOW HE'LL HUNT US DOWN, YOU AND ME.

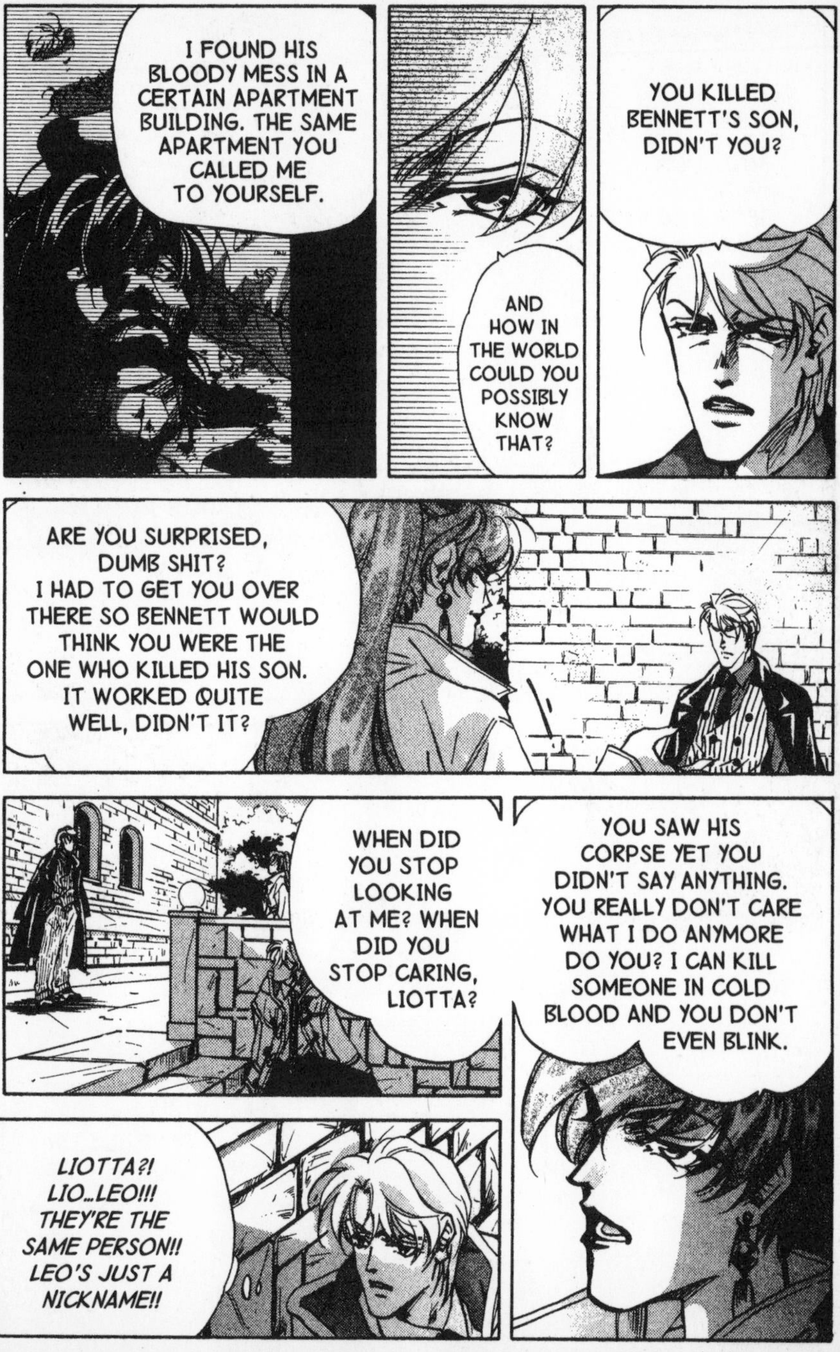
YOU KILLED BENNETT'S SON, DIDN'T YOU?
AND HOW IN THE WORLD COULD YOU POSSIBLY KNOW THAT?
I FOUND HIS BLOODY MESS IN A CERTAIN APARTMENT BUILDING. THE SAME APARTMENT YOU CALLED ME TO YOURSELF.
ARE YOU SURPRISED, DUMB SHIT? I HAD TO GET YOU OVER THERE SO BENNETT WOULD THINK YOU WERE THE ONE WHO KILLED HIS SON. IT WORKED QUITE WELL, DIDN'T IT?
YOU SAW HIS CORPSE YET YOU DIDN'T SAY ANYTHING. YOU REALLY DON'T CARE WHAT I DO ANYMORE DO YOU? I CAN KILL SOMEONE IN COLD BLOOD AND YOU DON'T EVEN BLINK.
WHEN DID YOU STOP LOOKING AT ME? WHEN DID YOU STOP CARING, LIOTTA?
LIOTTA?! LIO...LEO!!! THEY'RE THE SAME PERSON!! LEO'S JUST A NICKNAME!!

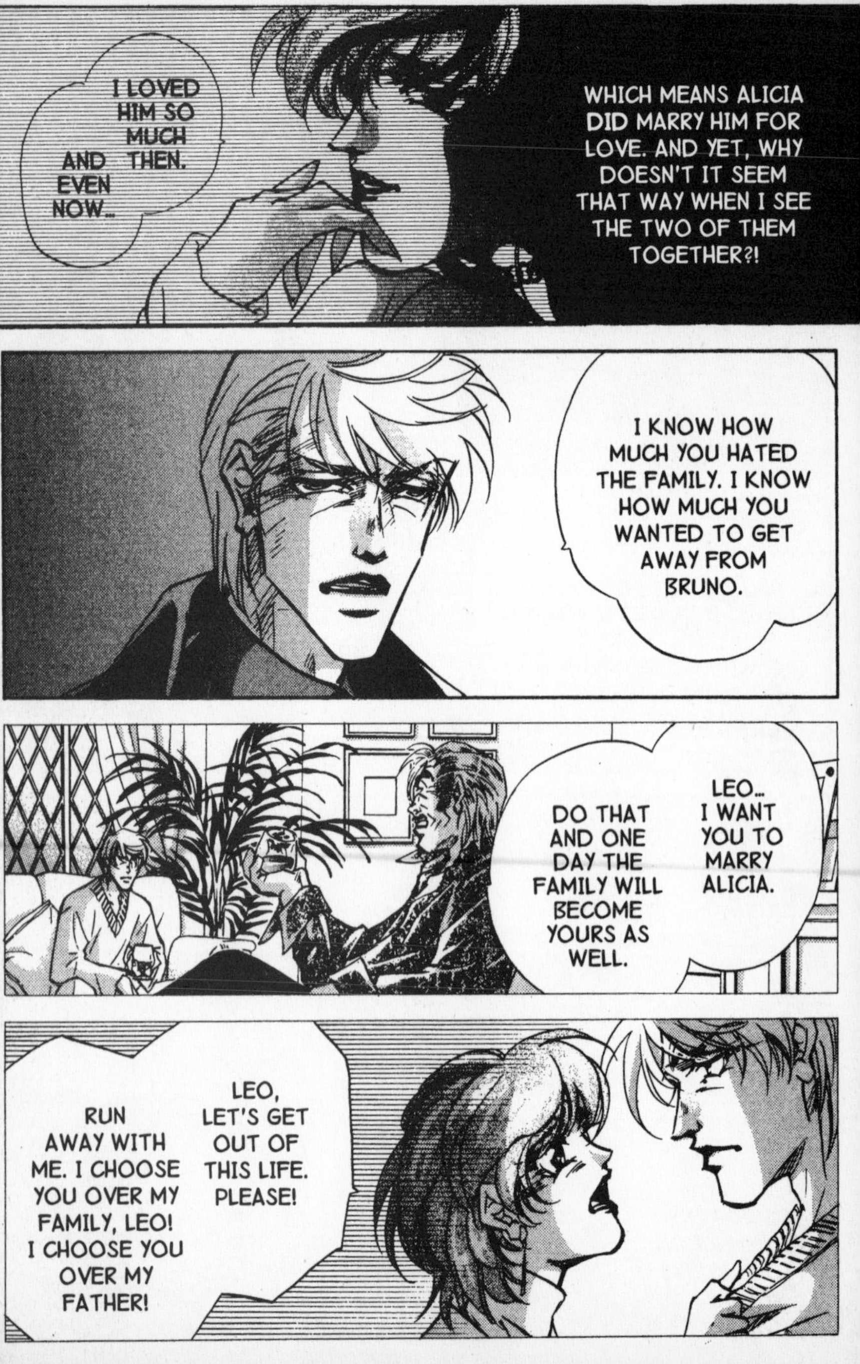
WHICH MEANS ALICIA DID MARRY HIM FOR LOVE. AND YET, WHY DOESN'T IT SEEM THAT WAY WHEN I SEE THE TWO OF THEM TOGETHER?!
I LOVED HIM SO MUCH THEN. AND EVEN NOW...
I KNOW HOW MUCH YOU HATED THE FAMILY. I KNOW HOW MUCH YOU WANTED TO GET AWAY FROM BRUNO.
LEO... I WANT YOU TO MARRY ALICIA.
DO THAT AND ONE DAY THE FAMILY WILL BECOME YOURS AS WELL.
LEO, LET'S GET OUT OF THIS LIFE. PLEASE!
RUN AWAY WITH ME. I CHOOSE YOU OVER MY FAMILY, LEO! I CHOOSE YOU OVER MY FATHER!

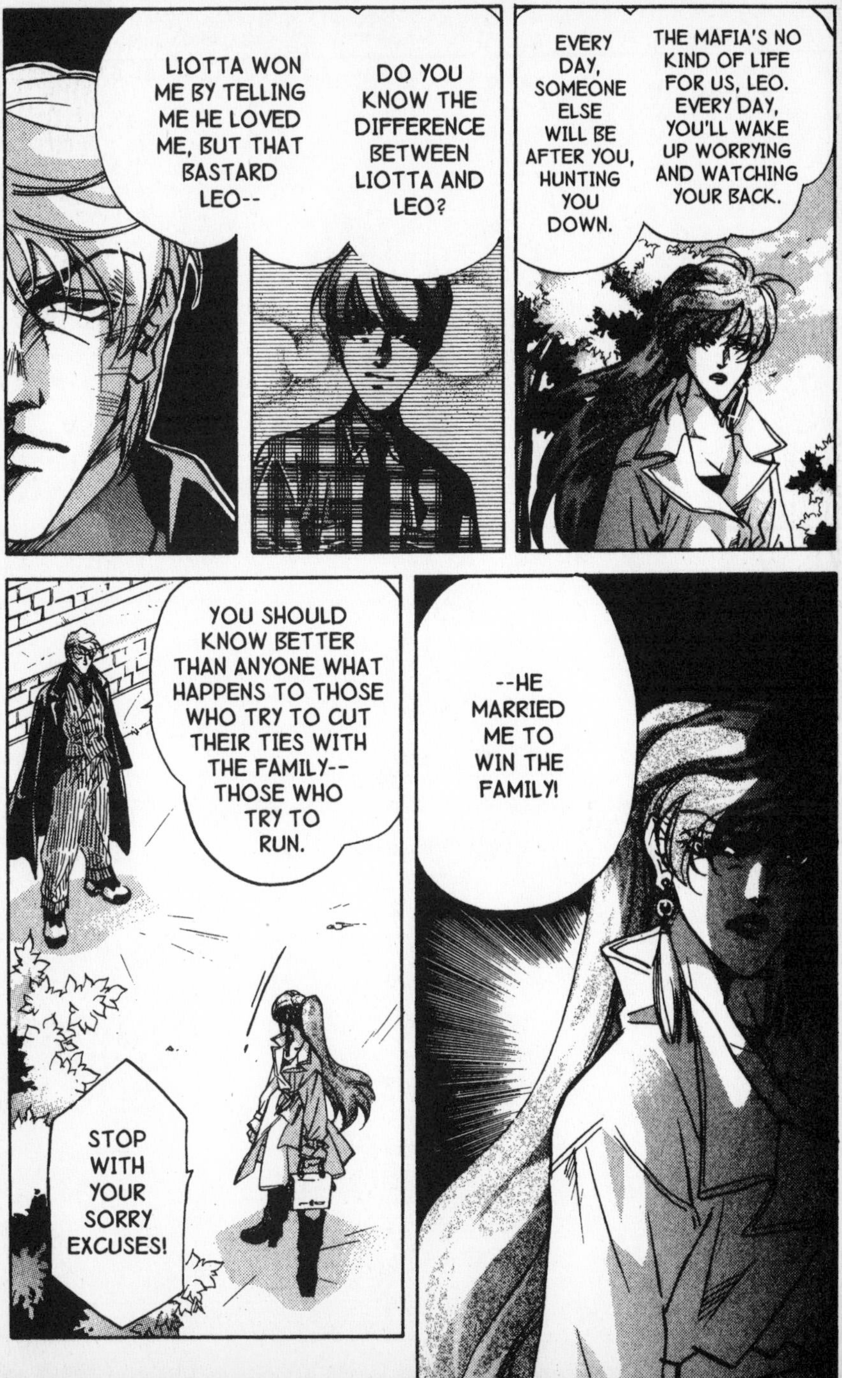
THE MAFIA'S NO KIND OF LIFE FOR US, LEO. EVERY DAY, YOU'LL WAKE UP WORRYING AND WATCHING YOUR BACK.
EVERY DAY, SOMEONE ELSE WILL BE AFTER YOU, HUNTING YOU DOWN.
DO YOU KNOW THE DIFFERENCE BETWEEN LIOTTA AND LEO?
LIOTTA WON ME BY TELLING ME HE LOVED ME, BUT THAT BASTARD LEO--
--HE MARRIED ME TO WIN THE FAMILY!
YOU SHOULD KNOW BETTER THAN ANYONE WHAT HAPPENS TO THOSE WHO TRY TO CUT THEIR TIES WITH THE FAMILY-- THOSE WHO TRY TO RUN.
STOP WITH YOUR SORRY EXCUSES!

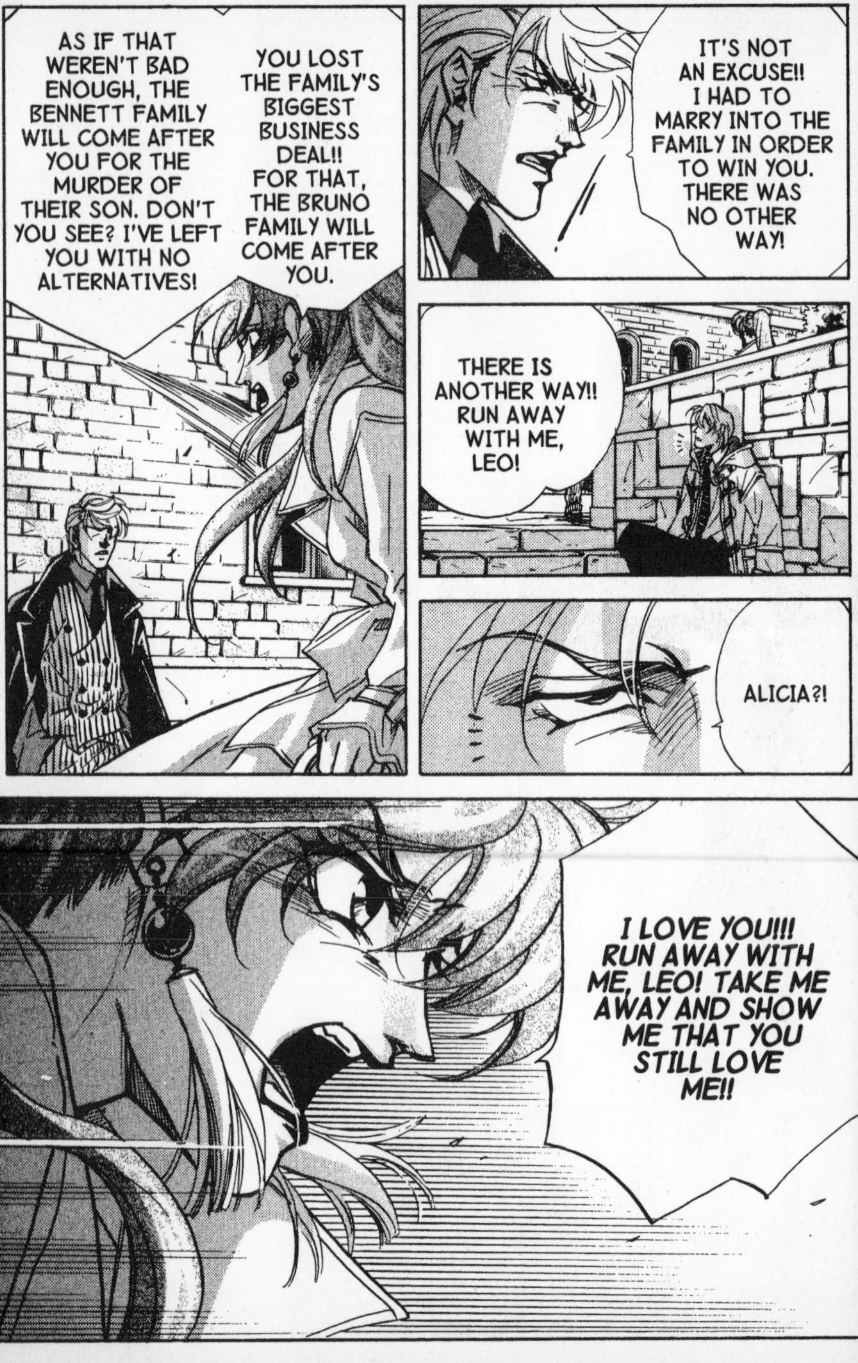
YOU LOST THE FAMILY'S BIGGEST BUSINESS DEAL!! FOR THAT, THE BRUNO FAMILY WILL COME AFTER YOU.
AS IF THAT WEREN'T BAD ENOUGH, THE BENNETT FAMILY WILL COME AFTER YOU FOR THE MURDER OF THEIR SON. DON'T YOU SEE? I'VE LEFT YOU WITH NO ALTERNATIVES!
IT'S NOT AN EXCUSE!! I HAD TO MARRY INTO THE FAMILY IN ORDER TO WIN YOU. THERE WAS NO OTHER WAY!
THERE IS ANOTHER WAY!! RUN AWAY WITH ME, LEO!
ALICIA?!
I LOVE YOU!!! RUN AWAY WITH ME, LEO! TAKE ME AWAY AND SHOW ME THAT YOU STILL LOVE ME!!

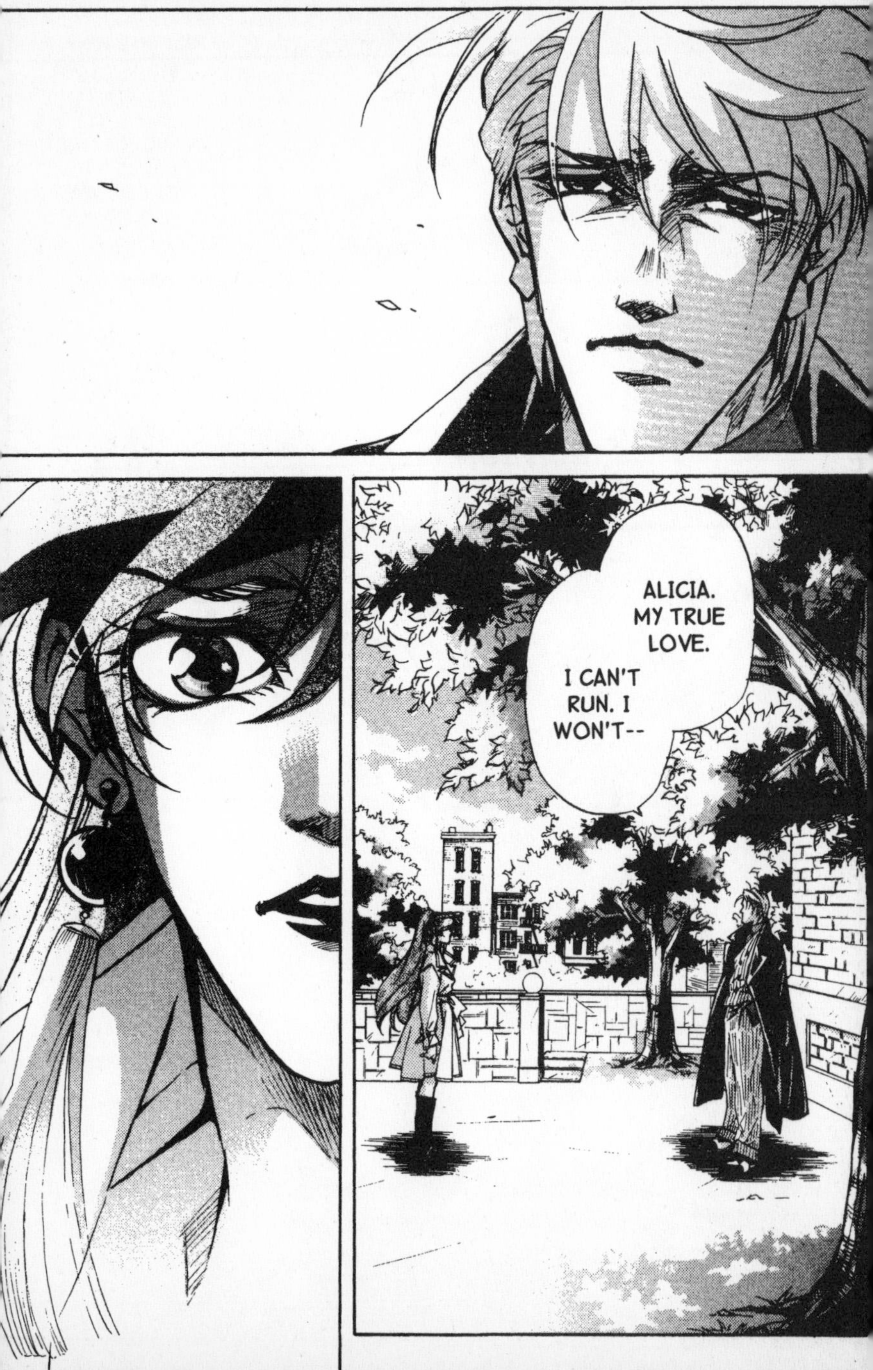
ALICIA. MY TRUE LOVE.
I CAN'T RUN. I WON'T--

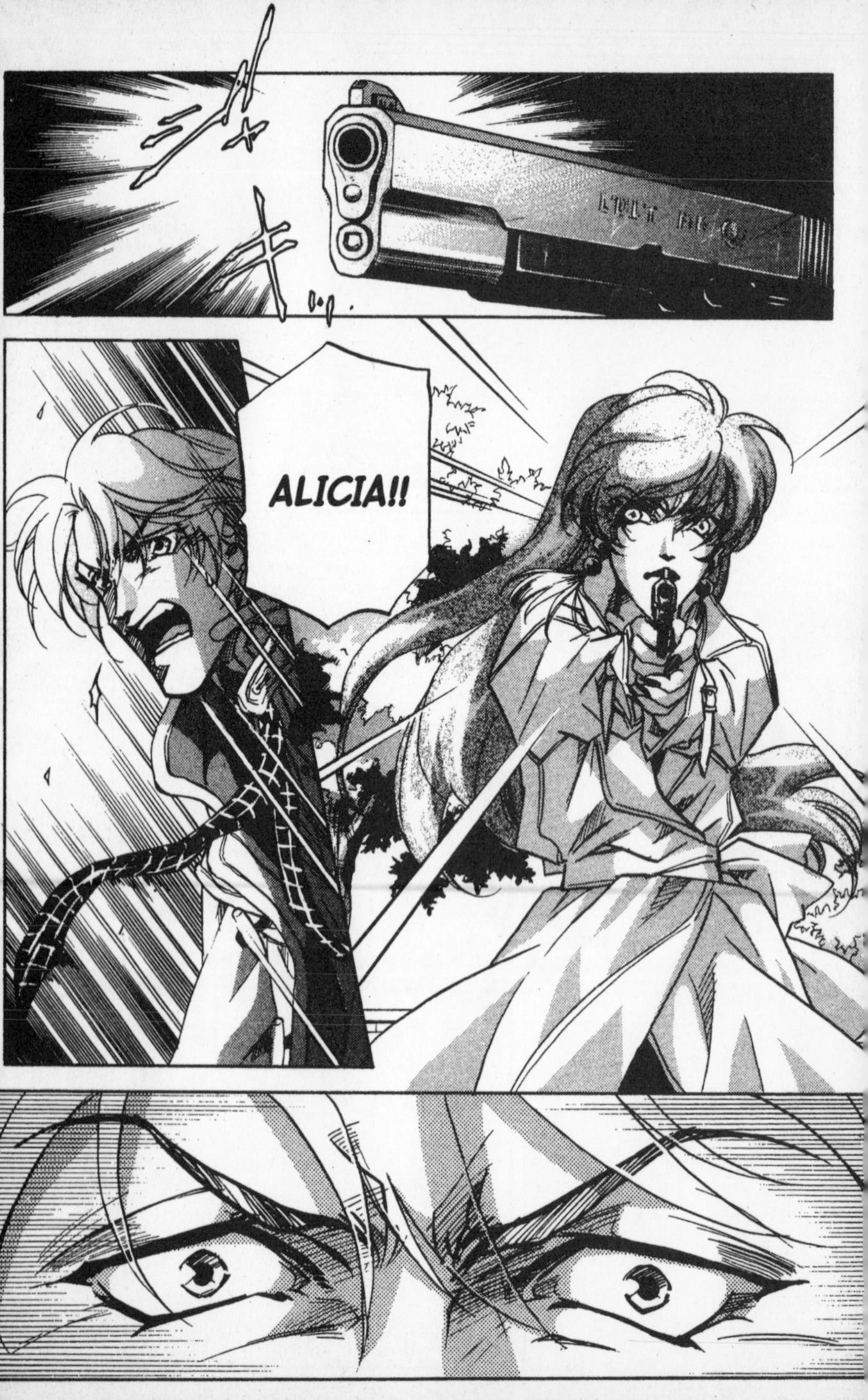
ALICIA!!

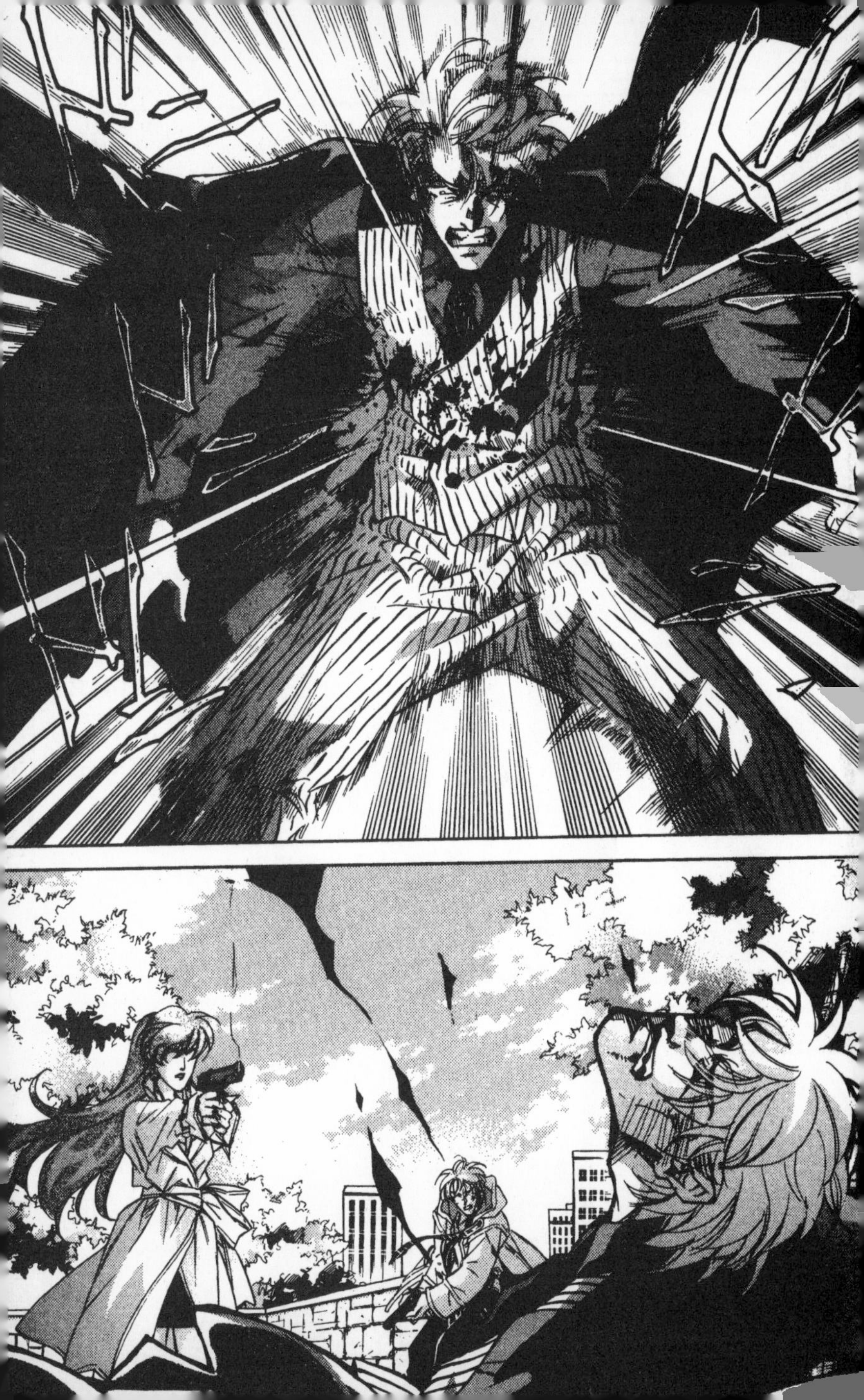

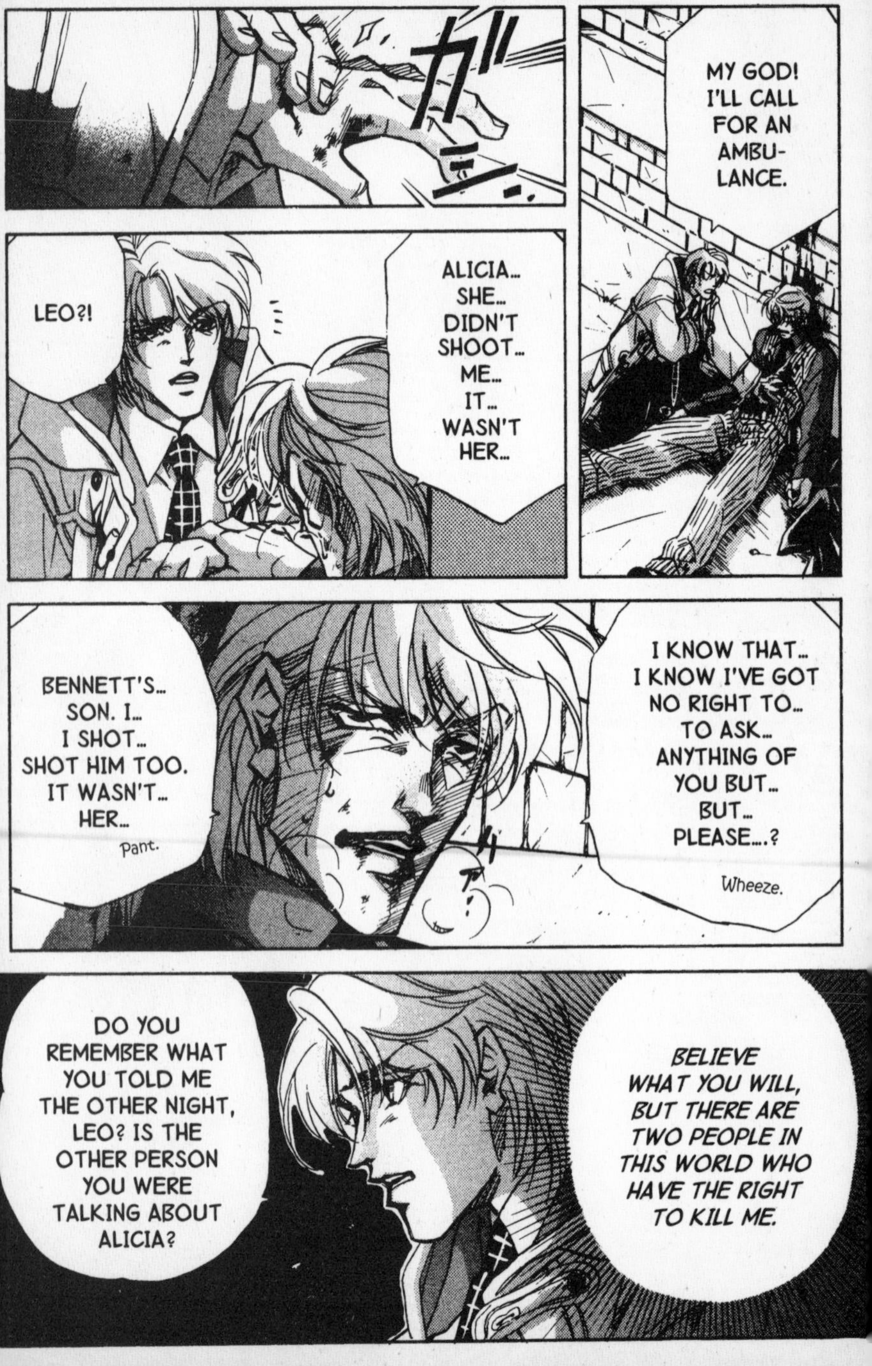
MY GOD! I'LL CALL FOR AN AMBU- LANCE.
ALICIA... SHE... DIDN'T SHOOT... ME... IT... WASN'T HER...
LEO?!
I KNOW THAT... I KNOW I'VE GOT NO RIGHT TO... TO ASK... ANYTHING OF YOU BUT... BUT... PLEASE....?
Wheeze.
BENNETT'S... SON. I... I SHOT... SHOT HIM TOO. IT WASN'T... HER...
Pant.
BELIEVE WHAT YOU WILL, BUT THERE ARE TWO PEOPLE IN THIS WORLD WHO HAVE THE RIGHT TO KILL ME.
DO YOU REMEMBER WHAT YOU TOLD ME THE OTHER NIGHT, LEO? IS THE OTHER PERSON YOU WERE TALKING ABOUT ALICIA?

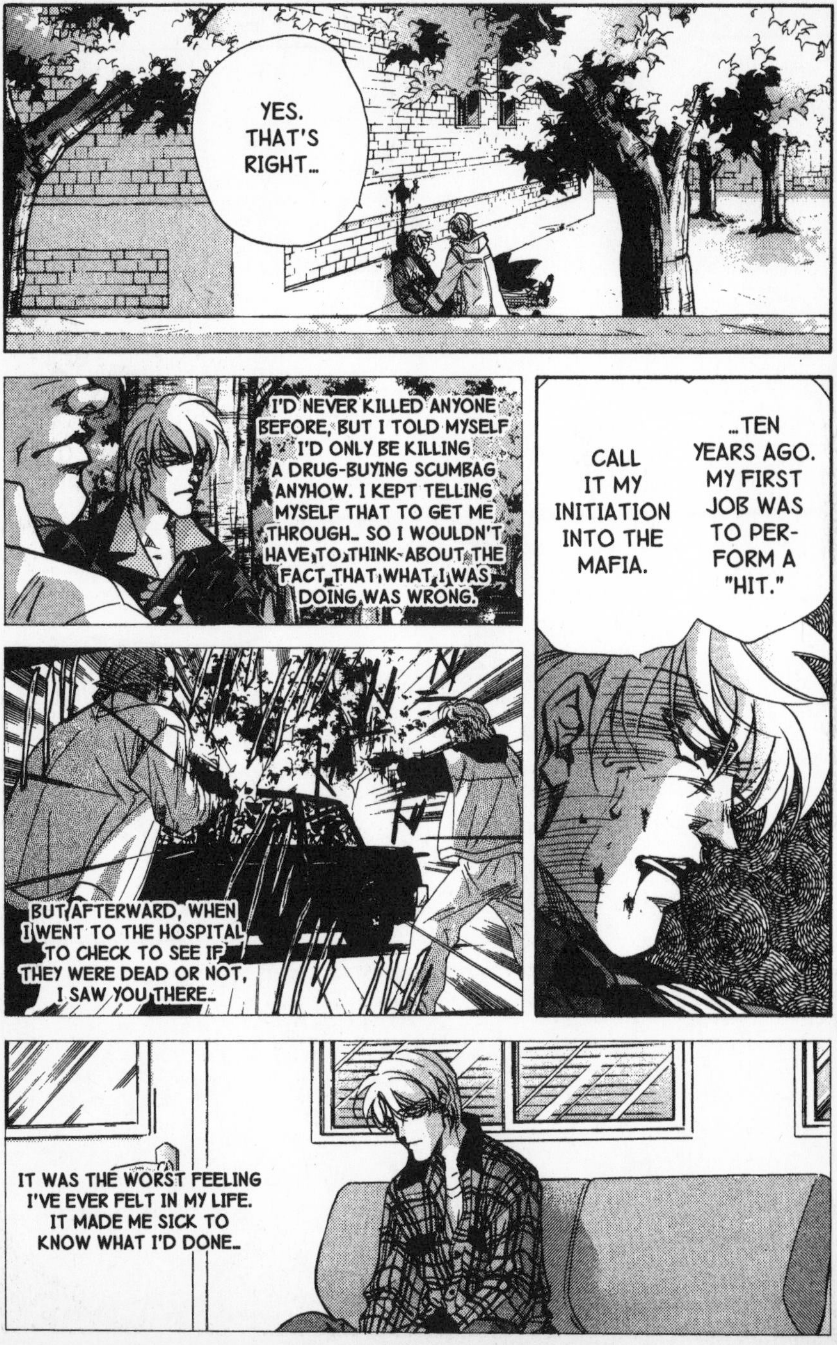
YES. THAT'S RIGHT...
...TEN YEARS AGO. MY FIRST JOB WAS TO PER-FORM A "HIT."
CALL IT MY INITIATION INTO THE MAFIA.
I'D NEVER KILLED ANYONE BEFORE, BUT I TOLD MYSELF I'D ONLY BE KILLING A DRUG-BUYING SCUMBAG ANYHOW. I KEPT TELLING MYSELF THAT TO GET ME THROUGH... SO I WOULDN'T HAVE TO THINK ABOUT THE FACT THAT WHAT I WAS DOING WAS WRONG.
BUT AFTERWARD, WHEN I WENT TO THE HOSPITAL TO CHECK TO SEE IF THEY WERE DEAD OR NOT, I SAW YOU THERE...
IT WAS THE WORST FEELING I'VE EVER FELT IN MY LIFE. IT MADE ME SICK TO KNOW WHAT I'D DONE...

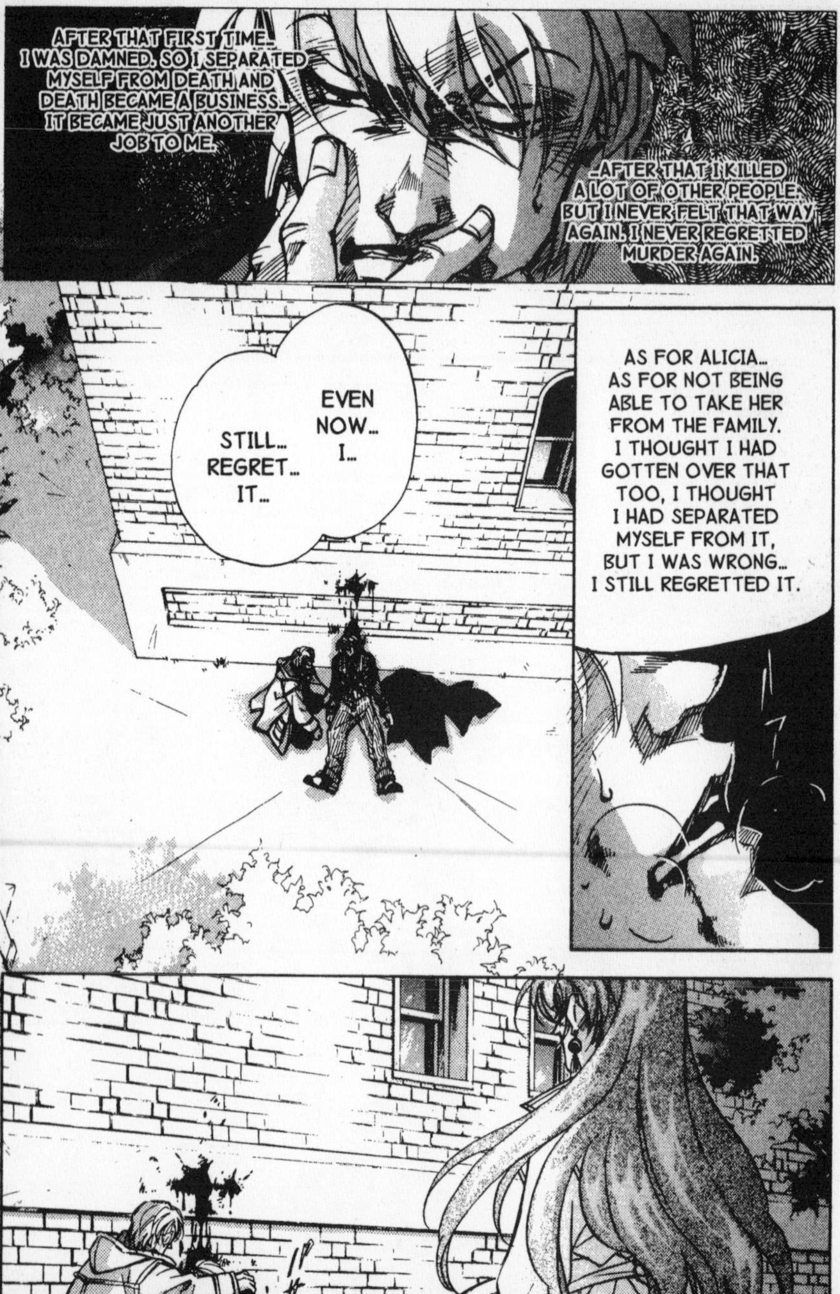
AFTER THAT FIRST TIME... I WAS DAMNED. SO I SEPARATED MYSELF FROM DEATH AND DEATH BECAME A BUSINESS... IT BECAME JUST ANOTHER JOB TO ME.
...AFTER THAT I KILLED A LOT OF OTHER PEOPLE. BUT I NEVER FELT THAT WAY AGAIN. I NEVER REGRETTED MURDER AGAIN.
AS FOR ALICIA... AS FOR NOT BEING ABLE TO TAKE HER FROM THE FAMILY. I THOUGHT I HAD GOTTEN OVER THAT TOO, I THOUGHT I HAD SEPARATED MYSELF FROM IT, BUT I WAS WRONG... I STILL REGRETTED IT.
EVEN NOW... I...
STILL... REGRET... IT...

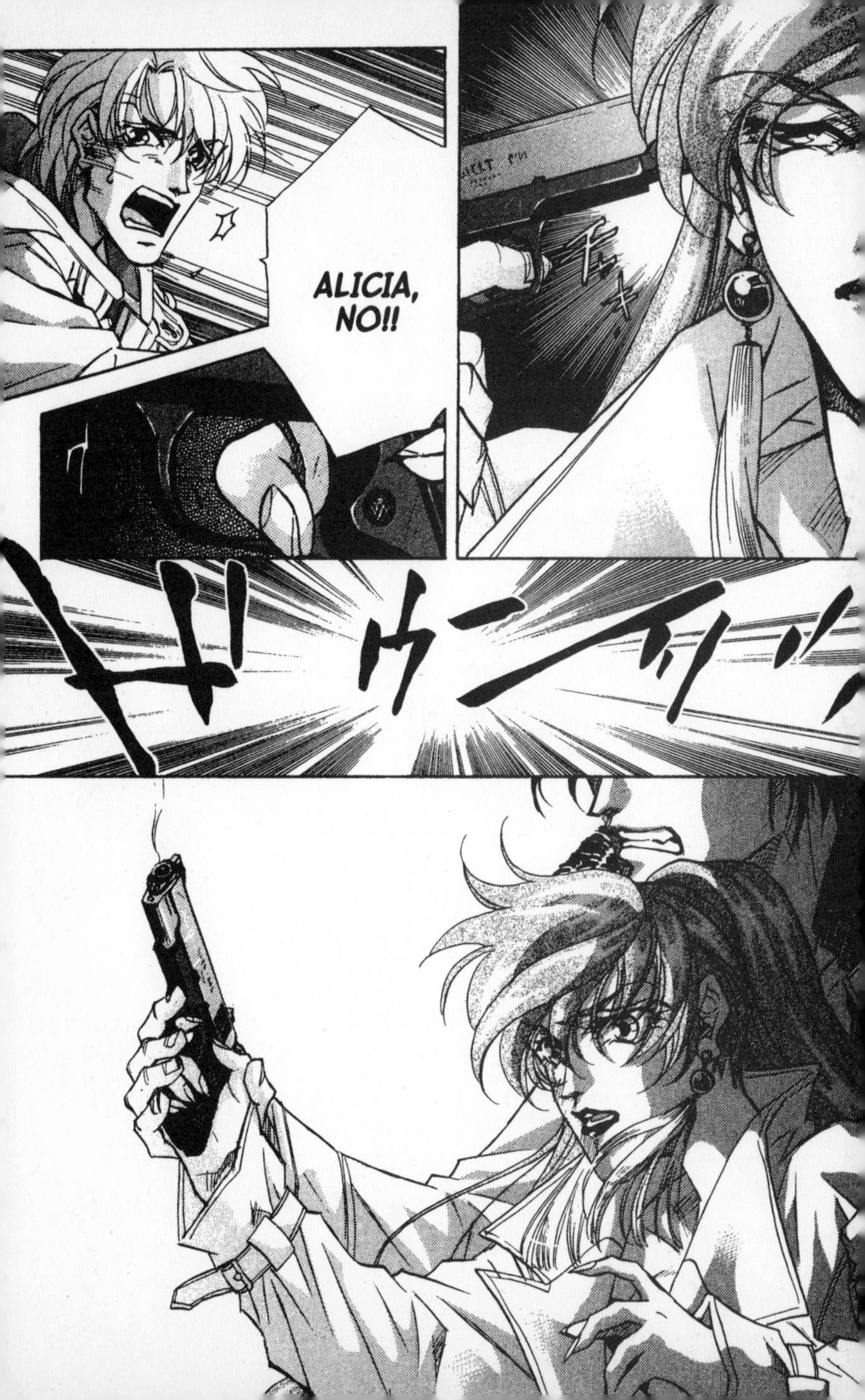
ALICIA, NO!!

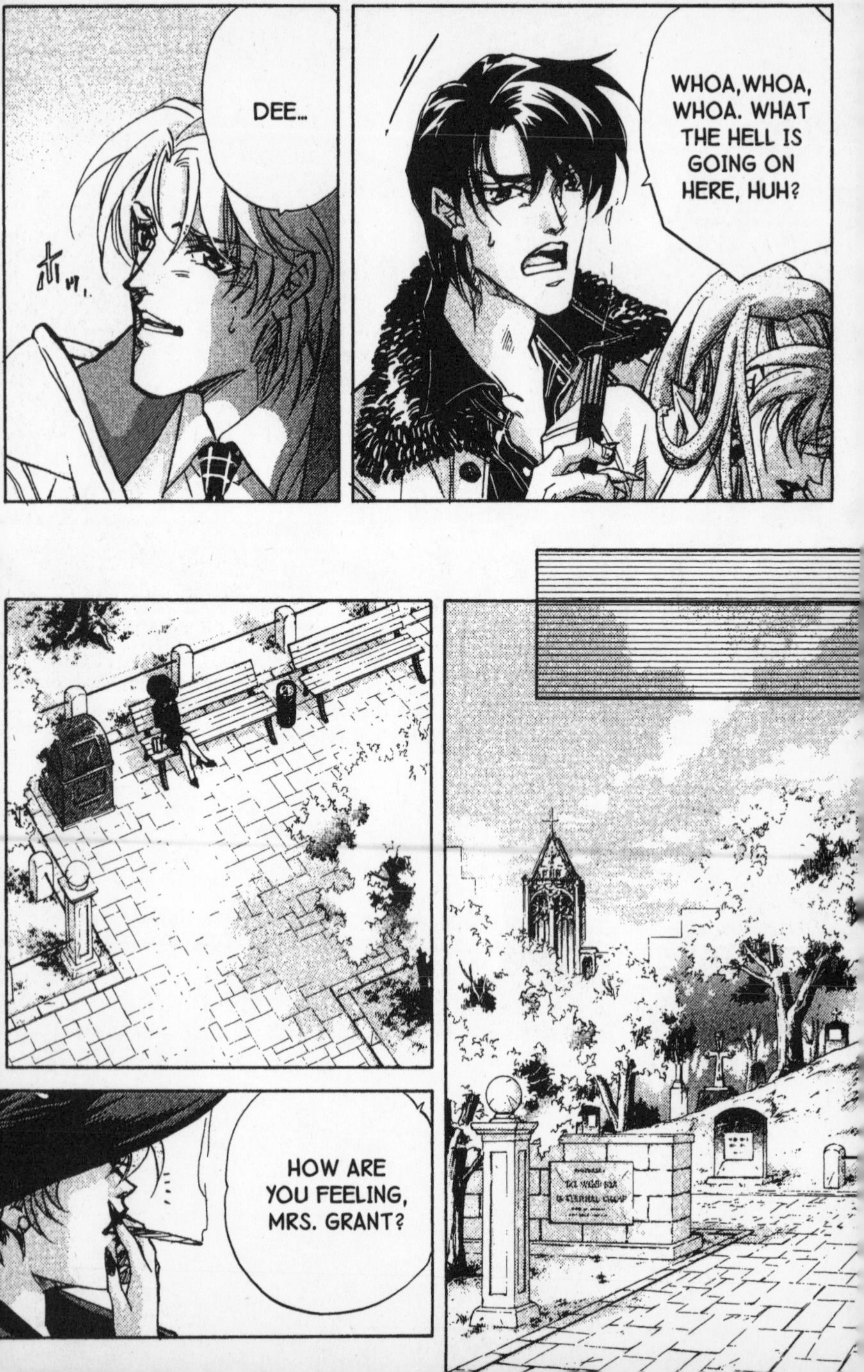
WHOA,WHOA, WHOA. WHAT THE HELL IS GOING ON HERE, HUH?
DEE...
HOW ARE YOU FEELING, MRS. GRANT?

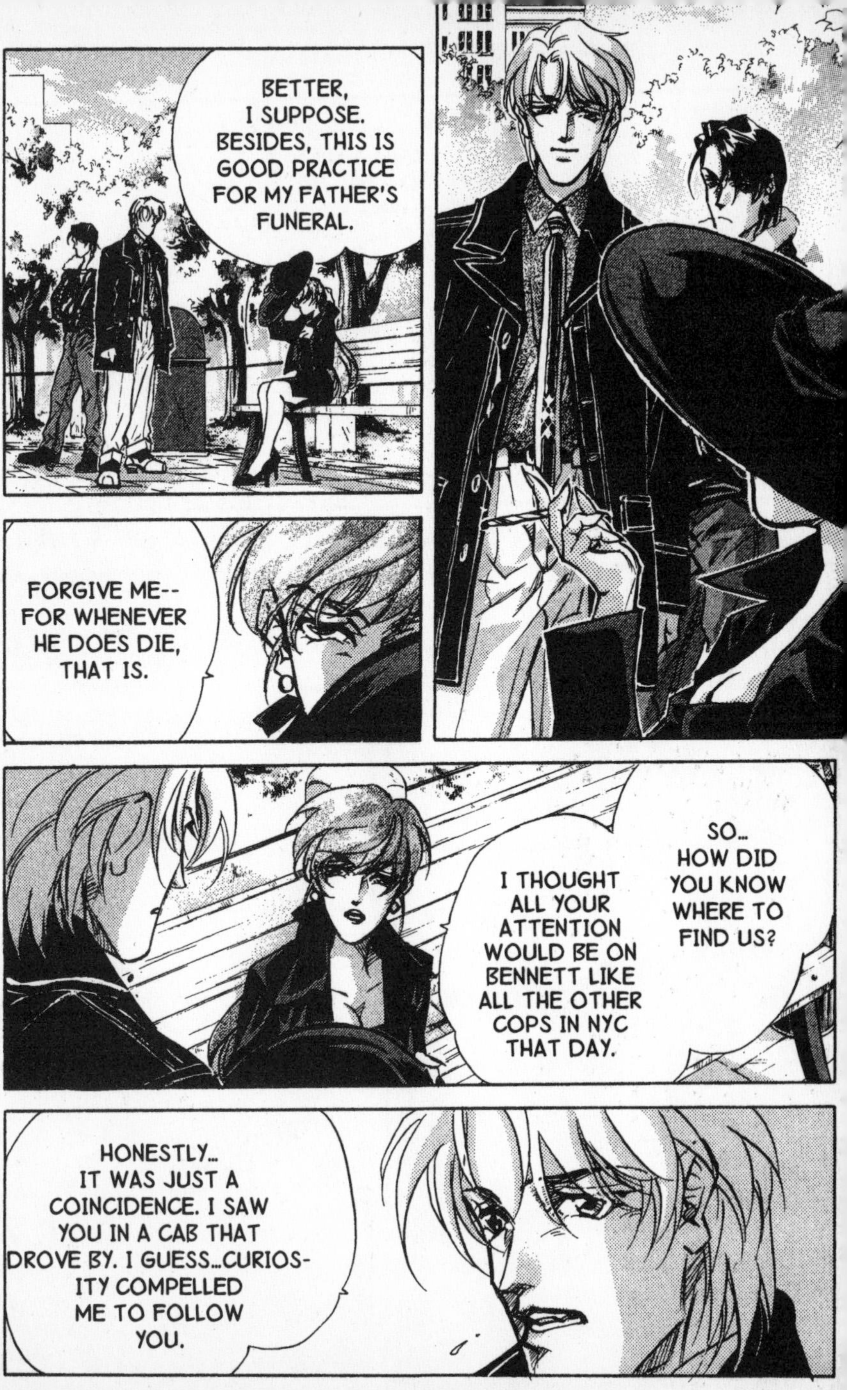
BETTER, I SUPPOSE. BESIDES, THIS IS GOOD PRACTICE FOR MY FATHER'S FUNERAL.
FORGIVE ME--FOR WHENEVER HE DOES DIE, THAT IS.
SO... HOW DID YOU KNOW WHERE TO FIND US?
I THOUGHT ALL YOUR ATTENTION WOULD BE ON BENNETT LIKE ALL THE OTHER COPS IN NYC THAT DAY.
HONESTLY... IT WAS JUST A COINCIDENCE. I SAW YOU IN A CAB THAT DROVE BY. I GUESS...CURIOS-ITY COMPELLED ME TO FOLLOW YOU.

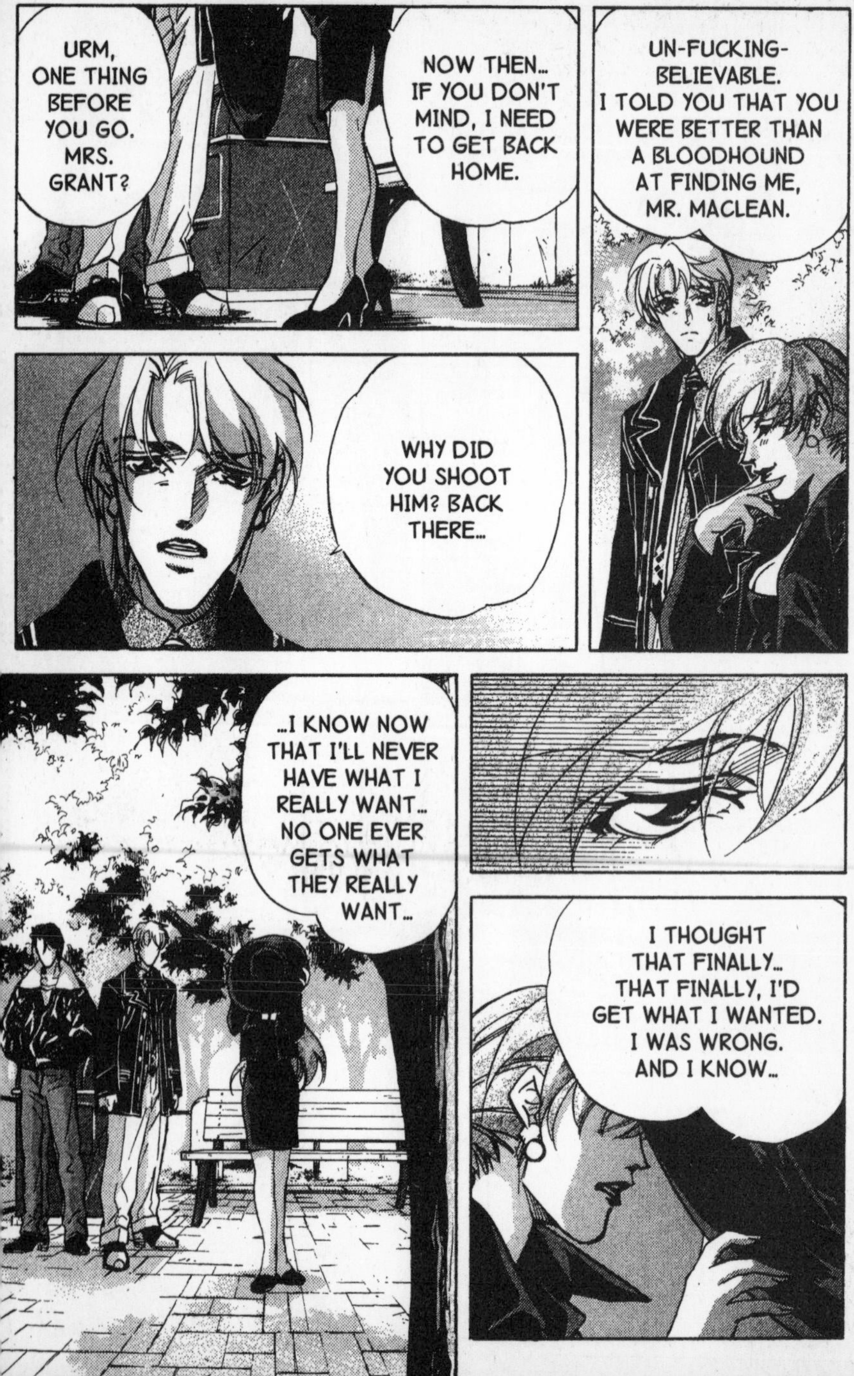
UN-FUCKING-BELIEVABLE. I TOLD YOU THAT YOU WERE BETTER THAN A BLOODHOUND AT FINDING ME, MR. MACLEAN.
NOW THEN... IF YOU DON'T MIND, I NEED TO GET BACK HOME.
URM, ONE THING BEFORE YOU GO. MRS. GRANT?
WHY DID YOU SHOOT HIM? BACK THERE...
I THOUGHT THAT FINALLY... THAT FINALLY, I'D GET WHAT I WANTED. I WAS WRONG. AND I KNOW...
...I KNOW NOW THAT I'LL NEVER HAVE WHAT I REALLY WANT... NO ONE EVER GETS WHAT THEY REALLY WANT...

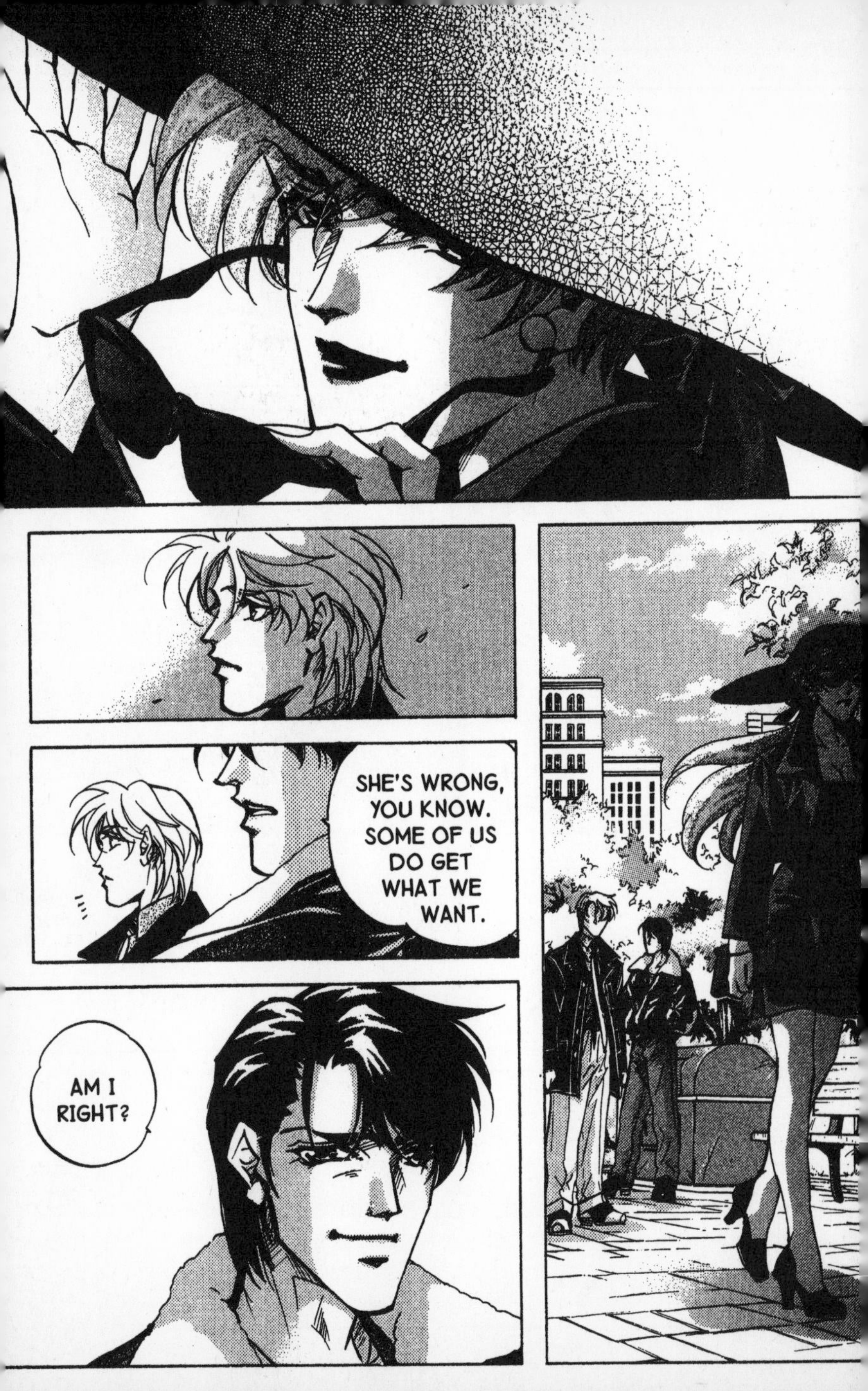
SHE'S WRONG, YOU KNOW. SOME OF US DO GET WHAT WE WANT.
AM I RIGHT?

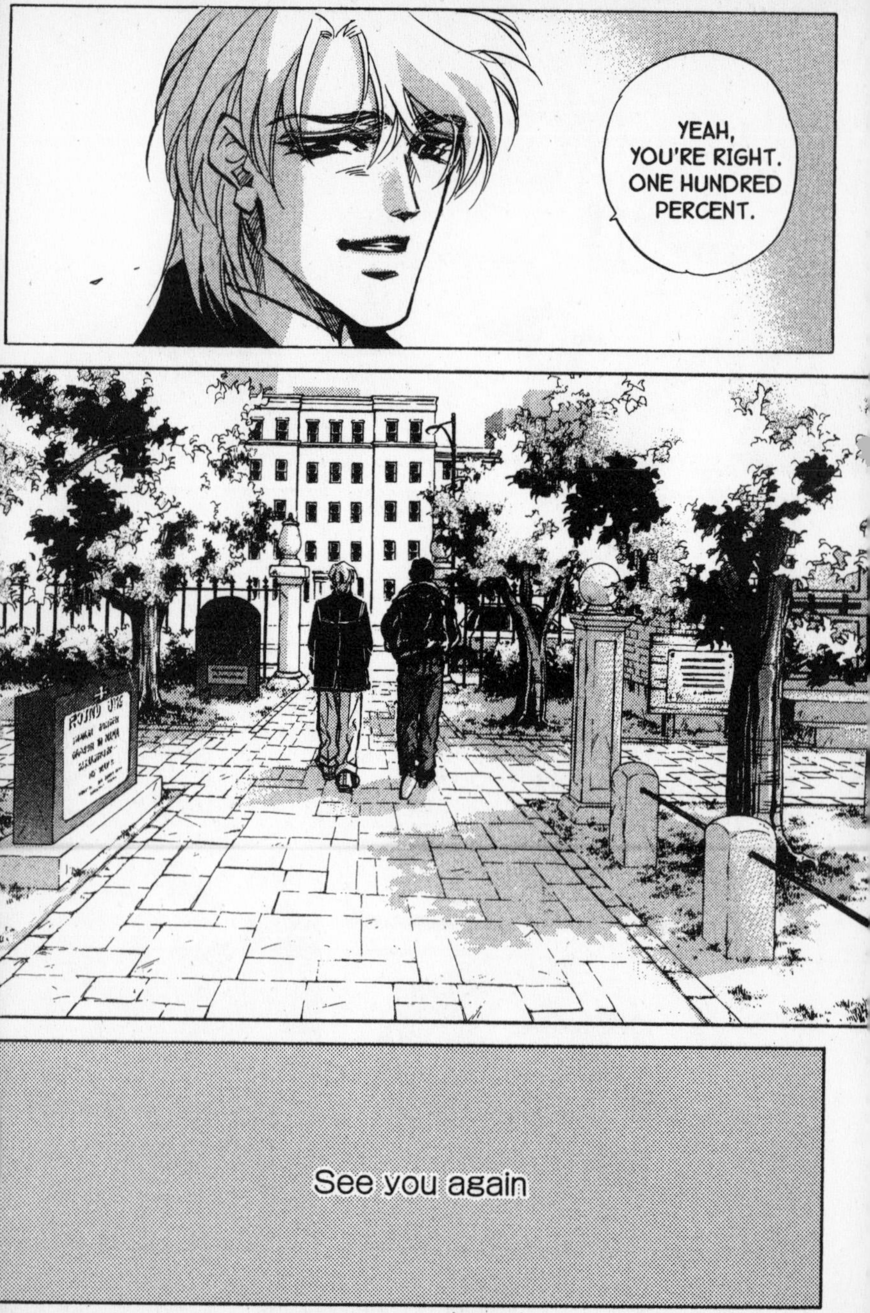
YEAH, YOU'RE RIGHT. ONE HUNDRED PERCENT.
See you again

FAKE act.19/The End.

FAKE

Act.20
SECOND CHANCE

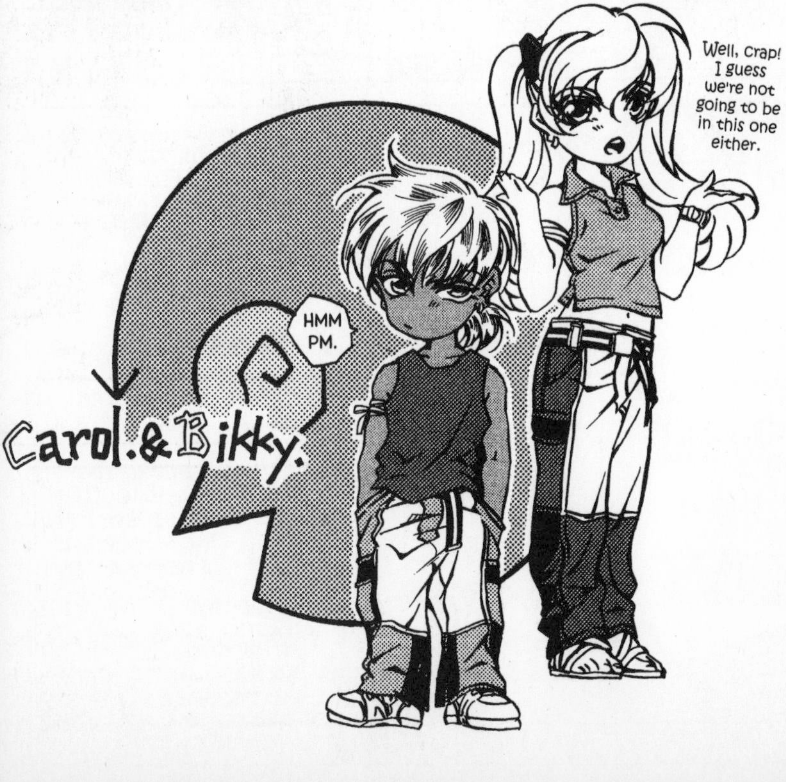
Well, crap! I guess we're not going to be in this one either.
HMM PM.
Carol.&Bikky.

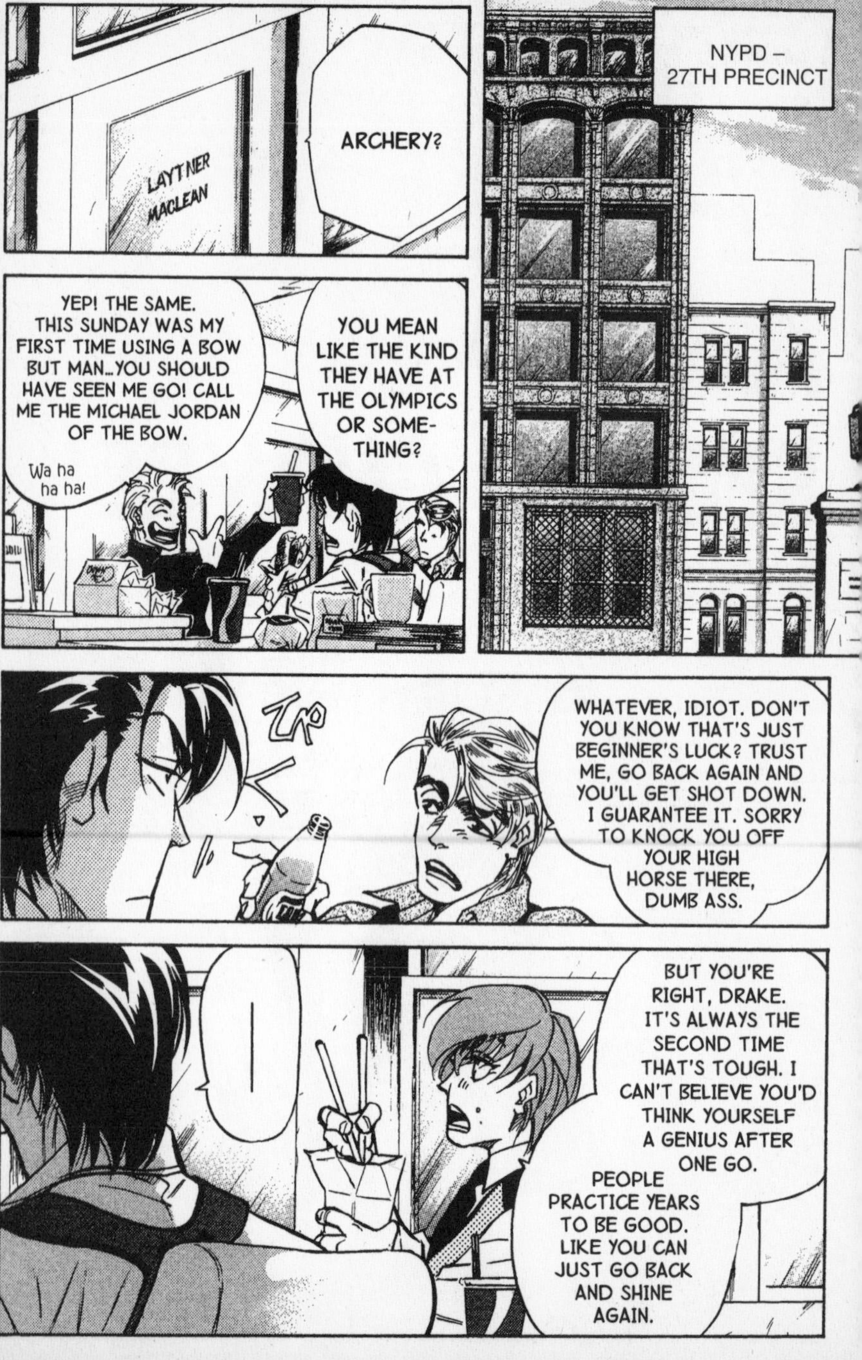
NYPD – 27TH PRECINCT
LAYTNER MACLEAN
ARCHERY?
YOU MEAN LIKE THE KIND THEY HAVE AT THE OLYMPICS OR SOME-THING?
YEP! THE SAME. THIS SUNDAY WAS MY FIRST TIME USING A BOW BUT MAN...YOU SHOULD HAVE SEEN ME GO! CALL ME THE MICHAEL JORDAN OF THE BOW.
Wa ha ha ha!
WHATEVER, IDIOT. DON'T YOU KNOW THAT'S JUST BEGINNER'S LUCK? TRUST ME, GO BACK AGAIN AND YOU'LL GET SHOT DOWN. I GUARANTEE IT. SORRY TO KNOCK YOU OFF YOUR HIGH HORSE THERE, DUMB ASS.
BUT YOU'RE RIGHT, DRAKE. IT'S ALWAYS THE SECOND TIME THAT'S TOUGH. I CAN'T BELIEVE YOU'D THINK YOURSELF A GENIUS AFTER ONE GO.
PEOPLE PRACTICE YEARS TO BE GOOD. LIKE YOU CAN JUST GO BACK AND SHINE AGAIN.

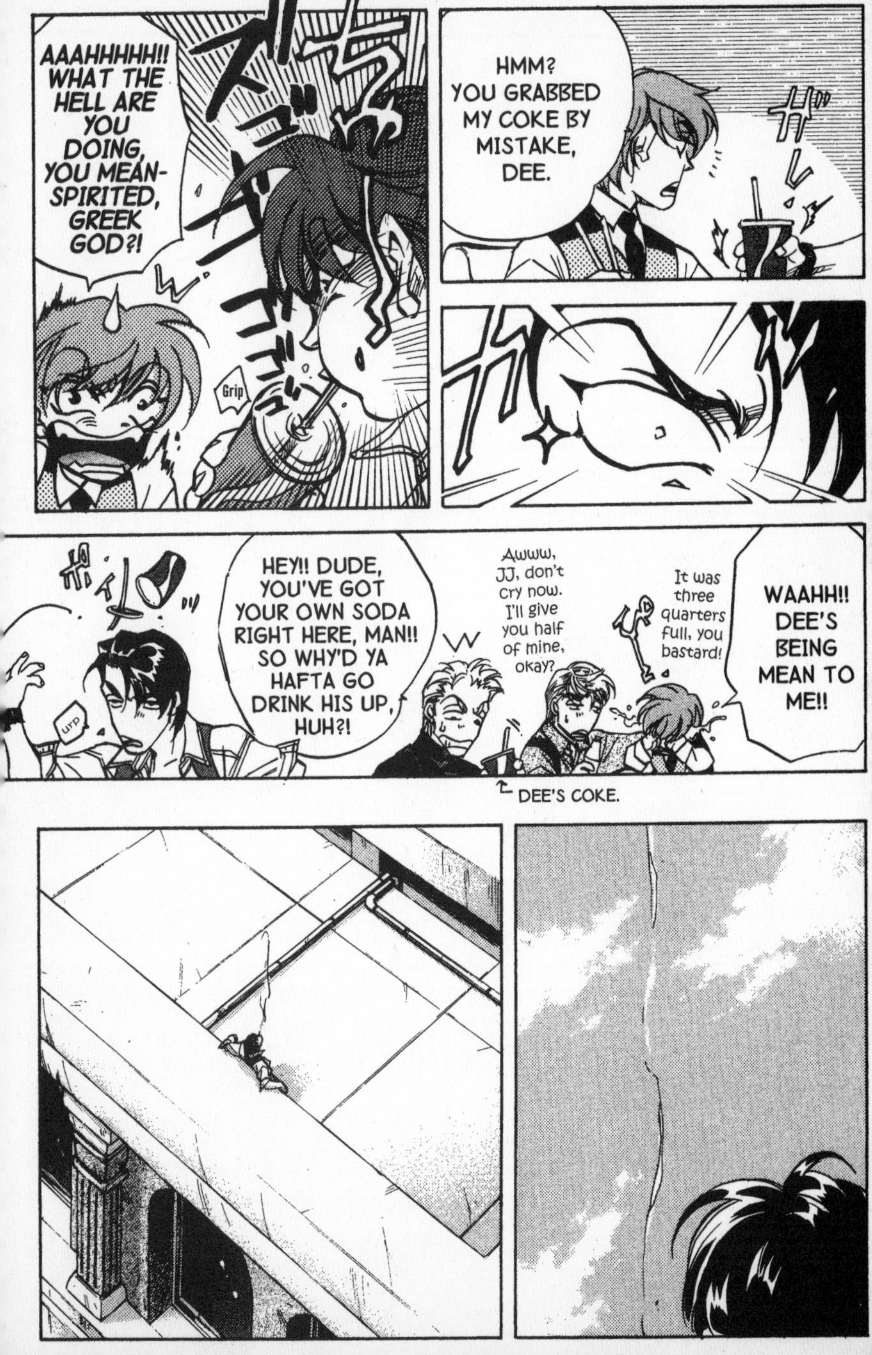
HMM? YOU GRABBED MY COKE BY MISTAKE, DEE.
AAAHHHHH!! WHAT THE HELL ARE YOU DOING, YOU MEAN-SPIRITED, GREEK GOD?!
Grip
WAAHH!! DEE'S BEING MEAN TO ME!!
It was three quarters full, you bastard!
Awww, JJ, don't cry now. I'll give you half of mine, okay?
HEY!! DUDE, YOU'VE GOT YOUR OWN SODA RIGHT HERE, MAN!! SO WHY'D YA HAFTA GO DRINK HIS UP, HUH?!
urp
DEE'S COKE.

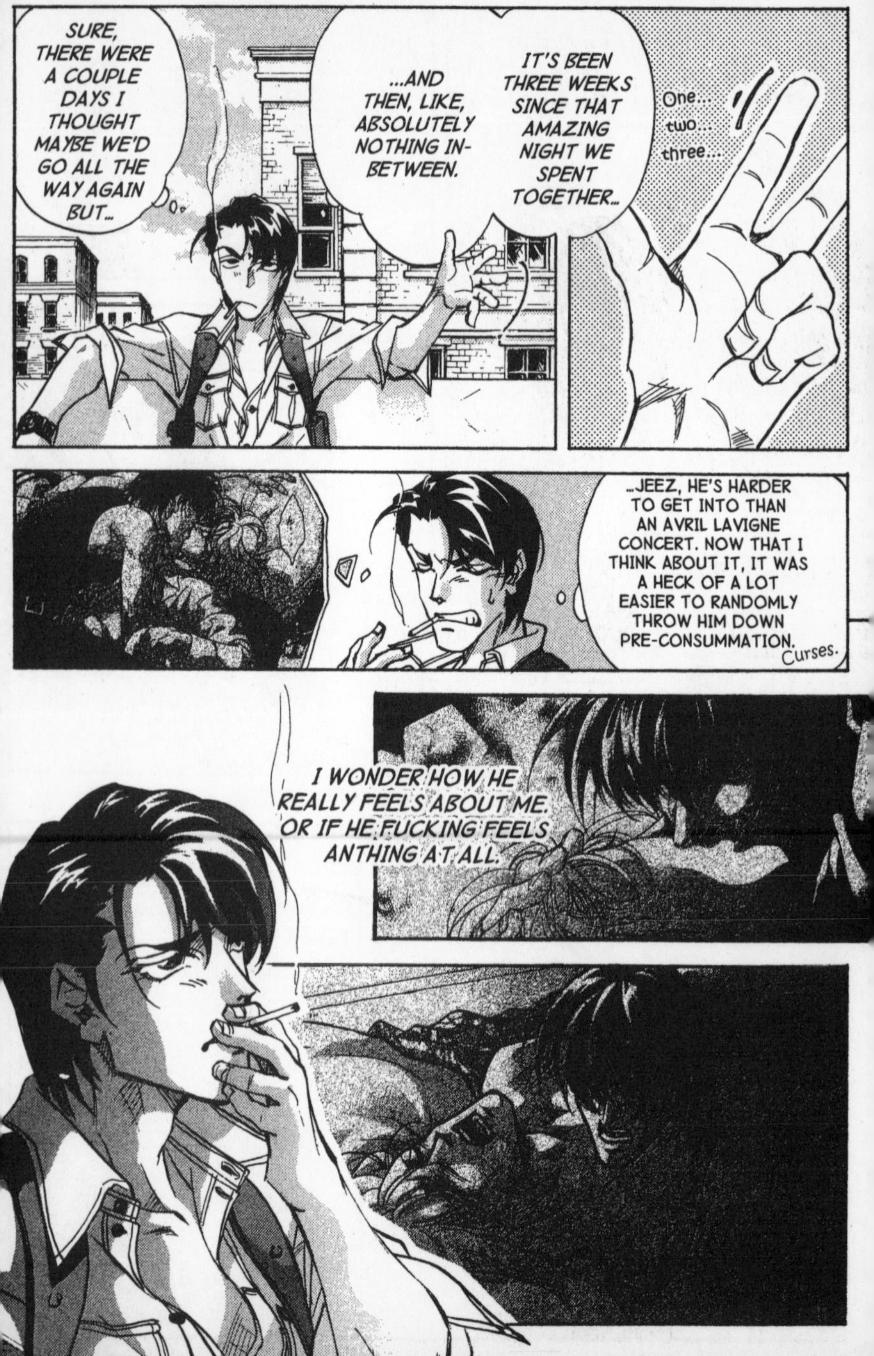
One... two... three...
IT'S BEEN THREE WEEKS SINCE THAT AMAZING NIGHT WE SPENT TOGETHER...
...AND THEN, LIKE, ABSOLUTELY NOTHING IN-BETWEEN.
SURE, THERE WERE A COUPLE DAYS I THOUGHT MAYBE WE'D GO ALL THE WAY AGAIN BUT...
...JEEZ, HE'S HARDER TO GET INTO THAN AN AVRIL LAVIGNE CONCERT. NOW THAT I THINK ABOUT IT, IT WAS A HECK OF A LOT EASIER TO RANDOMLY THROW HIM DOWN PRE-CONSUMMATION.
Curses.
I WONDER HOW HE REALLY FEELS ABOUT ME. OR IF HE FUCKING FEELS ANTHING AT ALL.

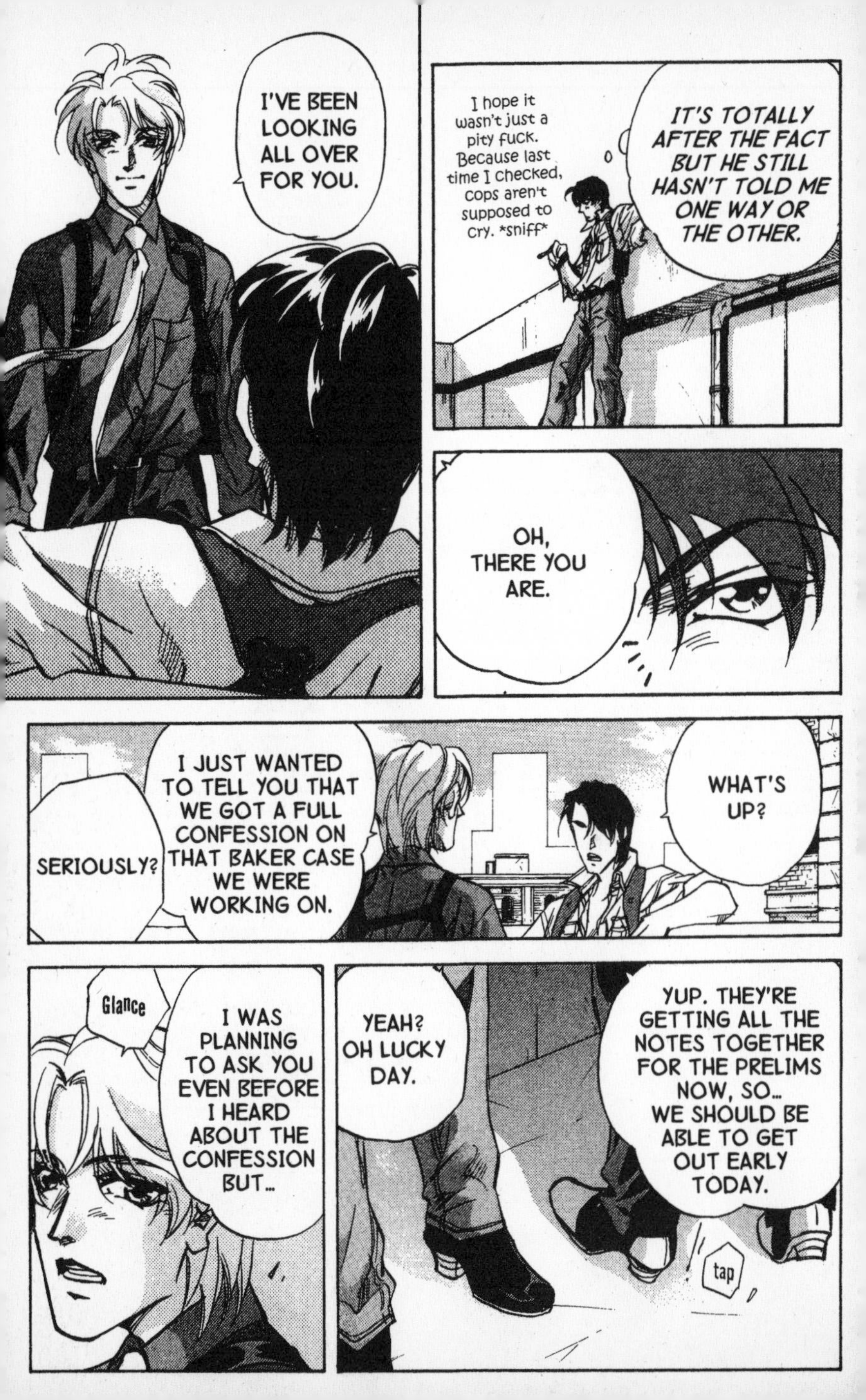
IT'S TOTALLY AFTER THE FACT BUT HE STILL HASN'T TOLD ME ONE WAY OR THE OTHER.
I hope it wasn't just a pity fuck. Because last time I checked, cops aren't supposed to cry. *sniff*
OH, THERE YOU ARE.
I'VE BEEN LOOKING ALL OVER FOR YOU.
WHAT'S UP?
I JUST WANTED TO TELL YOU THAT WE GOT A FULL CONFESSION ON THAT BAKER CASE WE WERE WORKING ON.
SERIOUSLY?
YUP. THEY'RE GETTING ALL THE NOTES TOGETHER FOR THE PRELIMS NOW, SO... WE SHOULD BE ABLE TO GET OUT EARLY TODAY.
YEAH? OH LUCKY DAY.
tap
I WAS PLANNING TO ASK YOU EVEN BEFORE I HEARD ABOUT THE CONFESSION BUT...
Glance

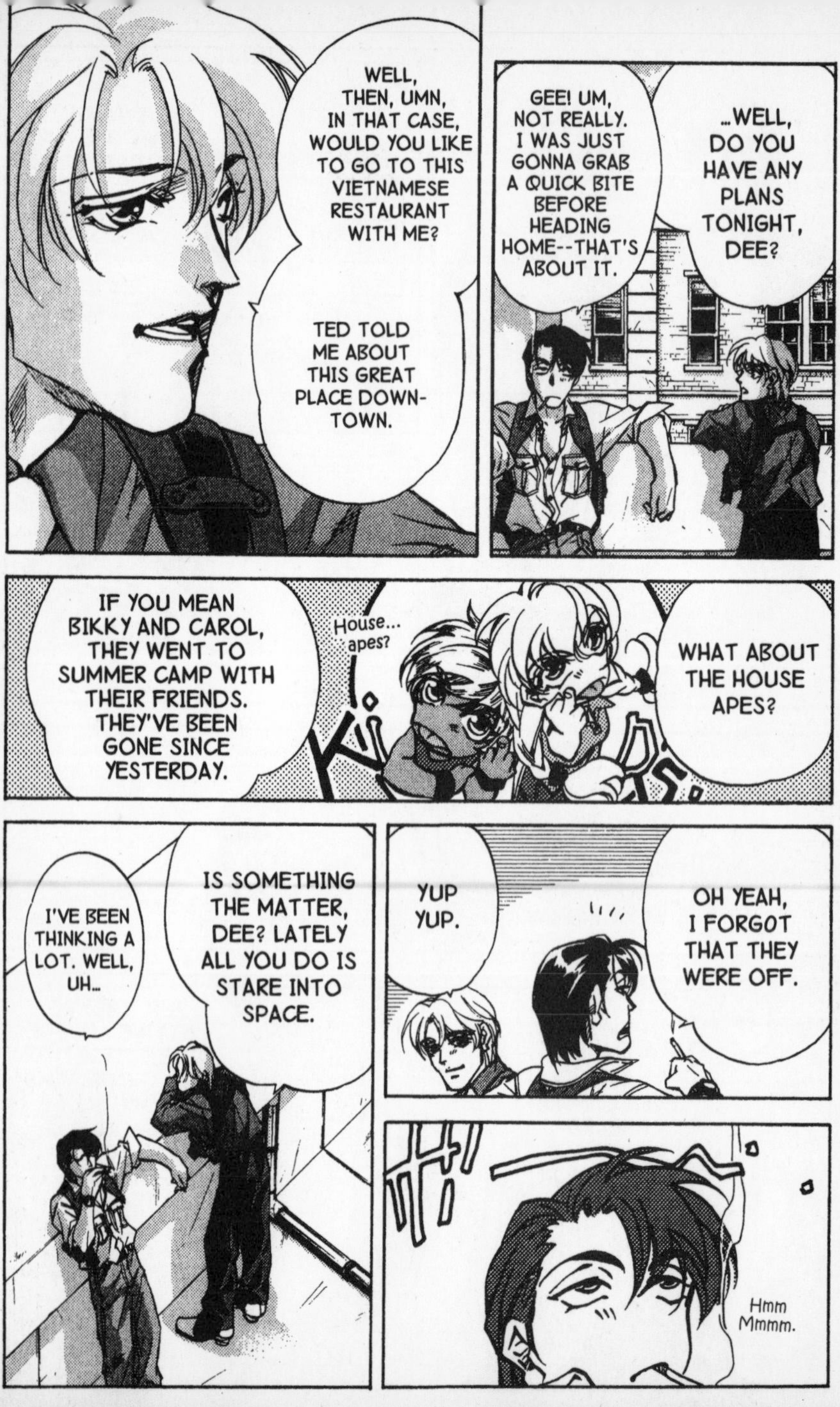
...WELL, DO YOU HAVE ANY PLANS TONIGHT, DEE?
GEE! UM, NOT REALLY. I WAS JUST GONNA GRAB A QUICK BITE BEFORE HEADING HOME--THAT'S ABOUT IT.
WELL, THEN, UMN, IN THAT CASE, WOULD YOU LIKE TO GO TO THIS VIETNAMESE RESTAURANT WITH ME?
TED TOLD ME ABOUT THIS GREAT PLACE DOWN-TOWN.
WHAT ABOUT THE HOUSE APES?
House... apes?
IF YOU MEAN BIKKY AND CAROL, THEY WENT TO SUMMER CAMP WITH THEIR FRIENDS. THEY'VE BEEN GONE SINCE YESTERDAY.
OH YEAH, I FORGOT THAT THEY WERE OFF.
YUP YUP.
Hmm Mmmm.
IS SOMETHING THE MATTER, DEE? LATELY ALL YOU DO IS STARE INTO SPACE.
I'VE BEEN THINKING A LOT. WELL, UH...

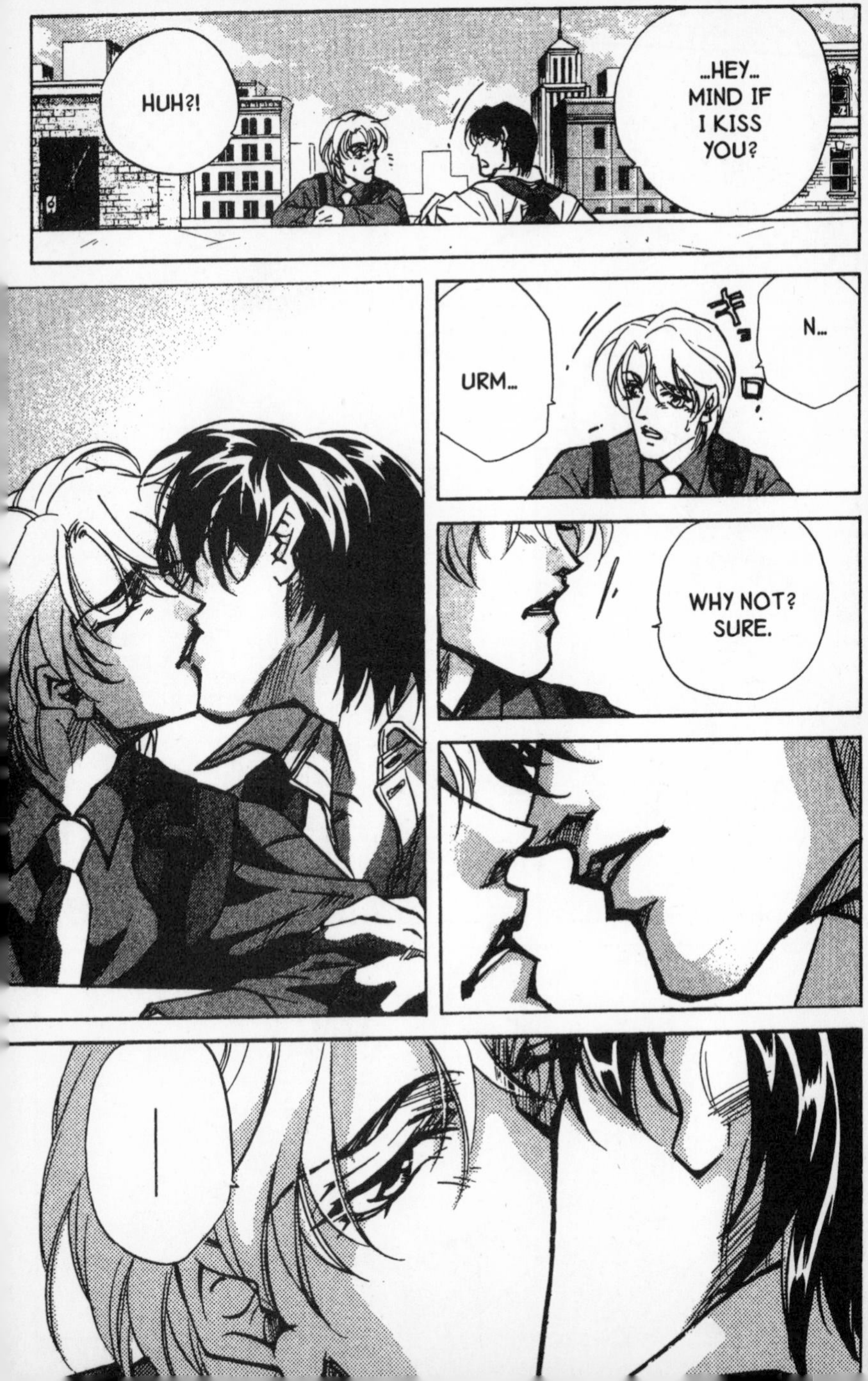
...HEY... MIND IF I KISS YOU?
HUH?!
N...
URM...
WHY NOT? SURE.

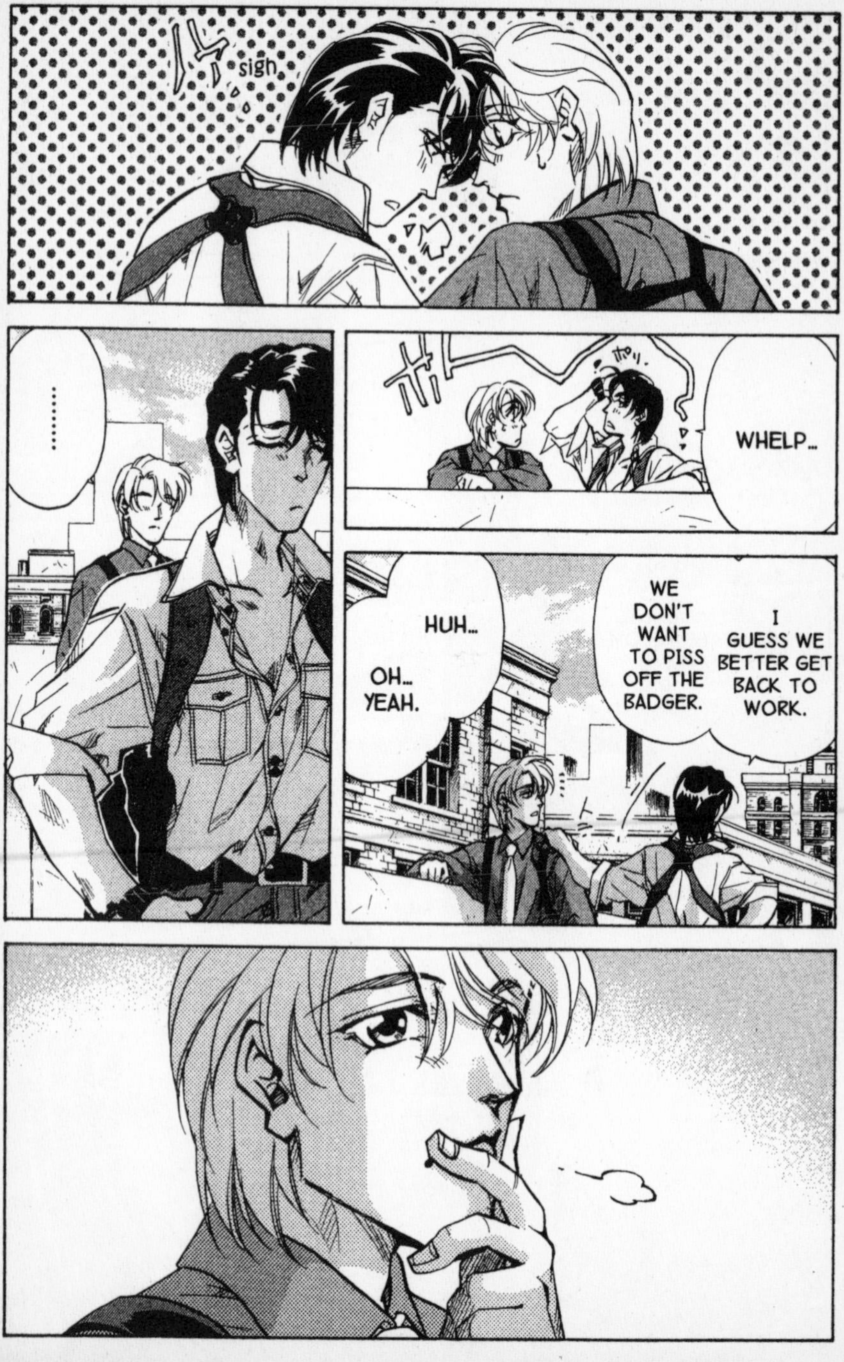
sigh
WHELP...
I GUESS WE BETTER GET BACK TO WORK.
WE DON'T WANT TO PISS OFF THE BADGER.
HUH...
OH... YEAH.
......

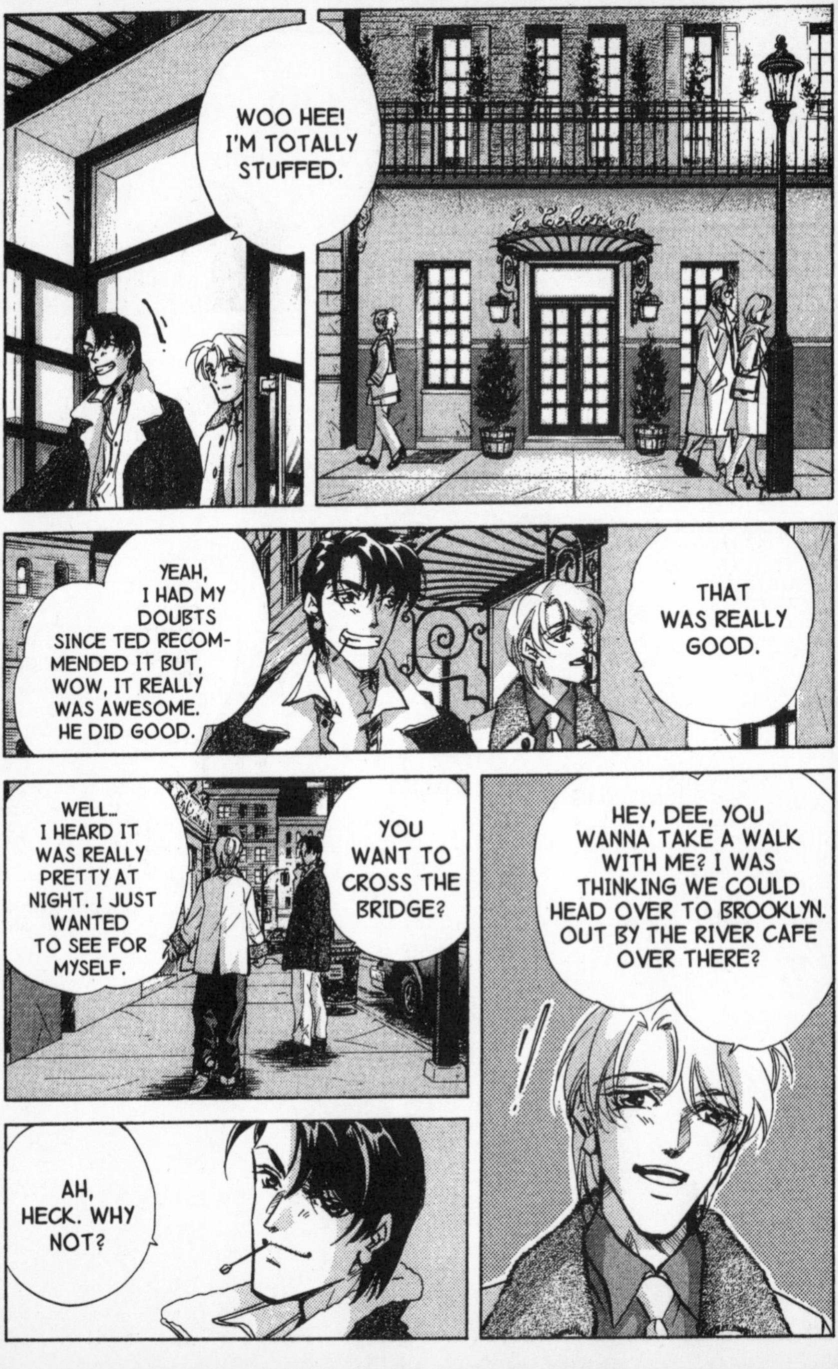
WOO HEE! I'M TOTALLY STUFFED.
THAT WAS REALLY GOOD.
YEAH, I HAD MY DOUBTS SINCE TED RECOM-MENDED IT BUT, WOW, IT REALLY WAS AWESOME. HE DID GOOD.
HEY, DEE, YOU WANNA TAKE A WALK WITH ME? I WAS THINKING WE COULD HEAD OVER TO BROOKLYN. OUT BY THE RIVER CAFE OVER THERE?
YOU WANT TO CROSS THE BRIDGE?
WELL... I HEARD IT WAS REALLY PRETTY AT NIGHT. I JUST WANTED TO SEE FOR MYSELF.
AH, HECK. WHY NOT?

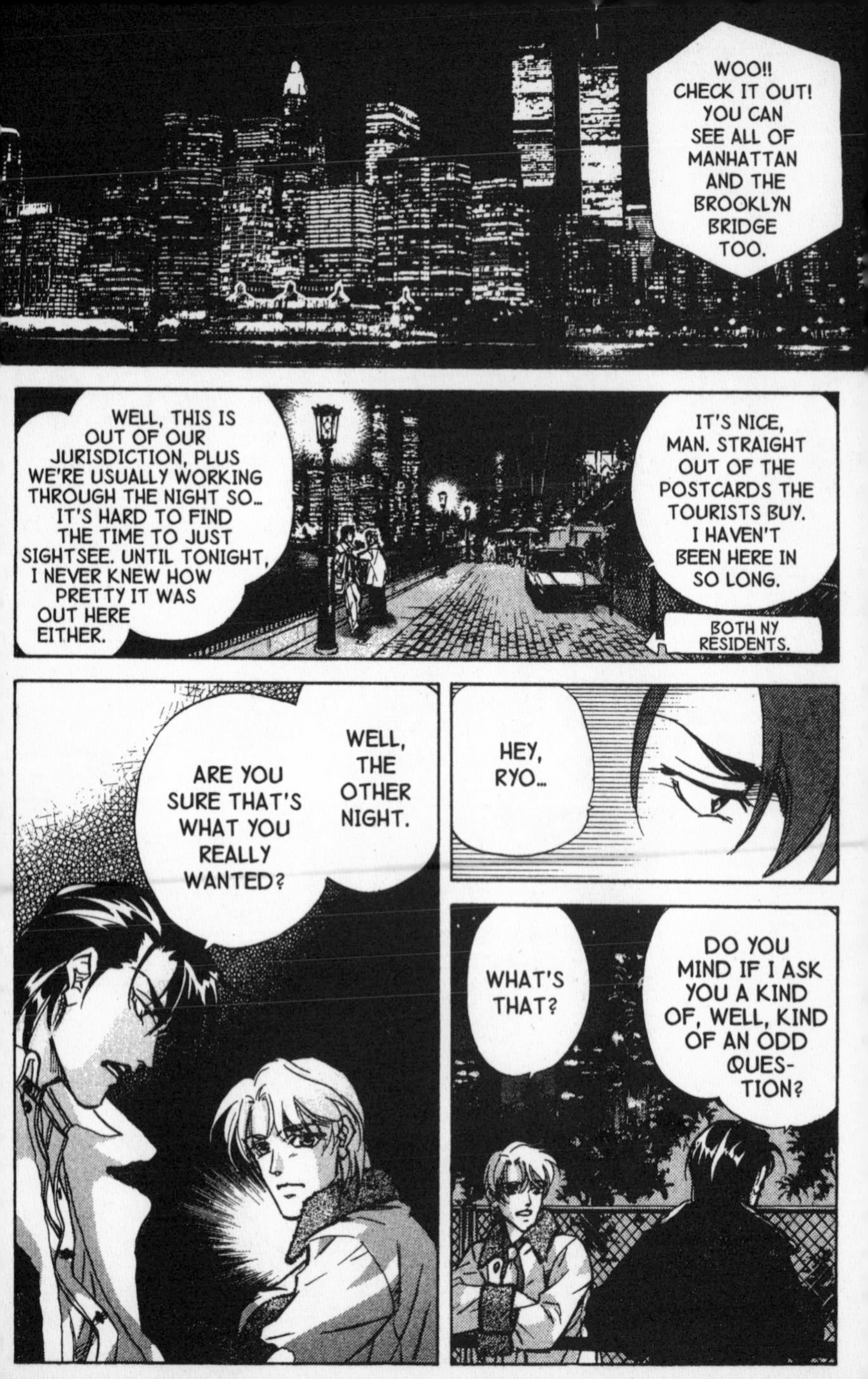
WOO!! CHECK IT OUT! YOU CAN SEE ALL OF MANHATTAN AND THE BROOKLYN BRIDGE TOO.
IT'S NICE, MAN. STRAIGHT OUT OF THE POSTCARDS THE TOURISTS BUY. I HAVEN'T BEEN HERE IN SO LONG.
WELL, THIS IS OUT OF OUR JURISDICTION, PLUS WE'RE USUALLY WORKING THROUGH THE NIGHT SO... IT'S HARD TO FIND THE TIME TO JUST SIGHTSEE. UNTIL TONIGHT, I NEVER KNEW HOW PRETTY IT WAS OUT HERE EITHER.
BOTH NY RESIDENTS.
HEY, RYO...
DO YOU MIND IF I ASK YOU A KIND OF, WELL, KIND OF AN ODD QUESTION?
WHAT'S THAT?
WELL, THE OTHER NIGHT.
ARE YOU SURE THAT'S WHAT YOU REALLY WANTED?

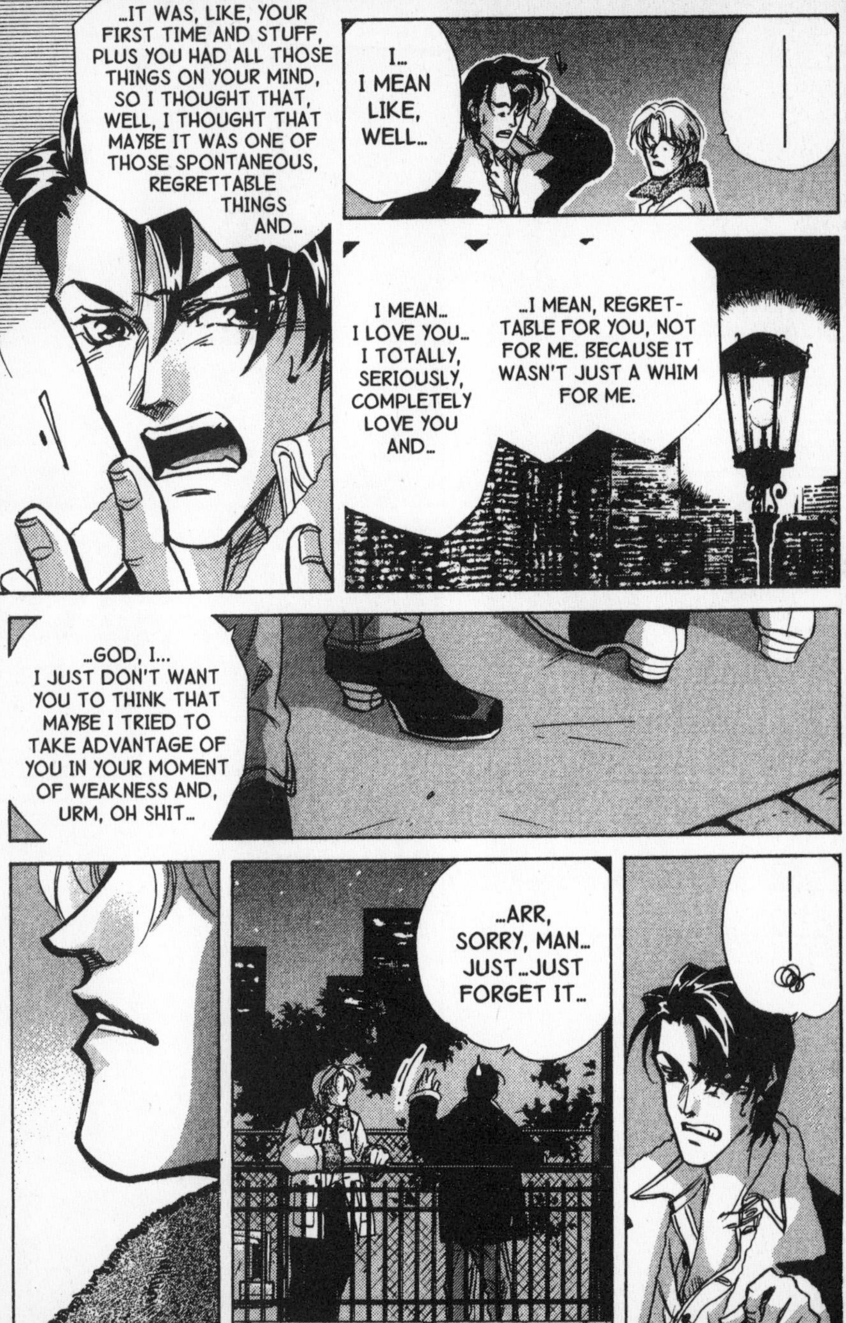
I... I MEAN LIKE, WELL...
...I MEAN, REGRET-TABLE FOR YOU, NOT FOR ME. BECAUSE IT WASN'T JUST A WHIM FOR ME.
I MEAN... I LOVE YOU... I TOTALLY, SERIOUSLY, COMPLETELY LOVE YOU AND...
...IT WAS, LIKE, YOUR FIRST TIME AND STUFF, PLUS YOU HAD ALL THOSE THINGS ON YOUR MIND, SO I THOUGHT THAT, WELL, I THOUGHT THAT MAYBE IT WAS ONE OF THOSE SPONTANEOUS, REGRETTABLE THINGS AND...
...GOD, I... I JUST DON'T WANT YOU TO THINK THAT MAYBE I TRIED TO TAKE ADVANTAGE OF YOU IN YOUR MOMENT OF WEAKNESS AND, URM, OH SHIT...
...ARR, SORRY, MAN... JUST...JUST FORGET IT...

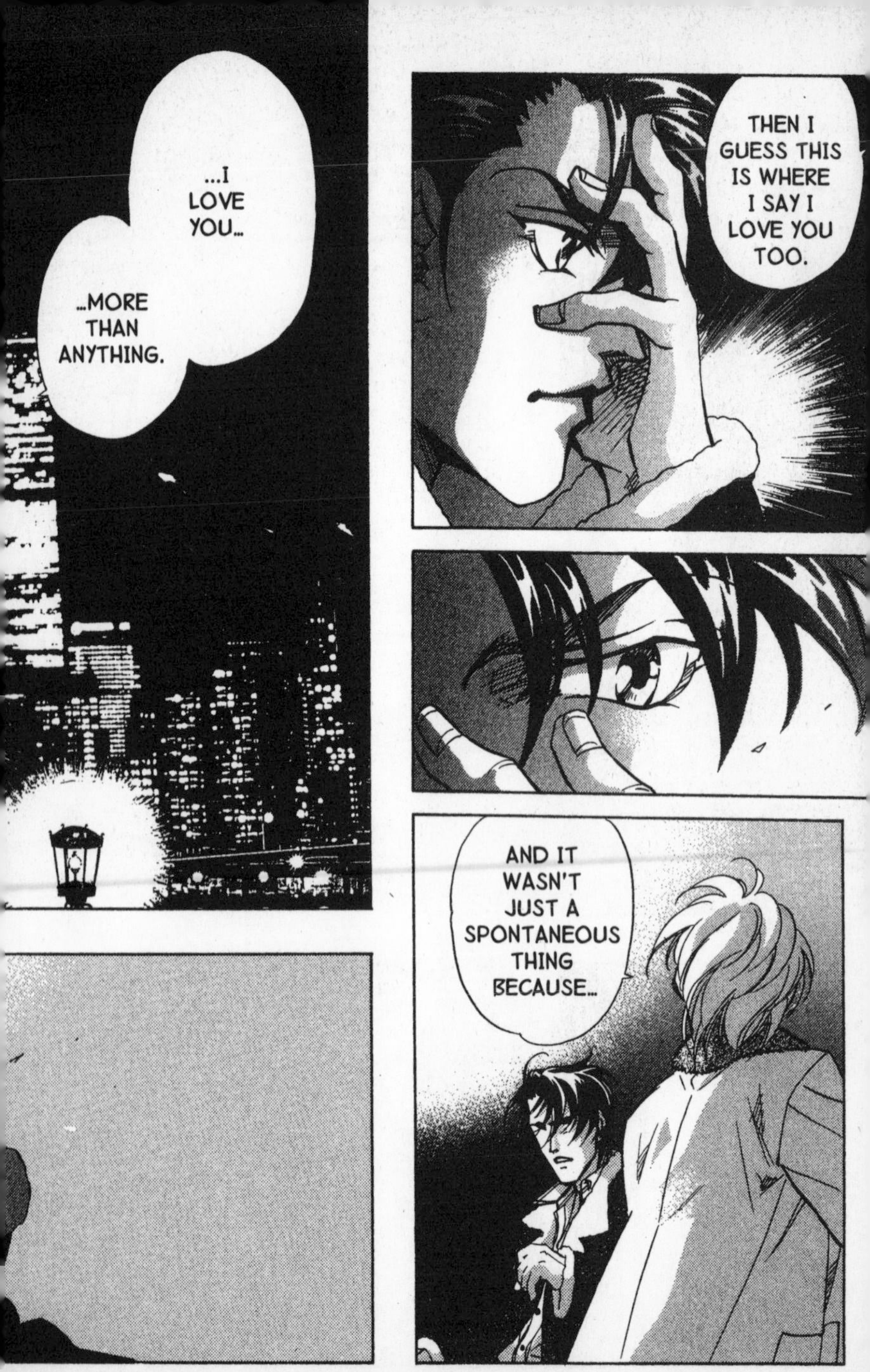
THEN I GUESS THIS IS WHERE I SAY I LOVE YOU TOO.
AND IT WASN'T JUST A SPONTANEOUS THING BECAUSE...
...I LOVE YOU...
...MORE THAN ANYTHING.

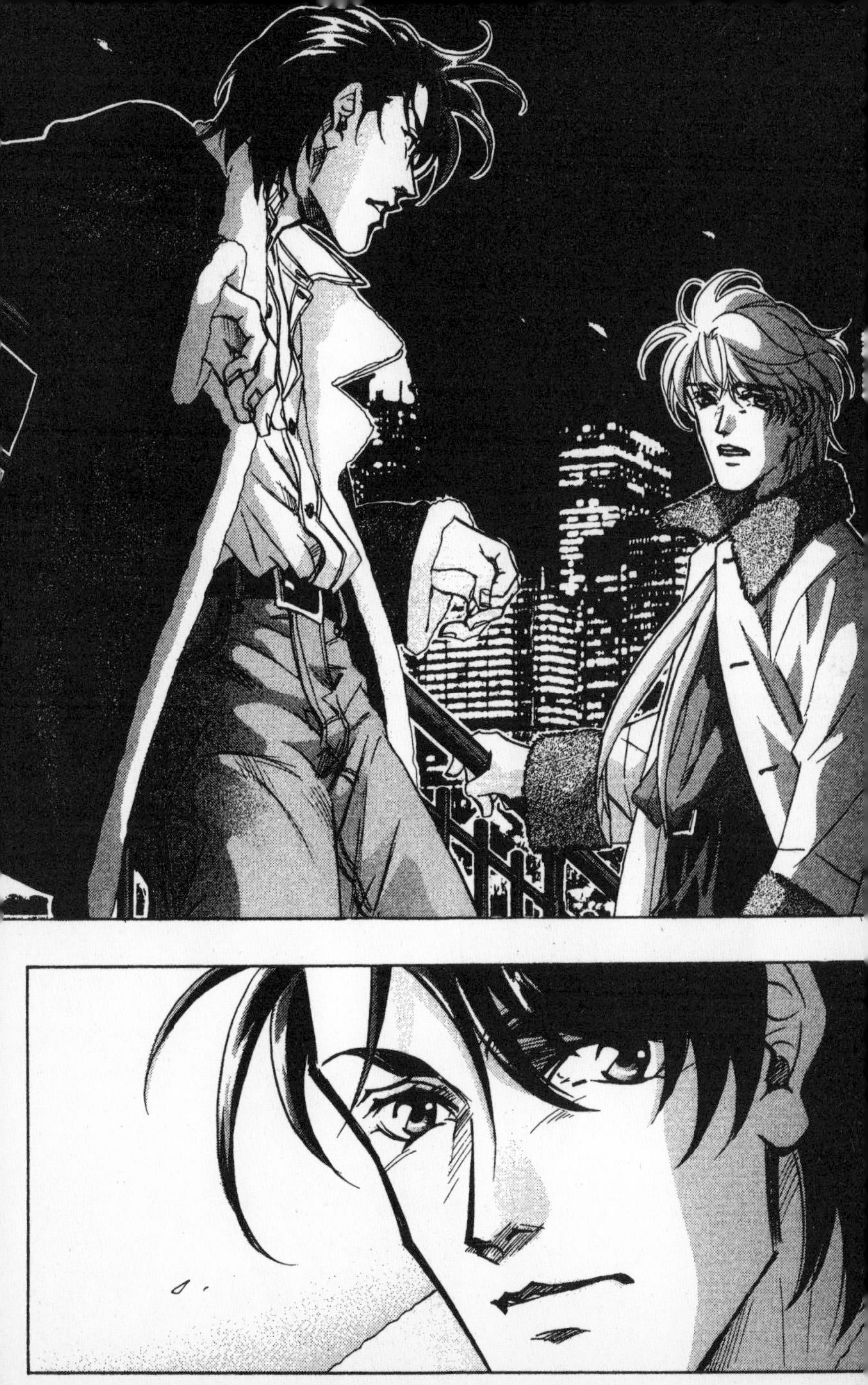

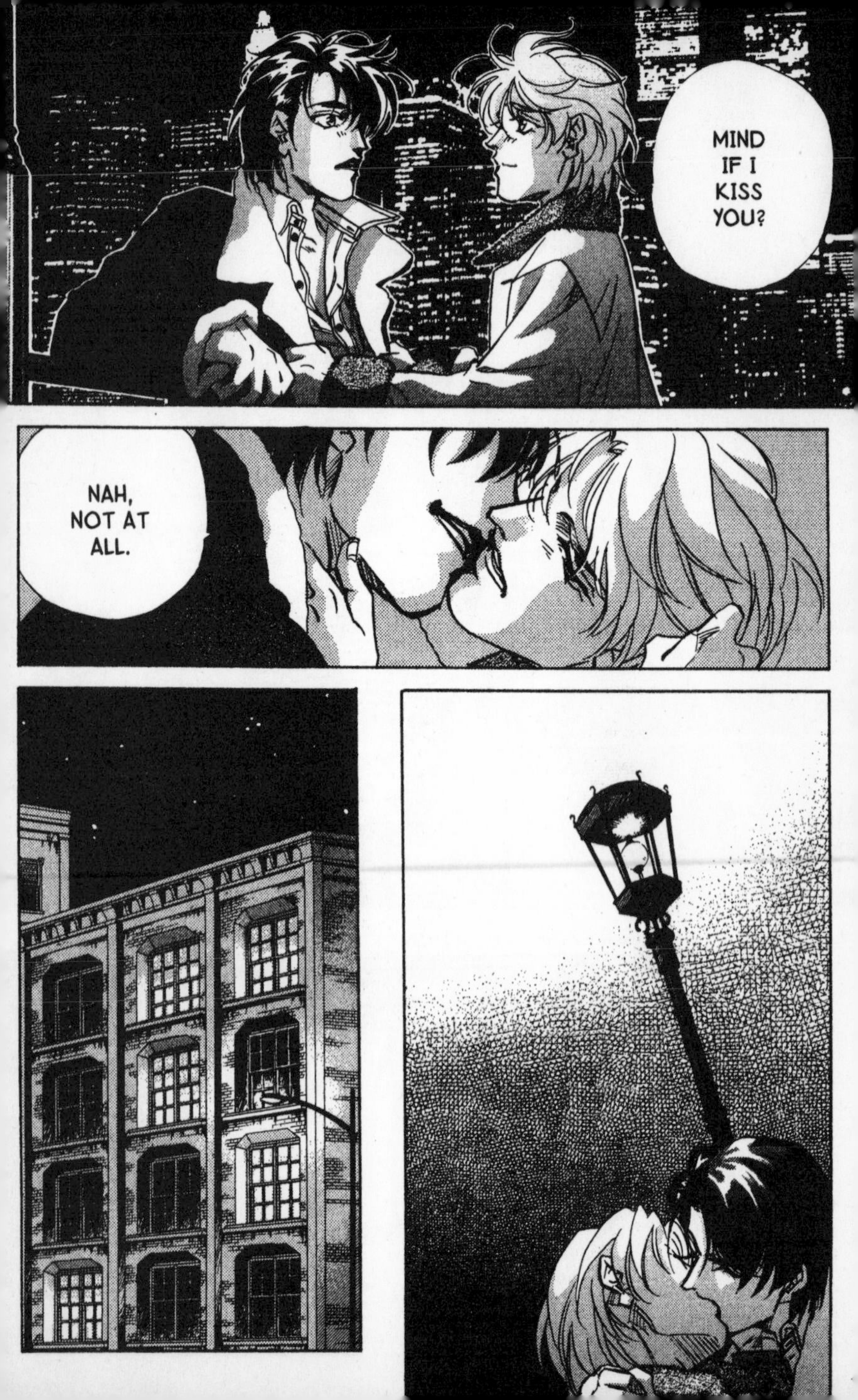
MIND IF I KISS YOU?
NAH, NOT AT ALL.

WHOA, WHOA, WAIT!!!
DEE... THAT'S THE DOOR... BE CAREFUL!!
DON'T WORRY. I GOT IT, OKAY? I SEE IT.
YOU SURE?!
DON'T TRIP ON THE RUG, EITHER. IT'S...

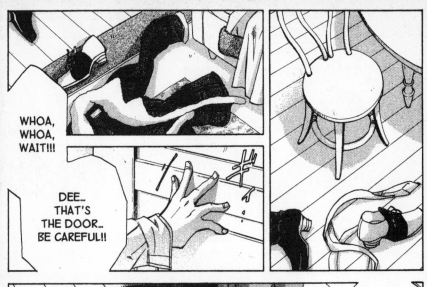

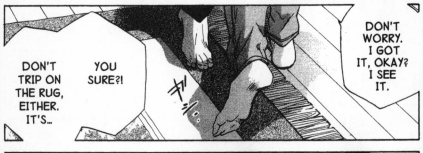

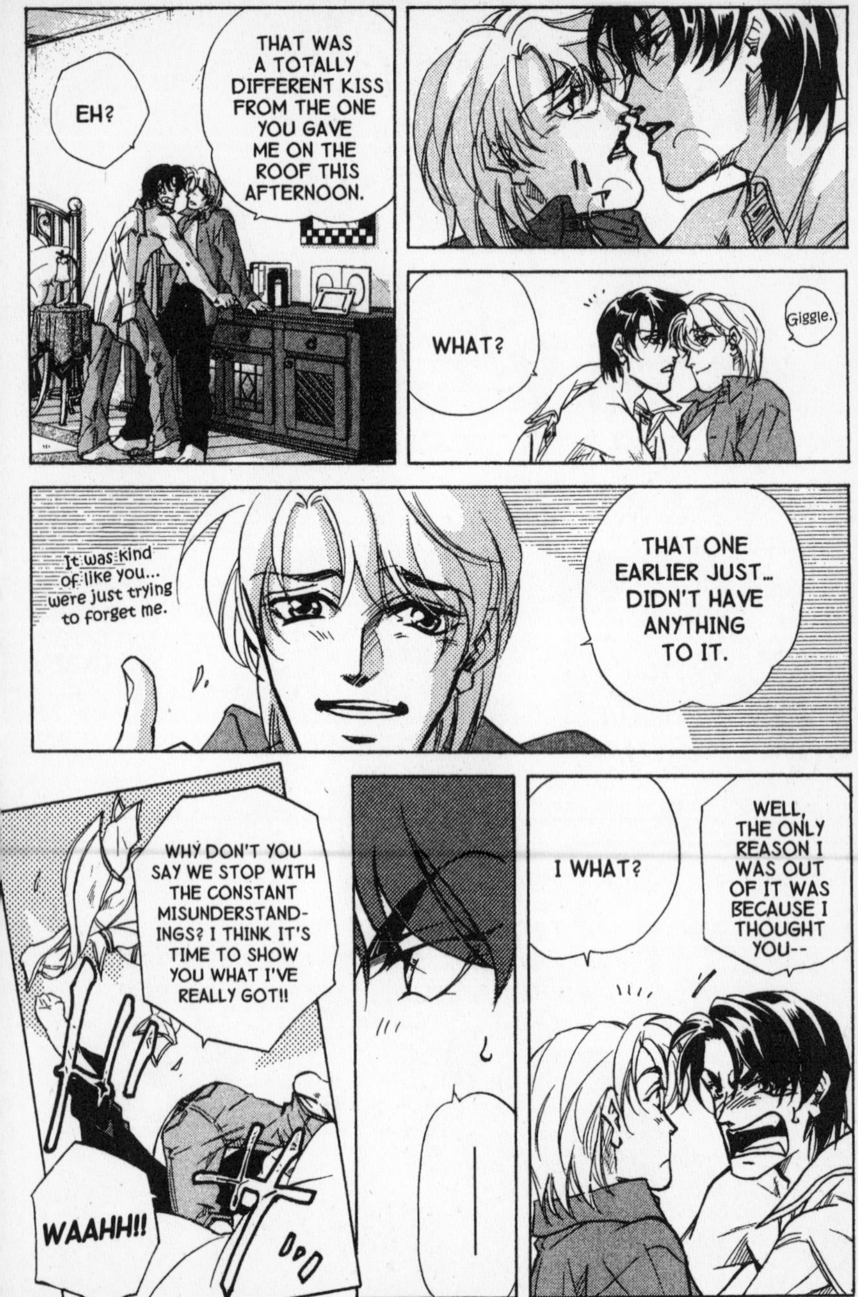
Giggle.
WHAT?
THAT WAS A TOTALLY DIFFERENT KISS FROM THE ONE YOU GAVE ME ON THE ROOF THIS AFTERNOON.
EH?
THAT ONE EARLIER JUST... DIDN'T HAVE ANYTHING TO IT.
It was kind of like you... were just trying to forget me.
WELL, THE ONLY REASON I WAS OUT OF IT WAS BECAUSE I THOUGHT YOU--
I WHAT?
WHY DON'T YOU SAY WE STOP WITH THE CONSTANT MISUNDERSTAND-INGS? I THINK IT'S TIME TO SHOW YOU WHAT I'VE REALLY GOT!!
WAAHH!!

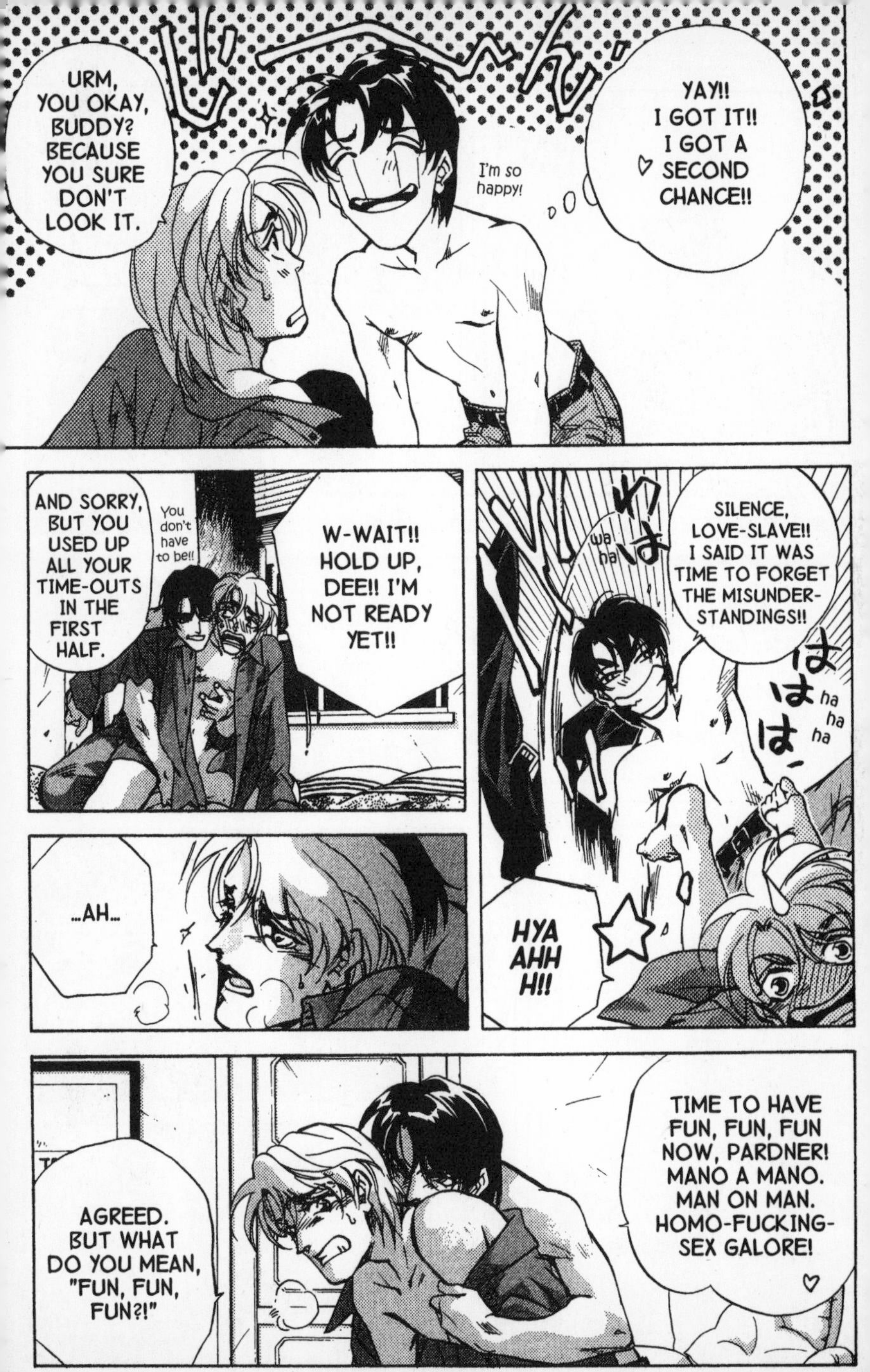
YAY!! I GOT IT!! I GOT A SECOND CHANCE!!
I'm so happy!
URM, YOU OKAY, BUDDY? BECAUSE YOU SURE DON'T LOOK IT.
わは
wa ha
SILENCE, LOVE-SLAVE!! I SAID IT WAS TIME TO FORGET THE MISUNDER-STANDINGS!!
ははは
ha ha ha
HYA AHH H!!
W-WAIT!! HOLD UP, DEE!! I'M NOT READY YET!!
AND SORRY, BUT YOU USED UP ALL YOUR TIME-OUTS IN THE FIRST HALF.
You don't have to be!!
...AH...
TIME TO HAVE FUN, FUN, FUN NOW, PARDNER! MANO A MANO. MAN ON MAN. HOMO-FUCKING-SEX GALORE!
AGREED. BUT WHAT DO YOU MEAN, "FUN, FUN, FUN?!"

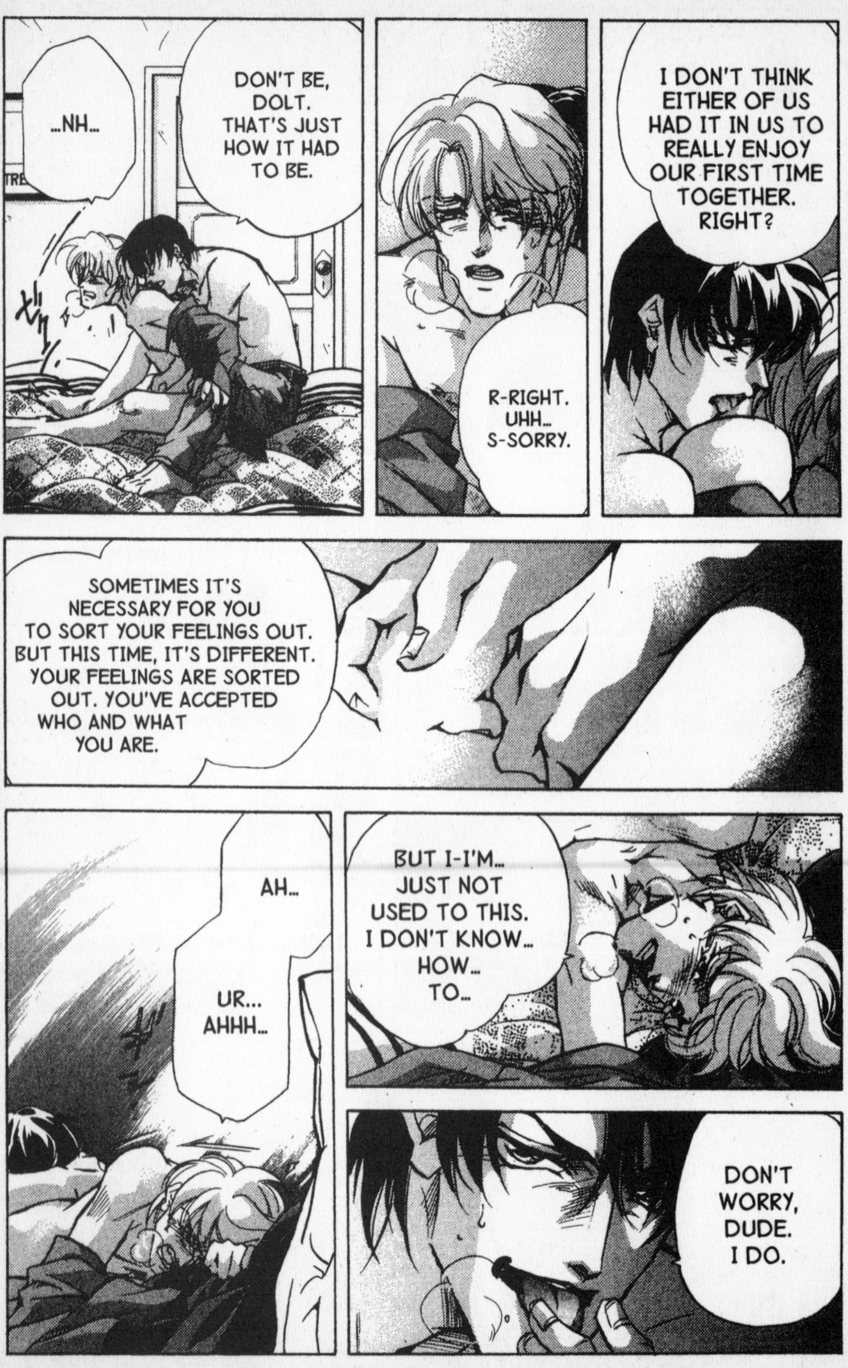
I DON'T THINK EITHER OF US HAD IT IN US TO REALLY ENJOY OUR FIRST TIME TOGETHER. RIGHT?
R-RIGHT. UHH... S-SORRY.
DON'T BE, DOLT. THAT'S JUST HOW IT HAD TO BE.
...NH...
SOMETIMES IT'S NECESSARY FOR YOU TO SORT YOUR FEELINGS OUT. BUT THIS TIME, IT'S DIFFERENT. YOUR FEELINGS ARE SORTED OUT. YOU'VE ACCEPTED WHO AND WHAT YOU ARE.
BUT I-I'M... JUST NOT USED TO THIS. I DON'T KNOW... HOW... TO...
DON'T WORRY, DUDE. I DO.
AH...
UR... AHHH...

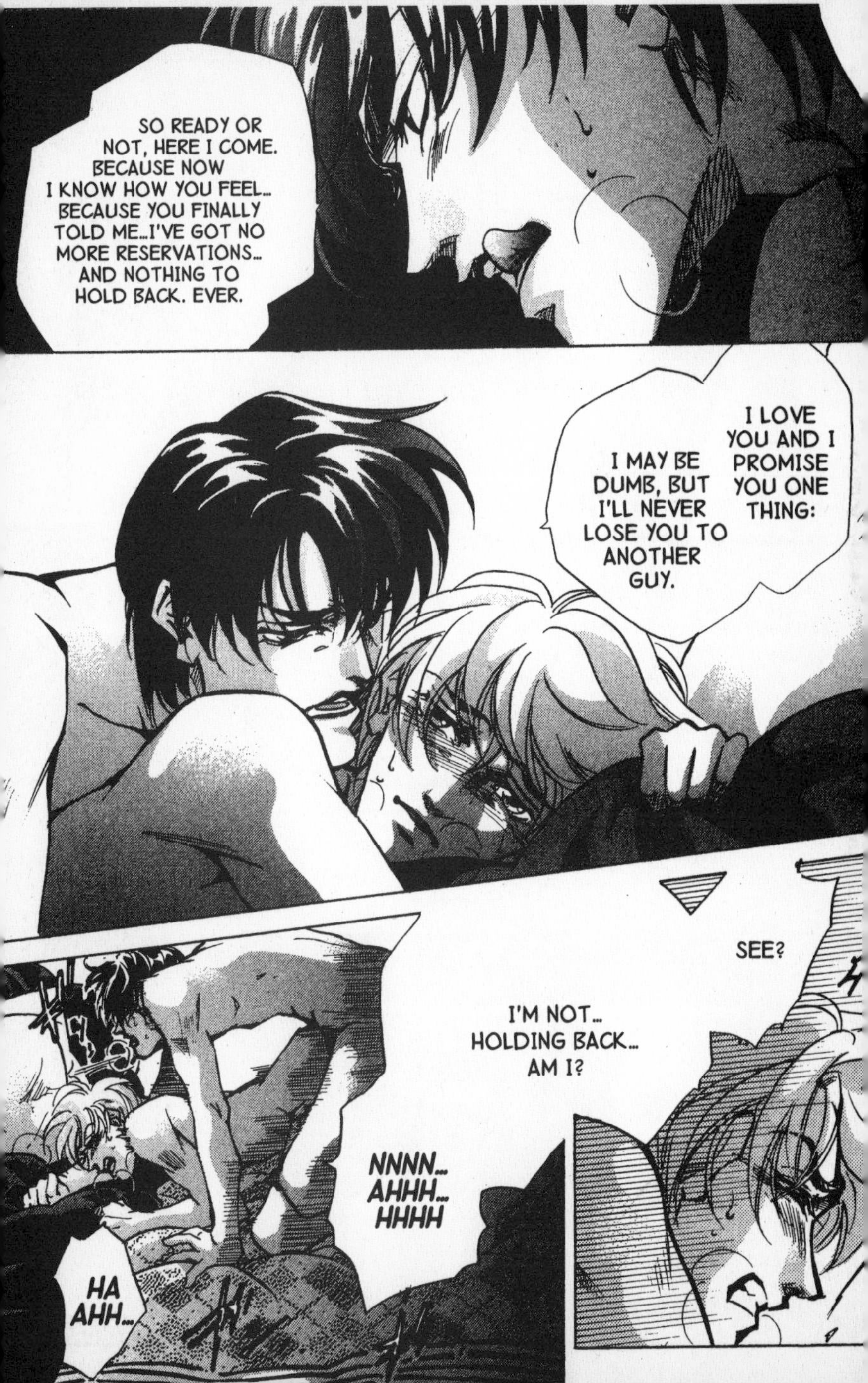
SO READY OR NOT, HERE I COME. BECAUSE NOW I KNOW HOW YOU FEEL... BECAUSE YOU FINALLY TOLD ME...I'VE GOT NO MORE RESERVATIONS... AND NOTHING TO HOLD BACK. EVER.
I LOVE YOU AND I PROMISE YOU ONE THING:
I MAY BE DUMB, BUT I'LL NEVER LOSE YOU TO ANOTHER GUY.
SEE?
I'M NOT... HOLDING BACK... AM I?
NNNN... AHHH... HHHH
HA AHH...

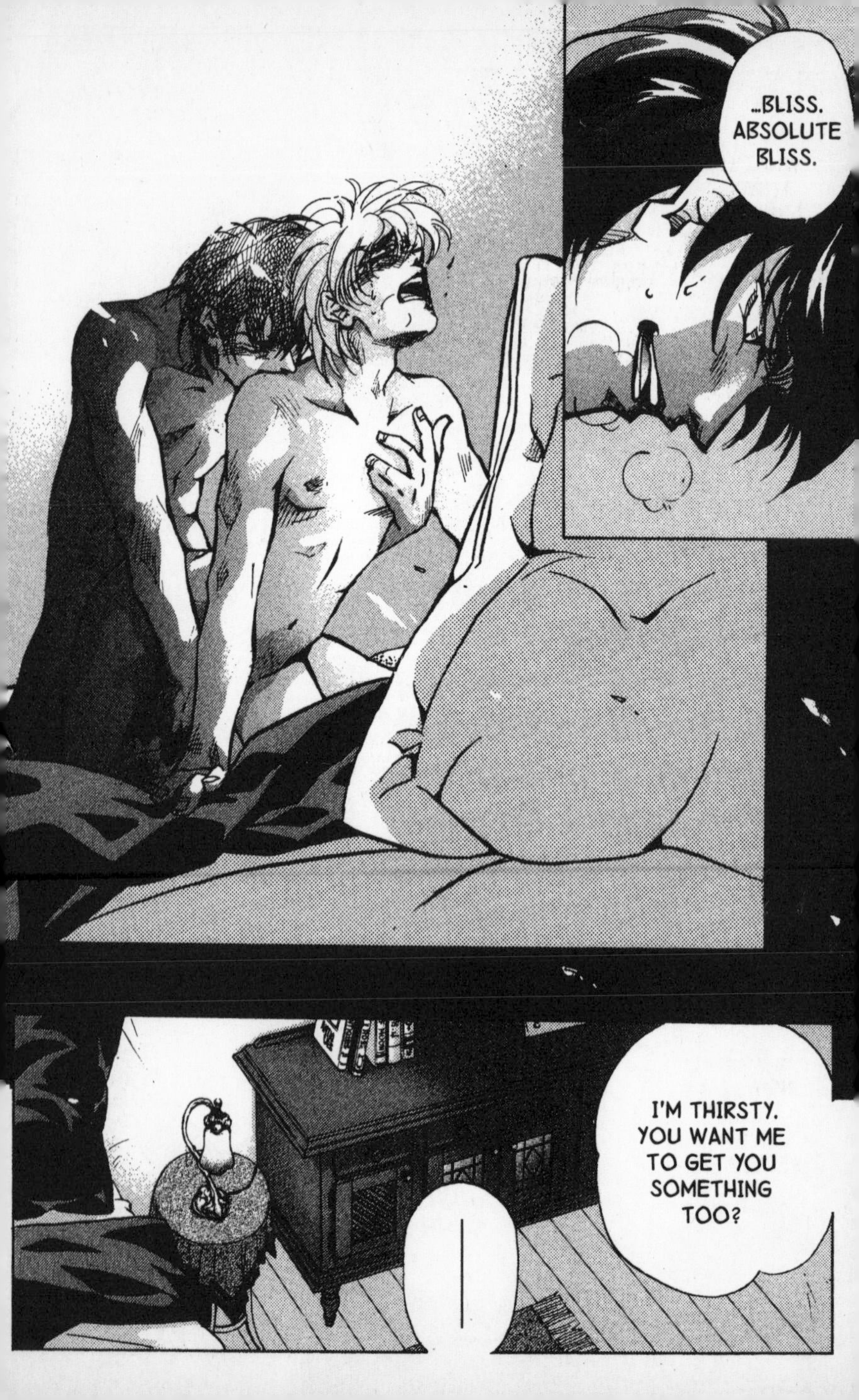
...BLISS. ABSOLUTE BLISS.
I'M THIRSTY. YOU WANT ME TO GET YOU SOMETHING TOO?
|

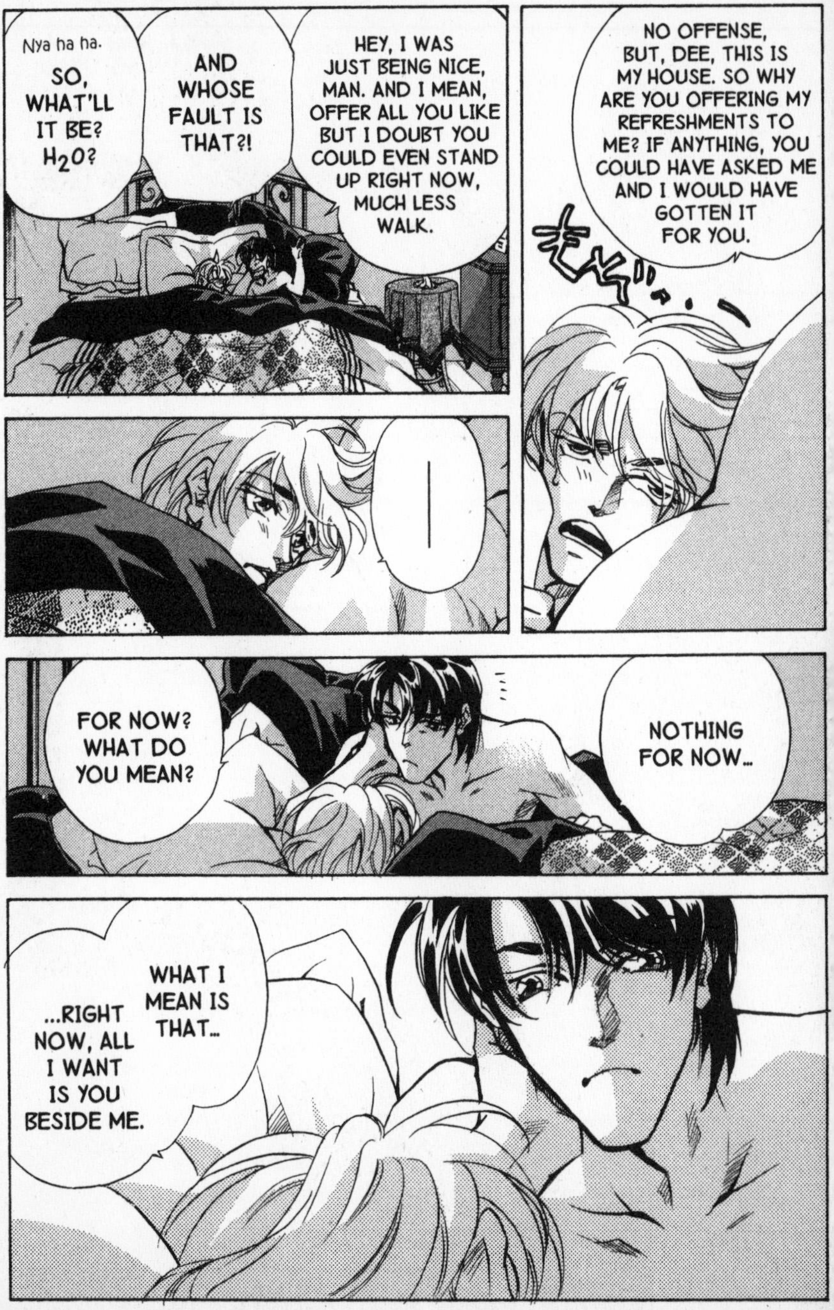
NO OFFENSE, BUT, DEE, THIS IS MY HOUSE. SO WHY ARE YOU OFFERING MY REFRESHMENTS TO ME? IF ANYTHING, YOU COULD HAVE ASKED ME AND I WOULD HAVE GOTTEN IT FOR YOU.
HEY, I WAS JUST BEING NICE, MAN. AND I MEAN, OFFER ALL YOU LIKE BUT I DOUBT YOU COULD EVEN STAND UP RIGHT NOW, MUCH LESS WALK.
AND WHOSE FAULT IS THAT?!
Nya ha ha.
SO, WHAT'LL IT BE? H_2O?
NOTHING FOR NOW...
FOR NOW? WHAT DO YOU MEAN?
WHAT I MEAN IS THAT...
...RIGHT NOW, ALL I WANT IS YOU BESIDE ME.

ALTHOUGH...

Y'KNOW, THAT SOUNDS GOOD...BUT INSTEAD OF ME BEING BESIDE YOU, HOWZ-ABOUT ME BEING ON TOP?

ACK! GET OFF, YOU CAVE MAN!! YOU'RE WAY HEAVY!!

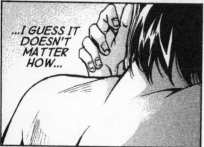

...I GUESS IT DOESN'T MATTER HOW...

...AS LONG AS I'M WITH YOU AND ONLY YOU... FOREVER...

FAKE act.20 SECOND CHANCE/The End

THERE ARE A LOT OF DANGEROUS SCENES IN VOL 7, SO DON'T SUE ME. OKAY?

THANK YOU SO MUCH FOR YOUR PURCHASE OF THIS COMIC. VOLUME 7 MARKS THE CONCLUSION OF THE "FAKE" STORYLINE, AND THOUGH IT SEEMS SHORT, IT'S TRULY BEEN A VERY LONG ROAD. SO FIRST AND FOREMOST, I WANT TO THANK YOU ALL SO MUCH FOR YOUR SUPPORT. "FAKE" BEGAN WITH THE SIMPLE THOUGHT: "HEY, I WANT TO DO A COP STORY!!" (AND TO BE QUITE HONEST, AT FIRST I TRULY REGRETTED GOING THE POLICE STORY ROUTE.) NOT TO MENTION THAT THE SCHEDULE BEXBOY GAVE ME FOR NEW EPISODES WASN'T THE MOST CONSISTENT, SO I WASN'T ABLE TO TURN OUT THE COMICS AS QUICKLY AS I WANTED TO. BUT STILL, EACH TIME THEY DID COME OUT, YOU GUYS WERE ALL THERE TO PURCHASE THEM!! SO AGAIN, THANK YOU SO VERY MUCH FOR YOUR PATIENCE AND SUPPORT.

I'VE HAD A VERY LONG RELATIONSHIP WITH THE CHARACTERS FROM "FAKE," SO I ADMIT, I HAVE A VERY, VERY SOFT SPOT IN MY HEART FOR ALL OF THEM. THEY HAVE MOVED MARVELOUSLY FOR ME, AND THROUGH THEM, I'VE BEEN ABLE TO STUDY AND LEARN MORE ABOUT THIS ART FORM KNOWN AS MANGA. BUT THERE'S SO MUCH THAT I WANT TO DO THAT, IN SPITE OF MY LOVE FOR THEM, I THOUGHT IT WAS A GOOD TIME TO TIDY UP ALL THE LOOSE ENDS OF THEIR STORY. BUT WHO KNOWS ABOUT THE FUTURE? I'M KINDA FICKLE, SO I'LL MOST LIKELY GO WHERE THE DAY TAKES ME. (SILENCE.) AT ANY RATE, IN MARCH OF 2001, I PLAN TO RELEASE A COLLECTION OF ILLUSTRATIONS IN WHICH I AM HOPING TO INCLUDE A BUNCH OF EXCLUSIVE "FAKE" IMAGES. (OPERATIVE WORD: HOPING.) SO PLEASE, IF THAT DOESN'T HAPPEN, LET ME OFF THE HOOK!

IN THE COLLECTION, I'LL ALSO BE FEATURING ILLUSTRATIONS I MADE THROUGH OTHER PUBLISHERS, SOME OF WHICH WILL ALSO BE COLLECTION-ONLY ORIGINALS, SO I WOULD VERY MUCH APPRECIATE IT IF YOU COULD KEEP AN EYE OUT FOR THAT AS WELL. (IT IS A BIT EXPENSIVE, THOUGH, SO SORRY!!)

EITHER WAY, I HOPE TO CONTINUE BEING A TRUE BLUE MANGA ARTIST UNTIL I DIE, SO I HOPE TO SEE YOU GUYS UNTIL THEN.

EVERY END IS A NEW BEGINNING.

おわりは はじまり

Current Hair Color: Ashe Blonde
Murrrr.

by まとば.

ALSO AVAILABLE FROM TOKYOPOP

ALSO AVAILABLE FROM ⚙TOKYOPOP®

MANGA

.HACK//LEGEND OF THE TWILIGHT
@LARGE
ABENOBASHI: MAGICAL SHOPPING ARCADE
A.I. LOVE YOU
AI YORI AOSHI
ANGELIC LAYER
ARM OF KANNON
BABY BIRTH
BATTLE ROYALE
BATTLE VIXENS
BOYS BE...
BRAIN POWERED
BRIGADOON
B'TX
CANDIDATE FOR GODDESS, THE
CARDCAPTOR SAKURA
CARDCAPTOR SAKURA - MASTER OF THE CLOW
CHOBITS
CHRONICLES OF THE CURSED SWORD
CLAMP SCHOOL DETECTIVES
CLOVER
COMIC PARTY
CONFIDENTIAL CONFESSIONS
CORRECTOR YUI
COWBOY BEBOP
COWBOY BEBOP: SHOOTING STAR
CRAZY LOVE STORY
CRESCENT MOON
CROSS
CULDCEPT
CYBORG 009
D•N•ANGEL
DEMON DIARY
DEMON ORORON, THE
DEUS VITAE
DIABOLO
DIGIMON
DIGIMON TAMERS
DIGIMON ZERO TWO
DOLL
DRAGON HUNTER
DRAGON KNIGHTS
DRAGON VOICE
DREAM SAGA
DUKLYON: CLAMP SCHOOL DEFENDERS
EERIE QUEERIE!
ERICA SAKURAZAWA: COLLECTED WORKS
ET CETERA
ETERNITY
EVIL'S RETURN
FAERIES' LANDING
FAKE
FLCL
FLOWER OF THE DEEP SLEEP
FORBIDDEN DANCE
FRUITS BASKET

G GUNDAM
GATEKEEPERS
GETBACKERS
GIRL GOT GAME
GIRLS EDUCATIONAL CHARTER
GRAVITATION
GTO
GUNDAM BLUE DESTINY
GUNDAM SEED ASTRAY
GUNDAM WING
GUNDAM WING: BATTLEFIELD OF PACIFISTS
GUNDAM WING: ENDLESS WALTZ
GUNDAM WING: THE LAST OUTPOST (G-UNIT)
HANDS OFF!
HAPPY MANIA
HARLEM BEAT
HYPER RUNE
I.N.V.U.
IMMORTAL RAIN
INITIAL D
INSTANT TEEN: JUST ADD NUTS
ISLAND
JING: KING OF BANDITS
JING: KING OF BANDITS - TWILIGHT TALES
JULINE
KARE KANO
KILL ME, KISS ME
KINDAICHI CASE FILES, THE
KING OF HELL
KODOCHA: SANA'S STAGE
LAMENT OF THE LAMB
LEGAL DRUG
LEGEND OF CHUN HYANG, THE
LES BIJOUX
LOVE HINA
LUPIN III
LUPIN III: WORLD'S MOST WANTED
MAGIC KNIGHT RAYEARTH I
MAGIC KNIGHT RAYEARTH II
MAHOROMATIC: AUTOMATIC MAIDEN
MAN OF MANY FACES
MARMALADE BOY
MARS
MARS: HORSE WITH NO NAME
MINK
MIRACLE GIRLS
MIYUKI-CHAN IN WONDERLAND
MODEL
MOURYOU KIDEN
MY LOVE
NECK AND NECK
ONE
ONE I LOVE, THE
PARADISE KISS
PARASYTE
PASSION FRUIT
PEACH GIRL
PEACH GIRL: CHANGE OF HEART

06.21.04T

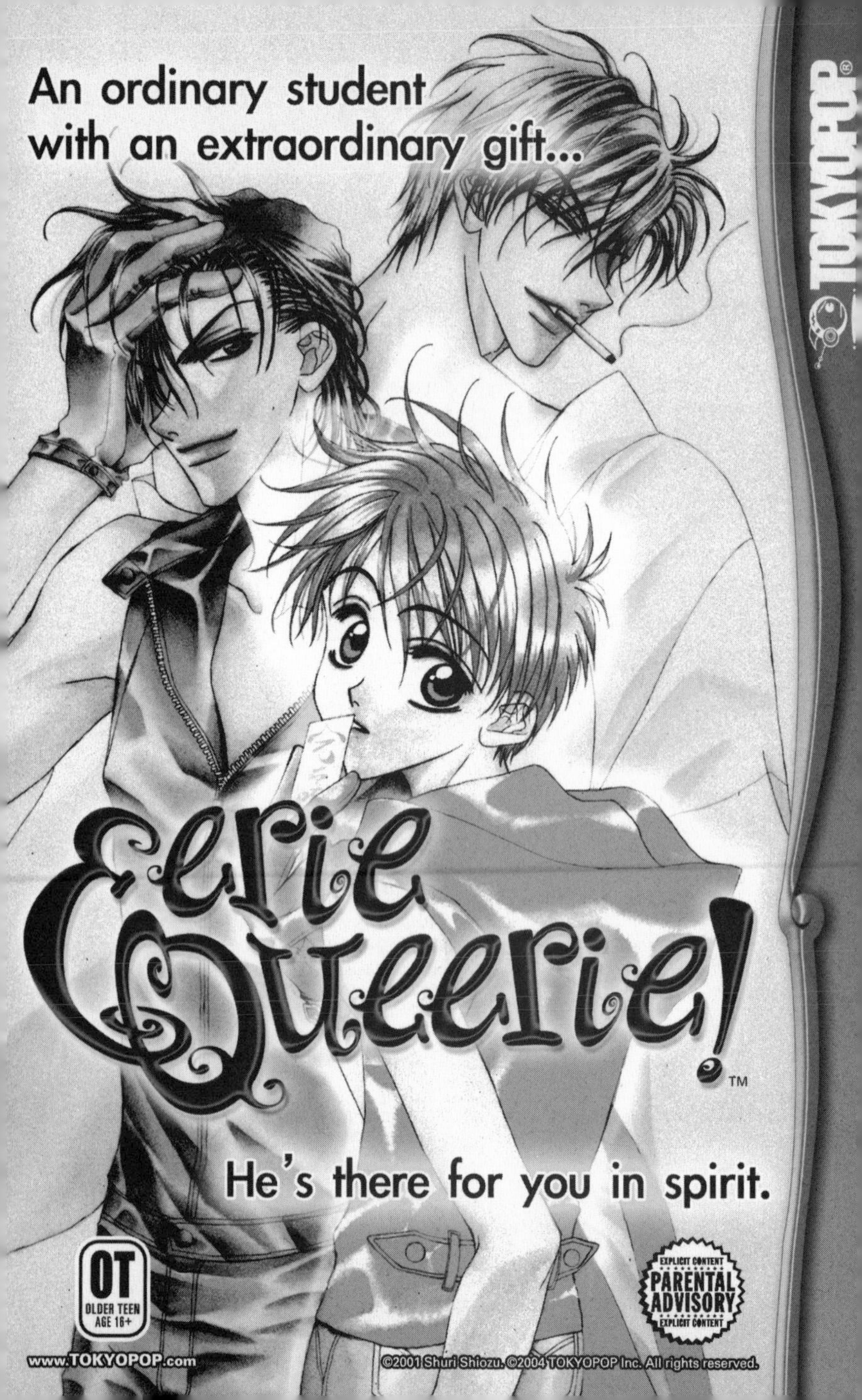

An ordinary student
with an extraordinary gift...
TOKYOPOP
Eerie Queerie!™
He's there for you in spirit.
OT
OLDER TEEN
AGE 16+
EXPLICIT CONTENT
PARENTAL ADVISORY
EXPLICIT CONTENT
www.TOKYOPOP.com
©2001 Shuri Shiozu. ©2004 TOKYOPOP Inc. All rights reserved.

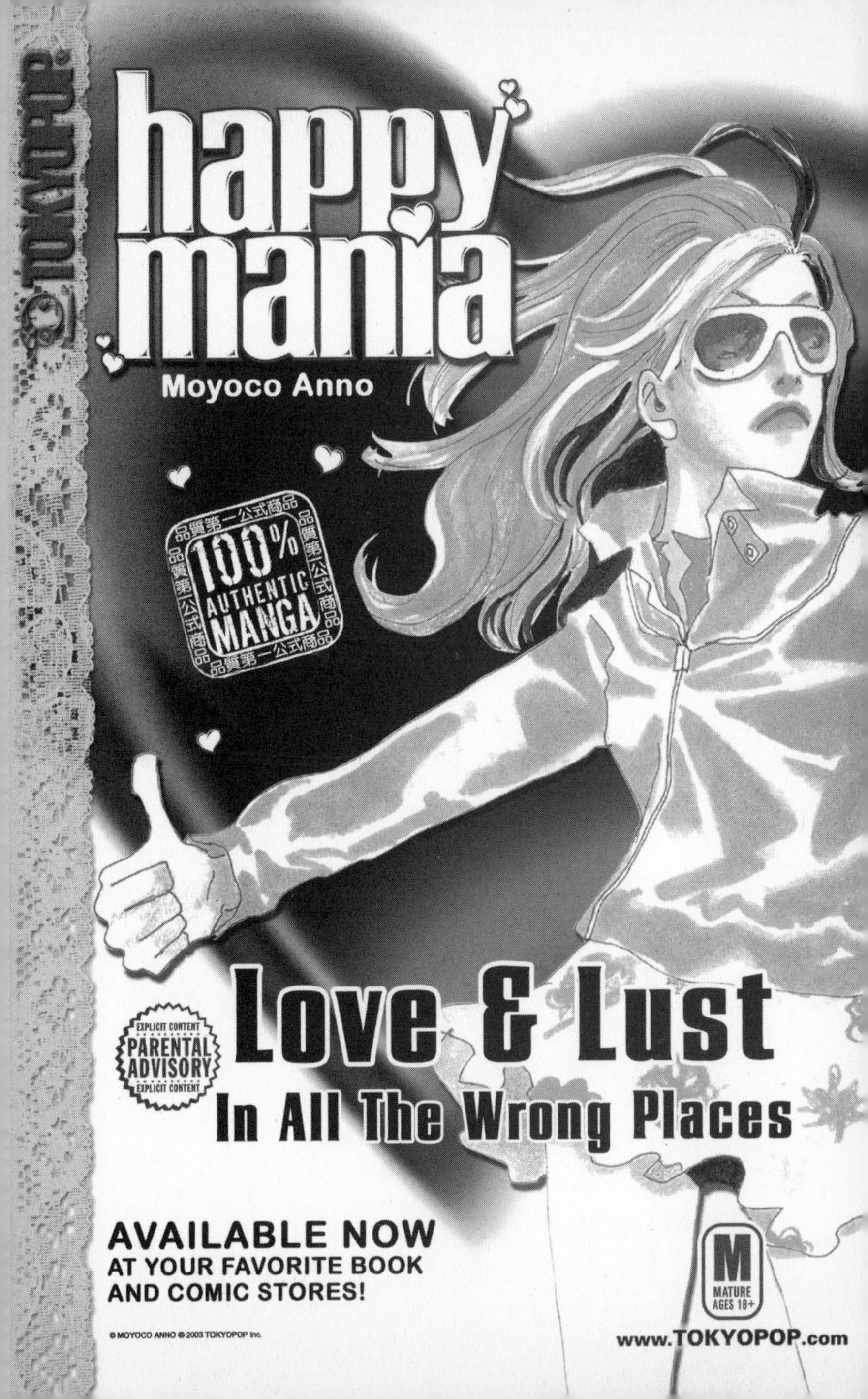
TOKYOPOP
happy mania
Moyoco Anno
品質第一公式商品
100% AUTHENTIC MANGA
EXPLICIT CONTENT PARENTAL ADVISORY EXPLICIT CONTENT
Love & Lust
In All The Wrong Places
AVAILABLE NOW
AT YOUR FAVORITE BOOK
AND COMIC STORES!
M
MATURE AGES 18+
© MOYOCO ANNO © 2003 TOKYOPOP Inc.
www.TOKYOPOP.com

The One I Love

watashi no suki na hito

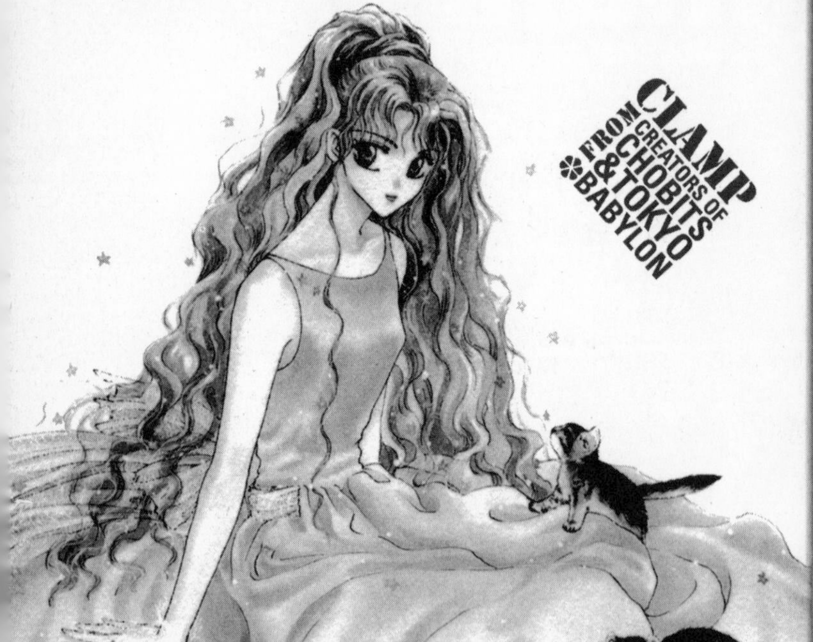

FROM CLAMP CREATORS OF CHOBITS & TOKYO BABYLON

breathtaking stories
of love and romance

T
TEEN
AGE 13+

www.TOKYOPOP.com

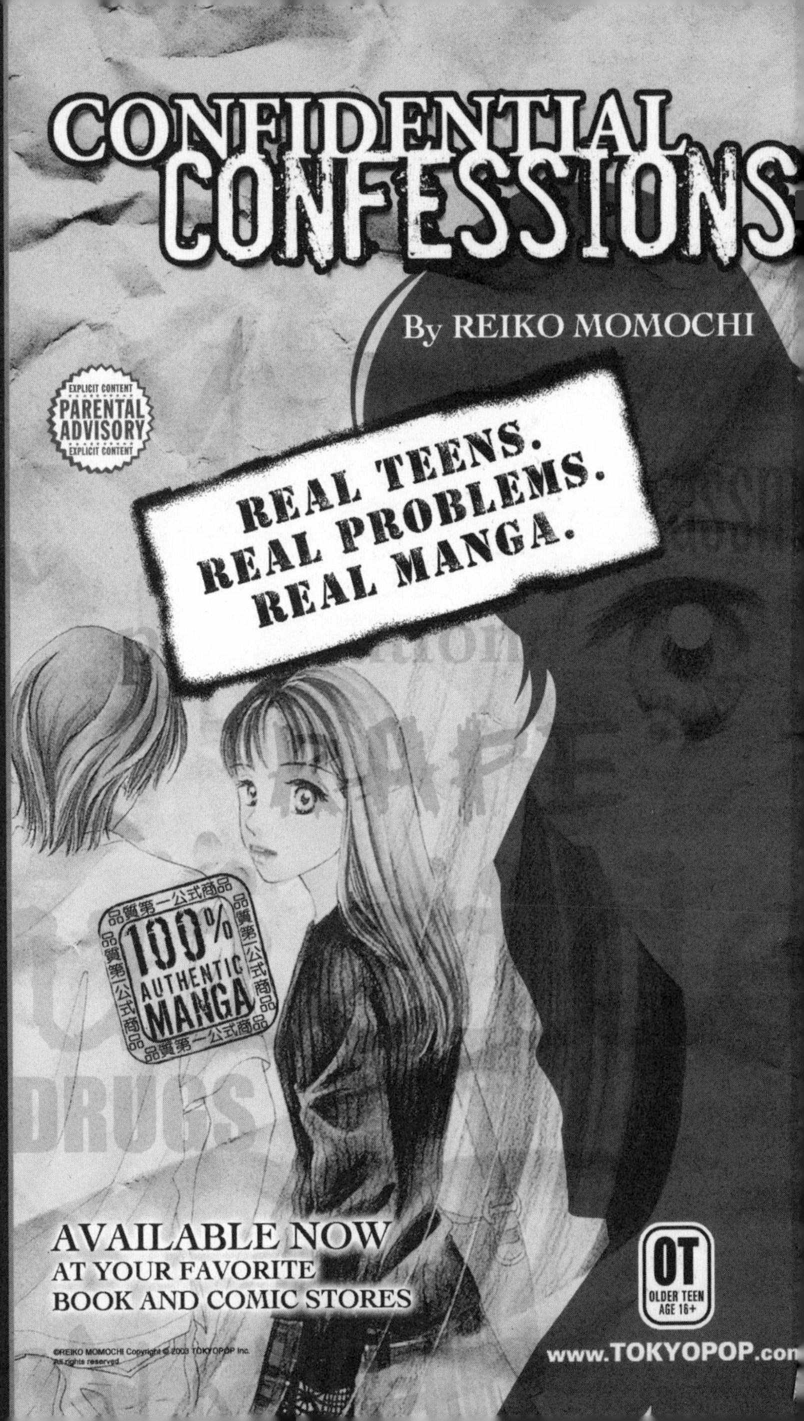
CONFIDENTIAL
CONFESSIONS
By REIKO MOMOCHI
EXPLICIT CONTENT
PARENTAL ADVISORY
EXPLICIT CONTENT
REAL TEENS.
REAL PROBLEMS.
REAL MANGA.
品質第一公式商品
100%
AUTHENTIC
MANGA
DRUGS
AVAILABLE NOW
AT YOUR FAVORITE
BOOK AND COMIC STORES
OT
OLDER TEEN
AGE 16+
©REIKO MOMOCHI Copyright © 2003 TOKYOPOP Inc.
All rights reserved
www.TOKYOPOP.com

STOP!

This is the back of the book.
You wouldn't want to spoil a great ending!

This book is printed "manga-style," in the authentic Japanese right-to-left format. Since none of the artwork has been flipped or altered, readers get to experience the story just as the creator intended. You've been asking for it, so TOKYOPOP® delivered: authentic, hot-off-the-press, and far more fun!

DIRECTIONS

If this is your first time reading manga-style, here's a quick guide to help you understand how it works.

It's easy... just start in the top right panel and follow the numbers. Have fun, and look for more 100% authentic manga from TOKYOPOP®!